prepare for u
change &

The Axia Age (Karl Jones)

buddhism

confucianism

christiany,

taoism

"profits over people & planet"

Critical Studies of Education

Volume 3

We live in an era where forms of education designed to win the consent of students, teachers, and the public to the inevitability of a neo-liberal, market-driven process of globalization are being developed around the world. In these hegemonic modes of pedagogy questions about issues of race, class, gender, sexuality, colonialism, religion, and other social dynamics are simply not asked. Indeed, questions about the social spaces where pedagogy takes place—in schools, media, corporate think tanks, etc.—are not raised. When these concerns are connected with queries such as the following, we begin to move into a serious study of pedagogy: What knowledge is of the most worth? Whose knowledge should be taught? What role does power play in the educational process? How are new media re-shaping as well as perpetuating what happens in education? How is knowledge produced in a corporatized politics of knowledge? What socio-political role do schools play in the twenty-first century? What is an educated person? What is intelligence? How important are socio-cultural contextual factors in shaping what goes on in education? Can schools be more than a tool of the new American (and its Western allies') twenty-first century empire? How do we educate well-informed, creative teachers? What roles should schools play in a democratic society? What roles should media play in a democratic society? Is education in a democratic society different than in a totalitarian society? What is a democratic society? How is globalization affecting education? How does our view of mind shape the way we think of education? How does affect and emotion shape the educational process? What are the forces that shape educational purpose in different societies? These, of course, are just a few examples of the questions that need to be asked in relation to our exploration of educational purpose. This series of books can help establish a renewed interest in such questions and their centrality in the larger study of education and the preparation of teachers and other educational professionals.

More information about this series at http://www.springer.com/series/13431

Jennifer M. Gidley

Postformal Education

A Philosophy for Complex Futures

Jennifer M. Gidley, PhD
Institute for Sustainable Futures
University of Technology Sydney
Ultimo, NSW, Australia

Critical Studies of Education
ISBN 978-3-319-29068-3 ISBN 978-3-319-29069-0 (eBook)
DOI 10.1007/978-3-319-29069-0

Library of Congress Control Number: 2016932891

Printed on acid-free paper

This Springer imprint is published by Springer Nature
The registered company is Springer International Publishing AG Switzerland

I dedicate this book to the memory of Joe L. Kincheloe (1950–2008) who invited and encouraged me to write this book a few months before his untimely death. Joe's radical love for the disenfranchised, his lively enthusiasm and the crazy wisdom in his writings on postformal education have inspired many of the ideas in my book.

Acknowledgements

I wish to acknowledge the influence of some of the brightest lights of last century: especially Rudolf Steiner, Jean Gebser and Sri Aurobindo for the gift of their inspirational integral evolutionary ideas; Michel Foucault, Jacques Derrida and Gilles Deleuze for their spiritual courage to write living philosophy.

I thank the pioneers of postformal reasoning, especially Michael Commons and Jan Sinnott, for challenging the orthodoxy of developmental psychology in the late 1970s and pushing forward with their research on postformal reasoning. I also thank the founders of postformal education Joe Kincheloe and Shirley Steinberg for their innovation and courage in extending critical pedagogy into multiple terrains.

I am grateful to innovative contemporary educators, such as Ron Miller, Tobin Hart, Kieran Egan and many others who think, write and work with the best interests of young people in mind, and creative and complex contemporary thinkers such as Ken Wilber, Ervin László, Hélène Cixous, Edgar Morin, Julia Kristeva, Basarab Nicolescu and many others whose work I have cited and for their inspiration.

I acknowledge with thanks the permission to use copyright images of Robert Bednarik for the palaeoart sections of Chapter 4.

I am deeply grateful to Earl de Blonville for his support and generosity of spirit throughout "the Springer book years" and for many illuminating dialogues about postformal reasoning and its significance for navigating uncertain, turbulent and complex futures. Last but not least, I thank my daughter Raina and my son Jesse for their love and ongoing encouragement of me and of my work.

Endorsements

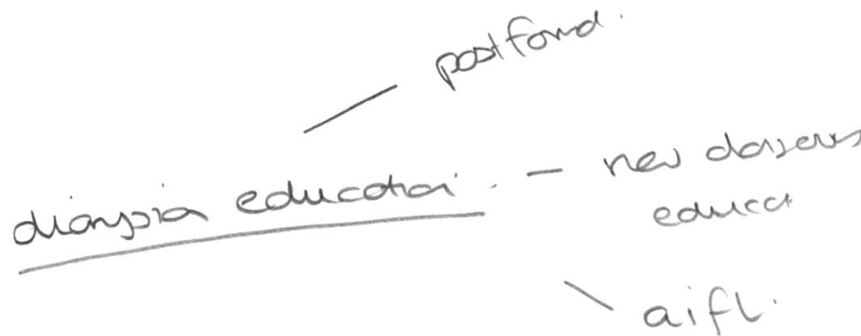

It is with great enthusiasm that I read Jennifer Gidley's masterful work that develops thought about education to a new level! The old, almost mechanistic, view of education must make way for what Gidley calls "postformal education" if we are to shape a rich future for human development. I'm surprised it took only ten years to write this amazing book, one that could turn thinking about education around.
I could not ask for a better application of postformal theory!

> – **Jan D. Sinnott, PhD, Professor of Psychology**, Towson University, Maryland, USA. Author of *The Development of Logic in Adulthood: Postformal Thought and Its Applications* (1998) Springer.

This is the book we have all been waiting for and should be read by educators, policy makers and everyone interested in the future through the transformative power of education in creating a wiser, more caring world with a vibrant future. This path-breaking book synthesizes the new thinking of philosophers in diverse areas of knowledge of the 20th century into a new model of integral education for a 21st century Integrative Age. There are many books on what is wrong with education but few on how to make fundamental systemic change.

> – **David K. Scott, PhD, Former Chancellor**, University of Massachusetts at Amherst. Leading thinker on integrating science and spirituality. Co-editor: *Integrative Learning and Action: A Call to Wholeness* (2006) Peter Lang Publishers.

Jennifer Gidley is one of the most provocative and important thinkers in education today. Her vision draws on the epic story of the evolution of consciousness as she presents us with the past, present and possible future of education. Interweaving ancient wisdom and the latest research, Gidley articulates an inspiring new and radical revisioning of the nature, mission, and role of education.

> – **Alfonso Montuori, PhD, Professor Transformative Studies Department**, School of Consciousness and Transformation, California Institute of Integral Studies, San Francisco. Editor: *Journeys in Complexity* (2014) Routledge.

An extraordinary triumph of scholarship that builds a bridge from the past to the future. It envisions futures of wisdom and gifts readers with everyday applicable concepts, empowering them to articulate a new world and language it into being.

– Earl de Blonville, FRGS, Founder Postformal Leadership "One of the top six leadership thinkers in Australia" – BRW 2012

This important book is a labour of love that brims with profound thought, wide ranging research, an overarching spiritual vision and commitment to an educational renaissance that is desperately needed around our troubled world. By linking the evolution of consciousness, aesthetic values, child-development, the art of teaching, post-formal thinking, contemplative insights and social commitment it is a resource of great value. For today's educational activists, who are concerned about the narrowness and over-competiveness that passes as educational policy in so many countries, it provides a solid and inspiring foundation for us to continue working in order to create an education that our children really need and deserve.

– Christopher Clouder, FRSA, Co-editor: *The Future of Childhood* (2000) Hawthorn Press. CEO – European Council for Steiner Waldorf Education (1991–2011). Pedagogical Director: Il Liceo dei Colli, Florence, Italy.

Contents

About the Author

Jennifer M. Gidley, PhD, is a psychologist, innovative educator and renowned futures researcher. She is President of the World Futures Studies Federation (UNESCO and UN Partner), the global peak body founded in Paris in 1973. In this capacity, she leads expert futures researchers, teachers and professional practitioners from over 60 countries. Jennifer was awarded the Chancellor's Gold Medal for Academic Excellence for her PhD on the evolution of consciousness in 2008. She has published dozens of academic papers, and her books include *The University in Transformation* (Ed.) (2000), *Youth Futures* (Ed.) (2002) and *The Future: A Very Short Introduction* (Oxford University Press, 2017). Jennifer founded and led an innovative private school in rural Australia over ten years (1985–1994). She has held academic positions in several Australian universities (1995–2012) and currently holds visiting academic posts in Australia and Europe.

List of Figures

List of Tables

Chapter 1
Introduction

1.1 Introduction

The book I offer you is about radical change. It explains why the current education model, which was developed in the 19th century to meet the needs of industrial expansion, is obsolete. It points to the need for a new approach to education designed to prepare young people for global uncertainty, accelerating change and unprecedented complexity. It argues that we need to fundamentally change our ways of thinking, and our ways of educating children and young people.

The challenges we face as human beings at the beginning of the 21st century are often intractable and increasingly "planet-sized". The overwhelming issues of global climate crisis, growing economic disparity, mass migration and the youth mental health epidemic reveal how dramatically the current education model has failed students, educators and global society as a whole, in that education is the bedrock of society and culture.

While so much has changed out of all recognition in the last hundred years, the institution of formal schooling still resembles the factory schools built to provide human fodder during the Industrial Revolution. Fundamentally, we are still educating our children as if we were living in the 19th century, albeit with a few added digital gadgets and online infotainment.

Furthermore, the type of thinking believed until the mid-20th century to be the highest form of thinking—what Jean Piaget called *formal operations*—is now known to be succeeded by other stages. Adult developmental psychologists in the USA have for decades been providing evidence that mature adult humans can develop higher-order reasoning than formal operations. They call this capacity: *postformal reasoning*.

Readers will learn about the impact on young people of both the global-societal challenges we face as a species and the failure of formal schooling to prepare them to meet those challenges. Our current ways of thinking, educating and running the world have left many young people depressed, with a loss of meaning, a sense of

J.M. Gidley, *Postformal Education*, Critical Studies of Education 3,
DOI 10.1007/978-3-319-29069-0_1

spiritual vacuum and feelings of disenchantment with the world they are inheriting. This *global youth problematique* has been discussed elsewhere (Gidley 2002a, 2011).

By reading this book, educators and others will become aware of the limitations of formal reasoning in addressing complex, systemic challenges. They will begin to appreciate the more complex, nuanced and paradoxical features of postformal reasoning and how such reasoning will help us to meet future planetary challenges with courage, imagination, wisdom, rather than relying on techno-fixes.

This book is not for the faint-hearted or those wanting to tinker with the edges of the outmoded schooling model. It raises a planet-wide call to deeply question how we actually think and how we educate. It charts a course towards a postformal education philosophy based on the most advanced and most significant developmental psychology and education research—as a foundation for educational futures.

A key question explored in this book is this: "If higher-order, more complex forms of cognition do exist, then how can we better educate children and young people so that more mature forms of reasoning appear at the appropriate life stage?"

Put simply, we cannot solve tomorrow's problems with yesterday's thinking.[1]

1.2 The Purpose of the Book

The book's main purpose is to articulate a new education philosophy designed to prepare young people for the complex futures already emerging in the 21st century. It does this by exploring the significant and intimate relationship between the evolution of consciousness and the futures of education.

A unique contribution of this book is to create a dialogue between the adult developmental psychology research on higher stages of reasoning (postformal reasoning) and today's most evolved education research and practice. The latter draws from the critical education literature on postformalism and a plethora of innovative educational approaches that support the evolution of new ways of thinking. I call these *postformal pedagogies* (Gidley 2009, 2012a, 2013).

This dialogue crosses the traditional disciplinary boundaries between adult developmental psychology research and educational research, laying foundations for a new postformal education philosophy. Such a far-reaching philosophy has the potential to awaken the creative, big-picture and long-term thinking that will help equip and future-proof young people to face tomorrow's challenges.

Early 21st-century challenges include significant global economic upheaval coupled with the dawning realisation of the potential threats to the habitability of

[1]Echoing Einstein's words of a century ago: "The significant problems we have cannot be solved at the same level of thinking with which we created them."

the earth's ecosphere posed by irreversible climatic stress. These challenges are compounded for educators and others working with children and young people. I am writing this book because I am inspired by a sense of urgency for education to evolve so that it can become a key player in meeting these challenges, which can be summarised as follows:

Challenge 1 The Global Problematique: The multidimensional planetary crises (environmental, psychological, socio-cultural and politico-economic);
Challenge 2 The Epistemological Problematique: The crisis of thinking and meaning underlying the planetary crises;
Challenge 3 The Global Youth Problematique: The psycho-social impact of the crises on young people;
Challenge 4 The Educational Problematique: The failure of the industrial, factory model of schooling to meet these challenges and the urgency for radical change.

While Challenge 1 is well beyond the scope of this book to address in detail, its influence cannot be overlooked because of its huge impact on the other three. To address these planetary crises, we need to look beneath the surface and address Challenge 2. The current crisis of thinking and meaning can only be addressed by radically and rapidly evolving our thinking. Many leading thinkers and researchers have been writing of this need for more evolved thinking. While the different disciplines push for what is needed from their own perspectives, very few have the breadth of vision to encompass the depth of change required. Educators need to know about the wide-ranging research on evolution of consciousness. This research includes the literature on planet-wide cultural evolution; the adult developmental psychology research on *postformal* reasoning; the *integral* studies literature; and the research on global mindset change or *megatrends of the mind* (Gidley 2010b). This book introduces these concepts and their importance for evolving education.

Challenge 3 refers to the alarming increases in youth mental health issues. For example, in Australia, currently one of the wealthiest nations in the world and arguably one of the least affected by the ongoing global financial turbulence, research indicates that 20–25% of young people suffer from some kind of mental health issue, including anxiety, depression and eating disorders.

While all these challenges inform my book, the primary focus is *the educational problematique* (Challenge 4). It should not be surprising that a 19th-century model of schooling cannot adequately deal with 21st-century challenges. What is surprising is that educators seem largely unaware of the research on the evolution of consciousness. Furthermore, there is a silence in educational research about the key role that education has to play in furthering the evolution of thinking and culture. Consequently, much educational research today remains trapped in the formal, modernist mindset that created the mainstream model of schooling. This disjuncture is arguably a consequence of the conceptual fragmentation that has arisen as a consequence of specialisation and conceptual territorialism.

French philosopher Edgar Morin sums up the education challenge as I do, by firmly linking it with the need to drastically change our thinking. He states:

> To articulate and organize, and thereby recognize and understand, the problems of the world, we need a reform in thinking … The education of the future is faced with this universal problem because our compartmentalised, piecemeal, disjointed learning is deeply, drastically inadequate to grasp realities and problems which are ever more global, transnational, multidimensional, transversal, polydisciplinary and planetary. (Morin 2001, p. 29)

1.3 Evolution of an Educator: A Brief Personal Narrative

> Humberto Maturana reminds us that everything that is said is said by *somebody*. (Montuori 2004, p. 353)

Since my own background, perspectives and biases are part of the tacit knowledge that comes through in this book, I want to be as transparent as I can about the various influences that may be informing my theories, even if not fully consciously. I will first provide some philosophical grounding for my decision to offer a brief personal narrative.

Philosopher David Couzens Hoy studied the history of consciousness from Kant and Hegel to Derrida and Foucault and notes the return of the subject in contemporary philosophical discourse. This is also the case in research that eschews modern scientific empiricism as a suitable research method for the social sciences. Taking a step back we need to be aware that the aim of modern scientific positivism was to arrive at "objective knowledge" not influenced by the "subjective" values of the researcher. In the process, scientific positivism effectively tried to eliminate the subjectivity of the researcher.

The emergence of post-positivism in the social sciences in the 1960s, along with critical theory, awakened the view that there is no such thing as values-neutrality in research, even in scientific positivism. This led to the claim that if the subjective values of the researcher are influencing the research, even if tacitly, then it is better to make these values and potential biases explicit.

The philosophical resurgence of interest in *subjectivity* has co-arisen with the emergence of transpersonal psychology (Zahavi 2004) and feminist literature, perhaps stimulated by Michel Foucault's seminal lectures on the *Hermeneutics of the Subject* (Foucault 1994, 2005). There is an emerging interest in the dialectical notion of *subjective-objective* ways of understanding reality (Benedikter 2005; Kegan 1994). Rudolf Steiner foreshadowed *subjective-objective* thinking over a century ago, in his *Philosophy of Freedom* (Steiner 1894/1964).

As a social science researcher, I support the idea that we cannot eliminate the subject—or self as researcher—in our research. Hence this brief personal narrative.

My first involvement with what I call evolutionary pedagogies—or postformal pedagogies—was almost forty years ago when I first encountered Rudolf Steiner's futures-oriented writings on education. The 1970s were exciting times intellectually and culturally as there was an influx of new ideas and cultural awakening. As a young psychologist-educator, I was influenced by writings from humanist and transpersonal psychologists, postmodern and feminist philosophers, and critical pedagogy theorists. There was a powerful shift of consciousness beginning to break into the formal academic world from the periphery at this time. My professional work in educational psychology already focused on marginal voices. In the 1970s I worked with teachers of young people who did not "fit into" mainstream education, and led a women's learning centre empowering "house-bound" women to take charge of their personal futures by re-entering employment and/or education.

As a professional psychologist-educator, I was aware of the serious limitations of the mainstream model of education and, as a mother, did not consider it suitable for my children. I decided to found a Steiner school but sought to transcend the conservative, cobweb-covered, 19th-century version of Steiner education. The school I founded and pioneered for ten years (1985–1994) was a contemporary, creative interpretation of Steiner's pedagogical writings (Steiner 1909/1965, 1967, 1971, 1981, 1982) adapted to late 20th-century, sub-tropical, rural Australia. I now see this as a "reconstructive postmodern" interpretation of Steiner. Thus, my implementation of Steiner was less traditional Waldorf and more... "creative self-transcendence... radical openness to new experience and novel conditions" (Miller 2000). I worked directly and authentically from Steiner's original teachings rather than any set Waldorf curriculum. I believe this is what Steiner intended teachers to do. I became aware intuitively and experientially of what a powerful and positive educational approach it can be. However, I was frustrated on the one hand by its marginalisation by academics and mainstream educators and on the other hand by dogmatism in some of the schools applying Steiner's evolutionary ideas.

In the 1990s I decided to re-enter the academy, with the aim of both testing my intuitions and finding appropriate language to create dialogue between Steiner's evolutionary pedagogy, mainstream education and the academy. My Master's research indicated that Steiner-educated students, while holding similar fears and concerns about the future to other students, had a stronger sense of empowerment and greater capacity to envisage positive preferred futures (Gidley 1998, 2002b). Over the next ten years, I continued to broaden and deepen my reading, researching and writing about educational and youth futures (Gidley and Inayatullah 2002; Gidley 2004, 2009, 2010a, 2012a, 2012b; Gidley et al. 2004). More recently, my efforts expanded to explore the impact on education of the evolution of culture and consciousness, through my doctoral research and associated publications (Gidley 2006, 2007a, 2007b, 2010b, 2010c, 2013).

Around 2000, I (re)discovered Ken Wilber's writing and found that his philosophy really resonated with my internalised Steiner philosophy. The more I read Wilber the more I was amazed at the similarity between Wilber's ideas and what Steiner had been writing a century earlier. I was stunned that in spite of Wilber's claims to be creating an "integral theory of everything", he had pretty much ignored one of the most integral figures of the 20th century—Rudolf Steiner. I undertook doctoral research on the relationships between their works. But as I began to follow up on some of the sources that Wilber referred to, I became drawn into their original writings as well (Aurobindo 1914/2000; Gebser 1949/1985).

As I searched the literature for others who may have brought these pioneers together academically, I realised that apart from Roland Benedikter's research on Steiner and Wilber (Benedikter 2005) (most of which is in German), no one else had undertaken any major research that incorporated the futures-oriented, integral contributions to evolution of consciousness of Steiner, Jean Gebser and Wilber.

My doctoral research, completed in 2008, provides important material for the chapters in this book, although new research has continued to inform it (Gidley 2008). As a scholar-activist—or *transformative intellectual* (Giroux 1992)—I focus on evolving education as the pragmatic ground of action for my research.

1.4 The Methodical Structure of the Book: *Difference and Repetition*

> There is no difference between what a book talks about and how it is made. Therefore a book also has no object. As an assemblage, a book has only itself, in connection with other assemblages and in relation to other bodies without organs. We will never ask what a book means, as signified or signifier; we will not look for anything to understand in it… Writing has nothing to do with signifying. It has everything to do with surveying, mapping, even realms that are yet to come. (Deleuze and Guattari 1987, pp. 4–5)

These words from Gilles Deleuze and Félix Guattari hint at my intention with this book. The book cannot be a final word on a new educational philosophy for the 21st century. But it can play a role in "surveying, mapping, even realms that are yet  to come". I intend that the book provokes, challenges and invites new conversations on educational futures better suited to tomorrow's uncertainties.

To aid understanding I am using Deleuze's method of *difference and repetition* (Deleuze 1968/1994). The reader who takes a quick glance through the Table of Contents of the book may get the impression that in some cases two chapters are overly repetitive. For example, the sub-headings of Chapters 2 & 3, and 5 & 6 are structurally quite similar. Yet the content is significantly different. This deliberate systematic arrangement of the material reflects a postmodern presentation form  creating a rhythmical pattern of difference and repetition. My aim to maximise understanding plays out in the multi-modal way that I present information, because I recognise that different readers have different cognitive and learning styles.

I try to strike a balance between organised structure and creative flow, between difference and repetition (Deleuze 1968/1994) and between breadth of overview and depth of gap-dives (Roy 2006). My writing is also multilayered and can be read at different levels of engagement.

1.5 What "Postformal Education: A Philosophy…" is about

The book is arranged in three interconnected parts of three/four chapters each.

Part I frames the book within the context of the evolution of consciousness. It situates contemporary education within the cultural evolution background

(Chapter 2) from which formal schooling emerged, discusses the developmental psychology notions of stage theory (Chapter 3) and outlines a brief evolution of school education (Chapter 4), pointing to the need for more conscious evolution of education.

Part II explores research by adult developmental psychologists who identify and conceptualise postformal stages beyond Piaget's formal operations (Chapter 5), examines the theories and practices of postformalism in education (Chapter 6) and undertakes a multi-faceted dialogue among the postformal reasoning features, the postformal pedagogies and key evolutionary themes, arriving at four core pedagogical values (Chapter 7).

Part III expands these four core pedagogical values—love, life, wisdom and voice—from philosophical, psycho-social and practical educational perspectives, articulating the paradox of my postformal education philosophy: while it involved quite complex theoretical analyses to develop, it is terribly simple to apply.

In Part I, I make the claim that education needs to evolve. Therefore, I need to show how education is both a product of culture and a creator of culture, and how it both contributes to psychological development as well as potentially hinders it. I do this by exploring theories of cultural evolution and individual psychological development before investigating how education is contextualised within these processes. In the first two chapters, I show how the evolution of consciousness affects both the cultural development of our human species (phylogeny) and the psychological development of the individuals within the culture (ontogeny).

In Chapter 2, I introduce the notion of the evolution of consciousness, its history and development. After discussing some of the challenges of cultural evolutionary work and why it is important to take a transdisciplinary approach, I discuss how the evolutionary discourse has been dominated by a narrow reading of Darwinian biological evolution and demonstrate why this approach is incomplete. This provides a counter-point for an exploration of the alternative evolutionary discourse with its philosophical origins in 18th-century German Romanticism and Idealism. You will meet researchers and great thinkers who since the turn of the 20th century began to re-integrate spiritual perspectives of consciousness into the biological evolution discourse. I introduce the contemporary notion that we can consciously participate in evolution and perhaps surprise you that this idea was first put forward by German romantic philosopher Friedrich Wilhelm Joseph Schelling in the late 18th century. While there are several theorists of cultural evolution, I focus on three: Steiner, Gebser and Wilber. The main body of the chapter presents cultural evolution through five stages using Gebser's model of archaic, magic, mythical, mental and integral structures of consciousness—the latter currently emerging.

Following on from the big picture of cultural evolution supported by evidence from a variety of fields, Chapter 3 offers an introduction to individual psychological development theories across childhood and adolescence. After discussing some of the challenges of consciousness research, including critiques of developmentalism, I present an overview of developmental theories from the field of psychology. This includes the concept of stage theory, in particular through the child and adolescent development theories of Jean Piaget. Following discussion on the limitations of

Piaget's stage theory, I introduce a series of complex socio-psychological phenomena that I call the *megatrends of the mind* (Gidley 2010b). Through a mapping exercise, I show that significant developments have occurred in most, if not all, of the major academic disciplines. Secondly, there is a gradual transcending of disciplinary specialisation, via inter-, multi- and transdisciplinary approaches. I demonstrate how these developments are *enactments* of new ways of thinking and new knowledge patterns that break through the limits of formal reasoning, as manifestations of the evolution of consciousness (Gidley 2007b). Finally, I introduce the notion of a transition beyond formal operations to postformal reasoning and point to adult developmental psychology theories for discussion in Chapter 5.

Chapter 4 offers what can only be mere fragments of the evolution of education so far, given the subject could easily fill not just one book but rather several volumes, particularly when you consider that education is a much broader concept than just "schooling". To take you beyond the limited framing of contemporary school education, I present education in its broader *cultural* context, as only one of the types of enculturation that adults provide for their young people. I propose three macro-historical phases of education—pre-formal, formal and postformal. Drawing on cultural evolutionary research, I trace thousands of years of informal enculturation of children (pre-formal education), speculating on how education may have been practised in these very early periods of human history. This provides the context for how education has developed from the past to the present and how it might develop into the future. I explain how universal formal education began as an integrated, human-centred, process of *bildung*—or development of the whole person—two hundred years ago in Germany and only later became influenced by the industrial era mindset whereby schools became little more than factories. Finally, I point to some 21st-century drivers of change and introduce two contrasting concepts: the *global knowledge economy* and *global knowledge futures*.

Part II focuses on adult developmental psychology research on higher stages of reasoning, today's most evolved education research and practice, and a dialogue between them. This dialogue reveals surprising links between play and wisdom, imagination and ecology, holism and love. These explorations are foundational to my postformal education philosophy and may theoretically empower contemporary educational innovations, by reframing them as postformal pedagogies.

Chapter 5 begins by introducing you to a range of theories of mature adult psychological development. You will meet several adult developmental psychologists who have been working since the 1970s in the field of positive adult development, particularly in the USA. These psychologists have been undertaking theoretical and empirical research to establish the validity of stages of reasoning beyond Piaget's formal operations. They use the term *postformal* to denote higher developmental stages beyond Piaget's *formal operations*. This chapter presents and discusses numerous features of postformal reasoning and then relates them to four evolutionary themes that emerged from my extensive research on the evolution of consciousness (Gidley 2007b).

- Theme 1 includes notions of conscious, compassionate spiritual development, via traditional religious and post-traditional approaches.
- Theme 2 includes discourses that transcend the static nature of formal thinking and promote the emergence of more fluid, life-enhancing, thinking, through process and poststructuralist philosophies, and the new sciences.
- Theme 3 involves the increasing complexification of human thinking. This includes two sub-streams that both explicitly identify new stages of consciousness: cultural evolution and developmental psychology.
- Theme 4 involves discourses that transcend disciplinary, linguistic and paradigmatic boundaries by pointing to how new thinking and reflection on language can empower multiple voices.

In Chapter 6, I begin by identifying three evolutionary waves of educational change throughout the 20th century. The third evolutionary wave suggests that education is in a transition from formal schooling to postformal pedagogies. In this chapter you will learn about a group of critical educational theorists and practitioners who have been researching what they call "post-formal" education in relation to critical and postmodern approaches to education. Leading post-formal educational researchers Joe Kincheloe and Shirley Steinberg proposed four key components of postformality that are introduced in this chapter. In addition to Kincheloe's postformalism, I introduce several other key theorists and a dozen or more postformal educational approaches. I indicate how these *postformal pedagogies* are contributing to the type of education so necessary today. I map these different approaches and explore relationships among them. I hope this chapter will reflect back to readers the diversity of approaches, thus deepening understanding among theorists and practitioners of postformal pedagogies.

Chapter 7 is where I begin to dig more deeply into the convergences and divergences between the psychology and education approaches to postformality. As a transdisciplinary boundary-worker, I work at the creative margins of a number of discourses, and in this chapter I engage in a series of dialogues among them. Firstly, I focus on the dialogue between cultural evolution and psychological development. Secondly, I undertake several dialogues among the developmental psychology literature and the education literature within the framing of educational futures. This chapter makes a very important contribution by commencing such in-depth dialogues in that I map the evolutionary themes discussed in Chapter 5 across the clusters of postformal reasoning qualities and postformal educational offerings to reveal four core pedagogical values that emerged from these intersections.

The four chapters of Part III develop and articulate the four core pedagogical values that are central to my postformal education philosophy. These four core values—love, life, wisdom and voice—arise from the cross-pollination between the evolution of consciousness themes, postformal reasoning and postformal pedagogies. The chapters show how, by building on the four core pedagogical values, education could facilitate the healthy evolution of consciousness. These values have emerged as being crucial to a caring, revitalised, wise and empowering education.

In Chapter 8 I express my vision of educating children for and with respectful and responsible love. The chapter reflects the centrality of love, care, relationships and community as expressed in all the major religions and spiritual traditions in which human love is a reflection of Divine Love. As such, love should not be underestimated as a significant developmental and evolutionary force in education. You will learn about the approaches of several contemporary educators who emphasise the importance of love, care and teacher presence. Chapter 8 also presents many examples from both theory and practice of how love might increasingly infuse school education with evolutionary force.

Chapter 9 illuminates the early 20th-century turn from mechanistic to organic worldviews, as reflected in the new sciences and postmodern philosophical discourse. This shift from static, mechanistic thinking to organic, living process-oriented thinking has a co-evolutionary relationship with the emerging postformal, integral consciousness. This chapter discusses how educational futures depend on a deep understanding of how the creative imagination can be more fully awakened. I argue for the significance of imagination in education to revitalise thinking and indeed education itself. I introduce numerous educators and theories that stress the significance of imagination in education and demonstrate how enlivening education may even assist the resuscitation of a dying planetary ecosystem.

The focus of Chapter 10 is wisdom and how to develop it educationally. I discuss research that indicates that the most acknowledged path to wisdom is through the cultivation of multi-perspectival, versatile standpoints. I explore numerous learning modes and approaches that can be activated including engaging with multiple intelligences, creativity and complexity, which are all steps to cultivating wisdom. Finally, I introduce several other ways of knowing that have been even more subjugated in educational discourse. In the "serious business" of education and learning, squeezed on either side by the audit culture and high-stakes testing, such concepts as laughter, humour, frivolity, dancing and happiness seem remote. Yet these creative human literacies are part of wisdom's educational smorgasbord.

In Chapter 11, I propose that in this electronic age of "voice" mail, "chat" rooms and "talking" computers, the least valued of the evolutionary forces is the human voice itself. The education of the speaking voice as an expression of *living* language can potentially empower—give voice to—the marginal in society. No matter how caring, imaginative and interesting our approach to children may be, unless we can transmit our authentic *presence* to them through our choice of words, our tone of voice, the timing of our silences, we may not facilitate the transformation we would like. You will be introduced to several significant 20th-century thinkers who have drawn attention to the evolutionary significance of self-reflection and creativity in language. Although educational theory has not significantly engaged with voice and language for their empowering force, we will see that voice and its partner, silence, are being rediscovered amid a cacophony of electronic sound bytes.

Finally, in Chapter 12, I reflect on the threads of my postformal educational philosophy, pointing to ways forward for teachers and others who want to educate

young people as complete human beings rather than tools for the economic machine. I suggest that by nurturing their wholeness of being, they will find within themselves the creativity, strength and courage to face the complex futures ahead.

1.6 Personal Reflections and Concluding Remarks

Personal Reflections. *About twenty years ago, I was trekking with my family in some reasonably remote Himalayan villages in the mountains of Nepal. Some of the local children discovered that I was at that time a teacher. They took me by the hand and excitedly ran away with me to show off with pride their new school. It was a dark little square room with straight rows of seats, a blackboard and some white chalk with each child having a little piece of black slate so they could "learn to write". I tried to look happy for them. But inwardly I was wondering how it is that only the driest crumbs of the industrial educational model, already failing Anglo-European children in droves, could be being offered to these lively Nepalese children. I later wondered if that is what is meant by the World Bank's "Education for All" agenda. And I'm certainly not suggesting that their situation could be improved by giving these little schools computers as well. Having been involved for ten years in founding, pioneering and teaching in a radically contemporised Steiner school in rural Australia, I knew learning could be otherwise. As a responsible participant in their (and my) joyous learning of every imaginable subject through stories, drawing, painting, singing, movement, drama, music, poetry, mythology and play, I have guided numerous children from the age of five or six to puberty. And... perhaps as a surprise to many mainstream teachers, the children also became literate and numerate in the process. But instead of just developing a narrow, functional literacy, they developed rich and broad literacies. They learned to read for meaning, to write creatively, to share, to respect nature, to imagine worlds beyond their immediate one, to have social confidence, a passionate love of learning and the courage to be the ones to change the world.*

In summary, in this book I hope to show you how an educational integration of love and reverence, with life-giving conceptual imagination and creative multi-modal methods, transmitted through an authentic human voice, can lay a strong foundation for the emergence of postformal reasoning later in life. In these times of complexity and global distress, it is imperative that we consciously evolve education.

References

Aurobindo, S. (1914/2000). *The life divine. 2nd American edition* (Originally published in the monthly review Arya 1914–1920). Twin Lakes: Lotus Press.

Benedikter, R. (2005). *Postmodern spirituality: A dialogue in five parts.* http://www.integralworld.net/index.html?benedikter1.html. Accessed 28 June 2006.

Deleuze, G. (1968/1994). *Difference and repetition* (First published in French 1968). New York: Columbia University Press.

Deleuze, G., & Guattari, F. (1987). *A thousand plateaus* (B. Massumi, Trans.). Minneapolis: University of Minnesota Press.

Foucault, M. (1994). *Ethics: Subjectivity and choice* (The essential works of Michel Foucault 1954–1984). London: Allen Lane, The Penguin Press.

Foucault, M. (2005). *The hermeneutics of the subject: Lectures at the Collège de France 1981–1982*. New York: Palgrave MacMillan.

Gebser, J. (1949/1985). *The ever-present origin*. Athens: Ohio University Press.

Gidley, J. (1998). Prospective youth visions through imaginative education. *Futures: The Journal of Policy, Planning and Futures Studies, 30*(5), 395–408.

Gidley, J. (2002a). Global youth culture: A transdisciplinary perspective. In J. Gidley & S. Inayatullah (Eds.), *Youth futures: Comparative research and transformative visions* (pp. 3–18). Westport: Praeger.

Gidley, J. (2002b). Holistic education and visions of rehumanized futures. In J. Gidley & S. Inayatullah (Eds.), *Youth futures: Comparative research and transformative visions* (pp. 155–168). Westport: Praeger.

Gidley, J. (2004). The metaphors of globalisation: A multi-layered analysis of global youth culture. In S. Inayatullah (Ed.), *The causal layered analysis (CLA) reader: Theory and case studies of an integrative and transformative methodology*. Taipei: Tamkang University.

Gidley, J. (2006). Spiritual epistemologies and integral cosmologies: Transforming thinking and culture. In S. Awbrey, D. Dana, V. Miller, P. Robinson, M. M. Ryan, & D. K. Scott (Eds.), *Integrative learning and action: A call to wholeness* (Studies in education and spirituality, Vol. 3, pp. 29–55). New York: Peter Lang Publishing.

Gidley, J. (2007a). Educational imperatives of the evolution of consciousness: The integral visions of Rudolf Steiner and Ken Wilber. *International Journal of Children's Spirituality, 12*(2), 117–135.

Gidley, J. (2007b). The evolution of consciousness as a planetary imperative: An integration of integral views. *Integral Review: A Transdisciplinary and Transcultural Journal for New Thought, Research and Praxis, 5*, 4–226.

Gidley, J. (2008). *Evolving education: A postformal-integral-planetary Gaze at the evolution of consciousness and the educational imperatives*. PhD dissertation Southern Cross University, Lismore.

Gidley, J. (2009). Educating for evolving consciousness: Voicing the emergency for love, life and wisdom. In *The international handbook of education for spirituality, care and wellbeing* (Springer international handbooks of religion and education series). New York: Springer.

Gidley, J. (2010a). Evolving higher education integrally: Delicate mandalic theorising. In S. Esbjörn-Hargens, O. Gunnlaugson, & J. Reams (Eds.), *Integral education: New directions for higher learning* (pp. 345–361). New York: State University of New York Press.

Gidley, J. (2010b). Globally scanning for megatrends of the mind: Potential futures of "Futures Thinking". *Futures: The Journal of Policy, Planning and Futures Studies, 42*(10), 1040–1048.

Gidley, J. (2010c). Postformal priorities for postnormal times: A rejoinder to Ziauddin Sardar. *Futures: The Journal of Policy, Planning and Futures Studies, 42*(6), 625–632.

Gidley, J. (2011). From crisis to confidence: The development of social and emotional education in Australia. In B. Hey (Ed.), *Social and emotional education: International analysis II* (pp. 69–101). Santander: Fundacione Marcelino Botin.

Gidley, J. (2012a). Evolution of education: From weak signals to rich imaginaries of educational futures. *Futures: The Journal of Policy, Planning and Futures Studies, 44*(1), 46–54.

Gidley, J. (2012b). Re-imagining the role and function of higher education for alternative futures through embracing global knowledge futures. In P. Scott, A. Curaj, L. Vlăsceanu, & L. Wilson (Eds.), *European higher education at the crossroads: Between the Bologna process and national reforms*. Dordrecht: Springer.

Gidley, J. (2013). Global knowledge futures: Articulating the emergence of a new meta-level field. *Integral Review: A Transdisciplinary and Transcultural Journal for New Thought, Research and Praxis, 9*(2), 145–172.

Gidley, J., Bateman, D., & Smith, C. (2004). *Futures in education: Principles, practice and potential* (AFI Monograph Series 2004: No 5). Melbourne: Australian Foresight Institute.

Gidley, J., & Inayatullah, S. (2002). *Youth futures: Comparative research and transformative visions*. Westport: Praeger.

Giroux, H. A. (1992). *Border crossing: Cultural workers and the politics of education*. New York: Routledge.

Kegan, R. (1994). *In over our heads: The mental demands of modern life*. Cambridge, MA: Harvard University Press.

Miller, R. (2000). Education and the evolution of the cosmos [Electronic version]. *Caring for new life: Essays on holistic education*.

Montuori, A. (2004). *Edgar Morin: A partial introduction. World Futures: The Journal General Evolution, 60*(5), 349–355.

Morin, E. (2001). *Seven complex lessons in education for the future*. Paris: UNESCO.

Roy, B. (2006). The map, the gap and the territory. *Integral Review: A Transdisciplinary and Transcultural Journal for New Thought, Research and Praxis, 3*, 25–28.

Steiner, R. (1894/1964). *The philosophy of freedom: The basis for a modern world conception (GA 4)* (M. Wilson, Trans., Rev. Ed.) (Original work published 1894). Spring Valley: The Anthroposophic Press.

Steiner, R. (1909/1965). *The education of the child in the light of anthroposophy (GA 34)* (2nd ed., G. & M. Adams, Trans.) (Original work published 1909). London: Rudolf Steiner Press.

Steiner, R. (1967). *The younger generation: Education and spiritual impulses in the 20th century (GA 217)* (R. M. Querido, Trans.) [13 Lectures Stuttgart, October 3 to 15, 1922]. New York: Anthroposophic Press.

Steiner, R. (1971). *Human values in education, lectures, 1924*. London: Rudolf Steiner Press.

Steiner, R. (1981). *The renewal of education through the science of the spirit: Lectures, 1920*. Sussex: Kolisko Archive.

Steiner, R. (1982). *The kingdom of childhood: Lectures, 1924*. New York: Anthroposophic Press.

Zahavi, D. (Ed.). (2004). *Hidden resources: Classical perspectives on subjectivity*. Exeter: Imprint Academic.

Part I
An Evolutionary Approach to Education

Chapter 2
Cultural Evolution: Past, Present and Futures

2.1 Introduction

In this chapter I offer a big picture overview of cultural history as a context for understanding our present situation in relation to education. Ever since human beings first appeared as *Homo sapiens* around 200,000 years ago, human life on earth has been in a state of continual change and gradual development. The way that human cultures and societies have evolved over macro time periods is intimately connected with individual psychological development, including degrees of consciousness and ways of knowing about the world. Furthermore, the evolution of human consciousness is deeply interwoven with the development of speech, language and art. The aesthetic sensibility of early humans, once expressed in bodily ornamentation, cave paintings, carvings and pictograms, gradually evolved over several millennia into more abstract forms of writing and, more recently, digital technology (see Chapter 4). In a similar manner, the enculturation of children was for millennia purely about cultural transmission—that is, passing on the values and traditions of the tribe or community to the next generation. I refer to this broad enculturation of children into the myths, mores and laws of their societies as pre-formal education. It is only in the last two to three hundred years that pre-formal enculturation of children by their families and tribes has been replaced by formal school education for the majority. But before we go into formal education in Chapter 4, I want to trace this fascinating story of cultural evolution for its relevance to understanding the background from which school education emerged.

After introducing the concept of evolution of consciousness and discussing the research challenges, I take a transdisciplinary approach to evolution, to overcome some of the limitations of Darwinian biological evolution. Three theorists of cultural evolution are chosen—Rudolf Steiner, Jean Gebser and Ken Wilber—with the structural framework being provided by Gebser's model. An overview of five major transitions of culture and consciousness are presented, the most recent being integral, which is emerging today.

J.M. Gidley, *Postformal Education*, Critical Studies of Education 3,
DOI 10.1007/978-3-319-29069-0_2

This chapter challenges the dominant evolution narrative by integrating perspectives beyond classical evolutionary biology. The purpose of the chapter is to lay the groundwork for creating conceptual bridges between cultural evolution and education as the book unfolds.

2.2 Evolution of Consciousness: The Cultural Dimension (Phylogeny)

> Without renewing our culture and consciousness we will be unable to transform today's dominant civilization and overcome the problems generated by its shortsighted mechanistic and manipulative thinking. . . The shift to a new civilization—depends on the evolution of our consciousness . . . a precondition of our collective survival. (László 2006, pp. 39, 77)

Hungarian-born systems scientist, Ervin László, prefaces his comments with a nod to Einstein and his famous words of a century ago. Like many researchers from psychology, philosophy, physics and cultural history, László claims that the challenges of our times require that we *consciously* evolve our consciousness. The diverse features of the emerging new consciousness are being articulated in the literature on postformal reasoning, integral studies and planetary consciousness, which I gather under the term *evolution of consciousness*.

The interconnectedness between cultural evolution of our species as a whole and individual psychological development needs to be teased apart before it can be fully appreciated. This chapter will focus on cultural evolution, known as phylogeny, and the next chapter will focus on individual psychological development, known as ontogeny. The interrelationships between the two areas will be developed in Chapter 7.

2.2.1 What is Cultural Evolution?

To put it simply, cultural evolution is the idea that human cultures develop and evolve in much the same way that species evolve. In very broad terms, most of the cultures around the planet today are much more complex and multi-faceted than the cultures of early hunters and gatherers or agriculturalists. Some may argue that the dominant culture of today is not an improvement on early cultures, in light of the environmental damage being committed in the name of development. On the other hand, we cannot deny that human creativity and ingenuity has led to some remarkable cultural products in terms of language, art, music, architecture, science and technology and much more. We are in the midst of a new human cultural renaissance that is emerging out of the damaging impacts of hyper-industrialisation, to give birth to an infinitely creative post-industrial, postformal, integral, planetary culture.

I will begin by briefly explaining how I am using the key terms *culture* and *evolution*, before discussing more theoretical issues.

By *culture* I mean all that constitutes societies including the myths, mores, rules and laws that develop over time across the whole of humanity and yet can be quite diverse geographically at any given point in time.

My use of the term *evolution* not only refers to Darwinian biological evolution but also includes socio-cultural, philosophical and spiritual perspectives.

2.2.2 What is Evolution of Consciousness?

The idea of the *evolution of consciousness* is not new. Towards the end of the 18th century, it was a core topic of interest among those philosophers who were later referred to collectively as the German idealists and romantics. Almost a century before Charles Darwin published his *Origin of Species* (Darwin 1859/1998), Johann Gottfried von Herder published *This Too a Philosophy of History for the Formation of Humanity* (Herder 1774/2002). In it Herder claimed that "there exist radical mental differences between historical periods, that people's concepts, beliefs, sensations, etc. differ in important ways from one period to another" (Forster 2001).

Herder's seminal ideas on the evolution of consciousness were extended in many ways by Johann Wolfgang von Goethe, Georg Wilhelm Friedrich Hegel, Friedrich Wilhelm Joseph Schelling, the Schlegel brothers and Novalis. These philosopher-poets were attempting to re-unite philosophy, art, science and Spirit and were also influenced by the push to democracy and individual freedom of the synchronously occurring French Revolution. The pre-Enlightenment idea of a unity of knowledge had been superseded during the European Enlightenment, especially by Immanuel Kant's three-part theory of knowledge, expressed in his three major philosophical works: *The Critique of Pure Reason* (Plato's Truth), *The Critique of Practical Reason* (Plato's Goodness) and *The Critique of Judgment* (Plato's Beauty).

Schelling was a central figure in the conscious re-integration of knowledge. In particular, Schelling's contribution foreshadowed current notions of conscious evolution (Teichmann 2005). Although inspired by *earlier* unitive worldviews, these integral philosophers also pointed *forward*, beyond the limitations of both pre-modern (pre-Enlightenment) mythic consciousness and formal, modernist (Enlightenment) rationality, towards a more conscious awakening of a postformal, integral consciousness. Contemporary philosophers David Ray Griffin and Arran Gare refer to this as constructive or reconstructive postmodernism, which Gare traces to Schelling (Gare 2002; Keller and Daniell 2002).

Yet the world was not ready for these r/evolutionary ideas. It would take two hundred years for the integrative philosophical movement pioneered by the German idealists and romantics to begin to make its mark on the world through the contemporary integral movement. Following close on the heels of the European Enlightenment, and in parallel with the dawning of integral evolutionary thinking in the German States, the Industrial Revolution was brewing in Britain. This key

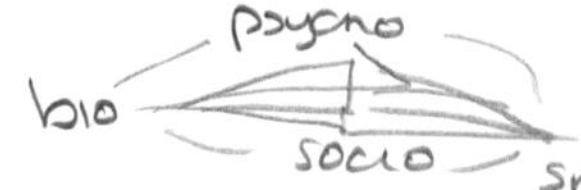

marker of early modernity was advancing its technological powers with tremendous socio-cultural force: both progressive and disruptive. Supported by the positivist worldview of scientific materialism and analytic philosophy, mechanistic notions of human nature cast a shadow on idealist and spiritual notions of human consciousness and culture, including education. Furthermore, since Darwin—and in spite of his under-appreciated writings on love and moral evolution (Loye 1998, 2004)—the dominant evolution discourse has emphasised materialistic biomechanical views of humanity, at the expense of more philosophical and spiritual views.

However, the evolution of consciousness is not just a biological concern. Swiss cultural philosopher Gebser wrote extensively about the shifts occurring in many disciplines in the first half of the 20th century, describing it as an indication of what he called a "mutation" to a new structure of consciousness (Gebser 1949/1985). Gebser's detailed examples of the features of the new consciousness—based on almost two decades of transdisciplinary research—provide a significant "academic footnote" to the extensive research on the evolution of consciousness undertaken by Steiner and Sri Aurobindo some decades earlier (Aurobindo 1914/2000; Steiner 1904/1959, 1926/1966). Steiner's research combined the history of ideas (across diverse cultures) with the evolutionary concepts of the German idealists and romantics. Sri Aurobindo's research was grounded in ancient Indian texts—contemporised by his study of German idealists (Gidley 2007; Kapoor 2007).

2.2.3 Challenges of Researching Evolution of Consciousness—Culturally

A major theoretical issue in researching cultural evolution last century was its perceived links with Auguste Comte and Herbert Spencer's contentious 19th-century models of social engineering (Comte 1855/2003; Spencer 1857). These ideologies were used to rationalise many racist and ethnocentric social abuses—including slavery, colonialism and ethnocide—and became known as *social Darwinism.*

Cultural anthropologists developed powerful critiques of these models, particularly following on from the early 20th-century shift to ethnographic field research. Their critiques include claims that cultural evolution models are ethnocentric, unilineal, too oriented towards technological materialism, privileging progress rather than preservation and speculative rather than evidence based.

For a few decades, the notion of evolution itself came under critique from anthropologists and critical social scientists. However, there has been a revival of interest as new, more integrative anthropological theories began to emerge, such as Marshall Sahlins' theory that there is both evolution of human culture in general—characterised by "growing complexity and unilinearity, with culture apparently leaping from one societal form to another", and specific evolution, "to account for the great variety in historical developments" of particular societies (Barnard and Spencer 1996/1998).

These challenging theoretical issues are discussed elsewhere in my doctoral research, in particular how Steiner, Gebser and Wilber dealt with these challenges (Gidley 2007).

2.2.4 *Why Darwinian Biological Evolution is Incomplete: A Cultural Diagnostic*

By the end of the 19th century, the entire evolution discourse had become dominated by the biologically based Darwinian evolution theory. Many contemporary evolutionary psychologists and anthropologists still base their research on what systems theorist/psychologist David Loye calls the "narrow version" of Darwinian evolutionary theory grounded in classical biology. According to Loye, Darwin's position with regard to human evolution, and particularly moral development, is more fully addressed in *Descent of Man,* which is relatively marginalised compared to *On the Origin of Species* (Darwin 1871/2004, 1872/2005; Loye 1998, 2004; Richards 1992).

Classical Darwinian evolution theory is also contested[1] from several other academic sources, which include:

- New biological approaches—such as self-organisation and emergentism—arising from chaos and complexity science (Deacon 2003; Goodenough and Deacon 2006; Swimme and Tucker 2006; Clayton 2006; Braxton 2006; Jantsch 1980; Russell 2000; Thompson 1991);
- Integral theoretic approaches that propose a dialectic between biological *evolution* and spiritual *involution* (Aurobindo 1914/2000; Combs 2002; Davidson 1992; Gebser 1970/2005; Hocks; Murphy 1992; Steiner 1971b; Wilber 2001; Gidley 2008);
- Integrative approaches that work towards an integration of evolutionary science and theology/spirituality (Clayton 2007; Esbjörn-Hargens and Wilber 2006; Cousins 1999; Stein 2006; Rolston III 2005, 1997; DeLashmutt 2005; Carr 2005; Clayton 2006; Scott 2007; Conway Morris 2007);
- Postmodern philosophical evolution theories (Rolston III 1997; Richards 1992, 2002);
- Systems theory approaches to evolution (Bocchi and Ceruti 2002; László 2006; Loye 1998, 2004);

[1]Proponents of the religious doctrine of *creationism* clearly also contest the Darwinian evolution theory. I do not enter the *evolution versus creationism* debate that still rages in schools in the USA. This is beyond the scope of my research, which builds on the well-established scientific and philosophical basis of evolutionary theory.

- Theological and religious literature, which includes intelligent design (Grace and Moreland 2002; Boivin 2001; Moreland 2001), theistic evolution (Carr 2005; DeLashmutt 2005; Teilhard de Chardin 1959/2002, 1959/2004) and *natural* theology (Conway Morris 2007; Rolston III 1997).

It is clear that classical biology is not the most comprehensive discipline for researching the richness and complexity of the evolution of culture and consciousness. The full range of human sciences needs to be involved to develop authentically *human* epistemologies. Tensions remain today within the cultural evolution discourse between the dominance of biology and the small but significant counter-thread of philosophical and spiritual approaches that have been active throughout the last century.

2.3 A Transdisciplinary Perspective on Human Culture

Cultural evolutionary work involves deep philosophical questions of far-reaching existential import. To deal with this requires a transdisciplinary approach drawing on a range of contemporary discourses including: consciousness studies, philosophy, cultural history, futures studies, psychology, spiritual studies and education. In this book I draw from diverse disciplinary fields to inform my research on the evolution of consciousness. Notwithstanding that biological notions of human nature are an advance on mechanistic notions, the complexity of human consciousness needs to be tackled in a transdisciplinary manner.

The transition from the 20th to 21st century heralded remarkable developments in our understanding of the nature of the universe. As Newtonian physics became overshadowed by the "new sciences", several pioneering thinkers took up the challenge to reconceptualise human nature in light of these radical paradigmatic shifts (Aurobindo 1909, 1914/2000; Bergson 1911/1944; Gebser 1949/1985, 1970/2005; Steiner 1926/1966; Teilhard de Chardin 1959/2004). I explore these developments in Chapter 3 as *megatrends of the mind.*

Researchers struggled to find suitable concepts to express what they saw as emergent changes in human consciousness, while minimising association with 19th-century social Darwinism. New concepts emerged such as evolution of consciousness (Steiner 1926/1966), creative evolution (Bergson 1911/1944), integral consciousness (Aurobindo 1909, 1914/2000), structures and mutations of consciousness (Gebser 1949/1985, 1970/2005) and noosphere (Teilhard de Chardin 1959/2004). Most of this work was overlooked in the social sciences, which seemed trapped in outmoded imitations of "old sciences". Ironically, social scientists have been slow to reframe human nature and its relationship to such a radically complex and mobile universe.

In spite of the challenges involved, outstanding early 20th-century thinkers have pointed to the increasing complexity of consciousness as an evolutionary quality (Aurobindo 1914/2000; Bergson 1911/1944; Gebser 1949/1985; Steiner 1926/

1966; Lovejoy 1936; Neumann 1954/1995; Teilhard de Chardin 1959/2004). Late 20th-century research lends support to Schelling's idea that we are now reaching a stage of development where we can consciously participate in evolution (Bamford 2003; Gidley 2006; Lachman 2003; Russell 2000; Thompson 1998). Several contemporary theorists have written on the evolution of consciousness, from a variety of perspectives (Combs 2002; Elgin and LeDrew 1997; Gidley 2007; László 2006; Thompson 1998; Wade 1996; Russell 2000; Jantsch 1980; Gangadean 2006a; Wilber 1981/1996).

In my research on megatrends of the mind (Gidley 2010), I attempt to cohere a number of these disparate discourses, many of which operate in isolation from each other, in contradiction to each other and even in competition with each other (See Chapter 3).

2.4 Selected Theorists of Cultural Evolution

From my analysis of the literature, I conclude that the three most important 20th-century theorists of the evolution of consciousness were Steiner, Gebser and Wilber. At first glance the integral approaches of Steiner, Gebser and Wilber discussed below may give an impression that they are simply modernist, unilinear, socio-evolution models packaged as something more. This is not the case (Gidley 2007, p. 31).

In this section I draw from an in-depth study of the writings of these three—each of whom point to the emergence of new stages, structures or movements of culture and consciousness that can be referred to as *integral* (Gidley 2007). Integral consciousness is another term for what developmental psychologists call *postformal reasoning* (Chapter 5).

2.4.1 Comparative Models: Steiner, Gebser and Wilber

> There are periods in human and cultural evolution when humanity passes through such fundamental transformations that our reality shifts and new patterns of thought are required to make sense of the unfolding human drama… The profound transformation we are now witnessing has been emerging on a global scale over millennia and has matured to a tipping point and rate of acceleration that has radically altered and will continue to alter our human condition in every aspect. We must therefore expand our perspective and call forth unprecedented narrative powers to name, diagnose, and articulate this shift (Gangadean 2006b, p. 382).

The notion that human consciousness *has* evolved is a largely undisputed claim. However, the idea that human culture and consciousness *are currently evolving* in such a way that we can *consciously participate* in this process is novel in academic circles. Integral philosopher Ashok Gangadean in the opening quotation encapsulates what many integral theorists have been voicing over the past decade. This research points to the emergence of a new type of consciousness that has been referred to by various terms, most notably, *postformal*, *integral* and/or *planetary*.

The major focus of this chapter is to broaden and deepen the readers' understanding of the significance of cultural evolution for education. What follows is an interpretive analysis and integration of the evolutionary writings of Steiner, Gebser and Wilber. My selection of these three was influenced by their comprehensiveness and how they complement each other. While Wilber's content is comprehensive—and his theory elegant—his areas of weakness are the areas of strength of Steiner and Gebser: participatory engagement and aesthetic sensibility. By contrast, Wilber's embrace of contemporary research and his accessible text complement the more historical nature of Steiner's and Gebser's contribution. More information on my rationale for choosing these three is published elsewhere (Gidley 2007).

Steiner's major contributions were that he was the first to write about an emergent new consciousness (Steiner 1904/1959). He wrote and lectured *extensively* on the evolution of consciousness, building on ancient Indian, Greek *and* particularly, German idealist and romantic lineages. Secondly, Steiner developed and published a comprehensive series of practices designed to awaken the new consciousness in humanity—particularly through education, contemplative practices and the arts (Steiner 1950, 1904/1959, 1964, 1909/1965, 1926/1966, 1966, 1986, 1971a, 1930/1983, 1904/1993, 1905/1981, 1982).

Wilber's major contributions so far have been: firstly, to synthesise, contemporise and popularise much of the earlier research[2]; and secondly, to theorise a framework designed to assist with the application of his integral theory to a range of disciplinary fields (Wilber 1981/1996, 1980/1996, 2000a, 2000b, 1995/2000, 2004, 2006). The most recent form of Wilber's framework is called AQAL—which refers to all quadrants, all levels, all lines, all states and all types, these being the five major dimensions of his theoretical framework (Wilber 2004). Thirdly, Wilber has popularised the need for *integral life practices*, already emphasised by Steiner and Sri Aurobindo and more recently in the USA by George Leonard and Michael Murphy, somewhat balancing his cognicentrism.

Gebser's major contributions were: firstly, to begin to academically formalise the emergent integral structure of consciousness; and secondly, to observe and note its emergence in the world in various disciplines and discourses in the first half of the 20th century (Gebser 1970/2005, 1949/1985, 1956/1996).

These three approaches provide very important perspectives on human development. In my analysis they are complementary peers, each stronger in one or another aspect. To be more precise, Gebser's model is very good in terms of cultural history and also in its rich and detailed descriptions of all the major structures including integral. Although Steiner's approach is inherently integrative, he rarely

---

[2]Wilber's omission of any substantial consideration of Steiner's extensive research on evolution of consciousness, other than a few brief comments, was a primary impetus for my inclusion of Steiner.

use the word *integral* explicitly to characterise his work. A major strength is the education system he founded which prepares children to develop new ways of thinking. Wilber's AQAL system is a comprehensive integral conceptual framework and may be used as a framework for analysis and design.

Because of my primary focus on these three major sources, my coverage of many significant theorists is of necessity brief. Wilber has quoted extensively from many other sources, but I have not in all cases been able to analyse his interpretation as I have done with his writings on Gebser.

2.4.2 Gebser's Structures of Consciousness

Gebser's view of cultural evolution is that the human species has undergone a number of transformations of our structures or modes of consciousness from the archaic, to the magic, to the mythical, to the mental/rational mode and is now in transition from the mental mode to the integral-aperspectival mode of consciousness. The five structures of consciousness that he identified are differentiated by "differing degrees or intensity of awareness" (Gebser 1949/1985). Gebser briefly summarised them as follows:

- *Archaic*—It is antecedent to any awareness of time and space and prior to magic consciousness and inhabits a zero-dimensional world. It is spiritually embedded in nature;
- *Magic*—It corresponds to deep sleep, does not know of time and space and has its domain in a one-dimensional world. It is vegetative, instinctual and vitalistic in nature;
- *Mythical*—It corresponds to dream states, knows time but not space and inhabits a two-dimensional world. It is psychic in nature;
- *Mental*—It corresponds to wakefulness, to life in time and space in a three-dimensional world. It is essentially rational in nature;
- *Integral*—It corresponds to aperspectival consciousness, comprising a world of four dimensions. It is essentially spiritual in nature (Gebser 1949/1985, p. 84).

Elsewhere, Gebser spoke about the integral-aperspectival consciousness as follows: "This space-time freedom…is spiritual; and in this sense the fourth dimension in all its plenitude is the initial expression of a concretion of the spiritual" (Gebser 1949/1985, p. 387).

For a rich understanding of the potential of integral consciousness to better understand how education needs to change today to foster the new consciousness, Gebser's *Ever-Present Origin* is a seminal text (Gebser 1949/1985). The remainder of this chapter is organised according to Gebser's five structures of consciousness—archaic, magic, mythical, mental and integral.

While it is impossible to know how archaic humans actually enculturated their children and young people, as we move through the different cultural-historical periods, we can begin to sense how enculturation began to crystallise into more

Table 2.1 Relationships among Approaches of Gebser, Steiner and Wilber

Time	Gebser Structures	Steiner Macrohistory	Wilber Synthesis
P A	Archaic (pre-history)	Pre-Diluvian, pre-history Spiritually embedded	Archaic-uroboric
S T	Magic (includes Ice Age)	Ancient Indian cultural era (7,000–5,000 BCE approx.) Ancient Persian cultural era (5,000–3,000 BCE approx.)	Magic-typhonic
	Mythical (pre-800 BCE)	Mythic and pictorial cultures Egyptian cultural era (3,000–800 BCE approx.)	Myth-membership
F U T	Mental-perspectival (800 BCE–1,500 CE)	Rational intellectual ego development Greco-Roman cultural era (800 BCE–1,500 CE)	Ego-rational
U R E	Integral-aperspectival (1,500 CE–future)	Consciousness soul/mind Current and future cultural era (1,500 CE–3,500+)	Vision-logic

Source: Gidley (2008)

definite and formal structures as our ways of thinking became more formalised (see Chapter 4). It will become obvious as the book unfolds that if we are to facilitate the awaking of new integral, postformal ways of thinking, we need to radically postformalise our education systems.

Some of the correspondences between Gebser's, Steiner's and Wilber's taxonomies and terminologies of cultural evolution are shown in Table 2.1.

2.5 Cultural Evolution from an Integrated Lens

> A cultural taxonomy derived from art is vastly superior to one derived from tools. After all, tools do not designate cultures; art does. (Bednarik 2003, p. 2)

The significance of *art*—rather than *tools*—as a basis for a new approach to cultural evolution has been proposed by Robert Bednarik, director of the *International Federation of Rock Art Organizations* (IFRAO) (Bednarik 2003). Bednarik proposes that instead of terms such as Palaeo*lithic* and Neo*lithic*—referring to the development of use of stone tools—the term *Palaeolithic* could be replaced by the term *Palaeoaesthetic*.

Surprisingly, the domain of *art*—or *aesthetic sensibility*—may be a more fruitful starting point for the creation of a new *panhuman*[3] narrative about the evolution of culture and consciousness. For a guide to the aesthetic development of humanity from two and a half million years ago until the classical period around 3,000 years

[3]The term *panhuman* comes from the Greek *pananthropinon*. It has been used in recent academic literature, particularly in reference to world art (Kimball 2004) and Greek poetry (Stathatou 2007).

ago, see Table 2.2. The importance of aesthetics in cultural evolution informs my speculations on early forms of education, to be further pursued in Chapter 4.

The study and application of *aesthetics* has been a relatively minor—but continuous—philosophical thread that stretches from at least the Platonic beginnings of Western philosophy up to the present time (Bosanquet 1892/2005). Educational philosopher and poet, Sir Herbert Read (1893–1968), proposed that aesthetic appreciation is fundamental to higher cognition. On the basis of the significance of art in developmental and evolutionary theory and following in the footsteps of German philosopher Friedrich Schiller (1759–1805), Read claimed that art/aesthetics should be the very *basis* of education (Read 1943; Schiller 1954/1977). Read's evolutionary pedagogy begs the question: Why has art/aesthetics remained—at best—a tangential thread in educational philosophy in the light of its apparent significance as an evolutionary catalyst?

Table 2.2 The Aesthetic Genealogy of *Pre-literate* Humanity

Gebser's Structures of Consciousness[a]	**Human Creative Abilities**	**Human Aesthetic Development**	**Broad Time Periods BP (and BCE)**
Pre-Homo hominins (pedestrial, manual) **Archaic humans** (aural, vocal) (***Homo sapiens***)	Becoming gradually human. . . Whole body rhythmic, vital Aesthetic enactment	Walking, hunting Collecting objects Migrating, use of fire Tools, dancing Chorusing, cooking Colouring, shaping Beading, burials Skin/fur clothing	2.5 mya[b] → 800,000 → 500,000 → 200,000 → 100,000 →
Magic connectionism (visual, musical, manual)	Emotional Visual Musical Manual Aesthetic enactment	Singing, sculpting, Petroglyphs, painting Musical instruments Speech Buildings, pottery, metal craft Linen, cotton, silk[c] Early pictograms	40,000 → 30,000 → 15,000 → 7,000 BCE → 3,500 BCE →
Mythical (oral, poetic, narrative, cosmetic)	Oratory narrative Poetic linguistic Manual Aesthetic enactment Literary	Stories/myths Logograms, poetry Architecture, painting Weaving, sculpture High art Proto-alphabets	3,000 BCE → 2,000 BCE → 1,400 BCE →

Source: Gidley (2008)

[a]Gebser does not distinguish what time period is referred to by his term *Archaic* consciousness, but it is likely that it includes pre-human hominins. He only gives chronologies from mythical onwards.

[b]"mya" refers to *million years ago*.

[c]The art of spinning and weaving flax into linen developed in Egypt c. 3,400 BCE; in India the spinning of cotton traces back to c. 3,000 BCE; in China, sericulture and silk spinning methods were initiated c. 2,640 BCE. http://www.india-crafts.com/textile/textile-history.html

The following fragments of the evolutionary narrative are primarily drawn from Gebser's approach, but also integrate insights from Steiner, Wilber, Bednarik and others. In Chapter 4, I discuss the aesthetic sensibilities of these early hominins and humans and speculate on how they may have enculturated their young.

It is clear from Table 2.2 that the invention and use of stone tools is only a very minor, albeit significant, part of the cultural evolution of early humans. Dancing, singing, colouring and shaping were all part of the activities of Gebser's Archaic humans, during the Palaeolithic (Old Stone Age) period, prior to *Homo sapiens*. This picture lends a good deal of support to Bednarik's proposal to change our terminology from *Palaeolithic* to *Palaeoaesthetic*.

Furthermore, during the period 7,000 to 3,000 BCE, referred to as Neolithic (New Stone Age), humans were already engaged in sculpting, painting, pottery, metal craft and building and were wearing linen, cotton and silk. Perhaps we could continue Bednarik's aesthetic reframing by replacing *Neolithic* with *Neoaesthetic*. In Gebser's model this is an era of transition between magical consciousness and mythical consciousness. For transdisciplinary contextual framing, see Table 2.3.

2.5.1 The Dawn of Humans: The Culture of Survival

> That original wisdom was an actually inspired wisdom, one that came to man from without, arising from divine worlds. (Steiner 1971a, p. 114)

> Dreamlessly the true men of earlier times slept. Chaung-tzu ca. 350 BCE. (cited in (Gebser 1949/1985, p. 44))

Scientific knowledge regarding the emergence of human beings on earth is fragmentary, somewhat incoherent, and still being uncovered.[4] To add to the challenge of transdisciplinary research in this area, there appears to be different nomenclature and timelines to classify the various geological and archaeological periods both between and within disciplines (see Table 2.3 for a rough guide to this territory).

2.5.1.1 Key Features of Archaic Consciousness

> The archaic-uroboric period. . .presents in a very global fashion the great transition from mammals in general to man in particular, and stands further as the great subconscious ground out of which the figure of the ego would eventually emerge. . . (Wilber 1981/1996, p. 33)

[4]Radiocarbon dating is only accurate back to c. 60,000 years BP. Fossils older than ~100,000 years do not yield measurable DNA samples. http://www.tufts.edu/as/wright_center/cosmic_evolution/docs/fr_1/fr_1_cult1.html

Table 2.3 Cultural Evolution: Geology, Biology, Archaeology, Anthropology and History

Geological[a] Epochs	**Evolution of *Homo sapiens*: Biology**		**Archaeology Anthropology and History[d]**	**Gebser's Structures of Consciousness**
Pliocene 5.3–1.8 million years BP[b]	***Homo habilis*** 2.5–1.5 m BP ***Homo erectus/ergaster*** 2 million–250,000 BP		**Palaeolithic** (Old Stone Age) **Lower** 2.5 million–120,000 BP	**Archaic** Hunter-gatherer Nomadic Tribal palaeo-art Song and speech Spiritual connection Embedded in nature and cosmos Natural dwellings
Pleistocene (Ice Age) 2 million–12,000 BP	***Homo neanderthalensis*** 250,000–30,000 BP	***Homo sapiens*** 200,000 BP –present	**Middle Palaeolithic** 300,000–30,000 BP	
	Cro-Magnon 40,000–12,000 BP		**Upper Palaeolithic** 30,000–12,000 BP	
Geo-climatic catastrophe: Younger Dryas, abrupt climate change[c] 13,000–11,500BP (9,500 BCE)			**Ice melt global floods: sea level rise 120 m** 13,000–11,500 BP (9,500 BCE)	**Magic** Ice Age cave dwellers Tribal cave art and carving Warming enabled agriculture and horticulture Farming communities Early settlements Stone and copper work Housing
Holocene 9,500 BCE– late 18th century			**Mesolithic** (Middle Stone Age) 10,000–8,000 BCE	
			Neolithic (New Stone Age) 7,000–3,000 BCE and **Copper Age** 5,000–3,000 BCE	
		Pre-modern	**Bronze Age** 3,000–1,200 BCE	**Mythical** Feudal Early city-states Bronze and iron work Early pictographic writing Hieroglyphic writing
			Iron Age 1,200 BCE–700 BCE	
			Classical and medieval history 700 BCE–14th century	**Mental/Rational** Civic life in cities Egos, heroes, empires Alphabets Formal thinking Philosophy
		Modern	**Renaissance to Modern Industrial Period** 15th century–19th century	**Integral** Renaissance Enlightenment values Democratic rights Nation-states to planetary Industrial to post-industrial
Anthropocene Late 18th century to present		**Post-modern**	**Post-Industrial Postmodern** 20th–21st century and beyond	

Source: Gidley (2008)

[a]Geological data *University of California Museum of Paleontology* http://www.ucmp.berkeley.edu/help/timeform.html

[b]Archaeological and anthropological data *Handbook of Human Symbolic Evolution* (Lock and Peters 1996/1999) and *Encyclopedia of Social and Cultural Anthropology* (Barnard and Spencer 1996/1998). Mesolithic, Bronze and Iron Ages (Schriek et al. 2007; Seger 2006; Zong et al. 2007). Historico-philosophical periods (Tarnas 1991, 2006).

[c]"BP" refers to "before 1950" in geological time scales up to and including 10,000 BP (8,000 BCE).

[d]Geoclimatic upheavals (Ambrose 1998, 2003; Carlson et al. 2007; Colman 2007; Tarasov and Peltier 2005; Kay 1977; Wood and Collard 1999).

As far as we can discover from the evolutionary narratives of Steiner, Gebser, Wilber and others, several features are associated with early humans—including pre-human hominins.

- It is almost universally agreed that early humans lived in a way that was embedded in nature. What is also posited by integral evolutionary theorists is that they were also embedded in their sense of a cosmos;

- There are two conflicting views in terms of the primitiveness versus innate spiritual wisdom of early humans. Wilber tends to subscribe more to the biologically primitive notion, whereas Gebser and Steiner refer to their spiritual wisdom—albeit not with the kind of consciousness we have today (Gidley 2008, pp. 55–56);
- Our main theorists describe this most primal of human cultures as a matriarchal culture, and this is supported by other theorists (Eisler 1987);
- There is also a general sense from the evolution of consciousness theorists that the earliest of humans lived in a kind of unconscious Eden/Paradise;
- The palaeoaesthetic sensibility and expression will be discussed in more detail in Chapter 4, as it provides some grounding for speculations on pre-formal education among early humans.

It is beyond the scope of this volume to expand on these features. Interested readers will find a more detailed coverage published elsewhere (Gidley 2007, pp. 52–58).

2.5.2 *The Age of Magic: The Culture of Art*

> 'Art' has always been associated with the early cultural 'success' of anatomically modern humans, and with the establishment of what appears to be a 'fully human' cultural pattern (Lock and Peters 1996/1999, p. 289).

This conventional archaeological statement has become outmoded with the increasing body of evidence of aesthetic development in early *Homo* species, such as *H. heidelbergensis* and *H. neanderthalensis,* and the growing interest in palaeoart outside of Europe. The last glacial age (c. 70,000–10,000 BCE) was a period of great development of culture and human consciousness. This is within the late Pleistocene age and up to the beginning of the current geological epoch—the Holocene that began c. 10,000 BCE (see Table 2.3).

2.5.2.1 Key Features of Magic Consciousness

> The magic "epoch" as we see it, not only encompasses an extended "era" but also a variety of modes of manifestation and unfolding that are only imprecisely distinguishable from one another. [Yet]...we shall consider all such modes to be manifestations of magic [consciousness]. (Gebser, 1949/1985, p. 46)

The evolutionary narratives of Steiner, Gebser, Wilber and others, identify the following features as being associated with what Gebser called magic consciousness.

- Spacelessness, timelessness, unitive interconnectedness, merging with nature. Gebser expands on these features with the following description: "The spaceless

and timeless phenomena arise from the vegetative intertwining of all living things [as] realities in the egoless magic sphere" (Gebser 1970/2005, p. 49, 51);
- All three narratives characterise the social groupings as being based on kinship ties, for example of the hunter-gatherers and nomadic peoples. Gebser explained that it was the "animal breeders as well as the hunting and nomadic cultures [that were] predominantly rooted in the magic culture" (Gebser 1949/1985, p. 305). The embeddedness in the tribe was linked to the egolessness of magic human;
- The humans of this era enacted a magic response to Nature, by "standing up to Nature" and becoming a "Maker" (Gebser 1949/1985, p. 48). As Wilber put it: "the more advanced individuals had magical powers related to what we would now call *shamanism*" (Wilber 1981/1996, p. 75, 339);
- The flourishing of art—music, song and painting. This aesthetic aspect is expanded in Chapter 4 as a basis for speculation on educational processes at the time.

These features cannot be expanded in a volume of this scope. A more detailed coverage has been published elsewhere (Gidley 2007, pp. 62–69).

2.5.2.2 Transition from Magic to Mythical

> Farming was the most obvious effect, or perhaps vehicle, of a deeper transformation in structures of consciousness: it was the earliest expression, that is, of a shift from magical-typhonic to what we call mythic-membership consciousness. (Wilber 1981/1996, p. 93)

Something of a cultural hiatus occurred between approximately 9,500 BCE (the end of the abrupt climate event—the Younger Dryas) and 8,000 BCE (the beginning of the Neolithic). This is not surprising considering the dramatic environmental change occurring, during which "most of the final (warming) transition may have occurred in just a few years" (Colman 2007, Abstract). Between the height of the cultural activity of the glacial period and the establishment of agricultural settlements in the fertile crescent of Mesopotamia—China's Yellow River and the Indus and Nile valleys—the sea level rose approximately 120 metres, with much of this occurring between 12,000 BCE and 8,000 BCE.[5] As the geo-climatic conditions began to stabilise, the climatic changes associated with the end of glaciation actually facilitated the development of farming of cereals and the domestication of sheep, goats, pigs and cattle through the warmer climate and flooding of river basins. This enabled the formation of farming communities and more settled living conditions for the next few thousand years. Further research is published elsewhere (Gidley 2008, pp. 70–80).

In Steiner's narrative about this transition period, he focused on the pre-history of Asia—particularly India—and Mesopotamia—Persia-Sumeria. He pointed to

[5]This dramatic sea level data is sourced from the Goddard Institute for Space Studies, NASA, New York. http://www.giss.nasa.gov/research/briefs/gornitz_09/

the significance of what he referred to as the ancient Indian and ancient Persian cultures of that time based on his claims that: (a) they provided continuous, genealogical links to a cultural tradition of ancient spiritual wisdom; (b) their philosophical and scientific traditions were foundational to later European philosophical, scientific and cultural developments; and (c) they were significant in enabling the refining and consolidating of important subtle aspects of human biological and psycho-spiritual development (Gidley 2008, pp. 70–80).

2.5.3 *The Age of the Great Myths: The Culture of Stories*

> Whereas the distinguishing characteristic of the magic structure was the emergent awareness of nature, the essential characteristic of the mythical structure is the emergent awareness of soul. (Gebser 1949/1985, p. 61)

As the transition from magic to mythical consciousness reached its climax, the cultural shift took place from increasingly settled and complex agricultural villages to what are regarded as the world's first cities. Archaeologically, the period to be considered here straddles the Bronze Age (3,000–1,200 BCE) and the Iron Age (1,200–700 BCE). A major cultural flourishing occurred in North Africa and the Middle East among the Chaldean, Babylonian, Assyrian and Egyptian people—the thirty dynasties of the high culture of dynastic Egypt spanned 2,400 years of this period (c. 3,000–600 BCE) (Shaw 2000, pp. 479–483). Gebser locates the emergence and development of the mythic structure of consciousness across this span (c. 3,000–800 BCE), which is almost identical to the timing of Steiner's third cultural period—the Egypto-Chaldean (c. 3,000–750 BCE). So, unlike the earlier developments, there is a great deal of consensus on the age of mythical consciousness.

2.5.3.1 Key Features of Mythical Consciousness

> The ancient Chaldean priests. . .were the custodians of profound wisdom, but for them these laws of nature were not merely abstract, nor were the stars merely physical globes. They looked on each planet as ensouled by a Being. . .a divine Being who gave it life. Thus the Egyptians and Chaldeans discerned that they were spirits living among spirits in a world of spirits. (Steiner 1986, p. 101)

Most of the following key features are identified in the narratives of Steiner, Gebser and Wilber. Since this period is approaching the time of oral history, which eventually became recorded history, there is a greater body of supportive literature.

- The development of complex mythology, requiring imagination and a new degree of cognitive coherence;
- The development of astronomy, calendars and other complex mathematical systems;

- A new relationship to death and burial, reflecting the beginnings of disconnectedness;
- The development of language systems including the first pictographic and logographic writing systems;
- The strengthening of a sense of cyclical temporality;
- Membership of large organised social groupings, resembling cities. Wilber also emphasises sociological factors, such as changing gender roles and relationships, and the impact of agricultural surplus on the development of new, more specialised, social roles, e.g., priests, administrators, educators (Wilber 1981/1996, p. 97, 102);
- Temple structures, especially pyramids, were appearing. Although Egypt is most renowned for pyramids, this was also the primary form of temple architecture of the later Meso-American and South American Incan civilisations and South-East Asia;
- The culmination of primarily matriarchal societies prior to the beginnings of patriarchy with the Greco-Roman civilisation (Eisler 2001).

More information on how these features became embedded in human culture between 3,000 BCE and 700 BCE has been published elsewhere (Gidley 2007, pp. 81–90).

2.5.4 The Age of Philosophy: The Culture of Reason

> The Greek subjective conscious mind, quite apart from its pseudostructure of soul, has been born out of song and poetry. From here it moves out into its own history, into the narratizing introspections of a Socrates and the specialized classifications and analyses of an Aristotle, and from there into Hebrew, Alexandrian and Roman thought. And then into the history of a world, which, because of it, will never be the same again. (Jaynes 1976, p. 292)

Between 800 BCE and 700 BCE, another major transformation of consciousness began to take place, with its most explicit and most articulated expression in Athenian Greece. From a formal academic perspective, this is the beginning of classical history in the west when literate cultures began to record their own histories. Historian of consciousness Julian Jaynes (1976) firmly placed the emergence of rationality and history within the ancient Greek culture. Although from a Western perspective Greece is almost universally credited with the development of philosophy *per se*, this is a Eurocentric stance. In China, India and elsewhere, major philosophical developments, indicating a shift in consciousness, were also occurring during this period.

Steiner, Gebser and Wilber identified the birth of Western philosophy in ancient Greece as a turning point between mythical consciousness and mental-rational consciousness.

What I am calling here mental-rational consciousness, the epitome of which is Aristotle's formal logic, is closely aligned to what Piaget calls "formal operations" to be discussed in Chapter 3.

2.5.4.1 Key Features of Intellectual-Mental-Rational Consciousness

> The irruption of the mental structure. . .it divides and thus destroys the image of the world, which is replaced by a conception of the world. (Gebser 1949/1985, p. 176)

Because of the temporal and spatial convergence of various events, this new consciousness became hybridised with several characteristics:

- The awakening of the independent ego, or individualism—the heroes;
- The birth of rational philosophy in Greece, through Thales, Socrates, Plato, Aristotle;
- The conceptualisation of the laws of formal logic by Aristotle (Aristotle 350 BCE);
- Beginnings of formal mathematics with Pythagoras;
- The inner-directness towards self-knowledge: "Know Thyself" (Delphi Oracle);
- The beginnings of the Axial Age (a term coined by German philosopher Karl Jaspers) with the birth of Confucianism, Taoism, Buddhism and Christianity;
- The development of the world's first democratic city-state in Athens in 500 BCE, followed by the formalisation of politics and legislation;
- The shift from picture-based writing to the more abstract writing using the Greek alphabet followed by the Roman alphabet;
-  The origins of formal elite education in the 4th century BCE with Plato's *Academy* and Aristotle's *Lyceum* sowing the first seeds of higher education.

More information on how the above features which emerged in human culture between 800 BCE and the modern era can be read elsewhere (Gidley 2007, pp. 91–101).

Because the narrative is now dealing with the period of formal history, there is much material available for each of the points above, but it is beyond the scope of this chapter to cover this in detail. There is a general consensus in the history of Western ideas that a major transition began around 800 BCE from mythical consciousness to intellectual-mental-rational consciousness—primarily in Greece and later in ancient Rome (Gangadean 2006a; Habermas 1979; Jaynes 1976; Tarnas 1991, 2006). The present narrative points to prior influences from surrounding regions such as Egypt and Mesopotamia. In spite of this flourishing of rational thinking in southern Europe, Gebser claimed that the mythic consciousness continued to operate in most of northern Europe for a much longer period of time than in southern Europe and indeed that the new intellectual consciousness took another 2,000 years to be fully developed. Wilber agrees with Gebser (and Habermas) that rationality emerged "in the middle of the first millennium BCE, but it reaches its fruition with the rise of the modern state, roughly the sixteenth century in Europe"

(Wilber 1995/2000, p. 184). Wilber is referring to the European Enlightenment in the 16th century.

The European Enlightenment consolidated in northern Europe the development of the formal, logical processes of thinking initiated in ancient Greece by Aristotle. A notable feature of the emergence of the formal-mental-rational mode of thinking is that it led to the splitting apart of earlier more unitive modes of consciousness into what we take for granted now as more or less separate faculties—speech, writing, visual arts and music. Prior to the 1st millennium BCE, these faculties were much more closely interwoven than they are in most 20th- and 21st-century *modernised* humans. Arguably, they will re-integrate in times to come.

The extensive developments that took place during the long period that the rational intellect was being developed in human culture have been published in more detail (Gidley 2007, pp. 91–101).

2.5.4.2 The Birth of Formal Logic: The Cultural Context

> The most indisputable of all beliefs is that contradictory statements are not at the same time true. (Aristotle 350 BCE, Book IV, Part 6 Para 3)

This proposition from Aristotle is the second of three principle Laws of Thought and is generally referred to as the *Law of Non-Contradiction*. Another of Aristotle's principles—referred to as the *Law of the Excluded Middle*—relates to the *either/or* notion and is also a fundamental principle of formal operations. These two Aristotelian principles, when taken together, represent a 2,000-year-old encapsulation of key tenets of Piaget's formal operations, which are based on an inherently binary mode of thought. Piaget's developmental psychology theories will be discussed in Chapter 3.

The post-Enlightenment dominance of formal reasoning over the pre-formal, mythic and pictorial forms of thinking became the trademark of Western scientific and academic thinking. Increasingly with globalisation formal reasoning has become the aspirational aim of mainstream education around the world. The Enlightenment values of rationality and empiricism led on to the Industrial Revolution in Britain and later continental Europe, which laid down an intellectual-cultural template for the next three hundred years—known as *modernism*.

From a socio-cultural and geo-political perspective, binary logic also served the development of nation-states. Such questions as "Who is a National?" and "Who is a foreigner?" are based on formal logic and have supported the cultural evolutionary formation of nation states. But nation-states, like agricultural settlements and tribes before them, are mere phases in a much bigger-picture human cultural evolution, and we—as a species—are arguably right in the middle of a major transition to a planetary imaginary. Gebser (1949/1985) proposed that instead of being fixed conceptions, nations could be "dynamic efflorescences of a larger cultural context" (Gebser 1949/1985) (p. 291). What type of thinking might we need to cultivate if we are to build a non-hegemonic, richly pluralistic and sustainable planetary culture that celebrates such "dynamic efflorescences" rather than homogenising diversity? This question is addressed in Chapter 5.

2.5.4.3 A Word about Hyper-Rationality and Hyper-Modernism

From the perspective of cultural evolution, we have come to the end of the cultural period during which the abstract rational intellect was the highest form of consciousness. Since the Renaissance new forms of consciousness have been breaking through, as evidenced by the accomplishments of the most mature and advanced thinkers on earth. As always in the process of major cultural transition, those who resist the new developments struggle to hold on to the dying past. It is often the case that those individuals and groups who are most successful and powerful in the old paradigm, and thus have the most to lose, are the ones who vehemently resist all signs of a new paradigm breaking through. Fear of change provides the context for the powers-that-be to dominate with deformed and reduced forms of "the old ways of thinking" while at the same time stifling initiatives that usher in the new paradigm. A good example of this today is the great lengths that the powerful coal and oil lobbies will go to in their collusion with the climate change deniers.

There is a widespread critique today that Western culture has become dominated by an increasingly reduced form of rationality—which has led to growing fragmentation, siloism, and the separation of intellect from ethics. An example of this is the dominant global economic model—economic rationalism—which privileges profits over people and planet.

Given the intimate relationship we have already discussed between the dawn of rationality in Europe, modernism and industrialism, it is perhaps not surprising that in the more recently industrialising regions of China, India, Latin America and Africa, the rush to "modernise" to catch up with the global north is associated with a kind of frenzied hyper-modernism, hyper-industrialisation and associated hyper-urbanisation. The rapid rate of China's hyper-urbanisation, and the socio-cultural challenges it produces, is a classic example.[6]

2.5.5 *The Age of Integration: The Integral Cultural Era*

> The aperspectival consciousness structure is a consciousness of the whole, an integral consciousness encompassing all time and embracing both man's distant past and his approaching future as a living present. (Gebser 1949/1985, p. 6)

[6]Kaiman, Jonathan (2014) "China's 'eco-cities': empty of hospitals, shopping centres and people", The Guardian, 14 April 2014. http://www.theguardian.com/cities/2014/apr/14/china-tianjin-eco-city-empty-hospitals-people

Paradoxically, the first glimmerings of the integral culture and consciousness structure can be observed with the flourishing of the Renaissance even prior to the consolidation of formal thinking with the European Enlightenment (Gebser 1949/1985). Steiner and Wilber both refer to a new movement of consciousness in the cultural phenomena of 15th–16th-century Western Europe. For Steiner, the early 15th century marks the beginning of the current cultural period during which we could consciously evolve new, more self-reflective thinking that he called *consciousness soul*.

The next cultural flourish of integral thinking emerged a century after the Enlightenment when the rational scientific worldview as a sole way of knowing began to be challenged by German philosophers and English poets. As noted earlier, the German idealist and romantic philosopher-poets paved the way for resurgence of interest in the ideals of Platonic (pre-Aristotelian) ancient Greece and more spiritually integrated cultures such as ancient India. During this period, Goethe was instrumental in developing an integral philosophy known as Weimar Classicism. During the late 18th century and early 19th century, philosophical seeds were sown whereby what Gebser called "deficient rationality" could be transcended by more integral, postformal reasoning. In particular, Hegel and Schelling were developing notions of the evolution of consciousness in their philosophical writings, while Goethe, Schiller and Novalis were doing so in their literary works.

In the last two hundred years, individuals who express an integration of their intellects with art, music and spirituality are regarded as exceptions and are often referred to as "Renaissance men/women". The structure of consciousness that is currently emerging reflects a re-integration of human faculties. Futures indicated would see language again become artistic, yet also rich with the conceptual content, organisation and clarity that may arise from the integration of postformal, complex, aesthetic creativity *and* formal conceptualisation.

Further support for the notion of an emerging change in culture and consciousness comes from a ten-year study undertaken in the USA, reporting on the rise of integral culture and identifying almost a quarter of Americans as *cultural creatives* (Ray 1996). In addition, a forty-three-nation World Values Survey, including Scandinavia, Switzerland, Britain, Canada and the USA, concluded that: "a new global culture and consciousness have taken root and are beginning to grow in the world"—the postmodern shift (Elgin and LeDrew 1997).

2.5.5.1 Key Features of Integral Consciousness

> Integrality must by its nature be complex, many-sided and intricate; only some main lines can be laid down in writing, for an excess of detail would confuse the picture. (Aurobindo 1997, 152, p. 359)

This new movement of consciousness is highly complex—with *complexity* itself being one of its most significant features. The following qualities have arisen from the three narratives and will be further developed in Chapter 5.

- Re-integration of the whole person—originary spiritual presence, magic vitality, mytho-poetic imagination, mental directedness—embodied/enacted through integral transparency;
- Integration of dualisms, such as spirituality and science, imagination and logic, heart and mind, female and male;
- Transcending of egotism;
- Transcending linear, mechanical, clock-time through concretion of time-awareness;
- Planetisation of culture and consciousness;
- Linguistic self-reflection and the re-enlivening of the word.

In Chapter 7 the above features of emergent integral consciousness will be shown in relationship to the key qualities of postformal reasoning (see Table 7.4). *Re-integration of the whole person* is a core theoretical focus of this research. Humans have become *brain-bound* during the establishment of the intellectual-mental-rational mode. An integrative imperative to awaken artistic and participatory modes of consciousness comes through strongly in both the content and style of Steiner's and Gebser's writings—and in Wilber's conceptual notion of the *Big Three* (Truth, Beauty, Goodness). The emergence of integral consciousness and culture has been discussed in depth in another publication (Gidley 2007, pp. 102–121). Its growing impact on education will be discussed in several subsequent chapters.

2.6 Pointing to Megatrends of the Mind

We have seen above that the type of thinking that led to the dominant, modernist worldview is formal operations or formal reasoning (Piaget 1955). As part of the emergence of the integral cultural era, throughout the 20th century, disruption to the dominant worldview has been arising across the knowledge spectrum from quantum physics, postmodern philosophy, humanist psychology to innovative pedagogies. These evolving mindsets have transformed science, philosophy, education and knowledge as a whole. What I call *megatrends of the mind* are signs of evolutionary change in human thinking that parallel many of the exponential trends in the external world, and this movement is now undeniable (Gidley 2010). Most academic disciplines have undergone major transformation, while knowledge categorisation is moving beyond disciplinary specialisation towards transdisciplinarity (Klein 2004; Nicolescu 2002).

Such thinking affects all domains of life through the growing awareness of quantum possibilities for sudden unexpected change, win-win dialogue instead of win-lose debate, collaborative leadership instead of top-down hierarchy, cultural pluralism, self-reflection and higher purpose. These megatrends of the mind are arising from the intersection between the emerging integral culture, discussed above, and the appearance of postformal reasoning in growing numbers of mature adults. The megatrends of the mind will be introduced and discussed in the next chapter.

2.7 Concluding Remarks

In this chapter I have taken a very long-term view of human culture and shown how humans as a whole have evolved in many ways over millennia, though not in a monocultural way. The significant shifts in culture and ways of thinking that we have observed took place across thousands of years. For example, the shift from mythic to mental-rational thinking began to emerge in Greece between 800 BCE and 600 BCE but did not reach its culmination until 2,000 years later in Europe.

The evidence from cultural evolution indicates that the new integral culture began to emerge in the European Renaissance and has been gradually emerging within leading individuals for five hundred years. Compared to its longer-term potential, we see it is only in its relative infancy. An analogy would be to compare what mental-rational thinking was like just five hundred years after Aristotle compared to what it became in Hegel.

A unique aspect of the new cultural consciousness is its multifaceted nature. Integral culture is pluralistic, interconnected, multiperspectival—indeed planetary—in its scope. While the mental mode in ancient Greece began with a few leading-edge philosophers discussing ideas in Plato's Academy in Athens, the new consciousness will be pluralistic and planetary in reach—aided by the interconnectedness created through advances in technology.

If indeed we are in the midst of the emergence of a new complex mode of reasoning, then how should we educate to assist this process? This is the core question of the book and it is hoped that by the end, the reader will at least have some tentative answers, and more importantly some radical new questions. If we can educate for postformal reasoning and integral culture, imagine how much more wise, loving and creative might our consciousness be across the planet in another 1,000 years?

References

Ambrose, S. (1998). Late Pleistocene human population bottlenecks, volcanic winter, and differentiation of modern humans. *Journal of Human Evolution, 34*(6), 623–651.

Ambrose, S. (2003). Did the super-eruption of Toba cause a human population bottleneck? Reply to Gathorne-Hardy and Harcourt-Smith. *Journal of Human Evolution, 45*(3), 231–237.

Aristotle. (350 BCE). *Book IV* (W. D. Ross, Trans.). *Metaphysics* (W. D. Ross, Trans.): The Internet Classics Archive.

Aurobindo, S. (1909). *Yoga and human evolution. In essays in philosophy and yoga: Shorter works – 1910–1950* (Vol. 16). http://www.aurobindo.ru/workings/sa/16/0004_e.htm. Accessed 8 July 2007.

Aurobindo, S. (1914/2000). *The life divine. 2nd American edition.* (Originally published in the monthly review Arya 1914–1920). Twin Lakes: Lotus Press.

Aurobindo, S. (1997). *Essays divine and human with thoughts and aphorisms: Writings from manuscripts 1910–1950.* Volume 12: The complete works of Sri Aurobindo. http://www.aurobindo.ru. Accessed 7 July 2007.

Bamford, C. (2003). *An endless trace; the passionate pursuit of wisdom in the west.* New York: Codhill Press.

Barnard, A., & Spencer, J. (Eds.). (1996/1998). *Encyclopaedia of social and cultural anthropology.* London: Routledge.

Bednarik, R. G. (2003). A global perspective of Indian Palaeoart. http://www.ifrao.com/wpcontent/uploads/2014/06/reddy3.pdf. Accessed 9 April 2016.

Bergson, H. (1911/1944). *Creative evolution* (A. Mitchell, Trans.). New York: Macmillan & Co.

Bocchi, G., & Ceruti, M. (2002). *The narrative universe* (Advances in systems theory, complexity, and the human sciences). Cresskill: Hampton Press.

Boivin, M. J. (2001). Feeling humans and social animals: Theological considerations for an evolutionary account of human emotion. *Journal of Psychology and Theology, 29*(4), 314–329.

Bosanquet, B. (1892/2005). *A history of aesthetic* (Original work published 1892). New York: Cosimo Books, Inc.

Braxton, D. M. (2006). Naturalizing transcendence in the new cosmologies of emergence. *Zygon: Journal of Religion and Science, 41*(2), 347–364.

Carlson, A. E., Clark, P., U., Haley, B. A., Klinkhammer, G. P., Simmons, K., Brook, E. J. et al. (2007). Geochemical proxies of North American freshwater routing during the Younger Dryas cold event. *Proceedings of the National Academy of Sciences of the United States of America, 104*(16), 6493–6494.

Carr, P. H. (2005). A theology for evolution: Haught, Teilhard, and Tillich. *Zygon: Journal of Religion and Science, 40*(3), 733–738.

Clayton, P. (2006). The emergence of spirit: From complexity to anthropology to theology [Boyle lecture 2006]. *Theology and Science, 4*(3), 291–307.

Clayton, P. (2007). In review: Required reading: A complex brighter horizon. *Harvard Divinity Bulletin, 35*(1). http://bulletin.hds.harvard.edu/articles/winter2007/complex-brighter-horizon. Accessed 9 Apr 2016.

Colman, S. M. (2007). Conventional wisdom and climate history. *Proceedings of the National Academy of Sciences of the United States of America, 1104*(16), 6500–6501.

Combs, A. (2002). *The radiance of being: Understanding the grand integral vision: Living the integral life.* St. Paul: Paragon House.

Comte, A. (1855/2003). *Positive philosophy of Auguste Comte* (H. Martineau, Trans.) (Original work published, 1855). Whitefish: Kessinger Publishing.

Conway Morris, S. (2007). Darwin's compass: How evolution discovers the song of creation. In *Gifford lectures, 2007, The University of Edinburgh, February 19th to 27th 2007.*

Cousins, E. (1999). The convergence of cultures and religions in light of the evolution of consciousness. *Zygon: Journal of Religion and Science, 34*(2), 209–219.

Darwin, C. (1859/1998). *On the origin of species by means of natural selection or the preservation of favoured races in the struggle for life* (Original work published 1859). Hertfordshire: Wordsworth Editions Limited.

Darwin, C. (1871/2004). *The descent of man and selection in relation to sex.* Whitefish: Kessinger Publishing.

Darwin, C. (1872/2005). *The expression of the emotions in man and animals.* Whitefish: Kessinger Publishing.

Davidson, J. (1992). *Natural creation or natural selection: A complete new theory of evolution.* Rockport: Element.

Deacon, T. W. (2003). The hierarchic logic of emergence: Untangling the interdependence of evolution and self-organisation. In B. Weber & D. Depew (Eds.), *Evolution and learning: The Baldwin effect reconsidered* (pp. 273–308). Cambridge, MA: MIT Press.

DeLashmutt, M., W. (2005). Syncretism or correlation: Teilhard and Tillich's contrasting methodological approaches to science and theology. *Zygon: Journal of Religion and Science, 40*(3), 739–750.

Eisler, R. (1987). *The Chalice and the Blade: Our history, our future*. New York: HarperCollins.

Eisler, R. (2001). Partnership education in the 21st century. *Journal of Futures Studies, 5*(3), 143–156.

Elgin, D., & LeDrew, C. (1997). Global consciousness change: indicators or an emerging paradigm. San Anselmo: Millennium Project.

Esbjörn-Hargens, S., & Wilber, K. (2006). Toward a comprehensive integration of science and religion: A postmetaphysical approach. In P. Clayton, & Z. Simpson (Eds.), *The Oxford handbook of religion and science* (pp. 523–546). Oxford: Oxford University Press.

Forster, M. (2001). Johann Gottfried von Herder. In E. N. Zalta (Ed.), *The Stanford encyclopedia of philosophy*: Stanford: Stanford University Press.

Gangadean, A. (2006a). A planetary crisis of consciousness: From ego-based cultures to a sustainable global world. *Kosmos: An Integral Approach to Global Awakening, 5*, 37–39.

Gangadean, A. (2006b). Spiritual transformation as the awakening of global consciousness: A dimensional shift in the technology of mind. *Zygon: Journal of Religion and Science, 41*(2), 381–392.

Gare, A. (2002). The roots of postmodernism: Schelling, process philosophy, and poststructuralism. In C. Keller & A. Daniell (Eds.), *Process and difference: Between cosmological and poststructuralist postmodernisms*. New York: SUNY Press.

Gebser, J. (1949/1985). *The ever-present origin*. Athens: Ohio University Press.

Gebser, J. (1956/1996). Cultural philosophy as method and venture (G. Feurstein, Trans.) (Original work published 1956). *Integrative Explorations Journal, 3*, 77–84.

Gebser, J. (1970/2005). *The invisible origin: Evolution as a supplementary process* (Translated from "Der unsichtbare Ursprung", 1970). http://www.cejournal.org/GRD/JeanGebser.htm-edn64. Accessed 6 May 2007.

Gidley, J. (2006). Spiritual epistemologies and integral cosmologies: Transforming thinking and culture. In S. Awbrey, D. Dana, V. Miller, P. Robinson, M. M. Ryan, & D. K. Scott (Eds.), *Integrative learning and action: A call to wholeness* (Studies in education and spirituality, Vol. 3, pp. 29–55). New York: Peter Lang Publishing.

Gidley, J. (2007). The evolution of consciousness as a planetary imperative: An integration of integral views. *Integral Review: A Transdisciplinary and Transcultural Journal for New Thought, Research and Praxis, 5*, 4–226.

Gidley, J. (2008). *Evolving education: A postformal-integral-planetary gaze at the evolution of consciousness and the educational imperatives*. PhD dissertation Southern Cross University, Lismore.

Gidley, J. (2010). Globally scanning for megatrends of the mind: Potential futures of "Futures Thinking". *Futures: The Journal of Policy, Planning and Futures Studies, 42*(10), 1040–1048.

Goodenough, U., & Deacon, T. W. (2006). The sacred emergence of nature. In P. Clayton (Ed.), *Oxford handbook of science and religion* (pp. 853–871). Oxford: Oxford University Press.

Grace, C. R., & Moreland, J. P. (2002). Intelligent design psychology and evolutionary psychology on consciousness: Turning water to wine. *Journal of Psychology and Theology, 30*(1), 51.

Habermas, J. (1979). *Communication and the evolution of society* (T. McCarthy, Trans.). Boston: Beacon Press.

Herder, J. G. v. (1774/2002). This too a philosophy of history for the formation of humanity (M. N. Forster, Trans.) (Original work published 1774). In M. N. Forster (Ed.), *Herder: Philosophical writings* (Cambridge texts in the history of philosophy). Cambridge: Cambridge University Press.

Hocks, R. (n.d.). The 'Other' postmodern theorist: Owen Barfield's concept of the evolution of consciousness. http://www.missouriwestern.edu/orgs/polanyi/TADWEBARCHIVE/TAD18-1/TAD18-1-fnl-pg27-38-pdf.pdf. Accessed 9 Sept 2006.

Jantsch, E. (1980). *The self-organising universe: Scientific and human implications of the emerging paradigm of evolution*. New York: Pergamon Press.
Jaynes, J. (1976). *The origin of consciousness in the breakdown of the bicameral mind*. Boston: Houghton Mifflin Company.
Kapoor, R. (2007). Auroville: A spiritual-social experiment in human unity and evolution. *Futures: The Journal of Policy, Planning and Futures Studies, 39*, 632–643.
Kay, P. (1977). Language evolution and speech style. In B. G. Blount & M. Sanches (Eds.), *Sociocultural dimensions of language change*. London: Academic.
Keller, C., & Daniell, A. (2002). *Process and difference: Between cosmological and poststructuralist postmodernisms* (SUNY series in constructive postmodern thought). New York: SUNY Press.
Kimball. (2004). *Four quarters of the Earth: A heuristic-hermeneutic inquiry into world art*. Graduate College of Union Institute and University, Cincinnatti, OH.
Klein, J. T. (2004). Prospects for transdisciplinarity. *Futures, 36*(4), 515–526.
Lachman, G. (2003). *A secret history of consciousness*. Great Barrington: Lindesfarne Books.
László, E. (2006). *The Chaos point: The world at the crossroads*. Charlottsville: Hampton Roads Publishing Company, Inc.
Lock, A., & Peters, C. R. (Eds.). (1996/1999). *Handbook of human symbolic evolution*. Oxford: Blackwell Publishers.
Lovejoy, A. O. (1936). *The great chain of being: A study of the history of an idea* (William James lectures series, 1933). Cambridge, MA: Harvard University Press.
Loye, D. (1998). *Darwin's lost theory of love: A healing vision for the new century*. Lincoln: iUniverse Inc.
Loye, D. (Ed.). (2004). *The great adventure: Toward a fully human theory of evolution* (SUNY series in transpersonal and humanistic). Albany: SUNY Press.
Moreland, J. P. (2001). Intelligent design psychology and evolutionary psychology: A comparison of rival paradigms. *Journal of Psychology and Theology, 29*(4), 361–377.
Murphy, M. (1992). *The future of the body*. Los Angeles: Jeremy P. Tarcher.
Neumann, E. (1954/1995). *The origins and history of consciousness* (Translated from the German by R. F. C. Hull). Princeton: Bollingen Series XLVII, Princeton University Press.
Nicolescu, B. (2002). *Manifesto of transdisciplinarity* (Translated by Karen-Claire Voss) (Suny series in Western Esoteric Traditions). New York: SUNY Press.
Piaget, J. (1955). *The child's construction of reality*. London: Routledge.
Ray, P. (1996). The rise of integral culture. *Noetic Sciences Review, 37*(Spring), 4.
Read, H. (1943). *Education through art*. London: Faber and Faber.
Richards, R. J. (1992). *The meaning of evolution: The morphological construction and ideological reconstruction of Darwin's theory*. Chicago: University of Chicago Press.
Richards, R. J. (2002). *The romantic conception of life: Science and philosophy in the Age of Goethe*. Chicago: University of Chicago Press.
Rolston III, H. (1997). Genes, genesis and God. *Gifford Lectures 1997*.
Rolston III, H. (2005). Inevitable humans: Simon Conway Morris's evolutionary paleontology. *Zygon: Journal of Religion and Science, 40*(1), 221–230.
Russell, P. (2000). *The global brain awakens: Our next evolutionary step*. Melbourne: Element Books.
Schiller, F. (1954/1977). *On the aesthetic education of man – In a series of letters* (First published in 1795). New York: Frederick Ungar Publishing.
Schriek, T. v. d., Passmore, D. G., Stevenson, A. c., & Rolao, J. (2007). The Paleography of Mesolithic settlement-subsistence and shell midden formation in the Muge valley, Lower Tagus Basin, Portugal. *Holocene, 17*(3), 369–385.
Scott, D. (2007). The nature of ultimate reality: The convergence of science and spirituality. In *5th international philosophy, science and theology festival, Grafton, Australia, 23rd June, 2007*.
Seger, J. D. (2006). Bronze and Iron Age Tombs at Tell Beit Mirsim (book review). *Bulletin of the American Schools of Oriental Research, 342*, 114–116.

Shaw, I. (2000). *Oxford history of ancient Egypt*. Oxford: Oxford University Press.
Spencer, H. (1857). Progress: Its law and causes. *The Westminster Review, 67*(April), 445–465.
Stathatou, X. (2007). The "Pananthropinon" Panhuman in the Poems Proino Astro (Morning Star) by Giannis Ritsos and the Last Supper by Nikiforos Vrettakos. *The International Journal of the Humanities, 5*(2), 121–128.
Stein, R. (2006). An inquiry into the origins of life on earth—A synthesis of process thought in science and theology. *Zygon: Journal of Religion and Science, 41*(1), 995–1016.
Steiner, R. (1904/1959). *Cosmic memory: Prehistory of earth and man (GA 11)* (1st English ed.) (K. E. Zimmer, Trans.) (Original work published 1904) San Francisco: Harper & Row.
Steiner, R. (1904/1993). *Knowledge of the higher worlds: How is it achieved? (GA 10)* (6th ed.) (D. S. Osmond, & C. Davy, Trans.) (Original German work published 1904) London: Rudolf Steiner Press.
Steiner, R. (1905/1981). *The stages of higher knowledge (GA 12)* (L. Monges, & F. McKnight, Trans. 1967) (Original work published 1905). Spring Valley: Anthroposophic Press.
Steiner, R. (1909/1965). *The education of the child in the light of anthroposophy (GA 34)* (2nd ed.) (G. & M. Adams, Trans.) (Original work published 1909). London: Rudolf Steiner Press.
Steiner, R. (1926/1966). *The evolution of consciousness as revealed through initiation knowledge (GA 227)* (2nd ed.) (V. E. W. & C. D., Trans.). [13 Lectures: Penmaenmawr, N. Wales, August 19–31, 1923] (Original published work 1926). London: Rudolf Steiner Press.
Steiner, R. (1930/1983). *Metamorphoses of the soul: Paths of experience: Vol. 1 (GA 58)* (2nd ed.) (C. Davy & C. von Arnim, Trans.) [9 Lectures, Berlin and Munich, March 14 to December 9, 1909] (Original work published 1930). London: Rudolf Steiner Press.
Steiner, R. (1950). *World history in the light of anthroposophy and as a foundation for knowledge of the human spirit (GA 233)* [8 Lectures, Dornach, Switzerland, December 24–31, 1923]. London: Anthroposophical Publishing Company.
Steiner, R. (1964). *The arts and their mission (GA 276)* (L. D. Monges & V. Moore, Trans.) [8 Lectures, Dornach, Switzerland and Oslo, Norway, May 18 to June 9, 1923]. Spring Valley: The Anthroposophic Press.
Steiner, R. (1966). *Man's being, his destiny and world evolution (GA 226)* (2nd ed.) (E. McArthur, Trans.) [6 Lectures, Christiania [Oslo], Norway, May 16 to 21, 1923]. New York: Anthroposophic Press.
Steiner, R. (1971a). *Ancient myths: Their meaning and connection with evolution (GA 180)* (1st English ed.) (M. Cotterell, Trans.) [7 Lectures, Dornach, Switzerland, Jan 4 to 13, 1918]. Toronto: Steiner Book Centre.
Steiner, R. (1971b). Evolution, involution and creation out of nothingness (GA 107) [Lecture, Berlin, June 17, 1909]. *Anthroposophical Quarterly, 16*(1, Spring), 2–10.
Steiner, R. (1982). *Meditatively acquired knowledge of man (GA 302a)* (T. van Vliet & P. Wehrle, Trans.) [4 Lectures, Stuttgart, Germany, Sept 15 to 22, 1920]. Forest Row: Steiner School Fellowship Publications.
Steiner, R. (1986). *At the gates of spiritual science (GA 95)* (2nd ed.) (E. H. G. & C. D., Trans.) [14 Lectures, Stuttgart, Germany, Aug 22 to Sept 4, 1906]. London: Rudolf Steiner Press.
Swimme, B., & Tucker, M. E. (2006). The evolutionary context of an emerging planetary civilization. *Kosmos: An Integral Approach to Global Awakening, 5*, 7–8.
Tarasov, L., & Peltier, W. R. (2005). Arctic freshwater forcing of the Younger Dryas cold reversal. *Nature, 435*, 662–665.
Tarnas, R. (1991). *The passions of the western mind*. New York: Random House.
Tarnas, R. (2006). *Cosmos and psyche. Intimations of a new world view*. New York: Viking.
Teichmann, F. (2005). The emergence of the idea of evolution in the time of Goethe. *Research Bulletin, 11*(1), 1–9.
Teilhard de Chardin, P. (1959/2002). *The phenomenon of man*. New York: Perennial.
Teilhard de Chardin, P. (1959/2004). *The future of man*. New York: Image Books, Doubleday.
Thompson, W. I. (Ed.). (1991). *Gaia 2: Emergence, the new science of becoming*. New York: Lindesfarne Press.

Thompson, W. I. (1998). *Coming into being: Artifacts and texts in the evolution of consciousness*. London: MacMillan Press Ltd.
Wade, J. (1996). *Changes of mind: A holonomic theory of the evolution of consciousness*. New York: SUNY Press.
Wilber, K. (1980/1996). *The Atman project: A transpersonal view of human development* (2nd ed.). Wheaton: Quest Books.
Wilber, K. (1981/1996). *Up from Eden: A transpersonal view of human evolution* (2nd ed.). Wheaton: Quest Books.
Wilber, K. (1995/2000). *Sex, ecology, spirituality: The spirit of evolution* (2nd ed., Rev.). Boston: Shambhala.
Wilber, K. (2000a). *Integral psychology: Consciousness, spirit, psychology, therapy*. Boston: Shambhala.
Wilber, K. (2000b). *A theory of everything: An integral vision for business, politics, science and spirituality*. Boulder: Shambhala.
Wilber, K. (2001). *Appendix 2: The nature of involution*. http://www.kenwilber.com/Writings/PDF/ResponsetoHabermasandWeis_CRITICS_2003.pdf. Accessed 28 Apr 2016.
Wilber, K. (2004). *Introduction to integral theory and practice: IOS basic and the AQAL map*. http://www.humanemergence.nl/uploads/2011/03/IOS-Basic-Intro-to-Integral.pdf
Wilber, K. (2006). *Integral spirituality: A startling new role for religion in the modern and postmodern world*. Boston: Shambhala Publications.
Wood, B., & Collard, M. (1999). The human genus. *Science, 284*(5411), 65–71.
Zong, Y., Chen, Z., Innes, J. B., & Chen, C. (2007). Fire and flood management of coastal swamp enabled first rice paddy cultivation in east China. *Nature, 449*(7161), 459–463.

Chapter 3
Psychological Development: Child and Adolescent

3.1 Introduction

Through our bird's eye view of cultural evolution over grand macro-historical time frames, we can see that the human species is undergoing a new evolutionary leap, of a more complex order than previous developments. For the first time in human history, we can become conscious of our own evolution and realise we are responsible for co-creating it. Co-evolution is both conscious and collaborative. This has very significant implications for scientific and other academic research, for our abilities to have long-range vision and for our abilities to comprehend and work with the complexity and interdependency that our current global-societal challenges demand. We see in this chapter these forces play out in individual psychological development.

While the previous chapter focused on the evolution of consciousness from the cultural perspective, this chapter focuses on the psychological, particularly cognitive, dimension of the evolution of consciousness. After introducing the concept of psychological development, I discuss some of the challenges in researching the evolution of consciousness from the psychological standpoint and point to the need for a transdisciplinary approach. I then offer an overview of child and adolescent cognitive development. These theories provide stepping stones for the adult developmental psychology research on higher stages of reasoning—postformal reasoning—that are discussed in Chapter 5. I point to the limitations of Piaget's model and introduce some evidence of widespread changes in thinking occurring across the knowledge sector over the last hundred years: megatrends of the mind. Finally, I tempt with a preliminary comparison of Gebser and Piaget—a dialogue to be continued in Chapter 7.

The purpose of the chapter is to create conceptual bridges between psychological development and the futures of education.

J.M. Gidley, *Postformal Education*, Critical Studies of Education 3,
DOI 10.1007/978-3-319-29069-0_3

3.2 Evolution of Consciousness: The Psychological Dimension (Ontogeny)

> The primary crisis on the planet now is a crisis of consciousness, and our global wisdom suggests that humanity is in a painful transformation toward a more healthful integral technology of mind that ushers in a new sustainable global civilization wherein the whole human family may flourish together on our sacred planet. (Gangadean 2006a, pp. 37–39)

I fully concur with philosopher Ashok Gangadean in the opening quote to this section that the crisis of our times is a crisis of consciousness. Until recently the literature on the evolution of consciousness has been dominated by evolutionary biology—in terms of the "evolution" aspect—and by cognitive sciences such as neuropsychology, in terms of the "consciousness" aspect. The idea of individual psychological development cannot be completely separated from cultural evolution, and yet to better understand psychological development, I will examine it separately in this chapter. The interrelationships among these two intertwined but distinct evolutionary streams will be discussed in Chapter 7.

3.2.1 What is Psychological Development?

> Cognitive development, then, is not a static, innate dimension of human beings; it is always interactive with the environment, always in the process of being reshaped and reformed. We are not simply victims of genetically determined, cognitive predispositions. (Kincheloe and Steinberg 1993, p. 300)

In simple terms, psychological development is the idea that all individuals develop over time from birth to adulthood through various stages of cognitive development. This theory underlay the early 20th-century work of Swiss psychologist Jean Piaget (1896–1980) in developing his theory of stages of cognitive development in childhood and adolescence (Piaget 1955). Piaget's work inspired several other child psychologists including his close collaborator, Barbel Inhelder (1913–1997), and Russian psychologist, Lev Vygotsky (1896–1934), who shifted the developmental emphasis from the individual to the socio-cultural context. Ironically, neither Piaget's nor Vygotsky's theories were taken up by educational psychologists and researchers until the 1960s and 1970s.

Kincheloe and Steinberg indicate in the opening quote that there are complexities to the idea of psychological, and particularly cognitive development, that we will tease out in the next section, and as we progress in this volume.

3.2.2 *Challenges of Researching Evolution of Consciousness: Psychologically*

There are many challenges that arise with attempting to research consciousness. The scope of this book will only allow for a brief outline of some key challenges. An overview of the theoretical issues and challenges in evolution of consciousness research has been published elsewhere (Gidley 2007, pp. 19–27).

3.2.2.1 Defining Consciousness

> [The] impressive progress of the physical and cognitive sciences has not shed significant light on the question of how and why cognitive functioning is accompanied by conscious experience. The progress in understanding the mind has almost entirely centered on the explanation of behavior. This progress leaves the question of conscious experience untouched. (Chalmers 1996, p. 25)

By *consciousness*, I mean the type of complex consciousness expressed through human thinking and language as it develops over time, both culturally (through cultural evolution) and individually (through psychological development).

In the opening quote, international consciousness studies researcher David Chalmers speaks about what he calls the *hard problem*, generally referred to in the consciousness studies literature as *phenomenal consciousness* or *qualia*. He distinguishes this from simple perceptual consciousness which he calls the *easy problem* (Chalmers 1995, 1996). Chalmers (1996) explains that psychological properties like learning and memory, while posing some philosophical issues, are primarily small technical issues that can be addressed through research and are thus an "easy problem".

My approach to consciousness in this book with respect to both cultural evolution and psychological development is a long way from the easy problem or the neurobiology-based *epiphenomenalism*,[1] which claims that consciousness is dependent primarily on the brain for its existence. This is why consciousness research requires a transdisciplinary approach.

3.2.2.2 Critiques of Developmentalism

> Post-formal thinking attempts to conceive cognition in a manner that transcends the essentialist and reductionist tendencies in developmentalism, coupling an appreciation of the complexity of self-production and the role of power with some ideas about what it means to cross the borders of modernist thinking. (Kincheloe et al. 1999a, p. 60)

---

[1] *Epiphenomenalism*. "[This] is the view that mental events are caused by physical events in the brain, but have no effects upon any physical events." http://plato.stanford.edu/entries/epiphenomenalism/

Paradoxically, there is a critique of developmental psychology coming from the educational researchers who founded the concept of postformal education (Kincheloe and Steinberg 1999; Kincheloe et al. 1999b). Kincheloe and others are critical of what they regard as the cultural hegemony of some developmentalist approaches, such as the privileging of white, Anglo, middle class participants by standardised IQ testing (Kincheloe et al. 1999b; Malott 2011).

This apparent contradiction between the developmental notion of postformal reasoning—as theorised by adult developmental psychologists—and the critique of developmentalism found in the postformal education of Kincheloe and Steinberg is merely a surface reflection of the paradoxes at the heart of the evolution of consciousness, and postformal reasoning in particular.

These paradoxes and other challenges will be discussed in more detail in Chapter 7, under *Paradoxes of Postformal Research.*

3.3 Selected Theories of Child and Adolescent Development

3.3.1 Child Development Theories with a Focus on Piaget

> Basically, the mental development of the child appears as a succession of three great periods. Each of these extends the preceding period, reconstructs it on a new level, and later surpasses it to an even greater degree... Finally, after the age of eleven or twelve, nascent formal thought restructures the concrete operations by subordinating them to new structures whose development will continue throughout adolescence and all of later life (along with many other transformations as well). (Piaget and Inhelder 1966/2000, pp. 152–153)

The notion that all individuals develop cognitively, over time, from birth to adulthood was fundamental to the work of Piaget, who is widely regarded as the "father of developmental psychology" particularly as it applies to children and adolescents. Clearly, there are other theorists of child development, who could be studied here, perhaps the most significant being Piaget's collaborator Inhelder, or Vygotsky whose work has been taken up by educational researchers because of its attention to the social and cultural factors that influence children's cognitive development. I choose to focus on the theories of Piaget because they are so foundational to so many other developmental theories, including those who followed his ideas, those who critiqued them and those such as the adult developmental psychologists discussed in Chapter 5 who went beyond his ideas to develop postformal stages of reasoning. I begin with a brief overview of Piaget's four stages of cognitive development.

3.3.1.1 The Sensori-Motor Stage (up to two years old)[2]

> We call it the "sensori-motor" period because the infant lacks the symbolic function; that is, he does not have representations by which he can evoke persons or objects in their absence...In the absence of language or symbolic function, however, these constructions are made with the sole support of perceptions and movements and by means of sensori-motor coordination of actions, without the intervention of representations or thought. (Piaget and Inhelder 1966/2000, pp. 3–4)

Piaget's sensori-motor level is the first of his four cognitive stages and is the type of cognition that Piaget claimed was operating in the newborn infant up to approximately eighteen months of age. He refers to the development of a sensori-motor, or "practical intelligence", during this period (Piaget 1972). This stage of development is pre-language, and thus the learning that takes place in this early stage of life is affective, rather than cognitive as such. Although this period (with its six sub-stages) lays important foundations for the cognitive and affective development in later life, it is of limited direct relevance to the main emphasis of this book.

3.3.1.2 Pre-operational Stage (from two to seven years of age)

> Once language has been acquired and symbolical play and mental imagery developed, or in other words, the symbolic function (more generally known as the semiotic function), actions turn inwards and become representation, this supposes a reconstruction and a reorganization on a new plane which will be that of representational thought. (Piaget 1972, p. 1)

Piaget characterises the key features of the pre-operational stage as being "ego-centrism", "precausality" and "animism". Piaget further distinguishes two periods within the pre-operational stage: symbolic and preconceptual thought, and secondly, intuitive thought. The first appears at the end of the sensori-motor stage at around eighteen months to two years. It is at this time that language first appears, or as Piaget put it, "the symbolic function that makes language acquisition possible" (Piaget 1950/1964, p. 123). During this period and until around four years of age, the child normally develops symbolic and preconceptual thought. In this period the child learns a great deal through imitation. Piaget explains that "truly representative imitation ... only begins with symbolic play because ... it presupposes imagery" (Piaget 1950/1964, p. 126). He goes further to say that: "It is important to note the role of imaginal symbols and to realize how far the [child] is, during his early childhood, from arriving at genuine concepts" (Piaget 1950/1964, p. 127).

During the second part of the pre-operational stage, which Piaget denotes with the term "intuitive thought", we see in the child from around four to seven years old "a growing conceptualization, which leads the child from the symbolic or pre-conceptual phase to the beginnings of the operation" (Piaget 1950/1964, p. 129). During this period the child continues "to supplement incomplete operations

[2] Piaget himself indicates that ages are always approximate in his theory.

with a semi-symbolic form of thought, i.e. intuitive reasoning" (Piaget 1950/1964, p. 129). It is important to distinguish this type of "intuitive thought" described by Piaget, which is found in the four to seven year old child, from the "intuition" referred to later in this book as a postformal reasoning quality in mature adults (see Chapter 5).

The logic of this period remains incomplete until the child is seven or eight years old. These internal actions or representations are still pre-operational and only later become "operational".

3.3.1.3 Concrete Operations (from seven/eight to eleven/twelve years of age)

> From 7–8 years, the child is capable of certain logical reasoning processes but only to the extent of applying particular operations to concrete objects or events in the immediate present: in other words, the operatory form of the reasoning process, at this level, is still subordinated to the concrete content that makes up the real world. (Piaget 1972, p. 4)

Piaget points to an important feature of the preoperational stage by which concrete operations can be distinguished. He notes that all three earlier stages (or part-stages)—the sensori-motor schema, the preconceptual symbol and the intuitive configuration—are "always 'centred' on a particular state of the object and a point of view peculiar to the subject [the child in question]" (Piaget 1950/1964, p. 142). By contrast, concrete operations no longer "issues from a particular viewpoint of the subject, but coordinates all the different viewpoints in a system of objective reciprocities" (Piaget 1950/1964, p. 142).

Now let us consider the characteristics of concrete operations that Piaget identifies to distinguish it from formal operations. Firstly, in terms of concrete operations the child still reasons in terms of objects "classes, relations, numbers, etc." instead of "hypotheses that can be thought out before knowing whether they are true or false" (Piaget 1972, p. 4). Secondly, concrete reasoning can only sort and combine by relating to neighbouring elements. There is no higher-level category or classification that allows for very different objects to be connected. Thirdly, they have a very limited capacity for reversal operations (Piaget 1972). Piaget also added that concrete operations are always "tied to action" or relative to concrete ideas, which he refers to as "internalised actions" (Piaget 1950/1964, p. 146).

In summary, he states that with concrete operations, up to the age of eleven or twelve, a "particular logical form is still not independent of its concrete content" (Piaget 1950/1964, p. 147).

3.3.2 Adolescent Development Theories, including Piaget

3.3.2.1 Piaget's Formal Operations

> In contrast [to concrete operations] hypothetical reasoning [formal operations] implies the subordination of the real to the realm of the possible, and consequently the linking of all

> possibilities to one another by necessary implications that encompass the real, but at the same time go beyond it. (Piaget 1972, p. 4)

The notion of adolescent psychology was largely discarded as stage theories of child development went out of vogue a few decades ago. Piaget himself referred to the fact that the psychology of adolescence was being reduced to the "psychology of puberty" with a consequent overlooking of the important "intellectual changes that occur during the period from 12 to 15 years" (Piaget 1972, p. 1).

In defining these "intellectual changes", Piaget makes the point that the ability to reason hypothetically is a crucial feature of formal operations. He refers to the "capacity to reason in terms of verbally stated hypotheses and no longer merely in terms of concrete objects" as the principle novelty of the formal operations period.

Piaget also characterised formal thought as consisting of the following:

> Reflecting (in the true sense of the word) on these operations and therefore operating on operations or on their results and consequently effecting a second-degree grouping of operations. (Piaget 1950/1964, p. 148)

From the perspective of classical Piagetian developmental psychology theory, the ability to distinguish binary categories is a necessary part of formal operations, and even part of the process of identity-formation in adolescence. An appropriate phase of adolescent development is to distinguish between "us" (peers) and "them" (parents). But as adult developmental psychologists have shown, higher-order ways of reasoning are far more complex than the binary of formal operations (see Chapter 5).

Formal reasoning, which finds some of its highest expressions in Newtonian classical physics and British analytical philosophy, provided the epistemological foundation for the dominant worldview of the 20th century. Formal reasoning is also fundamental to behaviourist psychology and the technological achievements of industrial society. The attainment of formal reasoning has been the highest goal of formal schooling to date. Along with the economic imperative, which entered the educational mindset in the industrial era, it continues to dominate today.

3.3.2.2 Storm and Stress and other "Waiting Room" Theories

> The study of adolescence is the Cinderella, the neglected person, of developmental psychology. It is the Forgotten Era, having been the focus of less than two per cent of research articles on human behavior for many years. (Collins 1991, p. 1)

The most frequently used conception of adolescence in the early 20th century was that of George Stanley Hall whose seminal psychological study of the period between puberty and adulthood at around twenty-one, used the phrase "storm and stress" taken from the German *Sturm and Drang* movement (Hall 1904). While the inevitability of adolescence as a period of storm and stress in traditional cultures is strongly contested (Broude 1995), it is questionable how long this will remain so with the pace of global cultural change and the globalisation of youth (Gidley 2001, 2004).

Late 20th-century models of adolescent psychology, originating in the materialistic natural sciences, did little more than provide a waiting room theory between childhood and adulthood. All theories about human nature (and therefore adolescence) are embedded in the broader socio-cultural (and more recently politico-economic) milieu in which they are conceived. This is highlighted by the shift to the term youth—a broader politico-economically defined category than adolescence—and raises the age level of the passage to adulthood for economic purposes.

3.3.2.3 A Return to Adolescent Stage Theory?

> The discovery of the self as something unique, uncertain and questioning in its position in life… [and] … The romantic concerns and hopes for the self's future. (Kohlberg and Gilligan 1971, p. 1052)

Stage theorists Lawrence Kohlberg (1927–1987) and Carol Gilligan also built on Piaget's theories in their 1970s writings on adolescence as both a role transition and stage of development. They made important links between the uniqueness and vulnerability of adolescence and the importance of being able to retain idealism and hope and a positive relationship to the future (Kohlberg and Gilligan 1971). Their opening quote identified two of the central phenomena of adolescence.

Although stage theory became unpopular with psychologists and educators for a number of decades, there was a return in the 1980s to a recognition of the importance of learning readiness and of the dangers of intellectually accelerating children beyond their biological maturity (Elkind 1981). Several educational approaches have retained an appreciation of developmental stages of childhood and adolescence. These include Steiner's pedagogical theories, which have parallels with the approaches of Piaget, Erikson and Kohlberg, and the educational approaches initiated by Maria Montessori in Italy and Aurobindo's followers in India.

Steiner education takes developmental stage theory into a comprehensive, coherent pedagogy in which three seven-year stages unfold up to adulthood at twenty-one. The first stage up to the change of teeth at around six or seven years is devoted primarily to developing the child's body, coordination and physical health by engaging the small child in a lot of activity that imitates real life: e.g. in the pre-school and kindergarten, they would learn to garden and make bread, to dance, sing, paint and make simple objects in ways that they increase their oral language, their confidence, and learn to be competent with many basic life activities. In the second stage, up to puberty, the emphasis in Steiner education is on providing diverse, multi-modal opportunities for children to learn in ways that engage their imaginations and creativity. This helps them to integrate what they learn into the larger context of life as a whole, to develop a love of learning and to find meaning in everything they learn about. It is only after puberty that young people are expected to learn in a fully abstract rational way. This ties in with Piaget's notion of formal operations emerging around puberty in optimum circumstances. In the Steiner secondary school, although students learn at the same academic level as their mainstream peers, there is a greater emphasis on aesthetics, creativity, practical ability and the integration of learning so that the whole person is involved. This approach is referred to in a number of later sections of the book, especially throughout Part III.

The role of stage theory in psychological development is also supported in contemporary holistic and integral education approaches, which will be discussed in Chapter 6. Perhaps this is also an indication that the moral and spiritual aspects of development are being called for again today.

3.3.2.4 Adolescence and Mental Health: What went Wrong?

> Young people who become depressed, suicidal or fatigued in response to the hopelessness that confronts the world are living symbolic lives. Their struggles with meaning are not just personal struggles. They are trying to sort out the problems of society, and their sufferings, deaths and ruptures are not just personal tragedies but contributions to the spiritual dilemmas of the world. (Tacey 2003, p. 176)

Something has gone horribly amiss today with society's handling of the adolescent period. Over the last two decades, it has become increasingly evident to educators, psychologists and other professionals working with young people that something is wrong with our enculturation processes. Research shows that many young people are experiencing high rates of mental health problems, particularly depression, anxiety, eating disorders and suicidality. The Australian Institute of Health and Welfare (AIHW) has produced a series of national statistical reports on young people aged twelve to twenty-four years (1999, 2003 and 2007). In their most recent report *Young Australians: their health and wellbeing 2007*, they found that:

> Mental disorders were the leading contributor to the burden of disease and injury (49%) among young Australians aged 15–24 years in 2003, with anxiety and depression being the leading specific cause for both males and females. (AIHW 1999, p. 23)

A large global study examined the statistics for suicide among adolescents in the fifteen to nineteen year age group across ninety countries. It was found that "In the 90 countries (areas) studied, suicide was the fourth leading cause of death among young males and the third for young females... Of the 132,423 deaths of young people in the 90 countries, suicide accounted for 9.1%" (Wasserman et al. 2005). In Australia about ten per cent of all suicides were teenagers, with suicide accounting for one in five deaths among people aged fifteen to thirty-five.[3] In the UK, "Suicide remains the most common cause of death in men under the age of thirty-five."[4] In 2013, the World Health Organisation estimated that "suicide, or self harm, will be the fifteenth leading cause of death across the globe in 2015, killing more than liver

[3] http://www.news.com.au/national/thousands-cry-for-help-each-year-threatening-self-harm/story-e6frfkp9-1226196098607

[4] http://www.mentalhealth.org.uk/help-information/mental-health-statistics/suicide/

cancer, stomach cancer and colon cancer."[5] In 2013 suicide was the tenth leading cause of death in the USA.[6] In China, suicide is currently the fifth leading cause of death. This is believed to be a result of the high-stakes testing for university entrance (Wang 2004).

3.3.2.5 Adolescent Theory in the 21st Century

Around the turn of the 21st century, new conceptions of adolescence began to emerge. Awareness of the impact of postmodern socio-cultural shifts led several educational writers to posit a noticeable change in children and young people that correlates with the transition from modernism to postmodernism. Various terms have been introduced such as *postmodern child* (Elkind 1998), *millennial child* (Schwartz 1999), *tomorrow's children* (Eisler 2000) and *21st-century children* (Almon 2000). More recently, there are claims about young people as fitting the profile of *Generation X, Generation Y, Millennial Generation* or *digital natives*. These framings are mostly *ad hoc* and somewhat conceptually naïve as they do not substantially integrate the evolution of consciousness literature or its educational significance. Unfortunately such labels are also used as part of cynical exercises in market research to ensure that the big corporates are not missing out on their share of the "millennial generation's fortune". Much more research is needed on such conceptualisations of young people.

3.3.3 Why Piaget's Theory is Incomplete: A Psychological Diagnostic

3.3.3.1 The Limitations of Formal Operations

> In its extreme form of exaggerated abstractness, it is ultimately void of any relation to life and becomes autonomous; empty of content and no longer a sign but only a mental denotation, its effect is predominantly destructive. (Gebser 1949/1985, p. 88)

With these words Gebser refers to what he calls the deficient manifestations of the mental structure of consciousness (his term for formal operations). Gebser decried the excesses of abstraction, which he claimed has become increasingly evident throughout the 20th century. Steiner also noted, "humanity had to go through the period of abstractions.... But [the abstract ideas] *must* be united again with reality" (Steiner 1971, p. 31). In lectures given in 1923, Steiner fore-sensed a looming planetary catastrophe if we do not re-vitalise our thinking.

> If [we do] not vitalize [our] thoughts, if [we] persist in harboring merely intellectualistic thoughts, dead thoughts, [we] must destroy the earth.... The destruction begins with the most highly rarified element ... ruining ... the warmth-atmosphere of the Earth ... and if

[5] http://www.who.int/healthinfo/global_burden_disease/projections/en/

[6] https://www.afsp.org/understanding-suicide/facts-and-figures

> [our] thoughts were to remain purely intellectualistic, [we] would poison the air, ruining in the first place, all vegetation. [Eventually, far in the future] it will be possible for [us] to contaminate the water. (Steiner 1972, pp. 90–91)

It is very challenging to realise that in less than a century, what Steiner anticipated might happen over a long period of time is well underway towards the catastrophe he foreshadowed—most notably "ruining ... the warmth-atmosphere of the Earth" with global warming and contamination of our oceans.

Decades after Steiner's forewarning, Gebser (1949/1985) also fore-sensed catastrophic problems of global proportions.

> The crisis of our times and our world is in a process—at the moment autonomously—of complete transformation, and appears headed toward an event, which, in our view can only be described as a "global catastrophe."... Either we will be disintegrated and dispersed, or we must resolve and effect integrality. (Gebser 1949/1985, p. xxvii)

Even two hundred years ago, German idealist Georg Hegel, as interpreted by contemporary philosopher Richard Tarnas, seems to portend the impending crisis. According to Tarnas, "Hegel suggested [that] a civilization cannot become conscious of itself, cannot recognize its own significance until it is so mature that it is approaching its own death" (Tarnas 1991, p. 445).

Many contemporary scholars highlight the urgency for change in consciousness (Elgin 1993; Gangadean 2006b; Gidley 2007; László 2006; Montuori 1999; Morin and Kern 1999).

3.3.3.2 Was *Formal Operations* a Mistake?

> Fragmented, compartmentalised, mechanised, disjunctive, reductionist intelligence breaks the 'world-complex' into disjointed fragments, fractures problems, separates what is connected, makes the multidimensional unidimensional. (Morin 2001, p. 35)

In the formal epistemological model, knowledge is contained in what have become known as *silos*, where even sub-fields within disciplines are often not familiar with each other's work. Specialisation brings with it an infinite regress into detail and the separation of knowledge into smaller fragments discussed in ever-narrowing discourses—an academic *Tower of Babel*. As Morin indicates in the opening quote, this creates significant challenges in relation to the complex problems of our times. These challenges can be addressed by taking a transdisciplinary approach.

So was the development of formal operations a mistake? An aberration? On the contrary, it was exactly the appropriate and necessary stage of cognitive development for humans as a thinking species to discover their individuality and freedom (Gidley 2006). The acquisition of formal operations among those scientists and philosophers at the leading edge of society during the European Enlightenment has been a powerful catalyst for increasing the scientific knowledge of the natural world that has developed since the Enlightenment. Tarnas argues that the development of rationality (formal operations), initiated by the ancient Greek philosophers in

Athens, has been one of the major accomplishments of Western civilisation (Tarnas 1991).

Its mechanistic expression through Newtonian physics has its limitations, however, the further we move beyond the physical sciences into the life sciences, and especially into the social sciences. The binary categorical nature of formal operations leads to dissection, specialisation and fragmentation of knowledge rather than synthesis and integration. The failure of much contemporary psychology, and indeed education, is that it is based on the primacy of formal operations and that it tries to emulate natural science in its approaches to the psyche, which cannot be measured in the same way as physical objects.

If formal reasoning has led to academic siloism and cultural divisiveness, the question must be asked: "Is formal operations itself the appropriate type of reasoning for re-integrating the fragmented knowledge systems?" The answer must be "No!" New ways of thinking, speaking and creating meaning need to be found, which raise our conceptual abilities to a higher level so we can meet and grasp complex futures.

3.4 A Transdisciplinary Perspective on Consciousness Development

For a fuller understanding of the evolution of consciousness, a transdisciplinary approach is required that includes branches of psychology other than neuropsychology, and also philosophy, history, sociology and so on. In addition, the implications of the evolution of consciousness for education need to be considered.

While the consciousness research of Chalmers and others has been going on in the biologically and neuro-scientifically oriented arena of the psychology discourse, in the more humanistic positive psychology stream, several adult developmental psychologists have been pushing the boundaries of developmental psychology into the fuzzy territory of transpersonal consciousness, wisdom and spiritual development (Commons et al. 1982; Labouvie-Vief 1990; Sinnott 1998; Bassett 2005; Sternberg 1998). Such approaches are discussed in Chapter 5.

As a response to the narrow approach of some consciousness researchers, a set of criteria was developed in 1992 at an *International Symposium on Science and Consciousness* held in Athens (Braud and Anderson 1998, p. 9). The symposium came up with eleven criteria that were regarded as appropriate in regard to undertaking research on human consciousness within the context of an *extended science*. I summarise below the key points for this research, from what Brian Josephson and Beverly Rubik reported (cited in (Braud and Anderson 1998, pp. 14–15):

- Consciousness should be studied "subjectively" as well as in terms of "objective data";
- Science as currently practised would be extended to include "the humanities and the arts" and possibly including insights from "spiritual or religious practices";

- "Science cannot be divorced from philosophy";
- We need to move from the "conventional fragmentary approach" of reductionism "to principles of complementarity and integration, from 'either/or' to 'both/and' thinking";
- The insights of science are "context dependent" and "all approaches to reality are relative";
- "The importance of intuition as a contributing factor [to] knowledge advances needs to be fully acknowledged";
- Quantity needs to be balanced with "the qualitative aspects of being and feeling";
- The scientific attitude of arrogance has fostered "dogmatism and scientism". This needs to be replaced by "humility... awe, wonder and delight in the cosmos ...[and] reverence for nature";
- Studies on consciousness must acknowledge "the inherent wholeness and unity of body/mind";
- Consciousness studies must be regarded as having equal status with physics;
- An extended science of consciousness would have "conscience"... "a science for the integrity of both people and planet ... translatable into action" (Braud and Anderson 1998, p. 9).

In light of these challenges and in particular the criteria for researching consciousness above, I now introduce research on what I call the *megatrends of the mind* as part of an extended psychology that points to postformal reasoning.

3.5 Megatrends of the Mind: Breaking through Formal Operations

> Great stress is laid on the limitations of thought, reason, and so on, and it is asserted that the limitation cannot be transcended. To make such an assertion is to be unaware that the very fact that something is determined as a limitation implies that the limitation is already transcended.' (Hegel, Logic, p. 134) cited in (Priest 1991)

What is Hegel getting at here? What limitations might he be referring to?

Speaking as one of the greatest philosophers in history, Hegel is referring to the limitations on thinking that comes from the belief that Aristotelian categorical logic (formal operations) is the highest form of reasoning. He is referring to what is sometimes called "Kant's Barrier" in which his great philosophical predecessor Immanuel Kant claimed that there were limits to what we can "know" (Kovác 2002). While this topic would be interesting to explore further, it roams too far outside the main themes in this book to pursue here. Suffice to say that when we look at the limits that the binary logic of formal operations places on our thinking, we can see that the megatrends of the mind discussed below represent many examples of how human thinking is breaking through formal logic within and across disciplinary boundaries.

While much literature has been published in the last few decades, particularly from the futures studies field, about megatrends and drivers of change in the world of external events, the idea of *megatrends of the mind* has been largely ignored (Gidley 2010a). I am aware that the term megatrends is mainly used in empirico-predictive contexts. However, I use the term megatrends paradoxically in a more metaphoric, interpretive sense. My deliberate appropriation of predictive terminology is intended to disturb, to highlight the degree to which the major shifts in thinking are at least as significant as the megatrends discussed in relation to external events.

As a way to try to organise this information, I propose a theoretical bifurcation between contemporary research that *enacts* new stages of consciousness without necessarily conceptualising it as such[7] and research that explicitly *theorises* new stage/s of consciousness development—either individual or socio-cultural (Gidley 2010a).

I begin with a very brief overview of disciplines that have *enacted* major developments in their dominant mode of thinking during the 20th century. This is followed in Section 3.5.2 by some major developments in transdisciplinary fields that are *enacting* new knowledge patterns. Section 3.5.3 explores academic research that explicitly *theorises* new modes of thinking or knowledge creation. Finally, Section 3.5.4 identifies key transversal concepts—postformal, integral and planetary—that when taken together can provide additional meta-coherence to an understanding of megatrends of the mind.

3.5.1 Enacting new Thinking: Shifts within Disciplines

Leading thinkers have begun to enact new ways of thinking to such a degree that most academic disciplines have undergone a major paradigm shift throughout the 20th century. These disciplinary shifts have been discussed elsewhere (Gidley 2010a).

3.5.1.1 Transitions within Science: Shifting Foundations

Within science, classical physics based on Newtonian mechanics has been surpassed by new physics theories such as Einstein's theory of relativity and the discoveries of quantum physics (Einstein 1920/2000; Zajonc 2004). Several adult developmental psychologists attribute the relativism of postformal thought to Einstein's relativity (Kramer 1983; Riegel 1973; Commons et al. 2008).

---

[7]This bifurcation is a rough guide and the two categories are not necessarily mutually exclusive.

Secondly, there has been a shift in scientific fundamentals from a dominant emphasis on physics to an engagement with new biological discourses arising from developments in general systems theory, chaos theory and complexity sciences (Bertalanffy 1969/1976; László 2007). The more fluid, life-oriented worldviews arising from this biological turn emphasise life as being "a complex adaptive system" (Swimme and Tucker 2006), "self-organising" (Jantsch 1980; Varela et al. 1993) and "emergent" (Goodenough and Deacon 2006).

3.5.1.2 Transitions within Philosophy: Shifting Ideas

A similar transition can also be observed in Western philosophical thought throughout the 20th century from modernism to postmodernism. The singular notion of philosophy—implying British analytic philosophy, linked to logical positivism—has been increasingly complemented by a greater philosophical pluralism (Mandt 1986). A philosophical turn from static mechanistic metaphors to organic, living, process metaphors of thinking arose in Einstein's time with Henri Bergson's *élan vital*, Alfred North Whitehead's *process philosophy*, Rudolf Steiner's *living thinking* and Edmund Husserl's *lifeworld* (Bergson 1911/1944; Steiner 1894/1964; Whitehead 1929/1985). Related philosophical developments include critical social theory, eco-philosophy, the *linguistic turn* in post-structuralism, the *historical turn* in hermeneutics and, more recently, the *religious/spiritual turn* in continental philosophy (Habermas 2008; Manoussakis 2006).

3.5.1.3 Transitions within Religion: Shifting Values

Over the last two decades, new rational discourses on spirituality, not limited by religious doctrines, have appeared. New forms of postmodern spirituality and religion have been proposed (Tacey 2003; Wilber 2006; Taub 2002). Australian researcher Gary Bouma identified a fundamental shift since the mid-1970s, in regard to religious authority, from the dominance of *reason* to the dominance of *experience and emotion*. This superseded what he called the previous "Protestant shift" from *tradition* to reason (Bouma 2006).

3.5.1.4 Transitions in Education: Shifting Pedagogies

Several evolutionary waves have affected education over the last century and will be discussed in Chapter 6. The third evolutionary wave heralds the transition from formal, factory-model education to a plurality of postformal pedagogies. The extension of mass education across most countries, referred to as the *Education for All* Agenda, is a mixed blessing. While it is unquestionably a positive development that more and more children globally are receiving an education, the question that needs to be asked is: "What kind of education are they receiving"? Another dramatic educational shift relates to the implications of the information age, including mass media, WWW and more recently, social networking (Gidley 2004; Grossman et al. 1999; Healy 1998; Steinberg and Kincheloe 2004; Thompson 1998).

3.5.1.5 Transitions in Psychology: Shifting Consciousness

Since the 1960s, major changes have occurred in the way that scientific research per se was conceived and practised. The emergence of post-positivism seeded a plethora of research methodologies and concepts better suited to social science research than the reductionist forms of empirical research. Social scientists developed and worked with a diverse range of qualitative methods that were increasingly sensitive to the social construction of reality, subjectivities, cultural differences and the presence in researchers themselves of taken for granted values and other forms of tacit knowledge (Berger and Luckman 1966). This sowed seeds for major shifts in the discipline of psychology: from behaviourist to humanist, even transpersonal, psychology; from clinical models to positive psychology notions of human potential; and from developmental notions of formal reasoning as the highest stage of thinking to several higher stages of postformal reasoning (Cook-Greuter 2000; Kegan 1994; Kohlberg 1990; Sinnott 1998) (see also Chapter 5).

3.5.2 Enacting new Knowledge Patterns: The Shift beyond Disciplines

In addition to these disciplinary shifts, there has been a growing movement beyond disciplinary specialisation, thus broadening and deepening ways of conceptualising knowledge. These *post-disciplinary* fields include futures studies (expanding time) and global and planetary studies (expanding space).

3.5.2.1 Expanding Disciplinary Boundaries

There has been a developing transition from disciplinary specialisation to multi-, inter-, transdisciplinary knowledge creation (Klein 2004; Nicolescu 2002). The coining of the term transdisciplinarity in the late 1960s has been attributed to Jean Piaget, though others such as Edgar Morin and Erich Jantsch were using the term around the same time (Nicolescu 2003).

3.5.2.2 Expanding our Sense of Time

The gradual transition from emphasis on the past to awareness of the value of futures thinking and foresight in many discourses has paralleled the emergence of futures studies as a field (Bell 1997/2003; Dator 2002; Slaughter and Inayatullah 2000). Steiner, Gebser and Wilber all refer to the changing views of time associated with different structures of consciousness.

3.5.2.3 Expanding our Sense of Space

There has been a growing call from progressive thinkers for a geo-political shift from the nation-state to a more global perspective that embraces planetary perspectives. The current times have been conceptualised as the *planetary era* by several researchers (Earley 1997; Gangadean 2006b; Gidley 2007; Molz and Gidley 2008; Montuori 1999; Morin and Kern 1999; Swimme and Tucker 2006).

3.5.3 Research that Identifies and Theorises new Stages of Consciousness

While noting the important distinctions between individual psychological development, and cultural evolution, several theorists acknowledge and theorise the important interrelationships between ontogeny and phylogeny. These include Steiner, Gebser, Wilber, Piaget and John Dewey to name a few. A core aim of this book is to increase understanding of this important interrelationship as *two* faces of the *one* evolution of human consciousness (Gidley 2007). These interrelationships will be covered in the complex dialogues presented in Chapter 7.

3.5.3.1 Adult Developmental Psychology

Since the 1970s, positive adult developmental psychology researchers have identified stages of *postformal* cognitive development. The adult developmental psychology discourse is primarily focused on mature individual development and has many sub-streams and facets. These are discussed as part of the evidence for postformal reasoning in Chapter 5.

3.5.3.2 Cultural Evolution

As we have seen in Chapter 2, following the pioneering research of Steiner, Sri Aurobindo, Gebser and Teilhard de Chardin, many researchers have identified an emergent stage of global culture—referred to as *integral* or *planetary* (Combs 2002; Russell 2000; Thompson 1998; Elgin and LeDrew 1997; Montuori 1999; Morin and Kern 1999; Nicolescu 2002; Gangadean 2006b; Earley 1997; Wilber 2000; Ray 1996; Gebser 1970/2005; Feuerstein 1987; Goerner 2004; Murphy 1992).

3.5.4 Approaches that Meta-Cohere new Consciousness

Finally, there are three discourses that attempt to meta-cohere these new ways of thinking and new knowledge patterns—postformal, integral and planetary. Each has a stronger emphasis in a particular domain.

The *postformal* psychology literature focuses on empirical and analytic articulation of higher stages of reasoning (see Chapter 5).

The *integral* studies literature emphasises the epistemological crisis and promotes integral thinking. Integral is a widely used term by several different schools of thought (Gidley 2010b). In Chapter 2, I discussed the integral theories inherent in Steiner's integral spiritual science, Gebser's integral-aperspectival cultural phenomenology and Wilber's integral-AQAL theoretical framework. There are other integral (Aurobindo 1914/2000; László 2007) and transdisciplinary theories (Nicolescu 2002; Morin and Kern 1999) which should be included in any integral studies overview. Within integral studies the main terms used to refer to the new consciousness include Gebser's *aperspectival*; Wilber's *vision-logic*, *centaur* and *AQAL*; and Steiner's *consciousness soul* or *spiritual soul* (see also Chapter 7).

The *planetary* consciousness literature emphasises the urgency of transnational collaboration around our planetary crises: ecological, politico-economic and socio-cultural (Earley 1997; Gangadean 2006b; Miller 2001; Montuori 1999; Morin and Kern 1999; Nicolescu 2002). The term planetary—which denotes an anthropo-socio-cultural and ecological framing—is used as a counterbalance to the more politico-economic term: globalisation. Many researchers who use the term planetary have been inspired by Teilhard de Chardin's notion of the *planetisation of mankind* (Teilhard de Chardin 1959/2004). Morin's *Planetary Era* began around five hundred years ago (Morin 2001; Morin and Kern 1999).

My philosophical interest in this book is to *think these threads together* as facets of the one emerging consciousness movement.

3.6 Piaget's Legacy for Adult Cognitive Development

Piaget's work had a seminal influence on the research of many psychologists who theorised adolescent and adult psychological development. Lawrence Kohlberg (1927–1987) extended Piaget's theories into the realm of moral development, and

Carol Gilligan in turn extended Kohlberg's work to include an understanding of gender influences on moral development (Gilligan 1982).

Other leading 20th-century developmental psychologists include Sigmund Freud (1856–1939) who proposed the theory of psycho-sexual stages of development, Erik Erikson (1902–1994) who extended Freud's psycho-sexual stages into eight psychosocial stages and Jane Loevinger (1918–2008) who built on Erikson's work to develop a theory of levels of ego development. Loevinger's work provided important foundations for adult developmental psychologists (Cook-Greuter 2000).

Piaget's theory, which he called genetic epistemology, also provided important theoretical and epistemological foundations for the research undertaken since the 1970s by developmental psychologists focusing on mature adult thinking (Commons et al. 1982; Labouvie-Vief 1990; Sinnott 1998). These research psychologists demonstrate that Piaget's developmental psychology has serious limitations with respect to mature adult reasoning. From this research the concept of postformal reasoning has developed.

3.6.1 A Preliminary Comparison of Gebser and Piaget

Before moving into the increasingly complex discussions on adult developmental psychology and postformal reasoning in Chapter 5, I explore the parallels between Gebser's five-structure model of cultural evolution, which points to the emergent integral consciousness in the current era, and Piaget's theory of cognitive development which stops at formal operations—awaiting the involvement of other researchers to take his theories further (see Table 3.1). Perhaps it is not surprising that Piaget himself makes the comment that opens the next section.

3.6.2 The Psychological Transition to Postformal Reasoning

> Piaget did suggest that beyond formal operations, there are postformal operations, or "operations to the nth power"... An early example of "operations to the nth power" is Piaget's statement that constructing axiomatic systems in geometry requires a level of thinking that is a stage beyond formal operations: "one could say that axiomatic schemas are to formal schemes what the latter are to concrete operations" (*Introduction à l'épisté mologie génétique, Vol. 1: La pensée mathématique*). (Campbell 2006)

This quote from Piaget's writings, cited by Campbell, suggests that Piaget did conceive of a higher stage of operations beyond formal operations (Piaget 1950). In another context, Piaget hints at the potential for extension beyond formal operations.

In a discussion of structuralism, in particular the "limits of formalisation" in mathematical and logical structures, Piaget makes the following provocative statement—given his own work had been finalised at formal operations: "the number of

Table 3.1 Parallels and Gaps between Gebser's and Piaget's Theories

Cultural Evolution (Phylogeny)	**Individual Development (Ontogeny)**
Jean Gebser (1905–1973) **Polish/Swiss Cultural Historian**	**Jean Piaget (1896–1980)** **Swiss Child Psychologist**
Archaic (Pre-history)	Sensori-motor (infant) Movement and sensory experience
Magical consciousness (Ice Age)	Pre-operational (two to six years) Magical thinking predominates
Mythic consciousness (Agrarian to Philosophic 500 BCE)	Concrete operations (seven to twelve years) Logic is practical and concrete
Mental/rational mode (500 BCE–1,500 CE)	Formal operations (twelve to eighteen years) Logic becomes abstract
Integral consciousness (1,500 CE > the future)	*What happens next?* *(eighteen and beyond?)*

operations open to human thought is not fixed and may, for all we know, grow" (Piaget 1971, p. 35). Piaget did not develop this line of thinking in his lifetime. The notion of postformal reasoning was to be left to others to develop (see Chapter 5).

Einstein gave us a clue to the emergence of postformal reasoning over one hundred years ago with his statement "The significant problems we have cannot be solved at the same level of thinking that created them." But what was Einstein hinting at? Did he have insight into higher stages of reasoning? Arguably the answer is yes. Perhaps best known for his theory of relativity, Einstein was definitely a postformal thinker who used more cognitive capacity than formal logic alone. Einstein, like a great many leading thinkers, used many other modes of thinking such as creativity, complexity, paradox, imagination and intuition. As Ervin László states:

> Bruno, Galileo, Copernicus, Kepler, and Newton himself had deep intuitive, even mystical streaks. Nor did intuition lack in the giants of twentieth-century science. As their writings testify, it was a leading element in the thinking of Einstein, Erwin Schrödinger, and Niels Bohr, as well as Wolfgang Pauli and Carl Jung, to mention a few. (László 2006, pp. 59–60)

All of these modes of thinking find their way into the psychology literature on postformal reasoning. Arguably, knowledge, understanding and attainment of postformal reasoning have the potential to move humanity out of the conflict-arousing binary deadlock towards postformal thinking qualities such as dialogue, creativity, reflexivity and paradoxical reasoning. These qualities are at the heart of postformal psychology and are steadily making their way into education.

Postformal reasoning will be discussed in more detail in Chapter 5, as it is fundamental to the postformal education philosophy put forward in this volume.

3.7 Concluding Remarks

In what may be considered by some readers a regressive move, I have revisited child and adolescent stage theory in this chapter, with a focus on Piaget. While I have shown the limitations of Piagetian stage theory beyond adolescence, I have also introduced the controversial idea that stage theory may have been thrown out prematurely by empirical psychology and formal education. What I suggest is needed is a careful reconsideration of stage theory, and the concept of developmentalism as a whole. A reconstructed developmentalism, without Euro-Anglo-centrism and narrow notions of intelligence, is a different notion altogether as we shall see in Chapters 5, 6 and 7.

After exploring psychological theories of child and adolescent development, I introduced some megatrends of the mind that have been occurring across the knowledge spectrum at the intersection between cultural evolution and individual development—sometimes called global mindset change.

Having journeyed through cultural evolution, individual psychological development and some of the contemporary hotspots where the two intersect, we are ready in the next chapter to take a ride through the evolution of education.

References

AIHW. (1999). *Australia's young people – Their health and well-being 1999*. Canberra: Australian Institute of Health and Welfare.

AIHW. (2003). *Australia's young people 2003: Their health and well-being*. Canberra: Australian Institute of Health and Welfare.

AIHW. (2007). *Young Australians: Their health and well-being 2007*. Canberra: Australian Institute of Health and Welfare.

Almon, J. (2000). The children of the 21st century. In C. Clouder, S. Jenkinson, & M. Large (Eds.), *The future of childhood*. Gloucestershire: Hawthorn Press.

Aurobindo, S. (1914/2000). *The life divine. 2nd American edition*. (Originally published in the monthly review Arya 1914–1920). Twin Lakes: Lotus Press.

Bassett, C. (2005, October). Wisdom in three acts: Using transformative learning to teach for wisdom [Electronic version]. In *Sixth international transformative learning conference, East Lansing, Michigan*. http://www.wisdominst.org/WisdomInThreeActs.pdf. Accessed 10 Apr 2016.

Bell, W. (1997/2003). *Foundations of futures studies I: History, purposes, knowledge*. New Brunswick: Transaction Publishers.

Berger, P. L., & Luckman, T. (1966). *The social construction of reality*. New York: Doubleday.

Bergson, H. (1911/1944). *Creative evolution* (A. Mitchell, Trans.). New York: Macmillan & Co.

Bertalanffy, L. v. (1969/1976). *General systems theory: Foundations, development, applications* (Rev. ed.). New York: George Braziller, Inc.

Bouma, G. (2006). *Australian soul: Religion and spirituality in the 21st century*. Cambridge: Cambridge University Press.

Braud, W., & Anderson, R. (1998). *Transpersonal research methods for the social sciences: Honoring human experience*. Thousand Oaks: Sage.

Broude, G. (Ed.). (1995). *Growing up: A cross-cultural encyclopedia* (Encyclopedias of the human experience). Santa Barbara: ABC-CLIO.

Campbell, R. L. (2006). Jean Piaget's genetic epistemology: Appreciation and critique. http://hubcap.clemson.edu/~campber/piaget.html

Chalmers, D. J. (1995). Facing up to the problem of consciousness. *Journal of Consciousness Studies, 2*(3), 200–219.

Chalmers, D. J. (1996). *The conscious mind: In search of a fundamental theory* (Philosophy of mind series). New York: Oxford University Press.

Collins, J. K. (1991). Research into adolescence: A forgotten era. *Australian Psychologist, 26*(1), 1–9.

Combs, A. (2002). *The radiance of being: Understanding the grand integral vision: Living the integral life*. St. Paul: Paragon House.

Commons, M. L., Richards, F. A., & Kuhn, D. (1982). Systematic and metasystematic reasoning: A case for levels of reasoning beyond Piaget's stage of formal operations. *Child Development, 53*(4), 1058–1069.

Commons, M. L., Ross, S., & Miller, J. G. (2008). Why postformal stages of development are not formal, but postformal. *INTEGRAL WORLD: EXPLORING THEORIES OF EVERYTHING: An independent forum for a critical discussion of the integral philosophy of Ken Wilber*. http://www.integralworld.net/commons1.html. Accessed 29 July 2015.

Cook-Greuter, S. R. (2000). Mature ego development: A gateway to ego transcendence. *Journal of Adult Development, 7*(4), 227–240.

Dator, J. (2002). *Advancing futures: Futures studies in higher education*. Westport: Praeger.

Earley, J. (1997). *Transforming human culture: Social evolution and the planetary crisis* (SUNY postmodern series in constructive postmodern thought). New York: SUNY Press.

Einstein, A. (1920/2000). Relativity: The Special and General Theory (Translated Robert W. Lawson). Bartelby.com.

Eisler, R. (2000). *Tomorrow's children*. Boulder: Westview Press.

Elgin, D. (1993). *Awakening earth*. New York: William Morrow and Co.

Elgin, D., & LeDrew, C. (1997). Global consciousness change: Indicators or an emerging paradigm. San Anselmo: Millennium Project.

Elkind, D. (1981). *The hurried child*. Reading: Addison Wesley.

Elkind, D. (1998). Schooling the postmodern child. *Research Bulletin, 3*(1), 1–9.

Feuerstein, G. (1987). *Structures of consciousness* (Integrative explorations journal). Lower Lake: Integral.

Gangadean, A. (2006a). A planetary crisis of consciousness: From ego-based cultures to a sustainable global world. *Kosmos: An Integral Approach to Global Awakening, V*(2), 37–39.

Gangadean, A. (2006a). Spiritual transformation as the awakening of global consciousness: A dimensional shift in the technology of mind. *Zygon: Journal of Religion and Science, 41*(2), 381–392.

Gebser, J. (1949/1985). *The ever-present origin*. Athens: Ohio University Press.

Gebser, J. (1970/2005). The invisible origin: Evolution as a supplementary process (Translated from "Der unsichtbare Ursprung", 1970). http://www.cejournal.org/GRD/JeanGebser.htm-edn64. Accessed 6 May 2007.

Gidley, J. (2001). Globalization and its impact on youth. *Journal of Futures Studies, 6*(1), 89–106.

Gidley, J. (2004). The metaphors of globalisation: A multi-layered analysis of global youth culture. In S. Inayatullah (Ed.), *The causal layered analysis (CLA) reader: Theory and case studies of an integrative and transformative methodology*. Taipei: Tamkang University.

Gidley, J. (2006). Spiritual epistemologies and integral cosmologies: Transforming thinking and culture. In S. Awbrey, D. Dana, V. Miller, P. Robinson, M. M. Ryan, & D. K. Scott (Eds.),

Integrative learning and action: A call to wholeness (Studies in education and spirituality, Vol. 3, pp. 29–55). New York: Peter Lang Publishing.
Gidley, J. (2007). The evolution of consciousness as a planetary imperative: An integration of integral views. *Integral Review: A Transdisciplinary and Transcultural Journal for New Thought, Research and Praxis, 5*, 4–226.
Gidley, J. (2010a). Globally scanning for megatrends of the mind: Potential futures of "Futures Thinking". *Futures: The journal of policy, planning and futures studies, 42*(10), 1040–1048.
Gidley, J. (2010b). An other view of integral futures: De/reconstructing the IF brand. *Futures: The journal of policy, planning and futures studies, 42*(2), 125–133.
Gilligan, C. (1982). *In a different voice: Psychological theory and women's development*. Boston: Harvard University Press.
Goerner, S. (2004). Creativity, consciousness, and the building of an integral world. In D. Loye (Ed.), *The great adventure: Toward a fully human theory of evolution* (pp. 153–180). Albany: SUNY Press.
Goodenough, U., & Deacon, T. W. (2006). The sacred emergence of nature. In P. Clayton (Ed.), *Oxford handbook of science and religion* (pp. 853–871). Oxford: Oxford University Press.
Grossman, D., Degaetano, G., & Grossman, D. (1999). *Stop teaching our kids to kill: A call to action against TV, movie and video violence*. New York: Random House.
Habermas, J. (2008). *Between naturalism and religion: Philosophical essays*. London: Polity Press.
Hall, G. S. (1904). *Adolescence* (Vols. 1 and 2). New York: Appleton.
Healy, J. M. (1998). *Failure to connect: How computers affect our children's minds – And what we can do about it*. New York: Touchstone.
Jantsch, E. (1980). *The self-organising universe: Scientific and human implications of the emerging paradigm of evolution*. New York: Pergamon Press.
Kegan, R. (1994). *In over our heads: The mental demands of modern life*. Cambridge, MA: Harvard University Press.
Kincheloe, J., & Steinberg, S. (1993). A tentative description of post-formal thinking: The critical confrontation with cognitive theory. *Harvard Educational Review, 63*(3), 296–320.
Kincheloe, J., & Steinberg, S. (1999). A tentative description of post-formal thinking: The critical confrontation with cognitive theory. In J. Kincheloe, S. Steinberg, & P. H. Hinchey (Eds.), *The post-formal reader: Cognition and education* (Vol. 63, pp. 55–90). New York: Falmer Press.
Kincheloe, J., Steinberg, S., & Hinchey, P. H. (Eds.). (1999a). *The post-formal reader: Cognition and education* (Critical education practice). New York: Falmer Press.
Kincheloe, J., Steinberg, S., & Villaverde, L. E. (1999b). *Rethinking intelligence: Confronting psychological assumptions about teaching and learning*. New York: Routledge.
Klein, J. T. (2004). Prospects for transdisciplinarity. *Futures, 36*(4), 515–526.
Kohlberg, L. (1990). Which postformal stages are stages? In M. L. Commons et al. (Eds.), *Adult development, volume 2: Models and methods in the study of adolescent and adult thought*. Westport: Praeger.
Kohlberg, L., & Gilligan, C. (1971). The adolescent as a philosopher: The discovery of the self in a postconventional world. *Daedelus, 100*(4), 1051–1086.
Kovác, L. (2002). Two cultures revisited. *World Futures: the Journal of General Evolution, 58*, 1–11.
Kramer, D., A (1983). Post-formal operations? A need for further conceptualization. *Human Development, 26*, 91–105.
Labouvie-Viet, G. (1990). Modes of knowledge and the organization of development. In M. Commons, C. Armon, L. Kohlberg, F. Richards, A, T. A. Grotzer, & J. D. Sinnott (Eds.), *Adult development, volume 2: Models and methods in the study of adolescent and adult thought* (pp. 43–62). Westport: Praeger.
László, E. (2006). *The Chaos point: The world at the crossroads*. Charlottesville: Hampton Roads Publishing Company, Inc.

László, E. (2007). *Science and the Akashic field: An integral theory of everything*. Rochester: Inner Traditions.

Malott, C. S. (2011). *Critical pedagogy and cognition: An introduction to a postformal educational psychology* (Explorations of educational purpose). Dordrecht: Springer.

Mandt, A. J. (1986). The triumph of philosophical pluralism? Notes on the transformation of academic philosophy. *Proceedings and Addresses of the American Philosophical Association, 60*(2), 265–277.

Manoussakis, J. P. (2006). *After god: Richard Kearney and the religious turn in continental philosophy* (Perspectives in continental philosophy). New York: Fordham University Press.

Miller, R. (2001). Making connections to the world: Some thoughts on holistic curriculum. *Encounter: Education for Meaning and Social Justice, 14*(4), 29–35.

Molz, M., & Gidley, J. (2008). A transversal dialogue on integral education and planetary consciousness: Markus Molz speaks with Jennifer Gidley. *Integral Review: A Transdisciplinary and Transcultural Journal for New Thought, Research and Praxis, 6*, 47–70.

Montuori, A. (1999). Planetary culture and the crisis of the future. *World Futures: the Journal of General Evolution, 54*(4), 232–254.

Morin, E. (2001). *Seven complex lessons in education for the future*. Paris: UNESCO.

Morin, E., & Kern, A. B. (1999). *Homeland earth: A manifesto for the new millennium* (S. Kelly, & R. Lapoint, Trans.) (Advances in systems theory, complexity and the human sciences). Cresskill: Hampton Press.

Murphy, M. (1992). *The future of the body*. Los Angeles: Jeremy P. Tarcher.

Nicolescu, B. (2002). *Manifesto of transdisciplinarity* (V. Karen-Claire, Trans.) (Suny series in western esoteric traditions). New York: SUNY Press.

Nicolescu, B. (2003). *Definition of transdisciplinarity* [Electronic version]. http://www.interdisciplines.org/interdisciplinarity/papers/5/24/1/language/en. Accessed 8 Mar 2008.

Piaget, J. (1950). *Introduction à l'épistémologie génétique* (Vol. 1: la pensée mathématique). Paris: Presses univ. de France.

Piaget, J. (1950/1964). *The psychology of intelligence*. London: Routledge and Kegan Paul.

Piaget, J. (1955). *The child's construction of reality*. London: Routledge.

Piaget, J. (1971). *Structuralism* (C. Maschler, Trans.). London: Routledge and Kegan Paul.

Piaget, J. (1972). Intellectual evolution from adolescence to adulthood. *Human Development, 15* (1), 1–12.

Piaget, J., & Inhelder, B. (1966/2000). *The psychology of the child*. New York: Basic Books.

Priest, G. (1991). The limits of thought – And beyond. *Mind, 100*(3), 361–370.

Ray, P. (1996). The rise of integral culture. *Noetic Sciences Review, 37*(Spring), 4.

Riegel, K. F (1973). Dialectical operations: The final period of cognitive development. *Human Development, 16*, 346–370.

Russell, P. (2000). *The global brain awakens: Our next evolutionary step*. Melbourne: Element Books.

Schwartz, E. (1999). *Millennial child: Transforming education in the twenty-first century*. New York: Anthroposophic Press.

Sinnott, J. D. (1998). *The development of logic in adulthood: Postformal thought and its applications*. New York: Springer.

Slaughter, R., & Inayatullah, S. (2000). The knowledge base of futures studies CD-ROM. In (Vols. 1–4). Brisbane: Foresight International.

Steinberg, S., & Kincheloe, J. (Eds.). (2004). *Kinderculture: The corporate construction of childhood.* Boulder: Westview Press.

Steiner, R. (1894/1964). *The philosophy of freedom: The basis for a modern world conception (GA 4)* (M. Wilson, Trans.) (Rev. ed.). (Original work published 1894). Spring Valley: The Anthroposophic Press.

Steiner, R. (1971). *Ancient myths: Their meaning and connection with evolution (GA 180)* (1st English ed.) (M. Cotterell, Trans.) [7 Lectures, Dornach, Switzerland, Jan 4 to 13, 1918]. Toronto: Steiner Book Centre.

Steiner, R. (1972). *The driving force of spiritual powers in world history (GA 222)* (1st English ed.) (D. Osmond & J. Collis, Trans.) [7 Lectures, Dornach, Switzerland, March 11 to 23, 1923]. Toronto: Steiner Book Centre.

Sternberg, R. J. (1998). A balance theory of wisdom. *Review of General Psychology, 2*(4), 347–365.

Swimme, B., & Tucker, M. E. (2006). The evolutionary context of an emerging planetary civilization. *Kosmos: An Integral Approach to Global Awakening, V*(1), 7–8.

Tacey, D. (2003). *The spirituality revolution: The emergence of contemporary spirituality*. Sydney: Harper Collins.

Tarnas, R. (1991). *The passions of the western mind*. New York: Random House.

Taub, L. (2002). *The spiritual imperative: Sex, age and the last caste*. Tokyo: Clear Glass Press.

Teilhard de Chardin, P. (1959/2004). *The future of man*. New York: Image Books, Doubleday.

Thompson, W. I. (1998). *Coming into being: Artifacts and texts in the evolution of consciousness*. London: MacMillan Press Ltd.

Varela, F., Thompson, E., & Rosch, E. (1993). *The embodied mind: Cognitive science and human experience*. Cambridge, MA: The MIT Press.

Wang, Z. (2004). *An antidote to modern test-oriented education: Toward a constructive postmodern education*. Paper presented at the Forum for Integrated Education and Educational Reform, Santa Cruz, CA.

Wasserman, D., Cheng, Q., & Jiang, G.-X. (2005). Global suicide rates among young people aged 15–19. *World Psychiatry: Official Journal of the World Psychiatric Association (WPA), 4*(2), 114–120.

Whitehead, A. N. (1929/1985). *Process and reality*. New York: Free Press.

Wilber, K. (2000). *Integral psychology: Consciousness, spirit, psychology, therapy*. Boston: Shambhala.

Wilber, K. (2006). *Integral spirituality: A startling new role for religion in the modern and postmodern world*. Boston: Shambhala Publications.

Zajonc, A. (Ed.). (2004). *The new physics and cosmology: Dialogues with the Dalai Lama* (Mind and life series). New York: Oxford University Press.

Chapter 4
Evolving Education: Pre-formal and Formal

4.1 Introduction

Since this volume is more concerned with futures of education than it is about educational history, only a brief sketch will be presented here about how education has developed in the past. Having provided a context for education with our journeys through cultural evolution and psychological development, we can now address education, from historical, contemporary and futures perspectives. Although the ideas about evolution of culture and cognitive development discussed in Chapters 2 and 3 have been developing in the collective psyche for at least two hundred years, the idea of educating children with the evolution of consciousness in mind has not reached education to any significant degree.

In the first part of this chapter, I make an ambitious attempt to present an overview of what education-as-enculturation might have been like thousands of years before we had formal schooling—even for the elite. I trace fragments of the evolutionary narrative that have been critically under-appreciated—the apparent aesthetic sensibilities of some early hominins and humans. This provides rich possibilities in terms of imagining how education as enculturation might have been enacted with the young ones in tribes and communities up to and including life in settlements. I then discuss the early introduction of formal elite schooling in Europe and a handful of other civilisation centres.

By the end of this chapter, it will be clear that formal, publicly funded, universal school education began little more than two hundred years ago in Europe with central Europe, particularly Moravia and Germany leading much of the world. It will be revealed that this original form of universal education was holistic, idealistic and evolutionary and that it was only after the Industrial Revolution that schooling began to resemble factories. This chapter will also explore the approaches of pioneers who broke the industrial education mould a century ago and reiterated the need to educate for conscious evolution.

J.M. Gidley, *Postformal Education*, Critical Studies of Education 3,
DOI 10.1007/978-3-319-29069-0_4

In relation to levels of education, this chapter relates primarily to school education although the evolutionary imperative also applies to higher education. I will not discuss the history of higher education in detail as it is particularly complex if we consider Indian, Chinese, Arab/Islamic and Israeli streams of higher education—some of which claim to have preceded the European universities.

The purpose of this chapter is primarily to contextualise the futures of education within the broad macro-historical development from pre-formal, to formal to postformal education.

4.2 Background to Evolution of Education

4.2.1 Culture, Consciousness and Education: Symbiotic Relationships

> The way we define thinking exerts a profound impact on the nature of our schools, the role that teachers play in the world, and the shape that society will ultimately take. (Kincheloe and Steinberg 1993, p. 301)

The evolution of human culture—and with it human consciousness—is intimately interwoven with the development of speech, language and writing. All of this has, over millennia, been part of the enculturation of children, which later became known as education.

To create healthy positive educational futures, we need to understand the deep past. To understand how we need to change education so that it is more suited to the 21st century, we need to understand how culture and consciousness have evolved over the millennia and where they seem to be going today. Only then do we really appreciate what we are educating young people for.

The concept of *education* for the purposes of this book is much broader than the concept of schooling. I want to place education in its broad *cultural* context, as only one of the types of enculturation that societies provide for their young people. In this respect, I draw on Foucault's archaeological concept of *savoir* for the broader cultural context or worldview, in contrast with *connaissance* in relation to the institution of education (Scheurich and McKenzie 2005). It is inevitable that the institution of education—schools, colleges and universities—will evolve as the broader cultural milieu evolves. Consequently, I have shifted my own research emphasis from educational futures to the evolution of culture and consciousness. I argue that there will be no substantial change to the system and institution of education without a change to the way we think and view the world as a global society.

The imperative to actually *educate* for conscious evolution was pioneered early last century (Aurobindo 1914/2000; Montessori 1973; Steiner 1909/1965, 1976). Although awareness of the role of education in awakening new forms of consciousness can be found today among integral and holistic educators (Miller 2000; Hart

2001), the imperative to educate children with the evolution of consciousness in mind has been largely overlooked.

4.2.2 Three Macro-Phases

Prior to the Industrial Revolution, which embedded modernist ideas into the socio-cultural fabric of Western society, education for the majority of children was not a formal process, even in the Western world. For the vast majority of the world's population, education was local and informal—or pre-formal. While formal schooling—along with formal thinking—did originate over 2,000 years ago—, most notably in ancient Greece—, this was elite education for the wealthy nobility, the clerics, the military officers and professions. We find elite education in ancient China from as long ago as 2,000 BCE and in ancient Greece from several hundred years BCE. This elite schooling was mostly gender specific—for boys only. There was also private tutoring and private institutional religious and military training in some cases.

In terms of evolutionary perspectives on school education, I have identified three macro-phases: *pre*-formal, formal and *post*formal. These phases can be compared with socio-cultural and geo-political development (see Table 4.1).

- A *pre*-formal phase must be taken from the beginnings of early human culture. During this period, children were enculturated by their extended families, tribes and communities. This has been the case for the vast majority of the world's population until around two hundred years ago.
- A *formal* phase of school education. Within this sketch of formal education are two sub-streams: elite schooling from at least 2,000 years ago and mass public schooling which began only two hundred years ago in Europe as a holistic

Table 4.1 Socio-Cultural, Geo-political and Educational Macro-Phases

Developmental Phases	***Prehistory to 18th Century***	***18th to 20th Century***	***20th to 21st Century >>***
Socio-cultural	Pre-modern: traditional indigenous, tribal	Modern: human rights and rule of law	Post-modern: complex, diverse and planetary
Geo-political	City-states: feudal: imperial and hierarchic	Nation-states: democratic or totalitarian	Global-planetary: multi-polar governance
Educational	*Pre*formal: community and family enculturation, elite tutoring, lycees, religious seminaries	*Formal*: mass schooling: bildung versus "factory-model" schools and universities	*Post*formal: holistic, developmental, networked, innovative, global education

Source: Adapted from Gidley (2009)

initiative, but since the Industrial Revolution saw schools being modelled on factories.[1]

- A *postformal* phase beginning in the 20th century. In parallel with the global spread of formal education, the third macro-phase—postformal—is emerging in which postformal pedagogies will ideally flourish throughout the 21st century.

The simple theoretical schema is not intended to suggest that there has been a unilinear or unidimensional development of culture, geo-politics or education. The reality is much more complex, multi-dimensional and recursive. This historical context provides both an understanding and a basis for critique of how global education is currently being implemented, particularly in the global south. The time frames of developmental phases depicted in Table 4.1 are more applicable at present to the global north. However, with the rapid growth of industrialisation, globalisation, urbanisation and global education in the rest of the world, it is important that newly industrialising nations do not uncritically adopt 19th-century Anglo-American formal educational models, as if they are the best available.

4.3 Pre-formal Education: Thousands of Years of Enculturation

For most of humanity's history, children received informal or *pre-formal* education through family, tribal and community enculturation. Informal education still exists in many parts of the world, so it is important to recognise that even when children are not attending school, they may well be taking part in semi-structured, culturally appropriate, informal education. The remainder of this section needs to be read in the light of the cultural evolutionary stages presented in Chapter 2. What I have done here is tease out of this deep history the development of human aesthetic sensibilities that is documented through archaeological, anthropological and other records. I do this for two reasons: firstly, because this macro-history is both fascinating and neglected; and secondly, it illuminates what are likely to have been the educational and enculturation processes that early human children might have experienced.

4.3.1 Archaic Enculturation: The Arts of Gathering, Colouring, Shaping

In order to speculate on what education as enculturation might have been like in the most primal of human ages, I will focus on the little-known evidence from

[1] Notwithstanding this, much of the world has yet to even develop from pre-formal to basic formal education. (The UNESCO "Education for All" Program is targeting this inequity.)

palaeoart. Several forms of rock art—manuports, use of coloured pigment, beads and petroglyphs—have been found to significantly pre-date the earliest European cave art. Rock scientist Robert Bednarik has documented archaeological discoveries indicating that the earliest palaeoart actually pre-dates *Homo sapiens* and can be attributed to the late Pliocene geological period (see Table 2.3). The earliest known manuport is the Makapansgat cobble from South Africa dated between 2.5 and 3 million years old (Bednarik 2003b) (see Figure 4.1). Although it is not an example of hand-modification of an object, the inherent values implied in the collection of such an iconic-shaped object suggest an incipient form of reflective consciousness, perhaps the first evidence of proto-aesthetic and symbolic thinking in pre-humans (Bednarik 2001/2007, p. 178). As an extension of the pastime of collecting interesting objects—and still within the pre-sapiens temporal range—it appears that *Homo ergaster/erectus* began to modify iconic natural objects. This may seem remarkable based on conventional archaeological views of the primitivism of *Homo ergaster/erectus*. The modifying of iconic objects—a type of proto-sculptural activity—appears to have begun approximately half a million years ago. One of the most notable is the human-shaped natural quartzite object, which has been modified by engraved markings and the addition of red pigment from *Tan-Tan*, Southern Morocco, dated 300,000–500,000 BP (see Figure 4.2) (Bednarik 2001/2007, 2003a, 2006).

The oldest known rock art, anywhere in the world, has been found only in the last few years in Auditorium Cave in Bhimbetka in India. Very simple in form, with a *cupule* (or small cup) and a long, meandering groove (see Figure 4.3), it is

Figure 4.1 Makapansgat Cobble (This image of the Makapansgat cobble is copyrighted by Robert G. Bednarik and is used with permission) South Africa >2.5 million BP

Figure 4.2 Earliest known Proto-Figure (This image of the Tan-Tan figurine is copyrighted by Robert G. Bednarik and is used with permission) Tan-Tan, Morocco >300,000 BP

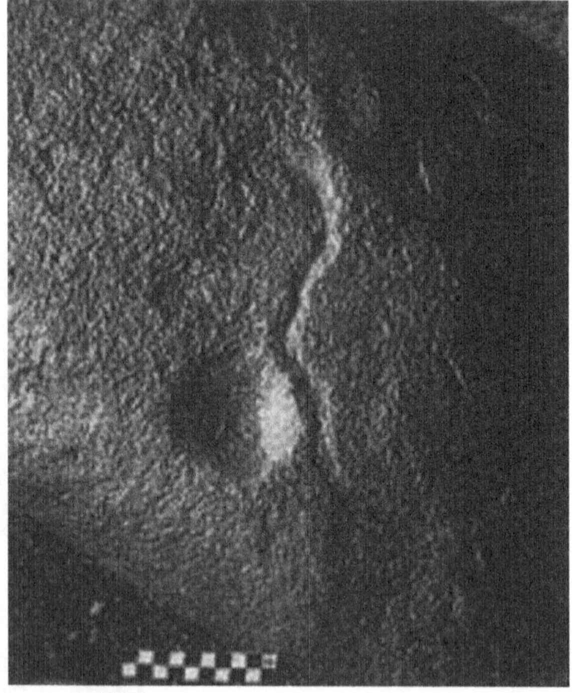

Figure 4.3 Earliest known Petroglyph (Earliest known petroglyph in the world, Auditorium Cave, Bhimbetka, dated very conservatively to earlier than 200,000 BP. This image is copyrighted by Robert G. Bednarik and is used with permission) Bhimbetka, India, >200, 000 BP

consistent with the Indian Acheulian age, 290,000–350,000 years ago (Bednarik 2003b). This ancient petroglyph is apparently the first representation of the two archetypal forms—a circle and a line—of which the entire world of form consists. The earliest hand-crafted objects that have been found suggest the beginnings of

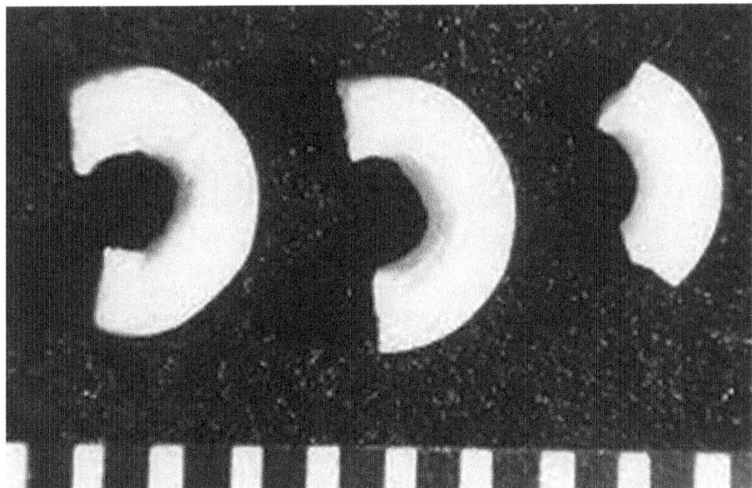

Figure 4.4 Ostrich Eggshell Beads (Ostrich eggshell beads image is copyrighted by Robert G. Bednarik and is used with permission) Libya c. 200,000 BP

body decoration. They include pendants made from ostrich eggshell beads, crafted 200,000 years ago in Libya, northern Africa (Bednarik 2007) (see Figure 4.4).

One can only imagine that children would have been a completely integral part of family and tribal life and would have been learning not only about survival but also the cultural rituals and aesthetic practices of their people from the very beginnings of their lives.

4.3.2 *Magic Enculturation: The Arts of Painting, Carving, Sculpture and Pottery*

It was believed until fairly recently that most petroglyphs were created during the Upper Palaeolithic period (35,000–12,000 BP). However, the engraved bone fragment pictured in Figure 4.5 is from the *Oldisleben 1* Site, Germany, possibly 120,000 years old. Another type of petroglyph (Figure 4.6) is a large limestone slab from a Neanderthal[2] infant's grave, La Ferrassie, France, bearing eighteen cupules on its underside, most of them in pairs. It is the earliest known rock art in Europe, about 40,000–70,000 years old (Bednarik 2003a, p. 98).

During the Upper Palaeolithic period in Europe, numerous types of art developed and consolidated that could be regarded as proto-writing particularly abstract and figurative rock engraving and paintings—as magical consciousness was beginning to give way to more symbolic, image-based forms of expression.

[2]*Homo neanderthalensis* appear to have been the first species to ceremonially bury their dead.

Figure 4.5 Engraved Bone Fragment (This image of the *Oldisleben 1* bone fragment is copyrighted by Robert G. Bednarik and is used with permission), Germany, c. 120,000 BP

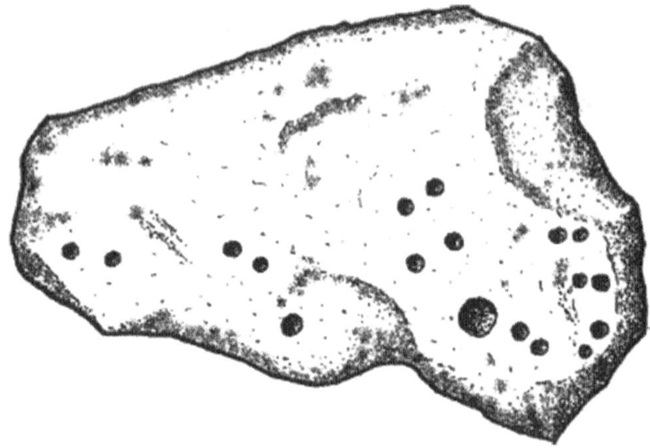

Figure 4.6 Neanderthal Child's Grave (This image of the limestone slab from the Neanderthal infant's grave, La Ferrassie, France, is copyrighted by Robert G. Bednarik and is used with permission), La Ferrassie, France >40,000 BP

Some of the earliest known rock art outside of Western Europe is sub-continental Indian and Australian (Gidley 2007, Appendix C).

The Upper Palaeolithic seemed to also mark the beginnings of what we could call sculpture. The so-called *Venus figurines* of the Eurasian Upper Palaeolithic are the earliest known sculptures, but there is much controversy about their dates as well as their meaning.

Two notable figurines are of ceramic and ivory, respectively. The *Venus of Dolní Věstonice*—about 11 centimetres tall—is reputedly the oldest known ceramic artefact in the world. It was found in 1925 between *Pavlov* and *Dolní Věstonice* in Moravia, Czech Republic (see Figure 4.7). The more famous *La Dame à la Capuche*—also sometimes called the *Venus of Brassempouy*—is a small, 3.5 centimetre ivory sculpture (see Figure 4.8) found in western France in the late 19th century (White 2006, p. 252).

In this era of cultural evolution, around 30,000 years ago, at least some members of our species were creating beautiful, intelligent artefacts. It is not hard to imagine the children growing up in such cultures would have learned from their elders the

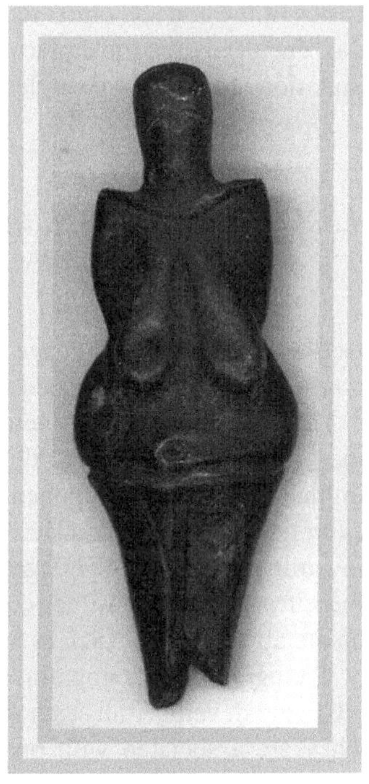

Figure 4.7 Venus of *Dolní Věstonice* (This image is in the public domain under the GNU Free Documentation License. http://en.wikipedia.org/wiki/Image:Venus_of_Dolni_Vestonice.png) Moravia, Czech Republic c. 27–31 ka

Figure 4.8 *La Dame à la Capuche* (This image is in the public domain. http://en.wikipedia.org/wiki/Image:Venus_of_Brassempouy.jpg) Brassempouy, France c. 22–28 ka

basics of the arts and crafts required to enhance and enrich their lives. In what form this enculturation took place is lost to pre-history. We can only imagine that imitation is likely to have played a large role.

4.3.3 *Mythical Enculturation: The Arts of Stories, Myths and Pictographs*

Gebser claimed that language development went through a three-stage sequence of *tone-image-sign* that echoed in the development of writing (Gebser 1949/1985, p. 156, Note 6). Steiner presented a similar three-stage process in that he referred to the first stage of language development as being related to our early attempts to imitate the sound component of what we experienced in the outside world—expressed as song and music; secondly, we begin to transform the sound experience inwardly into symbolic images—externalised as pictographs and hieroglyphs; only then, from a more abstract conceptual consciousness are we able to conceptually create abstract signs such as alphabets (Steiner 1930/1983, p. 9).

Pictograms and logograms began to emerge at the end of the fourth millennium BCE and developed in several regions during the second and third millennia BCE. They are associated with mythic consciousness by Steiner, Gebser and Wilber. Early pictographic writing has been found in Sumer, Egypt, China, Mesoamerica and the Indus Valley regions (Houston 2004).

The Indus script (see Figure 4.9) is a pictographic system that developed between 2,700 and 2,500 BCE as the Early Harappan culture transitioned into the Mature Indus Civilisation. Around 2,000–1,900 BCE the Indus Civilisation came to an end in the Indus Valley, which led also to the disappearance of the Indus script (Parpola 2005, p. 31).

Figure 4.9 Indus Script Pashupati (The Pashupati, Indus Valley seal with the seated figure termed Pashupati. The writing above it is in the mature Indus script. This image is in the public domain. https://commons.wikimedia.org/wiki/File:Shiva_Pashupati.jpg) Indus Valley 2,700–2,500 BCE

Figure 4.10 Pictographic Cuneiform (Sumerian inscription in monumental archaic style, ca. 26th century BCE. This image is in the public domain. http://en.wikipedia.org/wiki/Cuneiform_script) Sumer c. 2,600 BCE

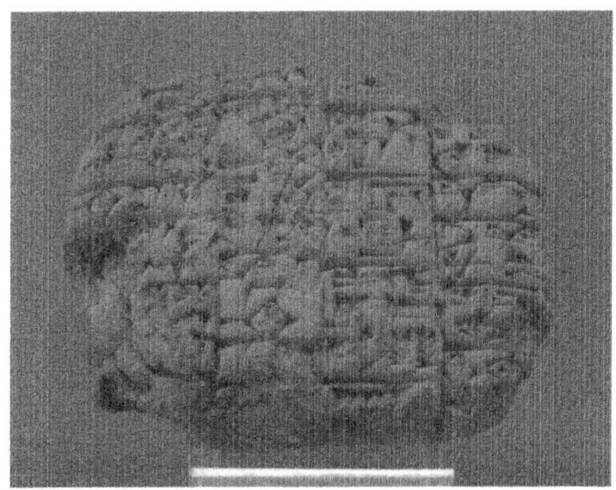

Figure 4.11 Cuneiform Clay *Letter* (Cuneiform letter sent by the high-priest Lu'enna to the king of Lagash (maybe Urukagina), informing him of his son's death in combat. This image is in the public domain.) Telloh (Girsu), Iraq c. 2,400 BCE

There were also earlier pictographic forms of writing on clay in Uruk perhaps as early as 3,300 BCE, which may have laid foundations for the later wedge-shaped cuneiform (Hooker 1990, p. 19) (see Figure 4.10).

Although preceded by earlier pictographic systems, the following are considered to be the first complete language-based writing systems: Sumerian cuneiform (see Figure 4.11), Egyptian hieroglyphs (see Figure 4.12), Chinese *hanji* (see Figure 4.13) and Mayan glyphs (see Figure 4.14). These four systems all appear to combine logographic, syllabic and determinative features.

The evolution of the first full alphabet[3] in Greece c. 800 BCE was followed by the Roman version—the alphabet used for English and most Western European

[3]Full alphabets consist of both consonants and vowels. Earlier proto-alphabets—called abjads—only consisted of consonants.

Figure 4.12 Papyrus of Ani (The *Papyrus of Ani* is the original Egyptian text of the *Egyptian Book of the Dead*. It is written in cursive hieroglyphs, usually reserved for religious texts. This image is in the public domain. http://en.wikipedia.org/wiki/Egyptian_hieroglyphs) Egypt, 19th Dynasty c. 1,300 BCE

Figure 4.13 Oracle Bone Script (Oracle bone about *the Sun*, from an exhibit at Chabot Space and Science Center in Oakland, California. This image is in the public domain under the GNU Free Documentation License. https://commons.wikimedia.org/wiki/File:OracleSun.jpg) China, Shang Dynasty c. 1,200 BCE

Figure 4.14 Mayan Glyphs (Maya glyphs in stucco at the *Museo de sitio* in Palenque, Mexico. This image is in the public domain. http://en.wikipedia.org/wiki/Mayan_glyphs) Palenque, Mexico c. 400–700 BCE

writing today. Linguists claim that the Greek alphabet developed from Egyptian hieroglyphs through a number of other proto-alphabets.

Speculation on education in the age of myths and stories suggests that children would have been educated through the stories that carried the culture with them. It is also obvious that once humans had developed such sophisticated language that it could be written down even in pictographic form, it would be a natural progression to pass this knowledge on to the children. While we do not know what form this passing on of knowledge took during the mythic period, we can speculate that the children of the elite would have learned the scripts of the day and that some would have been chosen to become apprentice scribes also.

4.4 Formal Education 1: 2,000 Years of Elite Formal Schooling

4.4.1 The Birth of European Elite Formal Schooling

The birth of formal thinking in ancient Athenian Greece paralleled the beginnings of formal education for the elite via Plato's *Academy* and Aristotle's *Lyceum* (see Chapter 2). Yet it would take another 2,000 years before formal education in schools and universities would be available and accessible to the majority of global citizens. Germany (the Prussian Empire at the time) was the place for the birth of mass education in the early 1800s. Wilhelm von Humboldt was the driver of this democratisation of education. This German model of education was founded on the ideals of everyone having an education—not the factory model (which came later) but an education based on idealist values—the development of the whole person or *Bildung* (meaning human development). We will return to this.

4.4.2 Fragments of Non-Western Elite Formal Schooling

It is even more outside the scope of this volume to attempt to present a full picture of the types of elite and generic education across diverse cultural landscapes prior to the introduction of mass formal schooling. In order to give just a taste of the diverse character of pre-modern, elite formal schooling, I have taken examples from three ancient non-European cultures: ancient China, ancient Egypt and ancient Aztec societies. These are presented as pointers for further research into the diversity of possible forms that education may take.

4.4.2.1 Elite Schooling in Ancient China

China has had an education system of some kind for several thousand years. During the feudal society of the Xia Dynasty (circa 2,070–1,600 BCE), there was a schooling system consisting of a central school called *xiao* and local schools called *xue* (Antonova and Rayevsky 2002, p. 9). These were elitist schools aimed at training the Chinese officials and as a result a special stratum of society was created—the literati (Antonova and Rayevsky 2002, p. 9). Confucius (551–479 BCE) himself initiated a number of private schools apparently to provide an alternative to the "official schools". He is said to have had more than 3,000 students (Antonova and Rayevsky 2002). Confucian philosophy was the primary content in all China's schools during this early feudal period (Antonova and Rayevsky 2002, p. 8).

4.4.2.2 Elite Schooling in Ancient Egypt

Archaeologists confirmed in 2001 that archaeological discoveries in Egypt in 1979 include an ancient school site dating back 1,700 years. The site was found in Amheida in the Dakhla Oasis, some 200 miles (322 km) west of the Nile, which was the ancient town of Trimithis. Ironically, the site is reported "to bear a striking resemblance to more modern classrooms as there are benches for students to sit on and lessons written on walls in Greek, which was widely spoken".[4] Based on the Greek quotations on the walls, the school was only for boys and probably the sons of the elite noblemen. Two quotations read: "Be bold, my boys; the great god [Hermes] will grant you to have a beautiful crown of manifold virtue"; and "Work hard for me, toils make men manly". Figure 4.15 is from c. 1,543 to 1,292 BCE.

[4]Article in the UK Daily Mail online titled: "Ancient Egyptian School Unearthed". http://www.dailymail.co.uk/sciencetech/article-2557632/Ancient-Egyptian-SCHOOL-unearthed-1-700-year-old-lesson-behave-walls.html#ixzz3GEXeCfbb

Figure 4.15 Prince's Schools in Ancient Egypt (This image is in the public domain under the GNU Free Documentation License. https://commons.wikimedia.org/wiki/File:Saq_Horemheb_08.jpg). Relief of Horemheb's Tomb, 18th Dynasty of Egypt: Saqqara.

4.4.2.3 Schooling in Aztec Societies

The Aztec culture, from the region that is now Mexico and surrounds, is arguably the first culture to introduce mandatory education for all children from the age of fifteen.[5] Prior to fifteen, children's education was the responsibility of the parents, who taught them the practical skills they would need for life. Because the society was arranged hierarchically according to a class system, there were two main types of schools that existed well before the Spanish arrived. Based on information sourced from the Mendoza Codex by Jacques Soustelle, the elite schools were the *calmecac,* which provided education for priests and officials and was primarily open for the children of dignitaries, though with occasional exceptions for children of merchants or commoners (Gvirtz and Beech 2008). These schools were run with rigid rules and strict discipline with children learning self-control, including fasting.

All the other children were educated in the *telpochcalli* schools which were less severe and were more concerned with training for battles (Gvirtz and Beech 2008). Apparently the girls did not learn to read or write, but rather were focused on

[5] http://www.aztec-history.com/aztec-inventions.html

Figure 4.16 Keeper of the Gods, Head of Calmécac School: Florentine Codex Book 2 (Image is in the public domain. http://www.mexicolore.co.uk/aztecs/aztec-life/aztec-education)

domestic, family and religious teachings. The Aztec culture thrived between the 12th and 16th centuries CE and was providing advanced college education well before the Spanish arrival in 1492 (Crum 1991) (Figure 4.16).

4.5 Formal Education 2: Two Hundred Years of Mass Formal Schooling

> The current modernistic and industrial definition of education is grossly inadequate to build capacity for individuals to critically and democratically participate in a postmodern society. (Horn 2004, p. 177)

This evolutionary narrative is primarily in reference to Anglo-European developments. However, these developments have influenced the globalising agenda to import the industrial model of education to the rest of the world, particularly via the "Education for All" agenda. This was precipitated by the United Nations Universal Declaration of Human Rights, over seventy years ago, which asserted that: "everyone has a right to education". In 1990, the World Bank, UNICEF, UNDP and UNESCO held a World Conference on "Education for All" in Jomtien, Thailand, creating the 1990 Jomtien World Declaration on Education for All. The Education for All (EFA) project, now run by UNESCO, has led to some success in increasing access to schooling for many children, and literacy rates have improved overall.

However, the challenges are far from over, with many complex issues at stake. Major challenges of the Education for All agenda include: (1) addressing the cultural implications of importing one system of education (largely Euro-American) into other cultures, (2) assessing whether the increased attendance at school is actually increasing learning and concomitant life opportunities (3) evaluating whether the dominant education model being imported can meet the needs of diverse futures in a rapidly changing world or whether in fact it needs a complete overhaul. These questions provide interesting directions for further research.

4.5.1 From Idealism to Industrialism

The current educational norm globally—compulsory formal schooling—did not exist until the 18th century. In the 17th century, Moravian educational theorist Johann Ámos Komenský (more frequently called by his Latin name Comenius) wrote the influential *Didactica Magna*, which proposed a three-tier universal schooling system for all children, but it was not implemented at that time (Dahlin 2006).

The first public education system was founded in 18th-century Prussia. Wilhelm von Humboldt, Prussian Minister of Education, shaped an education system that was committed to the development of the whole person and the ongoing evolution of consciousness (Holborn 1964). Humboldt's developmental and holistic education approach is referred to in German as *bildung*. According to the German *bildung* tradition, "philosophy and education are virtually synonymous terms that designate an ongoing process of both personal and cultural maturation".[6] Humboldt was influenced by the idealist philosophies of Goethe, Hegel, Schelling and Novalis; Schiller's aesthetic education (Schiller 1954/1977) and Johann Friedrich Herbart's integrative pedagogical system (Klein 2004).

However, by the middle of the 19th century, after the deaths of these leading German philosophers, the idealist-romantic educational project was largely hijacked by the gradual influence of the British Industrial Revolution, during which schools increasingly became training grounds to provide fodder for the factories. While it is acknowledged that England, like Germany, had its share of romantic poets such as Blake, Coleridge, Wordsworth, to name a few, their presence did not seem to influence educational thought in the way that the German romantics influenced the shaping of educational philosophy in continental Europe. The educational thought that developed in England from the 17th century until the late 19th century was dominated by concerns about "practical problems of the curriculum, teaching methods and school organisation" (Curtis and Boltwood 1953) in contrast to the more idealistic educational philosophy of German and

[6]http://www.philosophy.uncc.edu/mleldrid/SAAP/USC/pbt1.html

Swiss educators who were pre-eminently concerned with the development of the whole human being.

In its uptake of mass education, the USA was more influenced by the pragmatic, utilitarian model that developed in England, than the German *bildung* approach. Notwithstanding the different philosophies, theories and methods within mainstream formal education, there is a tacit industrial era template on which most contemporary educational institutions are based that has been the main influence on mass education in the global north for two hundred years (Dator 2000) and increasingly in the rest of the world.

As noted in Chapter 3, the growing global youth mental health epidemic suggests that this education model no longer adequately meets the needs of young people. The current global-societal challenges have a negative impact on the psycho-social wellbeing of young people, and formal education is ill equipped to meet these challenges. This raises the important question: "Why is this failed model being imported, somewhat uncritically, to the global south as *Education for All*"?

Paradoxically, the original holistic, developmental philosophy is re-emerging in the new futures-focused educational approaches discussed in Chapter 6.

4.5.2 Why Mass Formal Education is Incomplete: An Educational Diagnostic

> Modern schooling does not serve the spiritual unfoldment of the child. It serves capitalism, nationalism, and a reductionist worldview. It serves a society that is completely committed to meritocracy, where there's fierce competition between individuals to reach the top of a social hierarchy. (Miller 1999, pp. 190–191)

Formal school education seems trapped within industrial, mechanistic and economics metaphors. Its entrenchment hinders the development of the whole person and the appropriate development of new ways of thinking suitable for the complexity of our times. Such educational practices thwart the evolution of culture and consciousness in several ways:

- They fragment and compartmentalise knowledge in ways that many young people find meaningless (Eckersley et al. 2007; Gidley 2005; Miller 1993);
- They privilege one way of knowing (cognitive) over others, such as aesthetic, affective, contemplative, imaginative, intuitive, kinaesthetic, musical, inter- and intra-personal and participatory (Gardner 1996; Hart 1998; Noddings 2005; Rose and Kincheloe 2003; Kessler 2000; Zajonc 2006; Nava 2001; Nielsen 2006; Egan 1997);
- They are grounded in binary logic, supporting the status quo re the following binaries: science over literature, mathematics over art, intellectual over social-emotional qualities, materialistic over spiritual values and order over creativity (Abbs 2003; Finser 2001; Glazer 1994; de Souza 2006; Pridmore 2004; Johnson 2005; Chater 2006; Subbiondo 2005);

- They encourage the transmission of deadening, stale concepts rather than evoking a process of awakening mobile, living thinking (Deleuze and Conley 1992; St. Pierre 2004; Whitehead 1916/1967);
- They privilege the neoliberal, managerialist model of *education as commodity* over all other orientations (Giroux 2001; Morin and Kern 1999; Steinberg and Kincheloe 2004);
- They encourage neo-conservative research, linked to the audit culture and a scientistic approach to "evidence"—over complex, qualitative, creative inquiry (Denzin 2005; Kincheloe and Berry 2004; Lyotard 2004; MacLure 2006; Montuori 2006);
- They educate for the past, for forms of consciousness that are becoming outmoded and are no longer adequate for the complexity of post-industrial life on a fragile planet (Morin 2001; Miller 1993; Orr 1994; Giroux 1999/2005; Gidley 2007).

4.6 Drivers of Change in the 21st Century: Global Education

Several key drivers of change have arisen in education globally in recent decades. They include: awareness of global human rights, globalisation and corporatisation (particularly of higher education), the information revolution, the rise of the global south and the megatrends of the mind leading to new global knowledge futures.

4.6.1 Basic Education as a Human Right

As noted earlier, the *Education for All* meeting in Thailand, 1990, hosted by the World Bank and other UN agencies led to the rapid uptake of the idea of education as a basic human right. However, the actual provision of universal basic education is not only lagging but also fraught with difficulties in its implementation. Discussions about universal basic education also include changing notions of quality in which social justice and human potential may be used as alternative measures of quality (Gidley 2010). Such notions provide a balance to the high competition and high-stakes testing that drives the economics-driven model of US education and increasingly global education. The following associated drivers particularly impact the higher education sector.

4.6.2 Globalisation and Corporatisation of Higher Education

By the 1990s, the previous civic and cultural role of European higher education was eclipsed by "the economic rationale" (Huisman and Van der Wende 2004). The initial resistance from the sector weakened as globalisation intensified, driving global competitiveness via university league tables, as higher education became a commodity in the new "knowledge industry". In this market-sensitive environment, university administrators stripped back their core business, sacrificing academic tenure, non-commercial research and non-commercial disciplines, e.g. humanities. Higher education institutions, old and new, now compete for market share in the knowledge economy. But is competition the best way forward, given that some of the most creative, innovative and dynamic knowledge today is being produced *outside* universities?

On a positive note, the *European Commission Bologna Process*[7] is aimed towards cross-border initiatives, converging systems of higher education, preventing "brain drain" and fostering global talent flows (Huisman and Van der Wende 2004; Marginson 2007; Welch and Zhen 2008). Globalisation has also stimulated mobility (of students, academics and ideas) enabling new insights into diversity in higher education (Lunt 2008). Global education (incorporating terms such as international education, comparative education, postcolonial and planetary education) has arrived. In Chapter 11, I will explain how these globalising movements in education are all part of the flourishing of democratisation of education to empower marginal voices.

4.6.3 The Information Revolution

The corporate model of higher education was intensified by the rise of Information and Communication Technologies (ICTs). Although early virtual university models faltered, universities are moving in the direction of increasing their online offerings. With the evolution of ICTs over the last twenty years, online offerings have become more sophisticated, customised and multi-purpose. Many elite universities offer online classes gratis through Massive Open Online Courses (MOOCS). The economic benefits of online offerings are no longer about reducing the cost of education but about providing a competitive edge by luring students into fee-paying courses. A major tension with virtualisation is that academic redundancies will continue to increase as they have in other sectors (Inayatullah and Gidley 2000).

4.6.4 The Rise of the Global South

The rise of higher education provision in China, India, Malaysia and the Arab States is a significant development. In 2009 Malaysia educated "70,000 international

---

[7]"The *Bologna Process* aims to create a European Higher Education Area in which students can choose from a wide and transparent range of high quality courses and benefit from smooth recognition procedures." http://ec.europa.eu/education/policies/educ/bologna/bologna_en.html

students from more than 150 countries" including Indonesia, China and the Middle East (Sawahal 2009). While increasing Malaysia's economic profile, this reduces income from international students to the UK, North America and Australia, shifting the power balance. Malaysia is building a "129-hectare EduCity" to house eight universities (Sawahal 2009). It is also innovating by co-sponsoring the biennial Global Higher Education Forum (GHEF) with the UNESCO-founded International Association of Universities (IAU). The Qatar Foundation established the pioneering World Innovation Summit for Education (WISE) in 2009 under the patronage of its Chairperson, Her Highness Sheikha Moza bint Nasser. WISE is an "international, multi-sectoral platform for creative thinking, debate and purposeful action in order to build the future of education through innovation".[8]

Central Eastern Europe is also surging forward with evolutionary educational projects: an innovative ecopedagogy project is flourishing in Bulgaria[9]; educational futurists in Budapest, Hungary, ran futures education courses for young people (1999–2005) with UNESCO and the World Futures Studies Federation[10]; and the Executive Agency for Higher Education, Research, Development and Innovation (UEFISCDI), Bucharest, Romania, ran a three-year innovative programme involving international futures researchers to assist with transforming Romanian higher education by 2025. Officials in the Romanian Education Ministry decided they wanted a unique system, not a copy of the old Anglo-European industrial model that is already failing its own young people. UEFISCDI hosted a groundbreaking conference for all EU Education Ministers in 2012 to discuss European higher education futures. The published discussions are available in two volumes and make a pivotal contribution to the global education dialogue (Scott et al. 2012).

4.6.5 *Megatrends of the Mind and New Knowledge Patterns*

The systemic knowledge shifts of the last century, referred to as megatrends of the mind, were offered in Chapter 3 as evidence of the new consciousness breaking through across the whole knowledge sector. These diverse, yet interconnected disciplinary and post-disciplinary movements pave the way for the emergence of more complex, living and pluralistic approaches to knowledge futures. Education researchers, practitioners and policy-makers need to take serious account of these dramatic shifts in ideas and ways of organising knowledge. More complex, self-reflective, organic ways of thinking will be vital in re-shaping education so young people are better equipped for complex futures.

---

[8]http://www.wise-qatar.org/who-we-are

[9]Ecopedagogy is being developed through the Bulgarian Centre for Sustainable Local Development and Ecopedagogy. www.bcslde.org

[10]http://www.wfsf.org/our-activities/wfsf-futures-courses

4.7 From Global Knowledge Economy to Global Knowledge Futures

As the neo-conservative model of education tightens its grip globally through corporatisation of higher education, high-stakes testing and the audit culture of evidence-based research, the pluralism of alternative approaches continues to expand. This tension is an inevitable stage in the transition from formal systems to postformal futures.

4.7.1 The Global Knowledge Economy

> *Where is the wisdom we have lost in knowledge?*
> *Where is the knowledge we have lost in information*
> (T. S. Eliot 1934, *The Rock*, lines 12–13)

We hear a lot today about the *knowledge economy*, yet this economistic framing fails to attend to the richness and diversity of knowledge creation that is being enacted on a planetary scale. We also hear the term *information era* as if it were a complete encapsulation of the present phase of cultural evolution. The proponents of the information era generally fail to attend to the evolutionary move beyond mere information to new ways of knowing, new knowledge patterns and knowledge integration. At the close of the first decade of the 21st century, some of the most creative, innovative and dynamic knowledge around the globe is being produced and disseminated *outside* universities. Academic researchers and research councils need to take heed. Now that "knowledge production", "knowledge transfer" and "knowledge dissemination" have become core commodities of the increasingly competitive global knowledge market economy, how will universities and their research centres keep up?

While old-paradigm thinking retains its hold on educational institutions, the new knowledge paradigm is breaking through from the periphery. Private providers, social movements, niche research institutes, open source resources, edutainment and, of course, the ubiquitous information kaleidoscope of the World Wide Web make it increasingly difficult for the former guardians of knowledge production and dissemination—formal educational institutions—to compete for "market-share". But is competition the only way forward? Could the leadership of universities and research councils listen more deeply to the periphery—to the new, unorthodox developments in the creation and dissemination of knowledge?

4.7.2 Towards Global Knowledge Futures

> *One of the greatest problems we face today is how to adjust our way of thinking to meet the challenge of an increasingly complex, rapidly changing, unpredictable world. We must rethink our way of organising knowledge.* (Morin 2001, p. 5)

The two quotes opening this and the previous section speak of knowledge. The first is from American-British poet, T. S. Eliot, and the second is from French philosopher, Edgar Morin. Eliot bemoans the loss of wisdom while Morin hints at its re-awakening. Perhaps it takes the eye of an artist, a poet, to perceive the loss of wisdom in the stripped-down, prosaic pragmatism of the *information era*. Yet it is a philosopher—a lover of wisdom—who actively thinks towards more complex ways of organising knowledge in the *planetary era*.

In my reading of Morin's work it becomes immediately evident through the philosophical and poetic richness of his language and concepts that his notion of knowledge is already filled with the type of postformal, integral, planetary wisdom and foresight that is being gradually articulated in the frontier discourses discussed in this book. As Eliot indicates, the modern era of hyper-rationality and hyper-specialisation has been a reductive process in which the pre-modern unitive world-view of inherited, or revealed, wisdom has been superseded by bits—and, more recently, bytes—of information. In this context, the term "new knowledge" is often a cynical exercise to attract attention to new technologies.

In addition to the fragmentation, commodification of knowledge abounds as a socio-cultural by-product of globalisation. Borrowing heavily from industrial era metaphors, education is now marketed as the product in a globally competitive knowledge industry.

The insinuation of neoliberal economic theory into all walks of life—including education—has led to the reframing of education as a subset of the new "knowledge economy". In this new knowledge economy, we can witness nations and regions scrambling to grab market-share through creating "science parks", "education cities" and "knowledge hubs". The most disturbing aspect of this "globalisation of knowledge" is that it frequently reflects homogenisation. The McDonaldisation of education transplants outmoded models and approaches as if they were fast-food franchises with little regard to the quality of the learning experience for students or the cultural context in which the model is implanted. In the rush to the top of the globally competitive league tables, there appears to be a blind disregard for epistemological and cultural diversity, through alternative ways of knowing. Being embedded in the global economy, such approaches to global knowledge are also locked into short-termism, stasis and homogenisation (see Figure 4.17).

In contrast to the reductive and economistic ideologies underlying the notion of the *global knowledge economy*, I coin the alternative term *global knowledge futures*. It is intended to unsettle those who use the term knowledge reductively and/or prescriptively. My notion of global knowledge futures is framed within the understanding that human consciousness is evolving and that we can consciously participate. It includes research that eschews the mechanistic, instrumental, reduced

Figure 4.17 Global Knowledge Economy: Ideological Stasis and Homogenisation (Source: Gidley 2013)

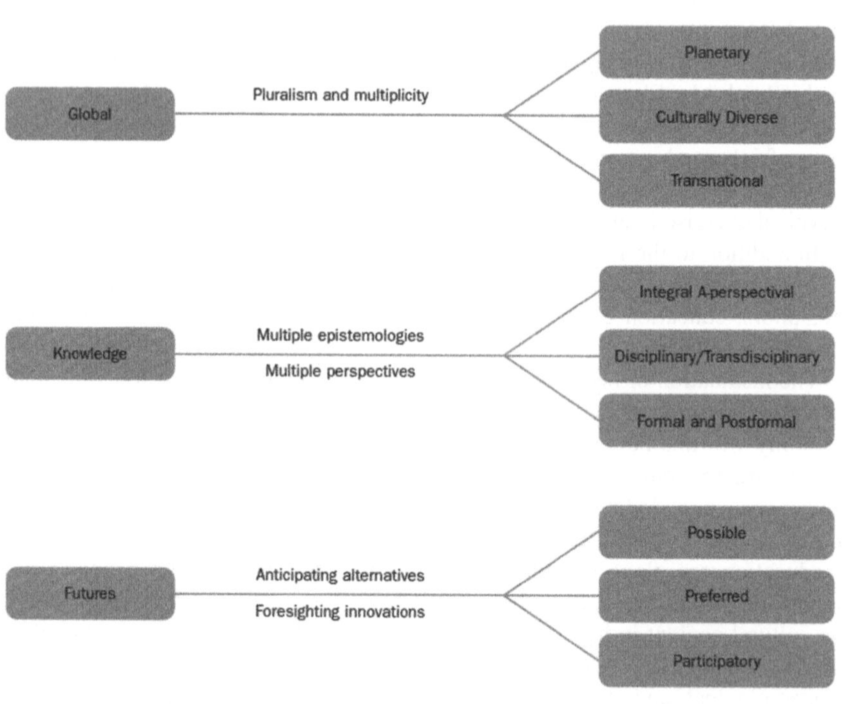

Figure 4.18 Global Knowledge Futures: Dynamic Unity in Dialogue with Diversity (Source: Gidley 2013)

versions of knowledge. It seeks to go beyond, to go deeper, to imagine longer time-scales and planetary spaces, to develop and enact more coherent futures of knowledge integration.

The term *global knowledge futures* can be distinguished from the hyper-modernist *global knowledge economy* in several ways (see Figures 4.17 and 4.18

for a graphical view). The cultural pluralism implied in my notion of global, and the ideological diversity in my notion of futures, fold back into the term knowledge, enriching it and opening it up to insights from the evolutionary discourses discussed in earlier chapters.

4.8 Concluding Remarks

I have talked a lot about the factory model of education in this chapter, and in previous chapters, as if it were the only model of mass formal education. I have discussed how this model is associated with the modernist worldview, formal reasoning and industrialisation.

However, if by mass formal education we mean the original model of universal and free public education proposed by Comenius in the 17th century and initiated by Humboldt in Germany in the 18th century, much can be gained from a careful study of this early pedagogy of human development—*Bildung*. After all, this model was first inspired by the unitive spiritual humanism of Comenius and later by the German idealist and romantic philosophers who were far more integrally aware than the educrats writing national curricula in the world for the past hundred years. When you consider that the inspirations for this original form of universal education included Pestalozzi's "head, heart and hands" approach, Herbart's integrative interdisciplinary pedagogy, Schiller's aesthetic educational approach, Schelling's co-evolution and the future-orientation of Novalis, there is a lot of relevance for today.

As we move through the chapters of this book, I will encourage you to gradually forget about models altogether and create living educational approaches that breathe with their local/global environment. Only in this way will the *connaissance* of institutional education become imbued with the *savoir* of evolving culture and consciousness.

References

Abbs, P. (2003). *Against the flow: The arts, postmodern culture and education.* London: RoutledgeFalmer.

Antonova, Y. V., & Rayevsky, D. S. (2002). Archaeology and semiotics (Russian language: English title/abstract). In A. V. Yevglevsky (Ed.), *Structural and semiotic investigations in archaeology: Volume 1* (Vol. 1). Donetsk: Donetsk University Press.

Aurobindo, S. (1914/2000). *The life divine.* 2nd American Edition (Originally published in the monthly review *Arya* 1914–1920). Twin Lakes: Lotus Press.

Bednarik, R. G. (2001/2007). *Rock art science: The scientific study of Palaeoart.* New Delhi: Aryan Books International.

Bednarik, R. G. (2003a). The earliest evidence of palaeoart. *Rock Art Research, 20*(2), 89–135.

Bednarik, R. G. (2003b). *A global perspective of Indian Palaeoart.* http://www.ifrao.com/wp-content/uploads/2014/06/reddy3.pdf. Accessed 9 Apr 2016.

Bednarik, R. G. (2006). Ранний и Средний Палеолит: возникновение семиотки. [The lower and middle palaeolithic origins of semiotics]. In A. Yevglevsky (Ed.), *Structural and semiotic investigations in archaeology (Russian language)* (Vol. 3, pp. 89–106, Structural and semiotic investigations in archaeology). Donetsk: Donetsk University Press.

Bednarik, R. G. (2007, November 23). *Email from Robert Bednarik*. Personal communication.

Chater, M. (2006). Just another brick in the wall: Education as violence to the spirit. *International Journal of Children's Spirituality, 11*(1), 47–56.

Crum, S. J. (1991). Colleges before Columbus: Mayans, Aztecs and Incas offered advanced education long before the arrival of Europeans. *Tribal College, 3*(2), 14.

Curtis, S. J., & Boltwood, M. E. (1953). *A short history of education*. London: University Tutorial Press.

Dahlin, B. (2006). *Education, history and be(com)ing human: Two essays in philosophy and education*. Karlstad: Karlstad University.

Dator, J. (2000). The futures for higher education: From bricks to bytes to fare thee well! In S. Inayatullah & J. Gidley (Eds.), *The university in transformation: Global perspectives on the futures of the university*. Westport: Bergin & Garvey.

de Souza, M. (2006). Educating for hope, compassion and meaning in a divisive and intolerant world. *International Journal of Children's Spirituality, 11*(1), 165–175.

Deleuze, G., & Conley, T. (1992). *The fold: Leibniz and the Baroque*. Minneapolis: University of Minnesota Press.

Denzin, N. (2005). The first international congress of qualitative inquiry. *Qualitative Social Work, 4*(1), 1105–1111.

Eckersley, R., Cahill, H., Wierenga, A., & Wyn, J. (Eds.). (2007). *Generations in dialogue about the future: The hopes and fears of young Australians*. Melbourne: Australian Youth Research Centre and Australia 21.

Egan, K. (1997). *The educated mind: How cognitive tools shape our understanding*. Chicago: The University of Chicago Press.

Eliot, T. S. (1934). *The rock*. London: Faber & Faber.

Finser, T. M. (2001). *School renewal: A spiritual journey for change*. Great Barrington: Anthroposophic Press.

Gardner, H. (1996). Probing more deeply into the theory of multiple intelligences. *NASSP Bulletin, 80*(583), 1–7.

Gebser, J. (1949/1985). *The ever-present origin*. Athens: Ohio University Press.

Gidley, J. (2005). Giving hope back to our young people: Creating a new spiritual mythology for Western culture. *Journal of Futures Studies, 9*(3), 17–30.

Gidley, J. (2007). The evolution of consciousness as a planetary imperative: An integration of integral views. *Integral Review: A Transdisciplinary and Transcultural Journal for New Thought, Research and Praxis, 5*, 4–226.

Gidley, J. (2009). Educating for evolving consciousness: Voicing the emergency for love, life and wisdom. In *The international handbook of education for spirituality, care and wellbeing* (Springer international handbooks of religion and education series). New York: Springer.

Gidley, J. (2010). From access to success: An integrated approach to quality higher education informed by social inclusion theory and practice. *Higher Education Policy, 23*, 123–147.

Gidley, J. (2013). Futures of education for rapid global-societal change. In F. González (Ed.), *Imagining the future*. Madrid: BBVA.

Giroux, H. A. (1999/2005). *Schooling and the struggle for public life: Democracy's promise and education's challenge*. Boulder: Paradigm Publishers.

Giroux, H. A. (2001). *Stealing innocence: Corporate culture's war on children*. New York: Palgrave Macmillan.

Glazer, S. (Ed.). (1994). *The heart of learning: Spirituality in education*. New York: Jeremy P. Tarcher/Putnam.

Gvirtz, S., & Beech, J. (2008). *Going to school in Latin America*. Westport: Greenwood Publishing Group.

Hart, T. (1998). A dialectic of knowing: Integrating the intuitive and the analytic. *Encounter: Education for Meaning and Social Justice, 11*, 5–16.

Hart, T. (2001). Teaching for wisdom. *Encounter: Education for Meaning and Social Justice, 14* (2), 3–16.

Holborn, H. (1964). *A history of modern Germany, 1648–1840*. Princeton: Princeton University Press.

Hooker, J. T. (1990). *Reading the past: Ancient writing from cuneiform to the alphabet*. London: Guild Publishing.

Horn, R. (2004). Building capacity for the development of a critical democratic citizenry through the redefinition of education. *World Futures, 60*, 169–182.

Houston, S. D. (Ed.). (2004). *The first writing: Script invention as history and process*. Cambridge: Cambridge University Press.

Huisman, J., & Van der Wende, M. (2004). The EU and Bologna: Are supra- and international initiatives threatening domestic agendas? *European Journal of Education, 39*(3), 349–357.

Inayatullah, S., & Gidley, J. (Eds.). (2000). *The university in transformation: Global perspectives on the futures of the university*. Westport: Bergin and Garvey.

Johnson, H. (2005). Counteracting performativity in schools: The case for laughter as a qualitative redemptive indicator. *International Journal of Children's Spirituality, 10*(1), 81–96.

Kessler, R. (2000). *The soul of education: Helping students find connection, compassion and character at school*. Alexandria: Association for Supervision and Curriculum Development.

Kincheloe, J., & Berry, K. (2004). *Rigour and complexity in educational research: Conceptualising the bricolage* (Conducting educational research). Berkshire: Open University Press.

Kincheloe, J., & Steinberg, S. (1993). A tentative description of post-formal thinking: The critical confrontation with cognitive theory. *Harvard Educational Review, 63*(3), 296–320.

Klein, J. T. (2004). Prospects for transdisciplinarity. *Futures, 36*(4), 515–526.

Lunt, I. (2008). Beyond tuition fees? The legacy of Blair's government to higher education. *Oxford Review of Education, 34*(6), 741–752.

Lyotard, J.-F. (2004). *The postmodern condition: A report on knowledge*. Manchester: Manchester University Press.

MacLure, M. (2006). The bone in the throat: Some uncertain thoughts on baroque method. *International Journal of Qualitative Studies in Education, 19*, 729–745.

Marginson, S. (Ed.). (2007). *Prospects of higher education: Globalization, market competition, public goods and the future of the university* (Educational futures: Rethinking theory and practice). Rotterdam: Sense Publishers.

Miller, R. (Ed.). (1993). *The renewal of meaning in education: Responses to the cultural and ecological crisis of our times (CD-ROM ed.)*. Brandon: Great Ideas in Education.

Miller, R. (1999). Holistic education for an emerging culture. In S. Glazer (Ed.), *The heart of learning: Spirituality in education*. New York: Putnam.

Miller, R. (2000). Education and the evolution of the cosmos [Electronic version]. In *Caring for new life: Essays on holistic education*. http://www.ctr4process.org/sites/default/files/pdfs/23_2Miller.pdf. Accessed 18 Apr 2016.

Montessori, M. (1973). *From childhood to adolescence*. New York: Schocken Books.

Montuori, A. (2006). The quest for a new education: From oppositional identities to creative inquiry. *ReVision, 28*(3), 4–17.

Morin, E. (2001). *Seven complex lessons in education for the future*. Paris: UNESCO.

Morin, E., & Kern, A. B. (1999). *Homeland earth: A manifesto for the new millennium* (S. Kelly, & R. Lapoint, Trans.) (Advances in systems theory, complexity and the human sciences) Cresskill: Hampton Press.

Nava, R. G. (2001). *Holistic education: Pedagogy of universal love* (M. N. Rios, & G. S. Miller, Trans., Foundations of holistic education series, Vol. 5). Brandon: Holistic Education Press.

Nielsen, T. W. (2006). Towards a pedagogy of imagination: A phenomenological case study of holistic education. *Ethnography and Education, 1*(2), 247–264.

Noddings, N. (2005). Caring in education. *The encyclopedia of informal education*. http://infed.org/mobi/caring-in-education/. Accessed 18 Apr 2016.

Orr, D. (1994). *Earth in mind: On education, environment, and the human prospect*. Washington, DC: Island Press.

Parpola, A. (2005, May 19). Study of the Indus script: Special lecture. In: *50th international conference of Eastern Studies Tokyo*. http://www.helsinki.fi/~aparpola/tices_50.pdf. Accessed 18 Apr 2016.

Pridmore, J. (2004). 'Dancing cannot start too soon': Spiritual education in the thought of Jean Paul Friedrich Richter. *International Journal of Children's Spirituality, 9*(3), 279–291.

Rose, K., & Kincheloe, J. (2003). *Art, culture and education: Artful teaching in a fractured landscape*. New York: Peter Lang.

Sawahal, W. (2009). *Knowledge hub in progress*. Malaysia: University World News.

Scheurich, J. J., & McKenzie, K. B. (2005). Foucault's methodologies: Archaeology and genealogy. In N. Denzin & Y. Lincoln (Eds.), *The sage handbook of qualitative research* (3rd ed., pp. 841–868). Thousand Oaks: Sage.

Schiller, F. (1954/1977). *On the aesthetic education of man—In a series of letters* (First published in 1795). New York: Frederick Ungar Publishing.

Scott, P., Curaj, A., Vlăsceanu, L., & Wilson, L. (Eds.). (2012). *European higher education at the crossroads—Between the bologna process and national reforms*. Dordrecht: Springer.

St. Pierre, E. A. (2004). Deleuzian concepts for education: The subject undone. *Educational Philosophy and Theory, 36*(3), 283–296.

Steinberg, S., & Kincheloe, J. (Eds.). (2004). *Kinderculture: The corporate construction of childhood*. Boulder: Westview Press.

Steiner, R. (1909/1965). *The education of the child in the light of anthroposophy (GA 34)* (2nd ed., G. & M. Adams, Trans.). London: Rudolf Steiner Press. (Original work published 1909)

Steiner, R. (1930/1983). *Metamorphoses of the soul: Paths of experience: Vol. 1 (GA 58)* (2nd ed., C. Davy, & C. von Arnim, Trans.) [9 Lectures, Berlin and Munich, March 14 to December 9, 1909] (Original work published 1930). London: Rudolf Steiner Press.

Steiner, R. (1976). *Practical advice to teachers: Lectures, 1919*. London: Rudolf Steiner Press.

Subbiondo, J. (2005). An approach to integral education: A case for spirituality in higher education. *ReVision, 28*(2), 18–23.

Welch, A. R., & Zhen, Z. (2008). Higher education and global talent flows: Brain drain, overseas Chinese intellectuals, and diasporic knowledge networks. *Higher Education Policy, 21*(4), 519–537.

White, R. (2006). The women of Brassempouy: A century of research and interpretation. *Journal of Archaeological Method and Theory, 13*(4), 251–304.

Whitehead, A. N. (1916/1967). *The aims of education*. New York: Free Press.

Zajonc, A. (2006). Cognitive-affective connections in teaching and learning: The relationship between love and knowledge. *Journal of Cognitive Affective Learning, 3*(1), 1–9.

Part II
Postformal Psychology and Education: A Dialogue

Chapter 5
Postformal in Psychology: Beyond Piaget's Formal Operations

5.1 Introduction

I expect that this chapter will be the most challenging of all the chapters for readers with limited prior knowledge of adult developmental psychology. It has certainly been the most challenging to write—largely because there is so much material on higher stages of reasoning, yet so little coherence of it to date. If you are a teacher of young children, you might even think you can skip this chapter but I urge you not to. For educators—or parents—of children of any age, it is vital to think about what childhood is leading to: What advanced forms of reasoning might be possible for the adults of tomorrow if given optimal opportunities to develop their potential fully? It is crucial to know about advanced forms of thinking that many of our children will need to embrace as adults simply to deal with life this century. It is a fundamental task for educators today to bring these insights into education.

In Chapters 2 and 3, I discussed the impact of the evolution of consciousness on human culture and thinking. In these chapters, I took a wide-angle lens to explore new qualities of thinking that are emerging first as part of cultural evolution and secondly through individual psychological development.

In this chapter we explore a range of adult development theories created by psychologists who saw beyond the limits of Piaget's cognitive model. I introduce the main researchers who have identified and described postformal reasoning qualities and reiterate the shift from formal to postformal reasoning. The postformal reasoning features they identify are listed, and from these I theorise and discuss twelve distinct postformal reasoning qualities.

By the end of this chapter, you will have a coherent picture of how postformal reasoning is conceptually aligned with four themes that I have distilled from the evolution of consciousness research.

J.M. Gidley, *Postformal Education*, Critical Studies of Education 3,
DOI 10.1007/978-3-319-29069-0_5

5.2 The Emergence of Adult Development Theories

> From a cognitive point of view, the passage from adolescence to adulthood raises a number of unresolved questions that need to be studied in greater detail. (Piaget 1972, p. 12)

This statement by Piaget towards the end of his life indicates that although his life's work involved building a theory of cognitive development that ended with adolescence, he himself was unconvinced that this was the last word on the matter.

This section offers a brief overview of psychological development theories that include stages beyond childhood and adolescence. These "adult development theories" belong to a complex area of psychology that I cannot comprehensively cover. What I do intend to do is the following:

- To offer a starting point for exploring a range of theories that go beyond Piaget's formal operations as the highest stage of cognitive reasoning; and
- To offer a rough guide to the spectrum of adult psychological development theories so that interested readers can pursue the references in greater depth.

The following sub-sections are not mutually exclusive. but rather I cluster groups of theories under themes to make some sense of the diversity. Some of these theorists appear in this chapter in relation to postformal features they have identified.

5.2.1 Adult Developmental Stage Theories

> The culture in which we find ourselves at the end of the twentieth century demands that we be capable of dialectical, post-ideological, transpersonal, fifth-order thinking... our children and students may be much more capable of it than our parents and teachers ever could be, and if we ignore this we will not make much contact with them... The observations on culture and consciousness which Lyotard was making in the seventies, and Kegan has been making in the nineties had already been made by Jean Gebser (1949) in the forties. (Neville 2006, pp. 5–6)

Since Sigmund Freud proposed his three-stage theory of psycho-sexual development (id, ego and super-ego) in the early 20th century, a string of developmental stage theorists have drawn on, adapted or rejected his theories. Erik Erikson extended Freud's psycho-sexual theory into eight psycho-social stages (see Table 5.1). Erikson's three later stages of mature adult development are discussed in Chapter 8 in relation to pedagogical love (Stages 6 and 7) and in Chapter 10 in relation to pedagogical wisdom (Stage 8).

Lawrence Kohlberg extended Piaget's cognitive theories into the domain of moral development, proposing three primary stages of pre-conventional, conventional and post-conventional morality—each with two sub-stages (Kohlberg 1981). His collaborator and critical friend, Carol Gilligan, further extended Kohlberg's work to acknowledge the different moral reasoning features observable among

Table 5.1 Erikson's Stages of Psycho-social Development

Stage	Psycho-social Crisis	Basic Virtue	Age
1	Trust vs. mistrust	Hope	Infancy (0–1½)
2	Autonomy vs. shame	Will	Early childhood (1½–3)
3	Initiative vs. guilt	Purpose	Play age (3–5)
4	Industry vs. inferiority	Competency	School age (5–12)
5	Identity vs. role confusion	Fidelity	Adolescence (12–18)
6	Intimacy vs. isolation	Love	Young adult (18–40)
7	Generativity vs. stagnation	Care	Adulthood (40–65)
8	Ego integrity vs. despair	Wisdom	Maturity (65+)

Source: Adapted from Erikson (1950/1985, 1959/1994)

female research participants (Gilligan 1982). Kohlberg was also a key figure in the development of postformal stage theory in his later life (Kohlberg 1990).

A related approach within adult development is "life-span psychology". German psychologist, Paul B. Baltes (1939–2006), was regarded by his peers to be a seminal figure in establishing life-span psychology and positive ageing as sub-disciplines of adult developmental psychology. Baltes edited/co-edited a series of publications on *Life-Span Development and Behaviour* from 1978 to 1990 (Baltes 1978). Several other theorists have pursued research in the area of life-span psychology and positive ageing (Labouvie-Vief 1980; Baltes et al. 1999; Thornton 2003). Other key researchers include Richard M. Lerner, co-editor of the four-volume *Handbook of Applied Developmental Science (2002)* and the two-volume *Encyclopedia of Applied Developmental Science (2004)*, and K. Warner Schaie who based his theory of adult cognitive development stages on longitudinal studies of adults throughout their life course (Schaie and Willis 2010).

Harvard psychologist Robert Kegan has developed a five-stage model of adult cognitive development which he referred to as "stages of development in 1982, orders of consciousness in 1994, and forms of mind in 2000" (Evans et al. 2010, p. 177). His model (Kegan 1994), referred to by Bernie Neville in the opening quote, is of interest to this research as it can be related isomorphically to Gebser's five structures of consciousness and Piaget's schema. Further parallels with Kieran Egan's imaginative education are discussed in Chapter 9 (see Table 9.3). We see in Table 5.2 that the gap at the upper limit of Piaget's theory—post-adolescence—becomes glaring beside Gebser's cultural and Kegan's adult cognitive theories.

5.2.2 *Ego Development Theories*

> Loevinger's achievement was to both hypothesise the stages of ego development and to develop an instrument that was able to reliably measure what stage of development an individual is probably operating from. (Hayward 2002, p. 7)

Table 5.2 Parallels between Jean Gebser, Jean Piaget and Robert Kegan

Gebser's Cultural Evolution	Piaget's Cognitive Stage Theory	Kegan's Orders of Thinking
Archaic (Pre-history)	Sensori-motor (infant) Movement and sensory	First order Impulsive mind
Magical consciousness (Ice Age)	Pre-operational (two to six years) Magical thinking	Second order Instrumental mind
Mythic consciousness (Agrarian to Philosophic > 500 BCE)	Concrete operations (seven to twelve years) Logic is concrete	Third order Socialised mind
Mental/rational mode (500 BCE–1,500 CE)	Formal operations (twelve to eighteen years) Logic becomes abstract	Fourth order Self-authoring mind
Integral consciousness (1,500 CE > the future)	*What happens next?* *(eighteen and beyond)*	Fifth order Self-transforming mind

Table 5.3 Jane Loevinger's Stages of Ego Development

Stage	Cognitive Style
Presocial	Autistic
Impulsive	Basic dichotomies
Self-protective	Dichotomous thinking
Conformist	Conceptual simplicity
Self-aware	Multiplicity
Conscientious (formal operations)	Conceptual complexity, patterning
Individualistic	Add: distinction of process and outcome
Autonomous	Increased complexity, ambiguity, contradiction

Source: Loevinger (1976, p. 24)

Ego development theories are also, in a sense, stage theories, but they have a more specific emphasis. Jane Loevinger (1918–2008) built on both Piaget's and Erikson's work to develop a theory of levels of ego development (see Table 5.3). Australian researcher Peter Hayward notes that "In the Piagetian scheme of cognitive development Loevinger's Conscientious ego stage correlates to Piaget's cognitive development stage of formal operational thinking" (Hayward 2002, p. 8).

Loevinger's work provided important foundations for other positive adult developmental psychologists (Cook-Greuter 2000; Wade 1996). Suzanne Cook-Greuter extends Loevinger's model into two higher levels. The post-conventional/postformal level includes: *construct-aware* and *unitive*. The higher level of *post*postconventional/ego transcendent reflects the *transcendent self* (Cook-Greuter 2000, 2008).

5.2.3 *Positive Psychology and Human Potential Theories*

> The field of positive psychology … is about valued subjective experiences: well-being, contentment, and satisfaction (in the past); hope and optimism (for the future); and flow and happiness (in the present). At the individual level, it is about positive individual traits: the capacity for love and vocation, courage, interpersonal skill, aesthetic sensibility, perseverance, forgiveness, originality, future mindedness, spirituality, high talent, and wisdom. At the group level it is about: … responsibility, nurturance, altruism, civility, moderation, tolerance, and work ethic. (Seligman and Csikszentmihalyi 2000)

The sub-discipline of positive psychology springs from the human potential movement. A founding figure is Abraham Maslow (1908–1970) whose original human potential theory covered five levels from a baseline of four deficiency needs: biological and physiological needs, safety needs, belongingness and love needs, and esteem needs, with one growth need: self-actualisation (Maslow 1956). His later theory extended to eight levels including the four deficiency needs and four growth needs: cognitive, aesthetic, self-actualisation and eventually transcendence (which involves helping others to self-actualise) (Maslow 1971).

Notable contemporary research in positive psychology includes Martin Seligman's theories of "learned hopelessness", "learned optimism" and "authentic happiness" (Seligman 1995); Mihaly Csikszentmihalyi's theories of "flow" in relation to being in states of happiness (Csikszentmihalyi 1990); and Barbara L. Fredrickson's work on positive emotions including love (Fredrickson 2013). The other emotions Fredrickson includes in her research are joy, gratitude, serenity, interest, hope, pride, amusement, inspiration and awe (Fredrickson 2013, pp. 4–6).

5.2.4 *Transpersonal Psychology*

> Transpersonal psychology is a truly integral psychology in that it systematically attempts to include and integrate the enduring insights of premodern religion, modern psychological science, and constructive postmodern philosophy in its investigation of exceptional human experiences and transformative capacities … [T]ranspersonal psychology takes a pluralistic, multi-layered, developmental approach. (Cunningham 2004, pp. 1–2)

Transpersonal psychology is effectively adult developmental psychology that allows for spiritual dimensions and/or transcendence. Like positive psychology, it had its roots in Maslow's work and other human potential theories. Transpersonal psychology, or what Maslow referred to as the fourth force in psychology, may well represent the psychology of the future that helps the discipline become the true "logos of the human psyche" humanist psychologist Gordon Allport envisioned it to be almost fifty years ago (Allport 1955/1969, p. 98).

After extensive research on definitions over twenty-three years of transpersonal psychology in the USA, it was defined by Susanne LaJoie and Michael Shapiro in 1992 as follows: "Transpersonal Psychology is concerned with the study of humanity's highest potential, and with the recognition, understanding, and realization of unitive, spiritual, and transcendent states of consciousness" (Lajoie and Shapiro 1992, p. 91).

Transpersonal researchers include Charles Alexander, Stanislav Grof, Roger Walsh, Frances Vaughan and Wilber (Grof 2000; Walsh and Vaughan 1993; Wilber 2000). There are also several developmental psychologists who include spiritual development as part of their study of higher cognition (Sinnott 1994; Cartwright 2001; Orme-Johnson 2000).

Although ego development and stage theories, positive psychology, human potential and transpersonal psychology theories all play a part in adult developmental psychology research, to explore them in depth would be tangential to the main focus of this book—the crucial relationship between postformal reasoning and education.

5.3 Postformal Reasoning in Adult Developmental Psychology

> *Postformal thought*.... is a kind of complex cognitive representational ability and logic developed during adulthood... To integrate the types of connections and their sometimes disparate or conflicting ideas successfully, yet preserve a concept of Self that is whole and a coherent strong center of events, postformal complex cognitive operations must be used. (Sinnott 2005, p. 30)

The term *postformal* is the most widely used psychological term to denote higher developmental stages beyond Piaget's *formal operations*. The first use of the term in this way was in a series of papers published from 1978. To date, most of the research in reference to the term *postformal* is the adult developmental psychology research (Yan and Arlin 1995; Sinnott 1994, 2005; Commons et al. 1990; Kohlberg 1990; Labouvie-Vief 1990; Sinnott 1998; Labouvie-Vief 1992; Kramer 1983; Commons and Richards 2002). *Postformal* in education is the focus of Chapter 6.

5.3.1 Terminology Issues

The literature on postformal reasoning shows a diversity of terminology, some of which is used interchangeably. Even within this specialised area of adult developmental psychology, there are sub-clusters of researchers who do not refer to each other's research. Individual writers use slightly different terms, indicating a lack of theoretical coherence, though most adult developmental psychologists use the term *postformal*—or *post-formal*—to refer to stages beyond Piaget's *formal operations* (Kohlberg 1990; Sinnott 1998; Kramer 1983; Commons and Richards 2002).

Cook-Greuter uses a variety of terms for what she often refers to collectively as third-tier development. She uses *postformal* "because it goes beyond the modern, linear-scientific Western mindset" and *post-conventional* after Kohlberg's third moral stage [which goes] "beyond the conventions of society by starting to question the unconsciously held beliefs, norms and assumptions about reality acquired during socialization and schooling" (Cook-Greuter 2008, p. 4). In other contexts Cook-Greuter uses *postsymbolic*, after Charles Alexander (Cook-Greuter 2000), and *postrepresentational* when she is speaking about awareness of the language habit (Cook-Greuter 2000, p. 228).

Kegan uses the term fifth-order thinking, which he links to the postmodern[1] mindset. However, Kegan introduces the idea of two types of postmodernism—a *deconstructive* and a later *reconstructive* form (Kegan 1994). Michael Commons and his colleagues have undertaken extensive research on postformal stages using Commons' Model of Hierarchical Complexity (Commons et al. 1998). Their model includes four distinct stages—systematic, metasystematic, paradigmatic and cross-paradigmatic—which they have theoretically articulated and empirically tested over decades (Commons and Ross 2008).

Educational researchers are more inclined to hyphenate post-formal (Kincheloe and Steinberg 1999; Kincheloe et al. 1999a; Villaverde and Pinar 1999) though there are no rules about this. These researchers also coined the terms *postformalism* and *postformality* (Kincheloe 2006). Joseph Chilton Pearce writes about *post-operations* (Pearce 1992), while Maclure refers to postfoundational research methods in the context of educational research (MacLure 2006).

The term *post-Piagetian* is a term sometimes used to refer to the general adult developmental psychology approach that reaches beyond the limits set by Piaget's notion that formal operations is the final stage of cognitive development (Cook-Greuter 1995). *Neo-Piagetian* is sometimes used in a similar way (Reams 2014). There is also a more specific use of the term by a group of developmental psychology researchers in the 1970s and 1980s who referred to themselves as neo-Piagetians. They included Juan Pascual-Leone, Robert Case, Kurt Fischer and Andreas Demetriou and primarily focused on the information-processing aspects of cognitive development, building on Piaget's work while critiquing it, extending it and refining its basic tenets. Some of them drew on the socio-cultural insights of Vygotsky.

Before putting the terminology issues to rest, I want to mention that Steiner and Wilber also coined terms for a postformal level of psychological development. In the early 1900s—prior to Gebser, Wilber or adult developmental psychology theories—Steiner wrote and lectured extensively about a stage of consciousness beyond abstract, formal, intellectual thinking. Steiner noted that this "self-reflective consciousness" is not only able to perceive and know the world but to become conscious of itself. He called this stage of development *consciousness soul*. Wilber frequently refers to postformal psychological development in his writing. But he

[1]Postmodernism includes complex attempts to find conceptual bridges between what has been called the "cosmological and poststructuralist postmodernisms" (Gare 2002; Keller and Daniell 2002).

also uses other terms including *vision-logic*, *integral* and *centaur* to refer to postformal reasoning (Wilber 2000). Vision-logic seems to be his preferred term. Steiner's concept of consciousness soul and Wilber's concept of vision-logic will be discussed in more detail in Chapter 7 for their ability to integrate psychological development and cultural evolution.

5.3.2 Key Researchers and their Approaches

> Although Piaget's interpretations capture a rich variety of performances during childhood, they fail to represent adequately the thought and emotions of mature and creative persons. (Riegel 1973, p. 346)

Many volumes have been published by a core group of research psychologists and psychiatrists who have been researching postformal reasoning for four decades. In this short space, I cannot hope to do justice to the breadth and depth of their work. What I will do is provide a rough chronology of important developments and introduce you to a few of the key players and the postformal reasoning qualities they have identified.

The first psychologist to write about the need to extend Piaget's formal operations to understand adult cognition was German-American psychologist Klaus F. Riegel. His most significant contribution was his paper on *dialectical operations*, which became recognised as one of the fundamental features of postformal reasoning. The paper is frequently cited as foundational to postformal research (Riegel 1973). To summarise his own work and how it differs from Piaget, Riegel states:

> Our own modification recognises dialectic conflicts and contradictions as a fundamental property of thought. In contrast to Piaget . . . the individual does not necessarily equilibrate these conflicts, but is ready to live with these contradictions. (Riegel 1973, p, 366)

Following Riegel's paper, Patricia Arlin proposed a Piagetian fifth stage related to *problem-finding* (building on from the problem-solving of formal operations) (Arlin 1975). In later work with Bernice Yan, Arlin extended her research to include other postformal qualities, including *dialectical thinking*, *relativism* and *reflective judgement* (Yan and Arlin 1995). It seems a movement had begun with adult developmental psychologists researching and writing about going "beyond Piaget's formal operations". The postformal features in these early papers included *unitary operations* (Koplowitz 1978), *contradiction*, *complexity*, *systemic* and *metasystemic reasoning* (Labouvie-Vief 1980; Commons et al. 1982).

The term postformal was first used in 1978 to explicitly represent a stage beyond Piaget's formal operations in a paper by Michael Commons and Francis Richards: "The structural analytic stage of development: A Piagetian postformal operational stage". It was presented at a conference of the Western Psychological Association, in San Francisco (Commons and Richards 1978). In 1981 Harvard University held the first of a series of Symposia on Post-Formal Operations: Reasoning in Late

Adolescence and Adulthood[2] at which Jan Sinnott presented a paper "Post-formal reasoning in interpersonal situations" (Sinnott 1981). Lawrence Kohlberg's work on stages of moral development was very influential on these early pioneers as was his contribution to theorising postformal stage theory (Kohlberg 1981, 1990; Kohlberg and Gilligan 1971).

Psychology professor, Jan Sinnott, along with Commons and Richards, is a pioneer of research into postformal reasoning. Although much has been published over forty years, particularly in edited volumes, Sinnott has actually developed and articulated her theory of "postformal thought" in a comprehensive authored book (Sinnott 1998). Although this book is now approaching twenty years old, it is a seminal text in the field—with insights that are not outdated. Sinnott's research, while grounded in decades of empirical research, includes philosophical, epistemological and socio-cultural observations to ground her theory in the "real world". By illuminating her psychological research with findings from the new physics, systems theory, and chaos and complexity theories, she builds a robust and convincing case for postformal thought. She also presents a variety of applications of postformal thought in areas of professional practice, including education. The features Sinnott (1998) highlights in her book are *complexity*, *creativity* (pp. 270–271), *paradox* (p. 39), *self-referential thought (reflexivity)* (pp. 33–39), *spirituality* (pp. 260–265) and *wisdom* (p. 33). Elsewhere she identified *relativism* as postformal (Sinnott 1984).

Another important paper from the early years is Deirdre Kramer's: "Post-Formal Operations: A Need for Further Conceptualization" (Kramer 1983). Attempting to synthesise the adult development literature that took either a Piagetian or neo-Piagetian line, Kramer identified three major characteristics of "post-formal operations": "(1) an understanding of the *relativistic, non-absolute* nature of knowledge; (2) an acceptance of *contradiction* as part of reality; and (3) an *integrative* approach to thinking" (Kramer 1983, pp. 91–92). Kramer also includes *contextualism* and *organicism*—which she links back to *integration* (Kramer 1983, p. 93). I use the term *ecological reasoning* to include Kramer's organicism.

By 1984 Commons and Richards and Cheryl Armon had produced an edited book called *Beyond formal operations Vol 1: Late Adolescent and Adult Cognitive Development* (Commons et al. 1984). It included Robert Sternberg's chapter on *higher-order reasoning* (Sternberg 1984) and Michael Basseches' extension of the dialectical line of thought of Riegel (Basseeches 1984).

Since the 1990s research into postformal reasoning has burgeoned. *Wisdom* stands out as a key quality of mature adult thought (Sinnott 1998; Pascual-Leone 2000; Sternberg 1990, 1998, 2005; Labouvie-Vief 1992; Bassett 2005a). A quality that has been uniquely identified by only one researcher is *construct-awareness*

[2]The series began as a Symposium on "Post-Formal Operations." The Second Harvard University Symposium on Beyond Formal Operations: The Development of Adolescent and Adult Thought and Perception, was held in 1985. The Third Harvard University Symposium on Beyond Formal Operations: Positive Development during Adolescence and Adulthood was held in 1987.

(Cook-Greuter 2000). It can be best understood as a facet of reflexivity, which I call *language reflexivity*. These qualities are now more fully explored.

5.3.3 Postformal Reasoning Qualities

The main features of postformal reasoning identified in the adult developmental psychology research are listed in the left-hand column in Table 5.4. However, since my research focus is broader than individual psychological development and includes cultural evolution and socio-cultural scanning of megatrends of the mind (introduced in Chapter 3), I contribute additional features.

Some of my contributions use more contemporary language or research, e.g. *ecological reasoning* (includes *organicism*) (Gidley 2007), *language reflexivity* (includes *construct aware*) (Gidley 2009). I add the term *higher purpose* for its importance in the postformal leadership research (de Blonville 2013a) as a neutral, secular quality—similar to *spirituality*. I add *dialogical reasoning* as a term to cover interpersonal and relational maturity as part of mature adult reasoning (Gangadean 1998). Finally, I add two qualities from the evolution of consciousness research: *pluralism*, linked with relativism and frequently used in research on epistemological paradigm shift (Gidley 2010a), and *futures reasoning* from the megatrends of the mind research (Gidley 2010a), noting that Seligman also uses *future mindedness* (Seligman and Csikszentmihalyi 2000).

In a preliminary process of sense making among the diverse postformal psychological features and as a basis for exploring their alignment with my broad evolutionary themes, I looked for *family resemblances* among them (Wittgenstein 1968). I theorise twelve core postformal qualities, some of which represent "clusters of qualities". In Table 5.4 the twenty-four features (left column) and the twelve synthesised qualities (right column) are arranged in alphabetical order.

5.3.4 Is Postformal Reasoning about Qualities or Stages?

An overriding question challenging researchers of postformal reasoning is to what extent qualities represent actual stage/s beyond formal reasoning and to what extent they represent merely different facets of one postformal stage. Because this is not a book entirely devoted to the research on postformal reasoning, such a question cannot be addressed in depth here. I offer some pointers for further study.

Kramer proposed that the three postformal qualities she identified (relativism, acceptance of contradiction and integration of contradiction into a larger whole) relate to "three distinct levels of thought that unfold over the entire life-span" (Kramer 1983, p. 93). Yet she did not go as far as to say that they represent structural changes—sometimes called *hard stages* (Kohlberg 1990).

Table 5.4 Delicate Theorising of Postformal Reasoning Qualities

Postformal Reasoning Features (Multiple Sources)	Postformal Reasoning Qualities (Gidley)
Complexity (Commons et al. 1998; Sinnott 1998; Labouvie-Vief 2006)	**Complexity** (incorporating paradox and contradiction)
Contradiction (Basseeches 1984; Riegel 1973; Kramer 1983)	
Context (Kramer 1983; Labouvie-Vief 2006)	
Creativity (Sinnott 1998; Sternberg 1999)	**Creativity** (incorporating problem-finding)
Dialectics (Basseeches 1984; Riegel 1973; Yan and Arlin 1995)	
Dialogical reasoning (Sonnert and Commons 1994; Galtung 1995)	**Dialogical reasoning** (incorporating dialectics, relationality)
Ecological thinking (Kramer 1983)	**Ecological reasoning** (incorporating context, process, organicism)
Futures thinking (Seligman and Csikszentmihalyi 2000; Gidley 2013)	**Futures reasoning** (incorporating foresight, future mindedness)
Higher purpose (Sinnott 2005; de Blonville 2013a)	**Higher purpose** (incorporating spirituality, values awareness)
Holism (Kramer 1983; Sinnott 1998)	
Imagination, mythopoesis (Bassett 2005b; Labouvie-Vief 2006)	**Imagination** (incorporating imaginal, mythopoesis)
Integration (Kramer 1983; Loevinger 1976)	**Integration** (incorporating holism, unitary thought)
Intuition (Cook-Greuter 2000)	**Intuitive wisdom** (incorporating wisdom, intuition)
Language reflexivity, Construct-awareness (Cook-Greuter 2000; Gidley 2009)	**Language reflexivity** (incorporating construct-awareness, voice, language sensibility)
Organicism (Kramer 1983)	
Paradox (Sinnott 1998)	
Pluralism (Gidley 2010a)	**Pluralism** (incorporating non-absolutism, relativism)
Problem-finding (Arlin 1975; Yan and Arlin 1995)	
Reflexivity (Sinnott 1998; Yan and Arlin 1995)	**Reflexivity** (incorporating self-reflection, self-references)
Relativism, non-absolutism (Kramer 1983; Sinnott 1984; Yan and Arlin 1995)	
Spirituality (Koplowitz 1990; Sinnott 1998; Cartwright 2001)	
Unitary thought (Koplowitz 1978)	
Values awareness (Kohlberg 1981)	
Wisdom (Sinnott 1998; Pascual-Leone 2000; Sternberg 1998; Bassett 2005a)	

Source: Gidley (2008)

Kohlberg and Armon introduced the distinction between hard and soft stages (Kohlberg and Armon 1984). In a later paper, Kohlberg argued that the hard stage model is needed to bring everything together because, in his view, education needs to be based on a coherent philosophy. He pointed to the need for more cross-cultural research if some kind of "cultural universality" is to be achieved within postformal stage theory with regard to its general applicability (Kohlberg 1990).

Commons developed a General Stage Model of postformal reasoning, now called the Model of Hierarchical Complexity. The model initially included systematic and metasystematic reasoning (Commons et al. 1982) with paradigmatic and cross-paradigmatic reasoning being added (Richards and Commons 1984). Commons claims that his model fulfils the purpose of specifying "hard stages" (Commons et al. 2008, Para 3). The Model is the most sophisticated of any that attempt to delineate stages. I refer to it where relevant but cannot in this context elaborate.

5.4 Reiterating the Shift from Formal to Postformal Reasoning

> Formal operations presume logical consistency within a single logical system. Within that single system, the implications of the system are absolute. Postformal operations resume somewhat necessarily subjective selection among logically contradictory formal operational systems, each of which is internally consistent and absolute. (Sinnott 1998, p. 25)

Aristotle was arguably the first to conceptualise and codify binary logic. Yet it took two millennia for much of humanity to adopt this way of thinking. The modernist worldview, which has contributed to both the advances and challenges of our times, is underpinned by the binary proposition that "every statement is either true or false and not both" (Klement 2005). Aristotle's binary logic, later conceptualised as a fundamental tenet of Piaget's formal operations, has underpinned the dominant mode of thinking now for centuries. In order to better understand the default tendency of the dominant worldview to cling to binary categorisations, we have contextualised its emergence in ancient Greece (Chapter 2) and shown how it is expressed in formal operations as part of individual psychological development in Chapter 3.

Western dualism was intensified in the 17th century by the French rationalist philosophy of René Descartes. Cartesian dualism—the mind/body split—pervades modern scientific positivism, analytic philosophy and formal education. The formal academic argument or thesis involves establishing the correctness of a particular concept or theory—and often the incorrectness of contradictory theories. Formal, binary or dualistic logic underpins all abstract, intellectual-rational thinking.

If our dominant mode of thinking is formal operations, based on binary logic, we may have trouble dealing with the tensions of a multi-perspectival world—we may feel overwhelmed by chaos, complexity and contradiction. When chaos, complexity and contradiction—signs of Ziauddin Sardar's "postnormal era"—are viewed in the context of the evolution of consciousness, the parallels with postformal reasoning qualities, complexity, paradox and creativity, become clear (Gidley 2010b; Sardar 2010). By embracing dialectics and paradox, the limitations of dualism can be transcended.

Postformal logics go beyond the *excluded middle* of Aristotelian formal logic. Holding in mind the paradox of contradictory truths—or non-truths—creates discomfort in the minds and emotions of people only accustomed to using formal logic. This raises the question of how we facilitate the ability of people today to think more complexly and to hold paradox in mind without constantly wanting a resolution of the tension through a reduction of the complexity to a binary. It is a global educational priority today to lay foundations in childhood and adolescence for the unfoldment of postformal logics in adults. This is the primary focus of the remainder of this volume.

5.5 Postformal Reasoning: Delicate Theorising of Twelve Qualities

Before bringing these qualities into dialogue with evolutionary themes, I give each quality meaning in this context, explaining how it was identified as postformal: through adult developmental psychology research, cultural evolution literature or epistemological shifts. I also point to educational relevance for later chapters.

5.5.1 Complexity: Incorporates Paradox and Contradiction

> One general aspect of post-formal thought is that one can conceive of multiple logics, choices, or perceptions of an event or relationship, even if seemingly paradoxical, in order to better understand the complexities and inherent biases in "truth". (Griffin et al. 2009, p. 173)

Complex thinking is the ability to hold multiple perspectives in mind while at the same time meta-reflecting on those perspectives and the potential relationships among them. It is a significant indicator of postformal reasoning in much of the adult development literature. Commons calls this metasystemic thinking—within his Model of Hierarchical Complexity (Commons et al. 1998).

Kincheloe and Steinberg regard complexity as a key feature of postmodern times that educators need to address (Kincheloe et al. 1999a). Cultural historians and philosophers view increasing complexity as a sign of development. The idea that organic processes are intrinsically more complex than mechanical processes is the basis of complexity theory (Morin 2005).

Paradox and contradiction go hand-in-hand with complex thinking (Commons et al. 1990; Commons and Richards 2002; Kramer 1983; Labouvie-Vief 1992; Riegel 1973; Sinnott 1998). Paradoxical reasoning refers to the ability to hold in mind the apparently illogical possibility that two contradictory statements can both be true—or indeed both false. This paradox of the *included middle* allows for *both/and* and *neither/nor* to be correct and is a key feature of transdisciplinarity (Nicolescu 2002). In contrast to Aristotle's Law of Non-Contradiction, Kramer notes a fundamental feature of postformal reasoning is "acceptance of contradiction" (Kramer 1983). Postformal approaches that emphasise complexity and paradox facilitate the cultivation of wisdom in education (see Chapter 10).

5.5.2 Creativity: Incorporates Problem-Finding

> Postformal thought . . . is linked to creative production by virtue of its . . . multiple views of reality and its multiple solutions, definitions, parameters, and methods during problem solving. . . the same sorts of processes [can be observed] under the rubrics of wisdom. (Sinnott, 1998, p. 271)

Creativity is the ability to see things from novel perspectives. Whitehead saw creativity as the ultimate category for understanding all other processes. Creation as movement into novelty is the basic process of existence (Hart 2006, p. 121).

Creativity supports wisdom and is a widely recognised postformal reasoning quality (Abbs 1994, 2003; Kaufman and Baer 2006; Kincheloe et al. 1999b; Montuori 1997; Montuori et al. 2004; Sinnott 1998; Sternberg 1999). Patricia Arlin was so convinced about the postformal nature of *problem-finding* as a component of creativity that she referred to it initially as a fifth Piagetian stage (Arlin 1975).

Cultural historians also emphasise creativity as an evolutionary quality. And yet, Arthur Koestler claimed that creativity is suppressed by the automatic routines of thought and behaviour that dominate our lives. Recent psychology research showing that creativity is declining during childhood, perhaps as a result of schooling, appears to support Koestler's claim (Kaufman and Sternberg 2006). Reversing this decline in creativity and other research on creativity in schools is the focus of Chapter 10.

5.5.3 Dialogical Reasoning: Incorporates Dialectics, Relationality

> Education is at heart a dialogical process. . . And dialogue, unlike a contest, is not about winning and losing but about ways of relating in which justice can be done to all who take part. (Biesta 2014, p. 3–5)

Dialogical reasoning is identified by Commons as being key to metasystemic reasoning in his General Stage Model (Sonnert and Commons 1994). Dialectical thinking is identified as a significant postformal feature (Commons et al. 1990; Baltes et al. 1999; Commons and Richards 2002; Kramer 1983; Labouvie-Vief 1992; Riegel 1973; Sinnott 1998).

Dialectics was a legacy of Hegelian philosophy that has been taken in different directions, for example, Marxist dialectical materialism and critical theory. Another direction of dialectics is the movement into dialogical reasoning or *dialogic imagination*—a term coined by Mikhail Bakhtin and developed by Julia Kristeva through her theory of intertextuality (Orr 2003). Dialogical reasoning is reflected in integral philosopher Ashok Gangadean's philosophy of *deep dialogue* (Gangadean 2006). Leading theoretical physicist David Bohm (1917–1992) created a widely used form of dialogue that came to be known as Bohm Dialogue (Bohm et al. 1991).

While formal thinking includes the ability to debate an argument, ending in win-lose, dialogical reasoning supports real win-win, in which we are free to really listen and finally hear the thoughts and views of others, as Gert Biesta indicates in the opening quote. Where formal research presents a formal argument to support a particular theory, postformal research involves dialogue among a plurality of perspectives, as we shall see in Kincheloe's *bricolage* (Chapter 7). For a discussion of the implications of dialogical reasoning in education, see Chapter 8.

5.5.4 Ecological Reasoning: Incorporates Context, Process, Organicism

> [The ecological perspective is a] "more spacious perspective, [through which] the Earth (and even the cosmos) are seen as interconnected, living systems". (Elgin and LeDrew 1997)

Ecological reasoning and its partners, *context* (or contextualisation) (Kramer 1983; Labouvie-Vief 2006), *organicism* (Kramer 1983) and *process*, are all features of Kincheloe and Steinberg's postformalism. These qualities also arise in postmodern philosophy, hermeneutics, futures studies and contemporary socio-cultural research.

Contemporary constructive or reconstructive postmodernisms draw on the organic, process philosophies of Bergson and Whitehead (Bergson 1911/1944; Whitehead 1929/1985). A few years before, in 1894, Rudolf Steiner stated his philosophical aim as being: "that knowledge itself shall become organically alive" (Steiner 1894/1964, p. xxix). The broadening of social science research beyond the positivist paradigm to the interpretive paradigm carried with it a shift from quantitative, especially statistical, forms of analysis to interpretive—particularly contextual, hermeneutic—forms of analysis (Denzin and Lincoln 2005).

Kincheloe viewed context as a major feature of his postformal philosophy (Kincheloe and Steinberg 1999) (see Chapter 6). Duane Elgin and Coleen LeDrew's (1997) study found that a new consciousness is growing in the world, showing two key features: self-reflexivity (see below) and an ecological perspective as described in the opening quote. The ecopedagogy movement is a prime example of ecological reasoning entering the education arena (Grigorov 2012) (see Chapter 9).

5.5.5 Futures Reasoning: Incorporating Foresight, Future Mindedness

> Make no mistake: envisioning the future is about the making of new myths, is about telling stories about the future that compel us to change our ways of doing and being in the multiple action-setting within which we organise ourselves. (Ziegler 1991, p. 526)

Positive psychologists Seligman and Csikszentmihalyi view *future mindedness* as central to wellbeing (Seligman and Csikszentmihalyi 2000). Although developmental psychologists undervalue futures reasoning as a postformal quality, the lack of it appears in clinical work. Psychological research links depression and suicide with a lack of ability to imagine a positive future (Abramson et al. 1989; Beck et al. 1975; Gidley 2001; Seligman 1995).

Thinking about the future has always been a part of human culture, but only in the past fifty years has it produced the academic field of futures studies (Masini 1993). While it is commonly thought that futures studies is an attempt to predict the future based on extrapolation from present day trends, this is only one of at least five approaches to futures research (Gidley et al. 2004; Gidley 2013).

What has changed in recent decades as a result of new thinking is that we no longer see the future as a single predetermined option, but rather we see ourselves as the creative agents of our desired futures, of multiple futures in a world of quantum possibility. What lies behind this changed perception is the evolution of human consciousness. Futures studies as a field begins where consciousness increases to embrace multiple future possibilities and where we become free to create a world of our choices. See also Chapter 9 for more about futures studies in education.

5.5.6 Higher Purpose: Incorporating Spirituality, Values Awareness

> Human nature has been sold short... man has a higher nature which is just as 'instinctoid' as his lower nature... this human nature includes the need for meaningful work, for responsibility, for creativeness, for being fair and just, for doing what is worthwhile, and for preferring to do it well. (Maslow 1971)

As early as 1971, Maslow was writing about "the farther reaches of human nature" which he describes as being linked with the highest of human values, such as "truth, beauty, efficiency, excellence, justice, perfection, order, lawfulness" (Maslow 1971, p. 238). *Altruism* is another way to express some of Maslow's values (Seligman and Csikszentmihalyi 2000).

Yet the individual human ego needs to be transformed by a higher order, spiritual consciousness or *higher purpose*. Danish theologian and existential philosopher, Søren Kierkegaard, wrote about this, as cited by Joseph Campbell: "The most tremendous thing that has been granted to man is: the choice, freedom. And if you desire to save it and preserve it there is only one way: in the very same second unconditionally and in complete resignation to give it back to God, and yourself with it" (Campbell 1968, pp. 197–198). Kierkegaard's comment can be taken as a statement about the importance of higher purpose in one's life. Higher purpose is identified as a core quality in postformal leadership (de Blonville 2013b).

When we relinquish ego-control, we become open to inspiration, through which our higher purpose in life can be revealed. Social entrepreneurship offers an important counter-value to the corporate model, which generally lacks higher purpose. The role of higher purpose in evolving education is discussed in Chapter 8.

5.5.7 Imagination: Incorporating Imaginal Thinking, Mythopoesis

> Since the beginning, imagination has been acknowledged as one of the most fundamental, if concealed, powers of humankind. Its elusive presence is accurately conjured up by Kant's famous words about 'an art hidden in the depths of nature... a blind but indispensable faculty of the human soul without which we would have no knowledge whatsoever'. (Kearney 1998, p. 1)

Although not strongly emphasised in the postformal adult development literature, *imagination* is linked with postformal development (Labouvie-Vief 1990; Bassett 2005b; Sinnott 2005). I regard it as a core—if tacit—component in the transition from formal to postformal thinking. Imagination enables the possibility of thinking beyond the already-known.

The significant role of imagination in higher-order thinking has been under-appreciated academically. Imagination enables conceptual vitality. Through imagination in our thinking, we not only enliven concepts, but we bring the significance of life back into centre focus in our lifeworld, enhancing vitality and wellbeing. Steiner specifically linked imagination with the cultivation of living thinking (Steiner 1904/1993).

A strong visual imagination is vital to envisioning alternative futures. From a futures studies perspective, it enables us to envision, and thus potentially create, authentically alternative futures. (Boulding 1988; Hutchinson 1996; Milojevic 2005; Polak 1973). The crucial role of imagination in my postformal education philosophy is discussed extensively in Chapter 9.

5.5.8 Integration: Incorporating Holism, Unitary Thinking

> Holism asserts that the universe is an undivided, interconnected whole, and that this whole embodies an all-encompassing creative source through many layers or contexts. (Miller 2005, Para 4)

Integration and holism are central to postformal thought. Kramer identified the ability to integrate contradiction into "an overriding whole" (Kramer 1983). Herb

Koplowitz proposed unitary operations as a stage beyond Piaget's formal operations (Koplowitz 1978). Integration denotes metasystemic thinking (Commons et al. 1982) and coordinating different frames of reference (Sinnott 1984).

Ron Miller grounds holistic education in epistemological holism, drawing on Anna Lemkow's (1990) *The Wholeness Principle*: "the oneness and unity of all life; the all-pervasiveness of ultimate Reality or the Absolute; the multi-dimensionality or hierarchical character of existence" (p. 23). The integration of human faculties such as *cognitive*, *affective* and *conative* assists in the development of wisdom (Sternberg 1998). Integral consciousness involves an integration of the whole person—head/brain/cognition, heart/love/feelings and limbs/hands/action (Gidley 2007).

Our world of specialisation and fragmentation requires the ability to integrate, synthesise and take a systems approach. Holism and integration are strong forces for countering atomism and reductionism in science. Karl Pribram, the neurosurgeon who developed the holonomic brain theory, pointed to the significance of holism theories in bringing "science and the spiritual disciplines into congruence" (Pribram 2006, p. 44). In Chapter 8 these will be discussed in relation to postformal pedagogies.

5.5.9 Intuitive Wisdom: Incorporating Wisdom, Intuition

> Intuition is the method of Bergsonism. Intuition is neither a feeling, an inspiration, nor a disorderly sympathy, but a fully developed method, one of the most fully developed methods in philosophy. (Deleuze 1988/2006, p. 13)

The postformal movement towards knowledge as wisdom returns what T.S. Eliot felt was lost in the pursuit of "knowledge" (Sternberg 1990, 1998, 2005; Labouvie-Vief 1992; Bassett 2005a; Prewitt n.d.). Pascual-Leone's later cognitive research has extended into the realms of "higher consciousness" to explore the effect of meditation on the development of wisdom (Pascual-Leone 2000).

In his study of Henri Bergson, Deleuze argues for the potential of intuition as a serious philosophical method. Steiner wrote extensively from 1904 about the cultivation of *imagination*, *inspiration* and *intuition* for developing higher cognitive faculties, regarding imagination as a foundation for intuition (Steiner 1904/1993), and, like Bergson, viewed intuition as one of his major methodologies. Kincheloe's "postformal intuition is… the ability to make swift and complex syntheses of the multiple forces and phenomena that one faces" (Kincheloe 2006, p. 134). Several central-eastern European thinkers highlight intuition as a way of knowing, including Russian-American sociologist, Pitirim Sorokin (Sorokin 1941/1992), and Hungarian philosopher of science, Michael Polanyi. Notions of the intuitive, tacit—and *personal knowledge*—were given momentum by Polanyi's (1958) seminal text. Hungarian systems scientist Ervin Lászĺó points to the intuition of great scientists

(László 2007). In Chapter 10, I discuss wisdom and its complex, multi-faceted role in my evolutionary postformal education philosophy.

5.5.10 Language Reflexivity: Incorporating Construct-Awareness, Voice, Language

> Thus, the determination of how high-end ego development stages fit into a full-spectrum model of consciousness depends in part on whether people can become aware of the language habit... (Cook-Greuter 2000, p. 228)

Language reflexivity is a subtle, advanced postformal quality (Gidley 2008). It is about being conscious of how we "language the world" to use Gadamer's phrase. Cook-Greuter (2000) uses the term *construct-aware* for the reflexive feature of postformal language development. She contrasts construct-awareness with: "the language habit...[which] can become a barrier to further development if it remains unconscious, automatic and unexamined... it is the first time in development that the ego is fully aware of its own defensive manoeuvres... because ego becomes transparent to itself" (Cook-Greuter 2000, p, 235).

Steiner and Gebser emphasised awareness of one's own language as a key feature of the new consciousness. Consciousness of language in the sense of historical context and power relations emerged as part of the *linguistic turn* (Rorty 1967). Continental philosophers, Ferdinand de Saussure and Ludwig Wittgenstein, contributed to the *linguistic turn* by focusing on language as philosophical content (Matthews 1996, p. 136), while others focused on linguistic reflexivity (Deleuze 1968/1994; Deleuze and Conley 1992; Derrida 1998, 2001; Kristeva 1986). The impact of language reflexivity in educational settings is discussed in Chapter 11.

5.5.11 Pluralism: Incorporating Non-Absolutism, Relativism

> In our situation of globalization, modern historical consciousness has developed into a postmodern kind of pluralistic consciousness... (Reynolds 2006, p. 2,4)

The concept of *pluralism* is underpinned by *relativism*, one of the first postformal qualities to be identified. Adult developmental psychologists found that mature adults using higher-order forms of thinking came to "the realization of the non-absolute, relative nature of knowledge" (Kramer 1983). This feature has been linked to Einsteinian relativity (Koplowitz 1978; Kramer 1983; Riegel 1973; Sinnott 1998). Relativism "is deemed to involve an acceptance of mutually incompatible systems of knowledge" (Kramer 1983, p. 92). It is thus inextricably linked with the acceptance of complexity, contradiction and paradox. Relativism paves the way for social and cultural pluralism in personal and civic spheres.

The notion of *pluralism* was introduced at the paradigmatic level through the historical philosophy of science of Thomas Kuhn and Paul Feyerabend, who argued: "science should be conceived as a developmental process, which takes place in a variety of historical circumstances using a variety of methods, rather than the implementation of an invariant, universal method" (Nola and Sankey 2000, p. 212). This shift led to *philosophical, epistemological and methodological pluralism.*

Methodological pluralism came as a sociological response to the dominance of scientific positivism (Marshal 1998) and is now common practice in British sociology (Payne et al. 2005). Some researchers associate methodological pluralism with holism (Morse and Chung 2003) and/or integral theory. The educational implications of pluralism are discussed in Chapter 11.

5.5.12 *Reflexivity: Incorporating Self-Reflection, Self-Referential Thought*

> [A]wakening of our unique capacity to be self-reflective—to stand back from the rush of life with greater detachment, observe the world and its workings non-judgmentally. (Elgin and LeDrew 1997)

Reflexivity (like creativity) is one of the most widely recognised postformal reasoning qualities (Abbs 1994, 2003; Kaufman and Baer 2006; Kincheloe et al. 1999b; Montuori 1997; Montuori et al. 2004; Sinnott 1998; Sternberg 1999). It is the ability to reflect on, and become conscious of, one's own thoughts, feelings and actions and thereby to become more conscious of one's underlying values. Sinnott calls this *self-referential thought* (Sinnott 1998, pp. 37–39), and Patricia King and Karen Kitchener studied the development of *reflective judgement* in advanced doctoral students and faculty. They describe it thus: "reflective thinking... reveals the assumption that one's understanding of reality is not given but must be actively constructed and that knowledge must be understood in relation to the context in which it is generated" (King and Kitchener 1993, pp. 31–32).

Elgin and LeDrew found a growing reflexivity in their meta-analysis. They called the emerging change in culture and consciousness the "reflective/living-systems" paradigm or perspective, and they described what they meant by reflexivity in the opening quote (Elgin and LeDrew 1997).

The formal empirical tradition requires that academic writing must be in the third person. However, this tradition has been gradually weakening, especially in the humanities. A counter-position has developed through the strengthening of feminist writing (Cixous 1991; Kristeva 1986), particularly since the *narrative turn* in interpretive research, whereby subjective first-person narratives may conversely marginalise third-person accounts—this is reflexivity at work in writing. In Chapter 11 we explore how to cultivate reflexivity in education as an evolutionary trait.

5.6 Postformal Psychology: In Light of Evolutionary Themes

> Where perspectival reason [formal operations] privileges the exclusive perspective of the particular subject, vision-logic *adds up all the perspectives*, privileging none, and thus attempts to grasp the integral, the whole, the multiple contexts... in a fluidly holonic and multi-dimensional tapestry. (Wilber 1995/2000, p. 403)

Wilber made this comment, after referring to the substantial research by developmental psychologists on postformal cognition. In summary, what unites all the perspectives is that they are all pointing to new ways of thinking that go beyond what is variously called formal operations, formal logic, binary logic, instrumental rationality or abstract intellectualism.

Before discussing the impact of the evolution of consciousness on education in subsequent chapters, I take a deeper look at the main themes that emerge from the evolution of consciousness literature. The discourses that support the emergence of new structures of consciousness can be organised into four "evolutionary themes".

I would like this clustering to be viewed as a type of *delicate theorising*[3] that has arisen from a postformal research process involving hermeneutic interpretation, not empirical analysis. This *postformal clustering* into themes is to be distinguished from *formal categorisation* into discrete territories as one might see in formal analysis. My attempts to cohere this diverse literature are a step in formulating my complex postformal education philosophy that supports the evolution of consciousness. A deeper and more comprehensive study of these four themes and how they emerged within the evolution of consciousness literature can be explored in my doctoral dissertation (Gidley 2008). I now demonstrate how each of these evolutionary themes interacts with postformal reasoning, as summarised in Table 5.5. In Chapter 6, I show how the evolutionary themes interact with postformal pedagogies (see Table 6.3).

In Chapter 7, I show the dynamic interrelationships among all these theoretical components (Table 7.9) and how they theoretically ground the four core pedagogical values that are central to my philosophy (Tables 7.10, 7.11, 7.12 and 7.13).

5.6.1 *Theme 1: Conscious, Compassionate, Spiritual Development*

A number of evolutionary approaches aim to facilitate the development of higher-order thinking through cultivating spiritual, contemplative and compassionate qualities. These approaches come primarily from the religious and spiritual traditions. Most involve a combination of study of spiritual texts and inner discipline.

[3]I coin the term *delicate theorising* in reference to Goethe's *delicate empiricism* (Holdrege 2005; Robbins 2006).

Table 5.5 Evolutionary Discourses, Themes and Postformal Reasoning Qualities

Evolutionary Discourses	*Theme Summary*	*Postformal Reasoning Qualities*
Discourses that facilitate higher-order thinking through cultivating spiritual, contemplative and compassionate qualities.	Theme 1: conscious, compassionate, spiritual development	Higher purpose Dialogical reasoning Integration
Discourses that transcend static, mechanistic thinking and promote fluid, organic, life-enhancing, thinking and being.	Theme 2: mobile, life-enhancing thinking	Imagination Ecological reasoning Futures reasoning
Discourses based on cultural evolution (phylogeny) and individual psychological development (ontogeny).	Theme 3: complexification of thinking and culture	Creativity Complexity Intuitive wisdom
Discourses that cross linguistic and paradigmatic barriers through reflexivity and multi-vocal awareness.	Theme 4: linguistic and paradigmatic boundary-crossing	Reflexivity Language reflexivity Pluralism

Source: Gidley (2009)

Given that in most religious traditions human love is a reflection of the Divine Love or God, the practice of integrating intellectual knowledge with the heart through love and compassion is a key theme. The majority of spiritually based approaches within the academic context still arise from traditional religious sources, many of which are theistic, even monotheistic, such as the Abrahamic religions: Christianity, Judaism and Islam. A critique is that many have pre-modern, dogmatic or sectarian notions of spiritual development, not having fully integrated the contributions of the modern human sciences (via formal operations), let alone the pluralism of postmodernity (via postformal reasoning). New more rational forms of postmodern spirituality are being discussed in the USA, Europe and Australia (Benedikter 2005; Habermas 2008; Manoussakis 2006; Tacey 2003).

The features of postformal reasoning that interact with this evolutionary stream are higher purpose, dialogical reasoning and integration.

5.6.2 *Theme 2: Mobile, Life-Enhancing Thinking*

This evolutionary theme includes discourses that promote mobile, life-enhancing thinking. The modernist, formal, scientific worldview, with its static "building block" universe of atoms, is based on Newtonian physics. It has been challenged by more fluid life-oriented worldviews grounded in Einstein's theories of relativity, quantum physics and, more recently, chaos and complexity theories. A parallel shift from the dominant emphasis on physics arose from the biological turn with notions of life as being "complex", "self-organising" (Jantsch 1980; Varela et al. 1993) and "emergent" (Goodenough and Deacon 2006).

Early 20th-century philosophers such as Whitehead, Bergson and Husserl pioneered the turn from static mechanistic metaphors to organic, living, process metaphors of thinking. Steiner, William James and John Dewey attempted to integrate these emerging organic, natural, biological understandings with positivist, analytical approaches (Dewey 1972; James 1897/1979; Steiner 1990). Their efforts were largely ignored in their day.

Ironically, in most contemporary academic settings, formal-analytical, and reductionist-pragmatic, philosophical discourses still hold academic power over the more aesthetic, process-oriented postmodern philosophies. Although earlier described as negative or nihilistic philosophies, both Jacques Derrida and Deleuze entertained a strongly life-affirmative element in their writings (Deleuze and Millett 1997; Derrida 2001). "To affirm... to create new values which are those of life, which make life light and active...", Deleuze, cited in (St. Pierre 2004).

The features of postformal reasoning that are aligned to this evolutionary stream are imagination, ecological reasoning and futures reasoning.

5.6.3 Theme 3: Complexification of Thinking and Culture

This theme draws from two complementary approaches that both point to complexification of human thinking and consciousness: cultural evolution at the species level (phylogeny) (see Chapter 2) and individual psychological developmental (ontogeny) (see Chapter 3). Both streams explicitly identify the emergence of new, more complex cultures and consciousness.

In Chapter 2 we discovered researchers who re-integrated biological evolution with more complex perspectives of consciousness and who pointed to the increasing complexity of consciousness as an evolutionary quality (Aurobindo 1914/2000; Gebser 1949/1985; Steiner 1926/1966; Teilhard de Chardin 1959/2004). We heard that we are reaching a stage of development where we can consciously participate in evolution through co-evolution (Bamford 2003; Gidley 2006; Lachman 2003; Russell 2000; Thompson 1998), foreshadowed by Schelling in the 1790s.

In this chapter we have seen how, since the 1970s adult developmental psychology researchers focusing on individual development, have identified *cognitive* stages beyond Piaget's fourth stage—formal operations. Under the collective term postformal, these researchers have enlightened us about mature postformal thinkers who consciously utilise imagination and creativity, complexity and paradoxical reasoning to name a few. And we discussed how they are likely to be better equipped to deal with chaos and contradiction while retaining psychological equilibrium

The features of postformal reasoning that I identify with this stream are creativity, complexity and intuitive wisdom.

5.6.4 *Theme 4: Linguistic and Paradigmatic Boundary-Crossing*

This evolutionary theme represents discourses that cross linguistic and paradigmatic boundaries. It would be worthwhile to explore the relationship between this theme and the cross-paradigmatic stage of Commons' Model of Hierarchical Complexity (Commons et al. 1998). This theme is expressed in the academic and educational movement beyond fragmentation and disciplinary isolationism and towards more integration—through transdisciplinarity approaches. A challenge that has emerged from the transdisciplinary literature is the difficulty in communicating across different disciplines, epistemologies and paradigms (Eckersley et al. 2006; Grigg et al. 2003). An important insight of French postmodern/poststructuralist philosophy is awareness of how we language the world. Arguably, this awareness that entered philosophy with the *linguistic turn* has not yet influenced formal education.

The features of postformal reasoning that I identify with linguistic and paradigmatic boundary-crossing are reflexivity, language reflexivity and pluralism.

5.7 Concluding Remarks

In summary, postformal reasoning is a mature mode of cognition, and postformal psychology is an emerging sub-field of positive psychology. They have significant implications for how we educate young people today and in the future. For the most part, the disciplinary divide between psychology and education has thwarted research on the importance of postformal reasoning for the maturing of education. This is discussed in the following Chapter 6. A deeper understanding of the potential importance of the various features of postformal reasoning for education is the focus of Part III of this volume.

References

Abbs, P. (1994). *The educational imperative: Defense of Socratic and aesthetic learning*. London: Routledge Falmer.

Abbs, P. (2003). *Against the flow: The arts, postmodern culture and education*. London: Routledge Falmer.

Abramson, L., Metalsky, G., & Alloy, L. (1989). Hopelessness depression: A theory-based subtype of depression. *Psychological Review, 96*(2), 358–372.

Allport, G. W. (1955/1969). *Becoming: Basic considerations for a psychology of personality*. Newhaven: Yale University Press.

Arlin, P. K. (1975). Cognitive development in adulthood: A fifth stage? *Developmental Psychology, 11*(5), 602–606.

Aurobindo, S. (1914/2000). *The life divine* (2nd American Edition) (Originally published in the monthly review *Arya* 1914–1920). Twin Lakes: Lotus Press.

Baltes, P. B. (1978). *Life-span development and behaviour* (Vol. 1). New York: Academic.

Baltes, P. B., Staudinger, U. M., & Lindenberger, U. (1999). Lifespan psychology: Theory and application of intellectual functioning. *Annual Review of Psychology, 50*, 471–507.

Bamford, C. (2003). *An endless trace; The passionate pursuit of wisdom in the west.* New York: Codhill Press.

Basseeches, M. (1984). *Dialectical thinking and adult development.* Norwood: Ablex.

Bassett, C. (2005a). Emergent wisdom: Living a life in widening circles. *ReVision: A Journal of Consciousness and Transformation, 27*(4), 6–11.

Bassett, C. (2005b, October). *Wisdom in three acts: Using transformative learning to teach for wisdom* [Electronic version]. In Sixth international transformative learning conference, East Lansing, Michigan.

Beck, A. T., Kovacs, M., & Weissman, A. (1975). Hopelessness and suicidal behaviour: An overview. *JAMA, 234*, 1136–1139.

Benedikter, R. (2005). *Postmodern spirituality: A dialogue in five parts.* http://www.integralworld.net/index.html?benedikter1.html. Accessed 28 June 2006.

Bergson, H. (1911/1944). *Creative evolution* (A. Mitchell, Trans.). New York: Macmillan & Co.

Biesta, G. J. J. (2014). *The beautiful risk of education.* Boulder: Paradigm Publishers.

Bohm, D., Factor, D., & Garrett, P. (1991). *Dialogue—A proposal.* [Electronic article]. http://www.david-bohm.net/dialogue/dialogue_proposal.html Accessed 31 July 2015.

Boulding, E. (1988). Image and action in peace building. *Journal of Social Issues, 44*(2), 17–37.

Campbell, J. (1968). *The masks of God: Creative mythology.* New York: Penguin Arkana.

Cartwright, K. B. (2001). Cognitive developmental theory and spiritual development. *Journal of Adult Development, 8*(4), 213–220.

Cixous, H. (1991). The laugh of the medusa. In R. Warhol & D. Price Herndl (Eds.), *Feminisms: An anthology of literary theory and criticism.* Piscataway: Rutgers University Press.

Commons, M. L., Armon, C., Kohlberg, L., Richards, F. A., Grotzer, T. A., & Sinnott, J. D. (Eds.). (1990). *Adult development, volume 2: Models and methods in the study of adolescent and adult thought.* Westport: Praeger.

Commons, M. L., & Ross, S. (2008). What postformal thought is, and why it matters. *World Futures, 64*, 321–329.

Commons, M. L., & Richards, F. A. (1978). *The structural analytic stage of development: A Piagetian postformal operational stage.* Paper presented at the Western Psychological Association, San Francisco.

Commons, M. L., & Richards, F. A. (2002). Organizing components into combination: How stage transition works. *Journal of Adult Development, 9*(3), 159–177.

Commons, M. L., Richards, F. A., & Armon, C. (Eds.). (1984). *Beyond formal operations: Vol. 1. Late adolescent and adult cognitive development* (Vol. 1). Westport: Praeger.

Commons, M. L., Richards, F. A., & Kuhn, D. (1982). Systematic and metasystematic reasoning: A case for levels of reasoning beyond Piaget's stage of formal operations. *Child Development, 53*(4), 1058–1069.

Commons, M. L., Ross, S., Miller, J. G. (2008). *Why postformal stages of development are not formal, but postformal.* Integral world: Exploring theories of everything: An independent forum for a critical discussion of the integral philosophy of Ken Wilber. [Electronic article]. http://www.integralworld.net/commons1.html. Accessed 29 July 2015.

Commons, M. L., Trudeau, E. J., Stein, S. A., Richards, F. A., & Krause, S. R. (1998). The existence of developmental stages as shown by the hierarchical complexity of tasks. *Developmental Review, 8*(3), 237–278.

Cook-Greuter, S. R. (1995). *Comprehensive language awareness: A definition of the phenomenon and a review of its treatment in the postformal adult development literature.* Boston: Harvard University.

Cook-Greuter, S. R. (2000). Mature ego development: A gateway to ego transcendence. *Journal of Adult Development, 7*(4), 227–240.

Cook-Greuter, S. R. (2008). Adapted and revised from mature ego development: A gateway to ego transcendence. . *Journal of Adult Development, 7*(4), 1–21.

Csikszentmihalyi, M. (1990). *Flow: The psychology of optimal experience*. New York: Harper Oerennial Modern Classics.

Cunningham, P. F. (2004). An integral psychology with a soul. *New England Psychological Association Newsletter, 21*(2), 1–4.

de Blonville, E. (2013a, May 31–June 2). *Is this the Dawn of Postformal Leadership? Adult development's theoretical contribution to a paradigm shift in the State of Global Leadership*. Paper presented at the European Society for Research in Adult Development 3rd annual symposium, Freiburg University, Germany.

de Blonville, E. (2013b). *Postformal Leadership for Innovative Millennials*. Paper presented at the World Futures Studies Federation 21st world conference, Bucharest, Romania, 26–28 June.

Deleuze, G. (1968/1994). *Difference and repetition* (First published in French 1968). New York: Columbia University Press.

Deleuze, G. (1988/2006). *Bergsonism* (Translated Hugh Tomlinson and Barbara Habberjam. Originally published in French as La Bergsonisme, 1966). Brooklyn: Zone Books.

Deleuze, G., & Conley, T. (1992). *The fold: Leibniz and the baroque*. Minneapolis: University of Minnesota Press.

Deleuze, G., & Millett, N. (1997). Immanence: A life... (Gilles Deleuze: A symposium). *Theory Culture & Society, 14*(2), 3–8.

Denzin, N., & Lincoln, Y. (2005). *The sage handbook of qualitative research* (3rd ed.). Thousand Oaks: Sage Publications.

Derrida, J. (1998). *Of grammatology*. Baltimore: The Johns Hopkins University Press.

Derrida, J. (2001). Structure, sign, and play in the Discourse of the human sciences. *Writing and Difference* (A. Bass, Trans.) (pp. 278–294). London: Routledge.

Dewey, J. (1972). *The early works, 1882–1898* (Vol. 5). Illinois: Carbondale and Edwardsville, Southern Illinois University Press.

Eckersley, R., Wierenga, A., & Wyn, J. (2006). *Flashpoints and signposts: Pathways to success and wellbeing for Australia's young people*. Canberra: Australia 21.

Elgin, D., & LeDrew, C. (1997). *Global consciousness change: Indicators or an emerging paradigm*. San Anselmo: The Millennium Project.

Erikson, E. H. (1950/1985). *Childhood and society*. New York: Norton.

Erikson, E. H. (1959/1994). *Identity and the life cycle*. New York: Norton.

Evans, N. J., Forney, D. S., Guido, F. M., Patton, L. D., & Renn, K. A. (2010). *Development of self-authorship* (Student Development in College, Theory, Research, and Practice, pp. 176–193). San Francisco: Jossey-Bass: A Wiley Imprint.

Fisher, C., & Lerner, R. (2004). *Encyclopedia of applied developmental science*. London: Sage.

Fredrickson, B. L. (2013). Positive emotions broaden and build. In P. Devine & A. Plant (Eds.), *Advances in experimental social psychology*. Elsevier: Burlington Academic Press.

Galtung, J. (1995). On dialogue as method: Some very preliminary notes. *Unpublished*, 2–22.

Gangadean, A. (1998). *Between worlds: The emergence of global reason* (Revisioning Philosophy, Vol. 17). New York: Peter Lang.

Gangadean, A. (2006). Spiritual transformation as the awakening of global consciousness: A dimensional shift in the technology of mind. *Zygon: Journal of Religion and Science, 41*(2), 381–392.

Gare, A. (2002). The roots of postmodernism: Schelling, process philosophy, and poststructuralism. In C. Keller & A. Daniell (Eds.), *Process and difference: Between cosmological and poststructuralist postmodernisms*. New York: SUNY Press.

Gebser, J. (1949/1985). *The ever-present origin*. Athens: Ohio University Press.

Gidley, J. (2001). An intervention targeting hopelessness in adolescents by promoting positive future images. *Australian Journal of Guidance and Counselling, 11*(1), 51–64.

Gidley, J. (2006). Spiritual epistemologies and integral cosmologies: Transforming thinking and culture. In S. Awbrey, D. Dana, V. Miller, P. Robinson, M. M. Ryan, & D. K. Scott (Eds.), *Integrative learning and action: A call to wholeness* (Studies in Education and Spirituality, Vol. 3, pp. 29–55). New York: Peter Lang Publishing.

Gidley, J. (2007). The evolution of consciousness as a planetary imperative: An integration of integral views. *Integral Review: A Transdisciplinary and Transcultural Journal for New Thought, Research and Praxis, 5*, 4–226.

Gidley, J. (2008). *Evolving education: A postformal-integral-planetary gaze at the evolution of consciousness and the educational imperatives.* PhD dissertation, Southern Cross University, Lismore.

Gidley, J. (2009). Educating for evolving consciousness: Voicing the emergency for love, life and wisdom. In *The International Handbook of Education for Spirituality, Care and Wellbeing* (Springer International handbooks of religion and education series). New York: Springer.

Gidley, J. (2010a). Globally scanning for megatrends of the mind: Potential futures of "Futures Thinking". *Futures: The Journal of Policy Planning and Futures Studies, 42*(10), 1040–1048.

Gidley, J. (2010b). Postformal priorities for postnormal times: A rejoinder to Ziauddin Sardar. *Futures: The Journal of Policy Planning and Futures Studies, 42*(6), 625–632.

Gidley, J. (2013). Global knowledge futures: Articulating the emergence of a new meta-level field. *Integral Review: A Transdisciplinary and Transcultural Journal for New Thought Research and Praxis, 9*(2), 145–172.

Gidley, J., Bateman, D., & Smith, C. (2004). *Futures in education: Principles, practice and potential* (AFI Monograph Series 2004, Vol. 5). Melbourne: Australian Foresight Institute.

Gilligan, C. (1982). *In a different voice: Psychological theory and women's development.* Boston: Harvard University Press.

Goodenough, U., & Deacon, T. W. (2006). The sacred emergence of nature. In P. Clayton (Ed.), *Oxford handbook of science and religion* (pp. 853–871). Oxford: Oxford University Press.

Griffin, J., Gooding, S., Semesky, M., Farmer, B., Mannchen, G., & Sinnott, J. (2009). Four brief studies of relations between postformal thought and non-cognitive factors: Personality, concepts of God, political opinions, and social attitudes. *Journal of Adult Development, 16*(3), 173–182.

Grigg, L., Johnston, R., & Milson, N. (2003). *Emerging issues for cross-disciplinary research: Conceptual and empirical dimensions.* Canberra: DEST, Commonwealth of Australia.

Grigorov, S. K. (2012). *International handbook of ecopedagogy for students, educators and parents: A project for a new eco-sustainable civilization.* Sophia: Bulgarian Centre for Sustainable Local Development and Ecopedagogy.

Grof, S. (2000). *Psychology of the future.* New York: SUNY Press.

Habermas, J. (2008). *Between naturalism and religion: Philosophical essays.* London: Polity Press.

Hart, T. (2006). From information to transformation: What the mystics and sages tell us education can be. In S. Inayatullah, I. Milojevic, & M. Bussey (Eds.), *Neohumanist educational futures: Liberating the pedagogical intellect.* Tamsui: Tamkang University Press.

Hayward, P. (2002). Resolving the moral impediments to foresight action. *Foresight, 5*(1), 4–10.

Holdrege, C. (2005). Editorial to Goethe's delicate empiricism. *Janus Head, 8*(1), 12–13.

Hutchinson, F. (1996). *Educating beyond violent futures.* London: Routledge.

James, W. (1897/1979). *The will to believe and other essays in popular philosophy.* Cambridge, MA: Harvard University Press.

Jantsch, E. (1980). *The self-organising universe: Scientific and human implications of the emerging paradigm of evolution.* New York: Pergamon Press.

Kaufman, J. C., & Baer, J. (2006). *Creativity and reason in cognitive development.* New York: Cambridge University Press.

Kaufman, J. C., & Sternberg, R. J. (Eds.). (2006). *The international handbook of creativity.* New York: Cambridge University Press.

Kearney, R. (1998). *Poetics of imagining: Modern to post-modern.* Edinburgh: University Press.

Kegan, R. (1994). *In over our heads: The mental demands of modern life*. Cambridge, MA: Harvard University Press.

Keller, C., & Daniell, A. (2002). *Process and difference: Between cosmological and poststructuralist postmodernisms* (SUNY Series in Constructive Postmodern Thought). New York: SUNY Press.

Kincheloe, J. (2006). *Reading, writing and cognition: The postformal basics* (Bold Visions in Educational Research). Rotterdam: Sense Publishers.

Kincheloe, J., & Steinberg, S. (1999). A tentative description of post-formal thinking: The critical confrontation with cognitive theory. In J. Kincheloe, S. Steinberg, & P. H. Hinchey (Eds.), *The post-formal reader: Cognition and education* (Vol. 63, pp. 55–90). New York: Falmer Press.

Kincheloe, J., Steinberg, S., & Hinchey, P. H. (Eds.). (1999a). *The post-formal reader: Cognition and education* (Critical Education Practice). New York: Falmer Press.

Kincheloe, J., Steinberg, S., & Villaverde, L. E. (1999b). *Rethinking intelligence: Confronting psychological assumptions about teaching and learning*. New York: Routledge.

King, P. M., & Kitchener, K. S. (1993). The development of reflective thinking in the college years: The mixed results. *New Directions for Higher Education, 84*, 25–42.

Klement, K. C. (2005). Propositional logic. *Internet Encyclopedia of Philosophy* [Electronic article]. http://www.iep.utm.edu/prop-log/. Accessed 16 Nov 2014.

Kohlberg, L. (1981). *Essays on moral development. Vol. I: The philosophy of moral development*. San Francisco: Harper & Row.

Kohlberg, L. (1990). Which postformal stages are stages? In M. Commons, C. Armon, L. Kohlberg, F. A. Richards, T. A. Grotzer, & J. D. Sinnott (Eds.), *Adult development, volume 2: Models and methods in the study of adolescent and adult thought*. Westport: Praeger.

Kohlberg, L., & Armon, C. (1984). Three types of stage models used in the study of adult development. In M. L. Commons, F. A. Richards, & C. Armon (Eds.), *Beyond formal operations: Vol. 1. Late adolescent and adult cognitive development* (Vol. 1, pp. 383–394). Westport: Praeger.

Kohlberg, L., & Gilligan, C. (1971). The adolescent as a philosopher: The discovery of the self in a postconventional world. *Daedelus, 100*, 1051–1085.

Koplowitz, H. (1978). Unitary operations: A projection beyond Piaget's formal operations stage. Unpublished manuscript, University of Massachusetts.

Koplowitz, H. (1990). Unitary consciousness and the highest development of mind: The relation between spiritual development and cognitive development. In M. Commons, C. Armon, L. Kohlberg, F. A. Richards, T. A. Grotzer, & J. D. Sinnott (Eds.), *Adult development, volume 2: Models and methods in the study of adolescent and adult thought*. Westport: Praeger.

Kramer, D. A. (1983). Post-formal operations? A need for further conceptualization. *Human Development, 26*, 91–105.

Kristeva, J. (1986). *The Kristeva reader*. New York: Columbia University Press.

Labouvie-Vief, G. (1980). Beyond formal operations: Uses and limits of pure logic in life-span development. *Human Development, 23*, 141–161.

Labouvie-Vief, G. (1990). Modes of knowledge and the organization of development. In M. Commons, C. Armon, L. Kohlberg, F. A. Richards, T. A. Grotzer, & J. D. Sinnott (Eds.), *Adult development, volume 2: Models and methods in the study of adolescent and adult thought* (pp. 43–62). Westport: Praeger.

Labouvie-Vief, G. (1992). Wisdom as integrated thought: Historical and developmental perspectives. In R. J. Sternberg & C. A. Berg (Eds.), *Wisdom: Its nature, origins, and development*. Cambridge: Cambridge University Press.

Labouvie-Vief, G. (2006). Emerging structures of adult thought. In J. J. Arnett & J. L. Tanner (Eds.), *Emerging adults in America: Coming of age in the 21st century*. Washington, DC: American Psychological Association.

Lachman, G. (2003). *A secret history of consciousness*. Great Barrington: Lindesfarne Books.

Lajoie, D. H., & Shapiro, S. I. (1992). Definitions of transpersonal psychology: The first twenty-three years. *The Journal of Transpersonal Psychology, 24*(1), 79–98.

László, E. (2007). *Science and the akashic field: An integral theory of everything*. Rochester: Inner Traditions.
Lerner, R. M., Jacobs, F., & Wertlieb, D. (2002). *Handbook of applied developmental science: Promoting positive child, adolescent, and family development through research, policies, and programs*. London: Sage.
Loevinger, J. (1976). *Ego development: Conceptions and theories*. San Francisco: Jossey-Bass.
MacLure, M. (2006). The bone in the throat: Some uncertain thoughts on baroque method. *International Journal of Qualitative Studies in Education, 19*, 729–745.
Manoussakis, J. P. (2006). *After God: Richard Kearney and the religious turn in continental philosophy* (Perspectives in Continental Philosophy). New York: Fordham University Press.
Marshal, G. (1998). *Methodological pluralism* (A Dictionary of Sociology). Oxford: Oxford University Press.
Masini, E. (1993). *Why future studies?* London: Grey Seal.
Maslow, A. H. (1956). Self-actualising people: A study of psychological health. In C. E. Moustakas (Ed.), *The self: Explorations in personal growth* (pp. 160–193). New York: Harper and Row.
Maslow, A. H. (1971). *The farther reaches of human nature*. New York: The Viking Press.
Matthews, E. (1996). *Twentieth century French philosophy*. Oxford: Oxford University Press.
Miller, R. (2005). Philosophical sources of holistic education [electronic version]. *Değerler Eğitimi Dergisi (Journal of Values Education), 3*(10), 9.
Milojevic, I. (2005). *Educational futures: Dominant and contesting visions*. London: Routledge.
Montuori, A. (1997). Reflections on transformative learning: Social creativity, academic discourse and the improvisation of inquiry. *ReVision, 20*(1), 34–37.
Montuori, A., Combs, A., & Richards, R. (2004). Creativity, consciousness, and the direction for human development. In D. Loye (Ed.), *The great adventure: Toward a fully human theory of evolution* (pp. 197–236). Albany: SUNY Press.
Morin, E. (2005). Restricted complexity, general complexity. In *"Intelligence de la complexite : Epistemologie et pragmatique", Cerisy-La-Salle, France, 26 Jun 2005*: Centre d'Etudes Transdisciplinaires. Sociologie, Anthropologie, Histoire Ecole des Hautes Etudes en Sciences Sociales. [Electronic article]. http://arxiv.org/pdf/cs/0610049v1.pdf. Accessed 11 Nov 2015.
Morse, J. M., & Chung, S. E. (2003). Toward Holism: The significance of methodological pluralism. *International Journal of Qualitative Methods, 2*(3), 13–20.
Neville, B. (2006). Out of our depth and treading water: Reflections on consciousness and culture. *Journal of Conscious Evolution, 2* [Electronic article]. http://cejournal.org/GRD/neville.htm. Accessed 18 Apr 2016.
Nicolescu, B. (2002). *Manifesto of transdisciplinarity* (K.-C. Voss, Trans.) (Suny series in Western Esoteric Traditions). New York: SUNY Press.
Nola, R., & Sankey, H. (2000). *After Popper, Kuhn and Feyerabend: Recent Issues in Theories of Scientific Method* (Australasian Studies in History and Philosophy of Science). Dordrecht: Kluwer Academic Publishers.
Orme-Johnson, D. W. (2000). An overview of Charles Alexander's contribution to psychology: Developing higher states of consciousness in the individual and society. *Journal of Adult Development, 7*(4), 199–215.
Orr, M. (2003). *Intertextuality: Debates and contexts*. Cambridge, UK: Polity Press.
Pascual-Leone, J. (2000). Mental attention, consciousness, and the progressive emergence of wisdom. *Journal of Adult Development, 7*(4), 241–254.
Payne, G., Williams, M., & Chamberlain, S. (2005). Methodological pluralism, British sociology and the evidence-based state: A reply to May. *Sociology, 39*(3), 529–533.
Pearce, J. C. (1992). *Evolution's end: Claiming the potential of our intelligence*. San Francisco: Harper.
Piaget, J. (1972). Intellectual evolution from adolescence to adulthood. *Human Development, 15* (1), 1–12.
Polak, F. (1973). *The image of the future* (E. Boulding, Trans.). San Francisco: Jossey-Bass.

Polanyi, M. (1958). *Personal knowledge: Towards a post-critical philosophy*. Chicago: University of Chicago Press.

Prewitt, V. (n.d.). The constructs of wisdom in human development and Consciousness. http://www.psy.pdx.edu/PsiCafe/Areas/Developmental/CogDev-Adult/OD-Wisdom.pdf. Accessed 7 Oct 2006.

Pribram, K. (2006). Holism vs Wholism. *World Futures: The Journal of General Evolution, 62*, 42–46.

Reams, J. (2014). A brief overview of developmental theory, or what I learned in the FOLA course. *Integral Review: A Transdisciplinary and Transcultural Journal for New Thought, Research and Praxis, 10*(1), 122–153.

Reynolds, T. E. (2006). *The broken whole: Philosophical steps toward a theology of global solidarity* (SUNY series in Theology and Continental Thought). New York: SUNY Press.

Richards, F. A., & Commons, M. L. (1984). Systematic, metasystematic, and cross-paradigmatic reasoning: A case for stages of reasoning beyond formal operations. In M. L. Commons, F. A. Richards, & C. Armon (Eds.), *Beyond formal operations: Vol. 1. Late adolescent and adult cognitive development* (Vol. 1, pp. 92–119). Westport: Praeger.

Riegel, K. F. (1973). Dialectical operations: The final period of cognitive development. *Human Development, 16*, 346–370.

Robbins, B. D. (2006). The delicate empiricism of Goethe: Phenomenology as a rigorous science of nature. *Indo-Pacific Journal of Phenomenology, 6*(Special Edition), 1–13.

Rorty, R. (1967). *The linguistic turn: Essays in philosophical method*. Chicago: University of Chicago Press.

Russell, P. (2000). *The global brain awakens: Our next evolutionary step*. Melbourne: Element Books.

Sardar, Z. (2010). Welcome to postnormal times. *Futures: The Journal of Policy Planning and Futures Studies, 42*(5), 435–444.

Schaie, K. W., & Willis, S. L. (2010). The Seattle longitudinal study of adult cognitive development. *ISSBD Bulletin, 57*(1), 24–29.

Seligman, M. E. P. (1995). *The optimistic child: A revolutionary approach to raising resilient children*. Sydney: Random House.

Seligman, M. E. P., & Csikszentmihalyi, M. (2000). Positive psychology. *American Psychologist, 55*(1), 5–14.

Sinnott, J. D. (1981). *Post-formal reasoning in interpersonal situations*. Paper presented at the Symposium on Post-Formal Operations, Harvard University.

Sinnott, J. D. (1984). Postformal reasoning: The relativistic stage. In M. L. Commons, F. A. Richards, & C. Armon (Eds.), *Beyond formal operations: Vol. 1. Late adolescent and adult cognitive development* (Vol. 1, pp. 298–325). Westport: Praeger.

Sinnott, J. D. (1994). Development and yearning: Cognitive aspects of spiritual development. *Journal of Adult Development, 1*(2), 91–99.

Sinnott, J. D. (1998). *The development of logic in adulthood: Postformal thought and its applications*. New York: Springer.

Sinnott, J. D. (2005). The dance of the transforming self: Both feelings of connection and complex thought are needed for learning. *New Directions for Adult and Continuing Education, 108* (Winter), 27–37.

Sonnert, G., & Commons, M. L. (1994). Society and the highest stages of moral development. *Politics and the Individual, 4*(1), 31–55.

Sorokin, P. (1941/1992). *The crisis of our age*. Oxford: Oneworld Publications.

St. Pierre, E. A. (2004). Deleuzian concepts for education: The subject undone. *Educational Philosophy and Theory, 36*(3), 283–296.

Steiner, R. (1894/1964). *The philosophy of freedom: The basis for a modern world conception (GA 4)* (M. Wilson, Trans.) (Rev. ed.). (Original work published 1894). Spring Valley: The Anthroposophic Press.

Steiner, R. (1904/1993). *Knowledge of the higher worlds: How is it achieved? (GA 10)* (6th ed.) (D. S. Osmond & C. Davy, Trans.) (Original German work published 1904). London: Rudolf Steiner Press.

Steiner, R. (1926/1966). *The evolution of consciousness as revealed through initiation knowledge (GA 227)* (2nd ed.) (V. E. W. & C. D., Trans.). [13 Lectures: Penmaenmawr, N. Wales, August 19–31, 1923] (Original published work 1926). London: Rudolf Steiner Press.

Steiner, R. (1990). *Toward imagination: Culture and the individual (GA 169)* (S. H. Seiler, Trans.) [7 Lectures, Berlin, June 6 to Jul 18, 1916]. New York: Anthroposophic Press.

Sternberg, R. J. (1984). Higher-order reasoning in postformal operational thought. In M. L. Commons, F. A. Richards, & C. Armon (Eds.), *Beyond formal operations: Vol. 1. Late adolescent and adult cognitive development* (Vol. 1, pp. 74–91). Westport: Praeger.

Sternberg, R. J. (1990). *Wisdom: Its nature, origins and development*. New York: Cambridge University Press.

Sternberg, R. J. (1998). A balance theory of wisdom. *Review of General Psychology, 2*(4), 347–365.

Sternberg, R. J. (1999). *Handbook of creativity*. New York: Cambridge University Press.

Sternberg, R. J. (2005, Winter). Older but not Wiser? The relationship between age and wisdom. *Ageing International, 30*(1), 5–26.

Tacey, D. (2003). *The spirituality revolution: The emergence of contemporary spirituality*. Sydney: Harper Collins.

Teilhard de Chardin, P. (1959/2004). *The future of man*. New York: Image Books, Doubleday.

Thompson, W. I. (1998). *Coming into being: Artifacts and texts in the evolution of consciousness*. London: MacMillan Press Ltd.

Thornton, J. E. (2003). Life-span learning: A developmental perspective. *International Journal of Aging and Human Development, 57*(1), 55.76.

Varela, F., Thompson, E., & Rosch, E. (1993). *The embodied mind: Cognitive science and human experience*. Cambridge, MA: The MIT Press.

Villaverde, L. E., & Pinar, W. F. (1999). Postformal research: A dialogue on intelligence. In J. Kincheloe, S. Steinberg, & L. E. Villaverde (Eds.), *Rethinking intelligence: Confronting psychological assumptions about teaching and learning* (pp. 247–256). New York: Routledge.

Wade, J. (1996). *Changes of mind: A holonomic theory of the evolution of consciousness*. New York: SUNY Press.

Walsh, R., & Vaughan, F. (1993). *Paths beyond ego: The transpersonal vision*. New York: Tarcher/Putnam Books.

Whitehead, A. N. (1929/1985). *Process and reality*. New York: Free Press.

Wilber, K. (1995/2000). *Sex, ecology, spirituality: The spirit of evolution* (2nd ed., Rev.). Boston: Shambhala.

Wilber, K. (2000). *Integral psychology: Consciousness, spirit, psychology, therapy*. Boston: Shambhala.

Wittgenstein, L. (1968). *Philosophical investigations*. Oxford: Basil Blackwell's.

Yan, B., & Arlin, P. K. (1995). Nonabsolute/relativistic thinking: A common factor underlying models of postformal reasoning? *Journal of Adult Development, 2*(4), 223–240.

Ziegler, W. (1991). Envisioning the future. *Futures, 23*(5), 516–527.

Chapter 6
Postformal in Education: Beyond the Formal Factory Model

6.1 Introduction

In the previous chapter, I identified and discussed the relationships among twelve clusters of postformal qualities and four themes arising from the evolution of consciousness. I now focus on the educational impact—both tacit and explicit—of these postformal evolutionary developments.

This chapter also continues from where Chapter 4 left us. Having traced the big picture of educational evolution through thousands of years of pre-formal enculturation and hundreds of years of formal education—both elitist and universal—we arrived at a number of drivers of change, which left us wondering where education should go to meet these challenges.

In this chapter, I first introduce three evolutionary waves of educational initiatives that have occurred over the last hundred years, some of which overlap with the drivers of change discussed in Chapter 4, and some of which are new initiatives. Before identifying numerous *postformal pedagogies*—and showing how they align to postformal reasoning qualities—I discuss the educational theory of "postformalism" developed by Joe Kincheloe and Shirley Steinberg. I then introduce other leading educational innovators who are developing evolutionary approaches, although not necessarily with any explicit reference to the postformal psychology research. Finally, I offer a more complex mapping of the relationships among the four evolutionary themes, the postformal qualities that relate to them and the diversity of postformal educational discourses (Gidley 2007a, 2009). This interpretive mapping continues throughout Chapter 7.

A major aim of the chapter is to map these different approaches, explore relationships among them, and reflect this out into the broader education discourse.

J.M. Gidley, *Postformal Education*, Critical Studies of Education 3,
DOI 10.1007/978-3-319-29069-0_6

6.2 The Emergence of Evolutionary Pedagogies

> The human task is not to become well-trained automatons or highly skilled manipulators of the physical world, but to become growing, questing, self-transcending agents of the evolution of spirit.
>
> ... If we are to move beyond our inherent resistance to self-transformation, we need to cultivate radical amazement rather than technological arrogance. This is the task of education in our time. (R. Miller 2000, Para 27)

You will recall from Chapter 4 that when universal public education began two hundred years ago in Germany, it was an integrative initiative that focused on the development of the whole person, and that this approach was gradually superseded by a more utilitarian model under the regime of the Industrial Revolution which swept across Europe and is still having its impact on the newly industrialising nations today.

What I now want to introduce is the minor stream of evolutionary educational initiatives that were reignited at the beginning of the 20th century and have been gathering strength for over one hundred years. I have observed three evolutionary waves of educational change since the beginning of the 20th century.

6.2.1 *First Wave: Pioneers from the Early 20th Century*

> The world was not created for us to enjoy, but we are created in order to evolve the cosmos. (Maria Montessori in *Education for a New World* cited in (R. Miller 2000, ¶ 1))

The opening words of Maria Montessori were cited by Miller as a pointer to the consciously evolutionary nature of the idealist form of education that she, Steiner, Aurobindo and John Dewey tried to reclaim from industrialism in the early 20th century. They were responding to their awareness that much of European and Anglo education had lost its initial idealist impulse and had succumbed to industrialism, secularism and materialism during the 19th century. These pioneers were attempting to re-integrate the philosophical and pedagogical insights of the German idealists and romantics who had inspired the original universal education impulse. The educational contributions of Steiner and Montessori in Europe, followed by Sri Aurobindo, in India indicate an interesting philosophical and circumstantial convergence. They were all futures-oriented in that they subscribed in some way to evolutionary notions of consciousness, culture and even cosmos. They all embraced spiritual[1] as well as scientific theories of evolution.

[1]Although honouring a spiritual as well as a material dimension to existence, none of these approaches is attached to a particular religious doctrine.

Steiner began in 1904 to write about the evolution of consciousness (Gidley 2007b, 2008). By 1909 he was beginning to shape his pedagogical theories around this notion, and by 1919 had founded his first school (Steiner 1904/1959, 1909/1965). Steiner integrated his comprehensive stage theory of human life-span development into education, well before Piaget developed his cognitive stage theories of child development (Piaget 1950/1964; Steiner 1909/1965, 1928/1972). A deeper genealogical exploration may indicate that Steiner was the proto-theorist for both life-span psychology and the psycho-spiritual development models being explored by adult developmental psychologists today.

In 1909, Sri Aurobindo began to write about evolution in relation to yoga and by 1914 began publishing his major treatise on the evolution of consciousness (Aurobindo 1909, 1914/2000). Sri Aurobindo's integral education initiative did not begin until 1943—via his spiritual collaborator in Pondicherry, India (The Mother 1955). Montessori, who in her later writings also referred to the evolutionary purpose of education, had already begun her first school in 1907 and published her first educational writings in 1916 (Montessori 1916/1964). Her philosophical alignment with the spiritual evolutionary perspectives of Steiner and Sri Aurobindo has already been noted. Although these three pioneers apparently had no physical contact with each other,[2] one could speculate that they were tapping into an important *zeitgeist*.[3]

Several contemporary educators have undertaken comparative studies of their approaches (Coulter 1991; Edwards 2002; Gidley 2007a; Marshak 1997; Miller 1990). All three have developed into global school movements—with Steiner-Waldorf and Montessori being the most extensive. All these approaches emphasise imagination, aesthetics, organic thinking, practical engagement, creativity, spirituality and other postformal reasoning qualities. Unfortunately, the dominant education model, with its economics-based managerialism and technological gadgetry masquerading as new educational approaches, largely overpowered them. In the case of Dewey's initiative, it has been appropriated in a reduced form by the mainstream US education system as so-called *progressive education*.

In a surprising development, the Australian Government, in creating its National Curriculum in 2009, decided to include and approve both Steiner[4] and Montessori educational curricula. The contribution of a postformal educational philosophy to the Steiner National Curriculum is discussed in Chapter 7.

[2]It is possible Sri Aurobindo and Steiner met in the early 20th century (Gidley 2008, p. 107).

[3]*Zeitgeist* is a German word meaning *time-spirit*, or *spirit of the times*. Schelling used the term in the late 18th century to refer to "the basic mood or current of an era" (Gebser 1996, p. 87).

[4]For information about the Australian Steiner Curriculum Framework, see Steiner Education Australia: http://steinereducation.edu.au/curriculum/

6.2.2 Second Wave: "Alternative" Education Emerges from the 1960s

> Education either functions as an instrument which is used to facilitate integration of the younger generation into the logic of the present system and bring about conformity or it becomes the practice of freedom, the means by which men and women deal critically and creatively with reality and discover how to participate in the transformation of their world." (Freire 1970, p. 15)

The *second evolutionary wave* of education alternatives arose in the late 1960s and 1970s, questioning the politics and practices of mainstream education (Freire 1970; Illich 1975; Neill 1960). It was sparked by the dramatic consciousness changes that erupted in 1968 with the student protests in Paris, followed rapidly by the 1969 Woodstock Peace Festival in the USA, which laid foundations for a global youth peace movement against the Vietnam War. These events also paralleled the arrival of futures studies on the academic scene, especially in Europe, with the journal *Futures* being founded in 1968 along with significant global meetings such as *Mankind 2000* that led to the forming of the World Futures Studies Federation (WFSF). These events coincided with the beginning of various "new age" movements, including participatory politics, new forms of music, east-west spiritual-philosophical dialogues, new gender relations, post-nuclear-family lifestyles and recreational use of designer drugs. These movements were taken up quite strongly in the Anglo countries, particularly in pockets of North America and Australia, where at least indirectly, ideas about the appropriateness of the factory model of formal education began to shift.

The 1970s to 1980s saw a flourishing of alternative education, including free schooling (Neill 1960), home schooling (Holt 1970), critical pedagogy (Freire 1970), de-schooling (Illich 1975) and a flurry of educational reforms within mainstream settings. Some of these initiatives were based on earlier theories such as Jean Piaget's constructivism and John Dewey's experiential education. All were critical of the formal, modernist model of mass education.

In many ways this second wave was very revolutionary—even anarchist. Some of these approaches opted right out of the formal schooling system (de-schooling, home schooling) rather than trying to create an alternative educational form. Most of these approaches still operate as minor threads. From the late 1980s, new more complex and comprehensive approaches were starting to emerge.

Recall Kegan's two-tiered view of postmodernism—deconstructive and reconstructive (Kegan 1994). From this perspective, I view the second wave as critically deconstructive (involving outright rejection of modernist education). The third wave discussed below was more reconstructive, nuanced and integrative—capable of distinguishing between what should be discarded of the old and what was worthy enough to be retained, rebuilt and perhaps transformed.

6.2.3 *Third Wave: The 21st Century is Postformal*

> The procedures that are built into our system of schooling—grading, standardizing, the herding of children from room to room at the sound of a bell, teachers who answer to a hierarchy of authority, the extraordinary influence of business leaders in what goes on in our classrooms—none of these things serve the spiritual unfolding of children or the building of community. (Miller 1999, pp. 190–191)

In this quote Ron Miller articulates both the critical, deconstructive and integrative reconstructive interests underlying his holistic educational approach. He also gives voice to the concerns of the rising movement of educators and researchers who resent and resist the colonisation of education by industrial, corporate and economic pressures. Paradoxically, as the neoliberal commodification of education tightened its grasp on mainstream education through an increasing emphasis on vocational skills and competencies, and the shift from education as cultural phenomena, to education as part of the *knowledge economy*, the range and scope of innovation has expanded.

The *third evolutionary wave* is the most significant and most powerful. A plethora of new evolutionary pedagogies have emerged over the last two decades. I use the terms postformal or evolutionary pedagogies as alternatives to *reform* or even *transformation* to highlight the scope of the transition we, as humans in a planetary era, are undergoing. Educational reform only tinkers at the surface of appearances—a bit like rearranging the deckchairs on the Titanic—while educational transformation is often limited by the philosophical perspective, ideology or paradigm it subscribes to. By contrast, the terms postformal and evolutionary connect education more consciously with evolution of consciousness, without which we can find no ways forward to meet and deal with complex futures.

I have identified over a dozen pedagogical approaches that demonstrate the influence of postformal reasoning qualities, either explicitly or implicitly. These include aesthetic and artistic education, complexity in education, critical and postcolonial pedagogies, environmental/ecological education, futures education, holistic education, imagination and creativity in education, integral education, planetary/global education, postformality in education, postmodern and poststructuralist pedagogies, spirituality in education, transformative education and wisdom in education. These make up the third wave of educational evolution. I will demonstrate in Chapter 7 why I call these evolutionary pedagogies postformal, when I map them alongside the postformal reasoning qualities I theorised in Chapter 5.

The diversity of postformal pedagogies has led to the emergence of pockets of educational theory, much of it arising from educational practice. Few educational theorists actually use the term *postformal education* (Horn 2001; Kincheloe et al. 1999a; Kincheloe and Steinberg 1993; Villaverde and Pinar 1999). However, if the term *postformal* is interpreted more broadly to include the impact of the wide range of postformal qualities, such as complexity, creativity, imagination, integration, spirituality and wisdom, to name just a few, then the picture opens up.

Most of these approaches sought to broaden education beyond the simple information-processing model based on a mechanistic view of the human being to a more holistic, creative, multi-faceted and participatory approach. Yet not all honour the multi-layered nature of the developing child, as part of a consciously evolving human species. These approaches are explored below and in Chapters 8, 9, 10 and 11.

6.3 Postformal Thought Emerging in Educational Theory

6.3.1 Post-formality of Joe Kincheloe and Shirley Steinberg

> Post-formality is life-affirming as it transcends modernism's disdain and devaluation of the spiritual... Postmodernism is the consummate boundary crosser, ignoring the no-trespassing signs posted at modernity's property line of certainty. It is possible that postmodernism and its socio-cognitive expression, post-formality, will lead us across the boundary dividing living and non-living. (Kincheloe and Steinberg 1993, p. 309)

In Chapter 2 I linked formal reasoning with the worldview of modernism. By contrast, the opening quote reveals how educational researchers Joe Kincheloe and Shirley Steinberg link post-formality with the worldview of postmodernism.

To reiterate: the dominant worldview uses primarily formal thinking to express its dualism and reductionism. The socio-cultural expression of this epistemology, in which formal education—with its emphasis on developing formal thinking—is situated, is modernism. By contrast, postformal consciousness can be linked to postmodernism and post-industrialism. Ken Wilber describes this connection by referring to postformal thinking using his term, vision-logic:

> Vision-logic (dialectical, dialogical, integral-aperspectival, interpenetration of opposites, intersubjective, feeling/vision) remains the cognitive goal, and aperspectival foundation of the moments of truth of the postmodern theorists. (Wilber 1995/2000, p. 679, Note 5)

Kincheloe and Steinberg were the first to introduce the notion of postformal thought into the education discourse. They later refer to their theoretical approach as postformalism, which they regard as a psycho-socio-political critical pedagogy. They began to articulate their theory of post-formality in their seminal article "A Tentative Description of Post-Formal Thinking: The Critical Confrontation with Cognitive Theory" (Kincheloe and Steinberg 1993). Interestingly, in this introduction to their theory they refer to it as a "post-Piagetian cognitive theory" (Kincheloe and Steinberg 1993, p. 296). They credit their theory with giving rise to a new "post-formal way of thinking" that could provide education practitioners with "a framework for reconsidering both curricular and pedagogical practices" (Kincheloe and Steinberg 1993, p. 296). They apparently use "post-Piagetian" in the sense of critiquing Piaget's project, rather than building on his work as some of the adult developmental psychologists have done (see Chapter 5: Section 5.3.1).

The article begins with a rather savage critique of formal thinking ("a la Piaget") and its limitations for the educational systems of the times. After noting Piaget's more situated approach to cognition in his later works, and referring briefly to two early post-Piagetian theorists Jean Lave (1988) and Valerie Walkerdine (1988), the authors refer to their own work as a "more critical post-formality grounded in our emancipatory system of meaning [which] does not cave in to relativistic social paralysis" (Kincheloe and Steinberg 1993, p. 298). They go on to develop their approach as one that "initiates reflective dialogue between critical theory and postmodernism—a dialogue that is always concerned with the expansion of self-awareness and consciousness" (Kincheloe and Steinberg 1993, p. 298).

In a subsequent article, Kincheloe refers to several important theoretical influences on their postformal education approach (Kincheloe et al. 1999c). While acknowledging his respect for the Piagetian tradition, he critiques what he sees as the "the part of it co-opted by Anglo-American mainstream educational psychology" (Kincheloe et al. 1999b, p. 9) and proceeds to acknowledge the influence of both Vygotskian psychology and "neo-Vygotskian situated cognition" (Kincheloe et al. 1999b, p. 10) and Deweyan progressivism on the theory of postformal education. He refers to the significant influence of the critical pedagogical theories of Paolo Freire and Henry Giroux on his efforts to "democratise intelligence" (Kincheloe et al. 1999b, p. 12) and validate marginalised ways of knowing. Other key influences on the development of his post-formal education theory include what Kincheloe calls the postmodern paradigm shift (Kincheloe et al. 1999b, p. 15), the transdisciplinary field of cultural studies, depth psychology and poststructuralist psychoanalysis, and Howard Gardner's theory of multiple intelligences (Kincheloe et al. 1999b, p. 21). Summarising the significance of these influences, Kincheloe claims: "To some degree all of the traditions referenced help us understand cognition and intelligence in a more contextualized and complex manner" (Kincheloe et al. 1999b, p. 23).

One of the complex aspects of Kincheloe and Steinberg's theory is that it has a paradoxical relationship to the notions of psychological development and intelligence, as they perceive these to be understood within the orthodoxy of psychology. I will discuss these issues in Chapter 7.

6.3.1.1 Core Components of Kincheloe and Steinberg's Post-formality

In articulating their theory of *post-formal thought* Kincheloe and Steinberg have identified what they see as four key components of post-formality in education:

- *Etymology*: Kincheloe and Steinberg explain etymology as "the exploration of the forces that produce what the culture validates as knowledge" (Kincheloe and Steinberg 1993, p. 302). Etymology is then further expanded into three other areas, which include the origins of knowledge; thinking about thinking through the play of imagination; and question-asking or problem detection.
- *Pattern*: They describe pattern as "the understanding of the connecting patterns and relationship that undergird the lived world" (Kincheloe and Steinberg 1993,

p. 302). This component is articulated by way of exploring deep patterns and structures: metaphoric cognition; mind-ecosystem links; and life-forces.
- *Process*: In this theory of post-formal thinking, process refers to "the cultivation of new ways of reading the world that attempt to make sense of both ourselves and contemporary society" (Kincheloe and Steinberg 1993, p. 302). Process is also identified with deconstruction, or the world as text; the integration of logic and emotion; and non-linear holism which goes beyond simple, reductionist, cause-and-effect models of knowledge.
- *Contextualisation*: The final component of their theory of post-formal thought is contextualisation, which involves "the appreciation that knowledge can never stand alone or complete in and of itself" (Kincheloe and Steinberg 1993, p. 302). Context is characterised as attending to the setting; it involves a dialectic between the particular and the general; and most importantly, it is about uncovering the role of power.

6.3.1.2 Application of Kincheloe and Steinberg's Post-formality

> As a critical theory (a social theoretical position concerned with transforming oppressive relations of power that lead to human suffering) of cognition, postformalism promotes thinking that leads to socio-political action. (Kincheloe 2006, p. 15)

A significant feature of Kincheloe and Steinberg's postformalism is that it is not just an abstract theory. It is a theory-in-action. As educational theorists, they are fine examples of Giroux's concept of the transformative intellectual (Giroux 1992).

In addition to Kincheloe and Steinberg's own research, they have worked with a number of colleagues whose involvement with the application of critical post-formality in education is noteworthy (Horn 2001; Malott 2011; Rose and Kincheloe 2003; Villaverde and Pinar 1999). However, these theorists cannot be discussed here.

In Chapter 7 I undertake a dialogue between the two types of postformalities: postformal reasoning in psychology and postformalism in education. I explore similarities and differences, potential points for integration and apparent irreconcilabilities. This includes a table mapping the relationships between postformal reasoning qualities and Kincheloe and Steinberg's postformalism (Table 7.6). Finally I propose a resolution, which distinguishes three different types of postformalities.

6.3.1.3 Kincheloe's *Bricolage*: Multilogicality in Research

> The bricolage understands that the frontiers of knowledge rest in the liminal zones where disciplines collide… the facilitation and cultivation of boundary work is a central theme of this process…a key aspect of 'doing bricolage' involves the development of conceptual tools for boundary work. (Kincheloe 2001, p. 688–691)

One of the concepts that Kincheloe places at the heart of postformalism is multilogicality. While it may seem to be an abstract, even esoteric, concept it is simply about multiple perspectives. As discussed earlier formal binary logic requires acceptance of the idea that only one of two "contradictory truths" can be correct. Postformalism allows for the complexity, paradox and contradiction of multiple—apparently contradictory—truths can all be valid within their own context.

Building on his conceptual work on the notion of *post-formal thinking* in education, Kincheloe expanded his postformalism and multilogicality into his complex educational research methodology: the *bricolage* (Kincheloe 2006, p. 152). Kincheloe's bricolage is both a theoretical approach and an overarching methodology that is highly suitable for educational research. His theorising of *bricolage* builds on Claude Lévi-Strauss' "understanding of the complexity and unpredictability of the cultural domain" (Kincheloe and Berry 2004, p. 25). Kincheloe refers to his features of *bricolage* as a *literacy of complexity* (Kincheloe and Berry 2004, pp. 25–27).

Although Kincheloe did not explicitly develop the theoretical links between his two theories, Table 6.1 demonstrates quite a strong interrelationship between Kincheloe's *bricolage* methodology and his theory of post-formality. It suggests that Kincheloe's conceptualisation of *bricolage* theoretically emerged from his conceptualisation of postformal thinking. However, this table should not be viewed

Table 6.1 A Comparison of Kincheloe's *Post-formal Thought and Bricolage*

Post-formal Thought in Education (Kincheloe and Steinberg 1999, pp. 62–81)	**Bricolage in Education Research** (Kincheloe and Berry 2004, pp. 25–29)
Etymology	
The origins of knowledge; Thinking about thinking and imagination; Problem detection	Multiple epistemologies; Interpretive aspect of knowledge; Discursive construction
Pattern	
Deep patterns and structures; Metaphoric cognition; Connection between mind and ecosystem	Explicate/implicate orders of reality; Fictive dimension of research; Living process in which cultural entities are situated
Process	
Deconstruction—the world as text; Logic-emotion links; Non-linear holism	Intertextuality; Ontology of relationships and connections; The utility of feedback loops
Contextualisation	
Attending to the contextual setting; Subtle interaction of particularity and generalisation; Uncovering the role of power.	Intersecting contexts; Contextual specificities and questioning of universalism; Cultural assumptions, power and knowledge.

Source: Gidley (2008)

as a formal categorisation of either. The information in Table 6.1 also demonstrates the postformal conceptual development of Kincheloe's *bricolage* in contrast to the notion of *bricolage* as mere eclecticism—mixing quantitative and qualitative methods—within what may be a formal research paradigm.

6.3.2 Evolutionary Ideas among other Educational Theorists

> All of the leading holistic thinkers identify the crisis of our time as an epistemological crisis. We are not arguing against technology as such, or against capitalism in itself. We are saying that underneath our political, social, and economic arrangements, the way modern culture defines and understands reality itself is faulty, and this flawed way of knowing gives rise to distorted, we might even say cancerous, forms of technology and economic organization. (Miller 2006, Para 6)

In these words, Ron Miller, one of the founders of holistic education, makes a critical connection between the epistemological crisis and its effects on society and culture, but without presenting a clear path forward. He points to the need for an alternative worldview or paradigm and is one of many who do so. In this volume I take this critical view further by showing that there is a new epistemology emerging and it is postformal. What I found when scanning the educational literature for new paradigm approaches is that innovative educators are highlighting many of the features of postformal reasoning that I have theorised in Chapter 5. Somewhat paradoxically, most of these alternative approaches operate in isolation from each other and are seemingly unaware of other quite similar approaches.

One of the most wide-ranging evolutionary approaches other than the postformal education of Kincheloe, Steinberg and colleagues is holistic education with its growing theoretical and research base (Martin 2004; Miller 2005). Holistic education theorist Ron Miller and psychologist/educator Tobin Hart are among those few contemporary educators who reflect postmodern and critical perspectives while also honouring the individual developmental, spiritual and socio-cultural evolutionary needs of children. Hart and Miller both contribute important insights for theorising postformal educational futures, while being careful not to put forward a "set curriculum" that could run the risk of being fundamentalised as some have done with Steiner's and Montessori's approaches.

Among other theoretical contributions, Miller points to two principles, freedom and structure, which he emphasises need not be in conflict with each other but held in a dialectical relationship where: "The student is not constrained by alien forces, but gladly participates in a structured world to which he or she feels connected" (Miller 2006).

Hart resists the counter-evolutionary weight of mainstream schooling, which he says has "focused on adaptation to the status quo rather than its transformation within (person) and without (culture and society)" (Hart 2006). By contrast, he points towards an education designed "for us to assist ourselves in our own evolution, enabling us to align with the rising currents of creation" (Hart 2006). Hart's theoretical model designed to align education to the evolution of consciousness is discussed in Chapter 10.

Several other holistic educators reflect postmodern, critical and postformal perspectives (Egan 1997; Forbes 2003; Hart 2001a, 2006; Kessler 2000; J. P. Miller 2000; Miller 2006; Neville 2001, 2006; Palmer 1998; Sloan 1983, 1992; Thompson 2001). These educators will be discussed in later chapters in the context of the postformal approach to which they are most aligned.

6.3.3 Tensions and Coherences between the New Approaches

> Now that governments in many countries have established a strong grip on schools through a combination of curriculum prescription, testing, inspection, measurement, and league tables, they are turning their attention to teacher education in order to establish total control over the educational system. (Biesta 2014, p. 121)

A major tension has been created by the powerful neo-fundamentalist backlash against alternative approaches in the Anglo countries from government-backed educrats who seek to dominate the educational agenda with scientism, economism and technicism—through their "audit culture" (MacLure 2006a). Further philosophical and theoretical coherence is needed to counter this and to facilitate more extensive sustainable educational transformation. Fortunately, there are several educational theorists and researchers who are attempting to expose and counter this reactionary neo-conservatism (Abbs 2003; Biesta 2014; Coryn et al. 2005; Denzin 2005; MacLure 2006a).

In the absence of coherence, the current piecemeal and ad hoc approach to educational alternatives may inadvertently support neo-conservatism (Coryn et al. 2005; Denzin 2005; Giroux 2003; MacLure 2006a). As Giroux (1992) stated, we need to "educate students to work collectively to make 'despair unconvincing and hope practical' by refusing the role of the disconnected expert, technician, or careerist and adopting the practice of the engaged and transformative intellectual" (p. 105). I wonder if this can be achieved unless as educators, philosophers, futurists, scientists, artists and integral theorists, we can find the living concepts and creative language to dissolve unnecessary boundaries (see Chapter 11).

Ironically, most of the innovative educators mentioned in this chapter take a single postformal reasoning quality as their focus, rather than taking a more integrated approach. I can see two possible reasons for this: firstly, adult developmental psychologists do not generally explore the implications of their findings for education; and secondly, most innovative educators appear unaware of the extensive body of psychological literature on postformal qualities even though they may be championing one or two of them. The significance of postformal thinking in education has been partially explored by some developmental psychologists

(Arlin 1999; Sinnott 1998; Sternberg 2001), but without reference to postformal education.

Various attempts have been made to integrate or cohere some of these divergences by building bridges between aesthetic, critical, postmodern and postformal (Kincheloe and Steinberg 1993; Rose and Kincheloe 2003); between and within holistic and integral (Gidley 2007a; R. Miller 2000; Miller 2005) and between some of the individual qualities, for example, postformal complex reasoning, ecology and creativity (Montuori 1997, 2003; Morin 2001).

This volume is a serious attempt to consciously bridge the gaps between theory and practice and between postformal psychology and postformal pedagogies.

6.4 The Shift from Formal Education to Postformal Pedagogies

> Formal operational thought would reflect mechanistic assumptions of linear causality, atomism, and determinism. Post-formal operational thought would reflect organismic assumptions about reciprocity and holism. (Kramer 1983, p. 94)

In her attempts to identify structural differences between formal operations and post-formal operational thought, Kramer points to the different underlying worldviews associated with each.

Other researchers look to the structural or paradigmatic shifts in philosophy, for example from Aristotelian formal logic to Hegelian dialectics (Riegel 1973); or in science, for example from Newtonian to post-Newtonian physics (Sinnott 1998, p. 29); or in terms of hierarchical complexity (Commons et al. 1998).

Kramer argues that "the distinction between formal operational thought as analytical, on the one hand, and post-formal operational thought as synthetic, on the other, is the major differentiating feature" (Kramer 1983, p. 96). She clarifies that an analytic perspective involves breaking the whole down into its parts, while the synthetic perspective maintains that "the system transcends and gives meaning to each of its parts" (Kramer 1983, p. 101). Taking Kramer's summary further, I add that analysis involves atomism, reductionism, segregation and specialisation, whereas synthesis involves holistic, integral, transdisciplinary and plural (see Table 6.2).

In the absence of research that systematically applies postformal reasoning to education, I offer a broad orientation to standard parameters and assumptions of education based on formal reasoning and indicate how postformal pedagogies may depart from these assumptions. The components used to identify postformal education in Table 6.2 include features from both the adult developmental psychology research and the post-formal educational theories. The distillation of all these features clarifies the conceptual shift from formal education to postformal pedagogies.

Table 6.2 The Shift from *Formal Education* to *Postformal Pedagogies*[a]

Formal Education[b]	Postformal Pedagogies
Atomistic, reductionist	Holonic, holographic, holistic
Simple mechanical structure	Complex organic structure
Straight line, sequential	Helix, progressive recapitulation
Instrumentalism	Multi-layered reflexivity
Formal logic: binary, dualistic, excluded middle	Postformal logics: dialectical, fuzzy, included middle, paradox
Disciplinary segregation, specialisation and territorialisation of knowledge	Transdisciplinary integration, pluralism and de-territorialisation of knowledge
Cognitive orientation, privileging of brain	Cognitive-affective-participatory, balancing brain, heart, limbs
Knowledge as static, objective content, information-based	Knowledge as process, subjective-objective capacity, wisdom-oriented
Values-neutral, secular	Values-oriented, spiritual
Language as objective tool, or pragmatic instrument of communication	Language as subjective-objective, imaginative, metaphoric medium
Methodological functionalism	Methodological pluralism
Analysis, data, results, conclusion	Interpretation, patterns, context, coherence
Argument, debate, win-lose	Dialogue, understanding, win-win
Researcher outside (etic) the research, third-person language	Researcher outside (etic)/inside (emic) the research, third-person and first-person language
Universal, timeless	Universal and particular, historical, contextual

Source: Gidley (2008)

[a]This table builds on an earlier comparison of formal research and postformal research typologies (Gidley 2008).

[b]These claims are quite consistent with assumptions and practices of *conventional approaches* to research from a transpersonal research methods perspective (Braud and Anderson 1998, pp. 4–5).

6.5 Postformal Pedagogies: Theorising Twelve Approaches

The development of any educational theory is complex territory, and clearly, to evolve forms of education that are authentically postformal is not a trivial matter. The only way that visionary, innovative educators can muster enough strength to enact the kind of meta-change that is required is through a *dialogue of pedagogies*. By enacting conversations among the rich pluralism of postformal pedagogies, we can begin to develop a picture of the rich tapestry of evolutionary change already happening.

My interest has been to identify and begin to cohere the plurality of emerging educational approaches that appear to support one or more postformal reasoning features and/or themes in the evolution of consciousness literature. By bringing them into dialogic relationship with each other, they can learn from each other, inspire each other and give strength to each other. This is what I mean by *evolving education*.

Table 6.3 Postformal Pedagogies: Clustering into Twelve Approaches

Aesthetic, artistic and poetic education: (Abbs 2003; Broudy 1987; Edwards 2002; Eisner 1985; Gidley 1998; Read 1943, 1954; Rose and Kincheloe 2003).
Critical, postcolonial, global and planetary: (Boulding 1990; Freire 1970; Gidley 2001; Giroux 1992, 1999/2005; Inayatullah and Gidley 2000; Jain et al. 2001; Kincheloe et al. 1999a; McLaren and Kincheloe 2007; Miller 2006; Morin 2001; Rose and Kincheloe 2003).
Complexity in education: (Davis 2004; Davis and Sumara 2006; Kincheloe and Berry 2004; Montuori 2003; Morin 2001; Sinnott 2005).
Creativity in education: (Egan 1990, 1997; Kaufman and Baer 2006; Kaufman and Sternberg 2006; Montuori 2006; Neville 1989; Sloan 1992; Sternberg 1999).
Ecological, environmental and sustainable: (Fien 1998; Jardine 1998; Ornstein and Ehrlich 1991; Orr 1994).
Futures and foresight education: (Dator 2002; Eisler 2001; Gidley et al. 2004; Hicks 2002; Hutchinson 1996; Milojevic 2005; Slaughter 2002; Gidley 2012a, 2012b).
Imaginative education: (Broudy 1987; Egan 1988, 1990; Eisner 1985; Neville 1989; Nielsen 2006; Nuyen 1998; Sloan 1992).
Integral and holistic education: (Adams 2006; Esbjörn-Hargens 2006; Forbes 2003; Gidley 2002, 2007a; Gunnlaugson 2004; Hart 1998; Kessler 2000; Miller 1990, 1999, 2000a, 2005; McDermott 2005; Nava 2001; Palmer 1998; Subbiondo 2005).
Postmodern and poststructuralist: (Abbs 2003; Elkind 1997, 1998; MacLure 2006a, 2006b; Nuyen 1998; Peters 1998; Sloan 1992).
Social and emotional education: (Clouder 2008; Gidley 2011; Goleman 1997; Graham and Fitzgerald 2007).
Spiritual, transformative and contemplative: (Bouma 2006; Chater 2006; de Souza 2006; Glazer 1994; Ferrer et al. 2005; Gidley 2007a; Hart 2000, 2001a; Miller 1999; Montuori 1997; Pridmore 2004; Scott 2000; Woods et al. 1997).
Wisdom education: (Arlin 1999; Bassett 2005; Gidley 2009; Hart 2001b; Sinnott 2005; Sternberg 2001).

Source: Gidley (2009, 2010) and Molz and Gidley (2008)

In addition to the specific post-formal education of Kincheloe, Steinberg and their colleagues, a plethora of educational approaches have emerged throughout the three evolutionary waves. By viewing these in the light of the postformal reasoning features (see Table 5.4), I identified around twenty evolutionary educational approaches and refer to these as postformal pedagogies (or evolutionary pedagogies).

In a similar sense-making process to that undertaken with the postformal reasoning qualities (Table 5.4), I clustered the postformal pedagogies into twelve groups of approaches based on how they reflected key postformal reasoning qualities.

This analysis also forms a basis for establishing how these educational approaches relate to the four evolutionary themes that I introduced in Chapter 5. Table 6.3 shows the twelve postformal pedagogical approaches with relevant references. Note that some of the items are internally clustered because the literature on these approaches strongly overlaps. This mapping will facilitate dialogue between postformal psychology and postformal education in Chapter 7. They are listed in alphabetical order in Table 6.3, prior to the deeper analysis in Chapter 7.

Each of these pedagogies is discussed in Chapters 8, 9, 10 and 11 in the context of the evolutionary theme that they support, and in relation to the core pedagogical values that anchor my postformal education philosophy. All are linked with new ways of thinking that are influencing both school and university education in an evolutionary way. A major challenge for the development of a postformal education philosophy is to cohere this diversity, without reducing its pedagogical richness.

6.6 Postformal Education: In Light of Evolutionary Themes

> A shift in educational orientation will manifest social changes. The evolution of society, the transcendence of existing social structures, rests in large measure with education. It is the creative function of education in all its work to look to the viability of its society in the present. To critique cultures, challenging injustices and inequities... However, currently our educational consciousness and imagination all too often work under the constraints of political ideologies more concerned with reproduction of culture and existing social structures than with social transformation. (Jenlink 2004, p. 226)

In Chapter 5 we explored four themes that emerged from the evolution of consciousness discourses and how they interacted with the twelve theorised postformal reasoning qualities. I now discuss how the twelve theorised postformal pedagogies intersect with the four evolutionary themes (Table 6.4). Figure 6.1 offers an alternative representation of these complex interactions. Although there is considerable overlap and interpenetration between and among the evolutionary themes and the postformal educational approaches, the latter have been clustered

Table 6.4 Evolutionary Discourses, Themes and Postformal Pedagogies

Evolutionary Discourses	*Theme Summary*	*Postformal Pedagogies*
Discourses that facilitate higher-order thinking through cultivating spiritual, contemplative and compassionate qualities.	**Theme 1:** Conscious, compassionate spiritual development	Spiritual, transformative and contemplative Social and emotional education Integral and holistic education
Discourses that transcend static, mechanistic thinking and promote fluid, organic, life-enhancing, thinking and being.	**Theme 2:** Mobile, life-enhancing thinking	Imaginative education Ecological, environmental and sustainable Futures and foresight education
Discourses based on cultural evolution and individual psychological development.	**Theme 3:** Complexification of thinking & culture	Creativity in education Complexity in education Wisdom education
Discourses crossing linguistic, and paradigmatic barriers through self-awareness and language reflexivity.	**Theme 4:** Linguistic and paradigmatic boundary-crossing	Postmodern and poststructuralist education Aesthetic, artistic and poetic education Critical, postcolonial, global and planetary

Source: Gidley (2009)

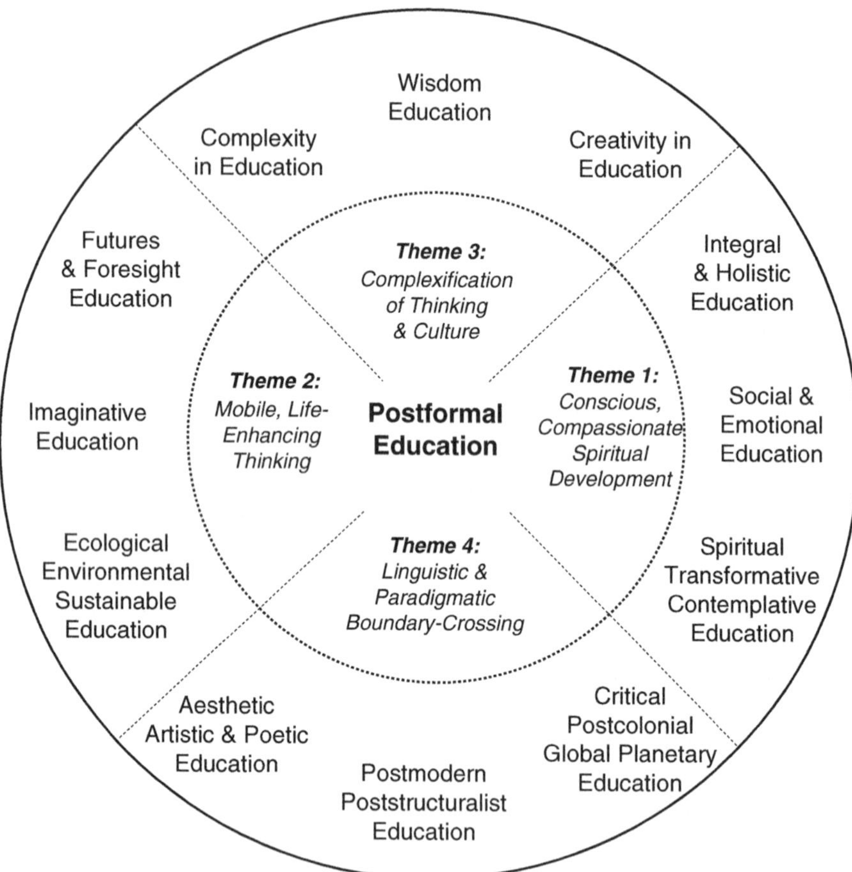

Figure 6.1 Postformal Pedagogies Interacting with Evolutionary Themes (Source: Adapted from: Gidley 2009)

under the evolution of consciousness theme that they appear to most strongly support.

In Chapter 7, I show how these postformal pedagogies align to the postformal reasoning qualities (Table 7.5) and explore other more complex interrelationships.

6.6.1 Educating for Conscious, Compassionate, Spiritual Development

This theme includes discourses that facilitate higher-order thinking through cultivating spiritual, contemplative and compassionate qualities. These may be religious, and particularly post-traditional and postmodern spiritual approaches that promote conscious, compassionate, spiritual development (see Chapter 5: Section 5.5.1). We saw in Chapter 5 how this theme interacts with the postformal reasoning qualities of higher purpose, dialogical reasoning and integration.

These evolutionary spiritual approaches are supported by educational styles that emphasise care, contemplation, empathy, love and reverence. Such approaches include spiritual, transformative and contemplative approaches; social and emotional education; and integral and holistic education. See summaries of these interactions in Table 7.9. All of these educational approaches and their interactions with the postformal qualities will be explored in Chapter 8.

6.6.2 *Educating for Mobile, Life-Enhancing Thinking*

This theme includes discourses that transcend static, mechanistic thinking and promote fluid, organic, life-enhancing thinking. Organic thinking is found in process philosophies; new science theories such as Einstein's relativity, quantum physics and systems science; and biology theories of chaos, complexity, self-organisation and emergence (see Chapter 5: Section 5.5.2). The postformal qualities that are associated with this theme are imagination, ecological reasoning and futures reasoning.

Several postformal educational approaches support this movement from lifeless *static* concepts to *living* thinking. In particular, vitality and wellbeing are nurtured by educational approaches that include imaginative education; ecological, environmental, and sustainable approaches; and futures and foresight education. See summaries of these interactions in Table 7.9. These educational approaches along with the postformal qualities that they nurture are discussed in Chapter 9.

6.6.3 *Educating for Complexification of Thinking and Culture*

This theme includes the two main streams within the evolution of consciousness discourse: cultural evolution and individual psychological development, which both explicitly identify the emergence of new modes of culture and consciousness. This theme interacts with the following postformal reasoning qualities: creativity, complexity and intuitive wisdom (see Chapter 5: Section 5.5.3).

There are specific educational theories addressed to the cultivation of wisdom, and in addition to those, this theme is addressed by educational styles that are creative, complex, multi-modal and paradoxical. These include approaches that emphasise creativity in education, complexity in education and wisdom education per se. See summaries of these interactions in Table 7.9. The many and varied educational offerings that encourage the development of these aspects of advanced postformal reasoning are detailed in Chapter 10.

6.6.4 Educating for Linguistic and Paradigmatic Boundary-Crossing

This theme includes discourses that cross linguistic and paradigmatic barriers through reflexivity and multi-vocal awareness. It relates to movement away from specialisation and towards integration. Through recognising the limits of reductionist research and academic siloism, a variety of transdisciplinary epistemological approaches have emerged. Postformal qualities that align with this theme include reflexivity, language reflexivity and pluralism (see Chapter 5: Section 5.5.4).

An evolutionary philosophy of education that can overcome this challenge requires tremendous sensitivity to linguistic, cultural and paradigmatic contexts. This advanced reasoning capacity of language reflexivity is nurtured by postmodern and poststructuralist pedagogies; aesthetic, artistic and poetic educational approaches; and critical, postcolonial, global and planetary education. See summaries of these interactions in Table 7.9. These educational approaches, their links with this theme and the associated postformal qualities they enhance are addressed in Chapter 11.

6.7 Concluding Remarks

Although there are numerous educational theorists who are working to change education in ways that move beyond the hegemony of the modernist schooling model, there is a lack of theoretical coherence in much of this literature. The remainder of this volume seeks to undertake the meta-cohering required to begin the formation of a postformal education philosophy. I have begun to show how several evolutionary educational approaches contribute to the kind of postformal education of the child that is needed in the fragmented world of the 21st century.

In the deeper analysis in Chapter 7, I show how I have theorised the postformal nature of the evolutionary pedagogies by aligning them to a postformal reasoning quality and how I situate them within the four evolutionary themes. In Part III, I synthesise the approaches into a living educational philosophy that can facilitate the awakening of mature, postformal reasoning at the appropriate life stage.

References

Abbs, P. (2003). *Against the flow: The arts, postmodern culture and education.* London: RoutledgeFalmer.

Adams, A. (2006). *Education: From conception to graduation. A systemic, integral approach.* Ph. D., California Institute of Integral Studies, California.

Arlin, P. K. (1999). The wise teacher: A developmental model of teaching. *Theory into Practice, 38*(1), 12–17.

Aurobindo, S. (1909). Yoga and human evolution. In *Essays in philosophy and yoga: Shorter Works: 1910–1950* (Vol. 16). http://www.aurobindo.ru/workings/sa/16/0004_e.htm. Accessed 8 July 2007.

Aurobindo, S. (1914/2000). *The life divine. 2nd American Edition* (Originally published in the monthly review Arya 1914–1920). Twin Lakes: Lotus Press.

Bassett, C. (2005, October). *Wisdom in three acts: Using transformative learning to teach for wisdom* [Electronic version]. In Sixth international transformative learning conference. East Lansing, Michigan.

Biesta, G. J. J. (2014). *The beautiful risk of education.* Boulder: Paradigm Publishers.

Boulding, E. (1990). *Building a global civic culture: Education for an interdependent world.* New York: Syracuse University Press.

Bouma, G. (2006, November 30). Souls are not shaken, just stirred. *Sydney Morning Herald.*

Braud, W., & Anderson, R. (1998). *Transpersonal research methods for the social sciences: Honoring human experience*. Thousand Oaks: Sage.

Broudy, H. S. (1987). *The role of imagery in learning.* Los Angeles: The Getty Centre for Education in the Arts.

Chater, M. (2006). Just another brick in the wall: Education as violence to the spirit. *International Journal of Children's Spirituality, 11*(1), 47–56.

Clouder, C. (2008). Introducing social and emotional education. In C. Clouder (Ed.), *Social and emotional education. An international analysis.* Santander: Fundacion Marcelino Botin.

Commons, M. L., Trudeau, E. J., Stein, S. A., Richards, F. A., & Krause, S. R. (1998). The existence of developmental stages as shown by the hierarchical complexity of tasks. *Developmental Review, 8*(3), 237–278.

Coryn, C. L. S., Schröter, D. C., & Scriven, M. (2005). A call to action: The first international congress of qualitative inquiry. *Journal of MultiDisciplinary Evaluation, 3*, 155–165.

Coulter, D. J. (1991). Montessori and Steiner: A pattern of reverse symmetries. *Holistic Education Review, 4*(2 (Summer)), 30–32.

Dator, J. (2002). *Advancing futures: Futures studies in higher education.* Westport: Praeger.

Davis, B. (2004). *Inventions of teaching: A genealogy.* Mahwah: Lawrence Erlbaum Associates.

Davis, B., & Sumara, D. (2006). *Complexity and education: Inquiries into learning, pedagogy and research.* Mahwah: Lawrence Erlbaum Associates.

de Souza, M. (2006). Educating for hope, compassion and meaning in a divisive and intolerant world. *International Journal of Children's Spirituality, 11*(1), 165–175.

Denzin, N. (2005). The first international congress of qualitative inquiry. *Qualitative Social Work, 4*(1), 1105–1111.

Edwards, C. P. (2002). Three approaches from Europe: Waldorf, Montessori, and Reggio Emilia. *Early Childhood Research and Practice, 4*(1) [Electronic article]. http://ecrp.uiuc.edu/v4n1/edwards.html. Accessed 20 Apr 16.

Egan, K. (1988). Metaphors in collision: Objectives, assembly lines and stories. *Curriculum Inquiry, 18*(1), 63–86.

Egan, K. (1990). *Romantic understanding: The development of rationality and imagination, ages 8–15*. London: Routledge.

Egan, K. (1997). *The educated mind: How cognitive tools shape our understanding*. Chicago: The University of Chicago Press.

Eisler, R. (2001). Partnership education in the 21st century. *Journal of Futures Studies, 5*(3), 143–156.
Eisner, E. (1985). *The educational imagination: On the design and evaluation of school programs* (2nd ed.). New York: Macmillan.
Elkind, D. (1997). Waldorf education in the postmodern world. *Renewal: A Journal for Waldorf Education, 6*(1), 5–9.
Elkind, D. (1998). Schooling the postmodern child. *Research Bulletin, 3*(1), 1–9.
Esbjörn-Hargens, S. (2006). Integral education by design: How integral theory informs teaching, learning and curriculum in a graduate program. *ReVision, 28*(3), 21–29.
Ferrer, J., Romero, M., & Albareda, R. (2005). Integral transformative education: A participatory proposal. *Journal of Transformative Education, 3*(4), 306–330.
Fien, J. (1998). Environmental education for a new century. In D. Hicks & R. Slaughter (Eds.), *World yearbook 1998: Futures education*. London: Kogan Page.
Forbes, S. H. (2003). *Holistic education: An analysis of its ideas and nature*. Brandon: Solomon Press/Foundation for Educational Renewal.
Freire, P. (1970). *Pedagogy of the oppressed*. New York: Herder and Herder.
Gebser, J. (1996). Psyche and matter: The validity of the dualistic hypothesis. *Integrative Explorations Journal, 3*, 86–89.
Gidley, J. (1998). Youth futures: Transcending violence through the artistic imagination. In S. Inayatullah & P. Wildman (Eds.), *Futures studies: Methods, emerging issues and civilizational visions. A multi-media CD ROM*. Brisbane: Prosperity Press.
Gidley, J. (2001). Globalization and its impact on youth. *Journal of Futures Studies, 6*(1), 89–106.
Gidley, J. (2002). Holistic education and visions of rehumanized futures. In J. Gidley & S. Inayatullah (Eds.), *Youth futures: Comparative research and transformative visions* (pp. 155–168). Westport: Praeger.
Gidley, J. (2007a). Educational imperatives of the evolution of consciousness: The integral visions of Rudolf Steiner and Ken Wilber. *International Journal of Children's Spirituality, 12*(2), 117–135.
Gidley, J. (2007b). The evolution of consciousness as a planetary imperative: An integration of integral views. *Integral Review: A Transdisciplinary and Transcultural Journal for New Thought, Research and Praxis, 5*, 4–226.
Gidley, J. (2008). *Evolving education: A postformal-integral-planetary gaze at the evolution of consciousness and the educational imperatives*. PhD dissertation, Southern Cross University, Lismore.
Gidley, J. (2009). Educating for evolving consciousness: Voicing the emergency for love, life and wisdom. In *The international handbook of education for spirituality, care and wellbeing* (Springer international handbooks of religion and education series). New York: Springer.
Gidley, J. (2010). Evolving higher education integrally: Delicate mandalic theorising. In S. Esbjörn-Hargens, O. Gunnlaugson, & J. Reams (Eds.), *Integral education: New directions for higher learning* (pp. 345–361). New York: State University of New York Press.
Gidley, J. (2011). From crisis to confidence: The development of social and emotional education in Australia. In B. Hey (Ed.), *Social and emotional education: International analysis II* (pp. 69–101). Santander: Fundacione Marcelino Botin.
Gidley, J. (2012a). Evolution of education: From weak signals to rich imaginaries of educational futures. *Futures: The Journal of Policy, Planning and Futures Studies, 44*(1), 46–54.
Gidley, J. (2012b). In P. Scott, A. Curaj, L. Vlăsceanu, & L. Wilson (Eds.), *Re-imagining the role and function of higher education for alternative futures through embracing global knowledge futures*. Dordrecht: Springer.
Gidley, J., Bateman, D., & Smith, C. (2004). *Futures in education: Principles, practice and potential* (AFI monograph series 2004: No 5). Melbourne: Australian Foresight Institute.
Giroux, H. A. (1992). *Border crossing: Cultural workers and the politics of education*. New York: Routledge.

Giroux, H. A. (1999/2005). Schooling and the struggle for public life: Democracy's promise and education's challenge. Boulder: Paradigm Publishers.

Giroux, H. A. (2003). *The abandoned generation: Democracy beyond the culture of fear*. New York: Palgrave Macmillan.

Glazer, S. (Ed.). (1994). *The heart of learning: Spirituality in education*. New York: Jeremy P. Tarcher/Putnam.

Goleman, D. (1997). *Emotional intelligence: Why it can matter more than IQ*. New York: Bantam.

Graham, A., & Fitzgerald, R. (2007, November 25–29). *Progressing the 'impact' agenda in education: Including children and young people in research*. In 2007 Australian association for research in education conference, 'proving or improving'. Fremantle.

Gunnlaugson, O. (2004). Towards an integral education for the Ecozoic Era. *Journal of Transformative Education, 2*(4), 313–335.

Hart, T. (1998). A dialectic of knowing: Integrating the intuitive and the analytic. *Encounter: Education for Meaning and Social Justice, 11*, 5–16.

Hart, T. (2000). Deep empathy. In T. Hart, P. Nelson, & K. Puhakka (Eds.), *Transpersonal knowing: Exploring the horizon of consciousness* (pp. 253–270). Albany: State University of New York Press.

Hart, T. (2001a). *From information to transformation: Education for the evolution of consciousness*. New York: Peter Lang.

Hart, T. (2001b). Teaching for wisdom. *Encounter: Education for Meaning and Social Justice, 14* (2), 3–16.

Hart, T. (2006). From information to transformation: What the mystics and sages tell us education can be. In S. Inayatullah, I. Milojevic, & M. Bussey (Eds.), *Neohumanist educational futures: Liberating the pedagogical intellect*. Tamsui: Tamkang University Press.

Hicks, D. (2002). *Lessons for the future* (Futures and education series). London: Routledge.

Holt, J. (1970). *How children learn*. Harmondsworth: Pelican.

Horn, R. (2001). Post-formal design conversation: Designing just and caring educational systems. *Systems Research and Behavioural Sciences, 18*(4), 361–371.

Hutchinson, F. (1996). *Educating beyond violent futures*. London: Routledge.

Illich, I. (1975). *Deschooling society*. London: Calder and Boyers.

Inayatullah, S., & Gidley, J. (Eds.). (2000). *The university in transformation: Global perspectives on the futures of the university*. Westport: Bergin and Garvey.

Jain, M., Miller, V., & Jain, S. (Eds.). (2001). *Unfolding learning societies: Deepening the dialogues* (Vol. April 2001, Vimukt Shiksha). Udaipur: The People's Institute for Rethinking education and Development.

Jardine, D. W. (1998). *To dwell with a boundless heart: Essays in curriculum theory, hermeneutics, and the ecological imagination* (Studies in the postmodern theory of education). New York: Peter Lang Publishing.

Jenlink, P. M. (2004). Education, social creativity, and the evolution of society. *World Futures, 60*, 225–240.

Kaufman, J. C., & Baer, J. (2006). *Creativity and reason in cognitive development*. New York: Cambridge University Press.

Kaufman, J. C., & Sternberg, R. J. (Eds.). (2006). *The international handbook of creativity*. New York: Cambridge University Press.

Kegan, R. (1994). *In over our heads: The mental demands of modern life*. Cambridge, MA: Harvard University Press.

Kessler, R. (2000). *The soul of education: Helping students find connection, compassion and character at school*. Alexandria: Association for Supervision and Curriculum Development.

Kincheloe, J. (2001). Describing the bricolage: Conceptualizing a new rigor in qualitative research. *Qualitative Inquiry, 7*(6), 679–692.

Kincheloe, J. (2006). *Reading, writing and cognition: The postformal basics* (Bold visions in educational research). Rotterdam: Sense Publishers.

Kincheloe, J., & Berry, K. (2004). *Rigour and complexity in educational research: Conceptualising the bricolage* (Conducting educational research). Berkshire: Open University Press.

Kincheloe, J., & Steinberg, S. (1993). A tentative description of post-formal thinking: The critical confrontation with cognitive theory. *Harvard Educational Review, 63*(3), 296–320.

Kincheloe, J., & Steinberg, S. (1999). A tentative description of post-formal thinking: The critical confrontation with cognitive theory. In J. Kincheloe, S. Steinberg, & P. H. Hinchey (Eds.), *The post-formal reader: Cognition and education* (Vol. 63, pp. 55–90). New York: Falmer Press.

Kincheloe, J., Steinberg, S., & Hinchey, P. H. (Eds.). (1999a). *The post-formal reader: Cognition and education* (Critical education practice). New York: Falmer Press.

Kincheloe, J., Steinberg, S., & Villaverde, L. E. (1999b). The foundations of a democratic educational psychology. In J. Kincheloe, S. Steinberg, & L. E. Villaverde (Eds.), *Rethinking intelligence: Confronting psychological assumptions about teaching and learning*. New York: Routledge.

Kincheloe, J., Steinberg, S., & Villaverde, L. E. (1999c). *Rethinking intelligence: Confronting psychological assumptions about teaching and learning*. New York: Routledge.

Kramer, D. A. (1983). Post-formal operations? A need for further conceptualization. *Human Development, 26*, 91–105.

Lave, J. (1988). *Cognition in practice: Mind, mathematics and culture in everyday life*. New York: Cambridge University Press.

MacLure, M. (2006a). The bone in the throat: Some uncertain thoughts on baroque method. *International Journal of Qualitative Studies in Education, 19*(6 November–December), 729–745.

MacLure, M. (2006b). Entertaining doubts: On frivolity as resistance. In J. Satterthwaite, W. M. Martin, & L. Robert (Eds.), *Discourse, resistance and identity formation*. London: Trentham.

Malott, C. S. (2011). *Critical pedagogy and cognition: An introduction to a postformal educational psychology* (Explorations of educational purpose). Dordrecht: Springer.

Marshak, D. (1997). *The common vision: Parenting and educating for wholeness*. New York: Peter Lang.

Martin, R. A. (2004, April). Holistic education: Research that is beginning to delineate the field. In *American education research association*. San Diego, California.

McDermott, R. (2005). An Emersonian approach to higher education. *ReVision: A Journal of Consciousness and Transformation, 28*(2), 6–17.

McLaren, P., & Kincheloe, J. (Eds.). (2007). *Critical pedagogy: Where are we now?* (Counterpoints: Studies in the postmodern theory of education). New York: Peter Lang.

Miller, R. (1990). *What are schools for? Holistic education in American culture*. Brandon: Holistic Education Press.

Miller, R. (1999). Holistic education for an emerging culture. In S. Glazer (Ed.), *The heart of learning: Spirituality in education*. New York: Putnam.

Miller, J. P. (2000). *Education and the soul: Towards a spiritual curriculum*. Albany: State University of New York Press.

Miller, R. (2000). Education and the evolution of the cosmos. *Caring for new life: Essays on holistic education* [Electronic version]. http://www.ctr4process.org/sites/default/files/pdfs/23_2Miller.pdf. Accessed 6 Dec 2006.

Miller, R. (2005). Philosophical sources of holistic education [Electronic version]. *Deðerler Eðitimi Dergisi (Journal of Values Education), 3*(10), 9.

Miller, R. (2006). Making connections to the world: Some thoughts on holistic curriculum [Electronic version]. *Encounter: Education for Meaning and Social Justice, 19*(4). http://ojs.great-ideas.org. Accessed 20 Apr 16.

Milojevic, I. (2005). *Educational futures: Dominant and contesting visions*. London: Routledge.

Molz, M., & Gidley, J. (2008). A transversal dialogue on integral education and planetary consciousness: Markus Molz speaks with Jennifer Gidley. *Integral Review: A Transdisciplinary and Transcultural Journal for New Thought, Research and Praxis, 6*, 47–70.

Montessori, M. (1916/1964). The Montessori method. New York: Schoken Books.
Montuori, A. (1997). Reflections on transformative learning: Social creativity, academic discourse and the improvisation of inquiry. *ReVision, 20*(1), 34–37.
Montuori, A. (2003). The complexity of improvisation and the improvisation of complexity: Social science, art and creativity. *Human Relations, 56*(2), 237–255.
Montuori, A. (2006). The quest for a new education: From oppositional identities to creative inquiry. *ReVision, 28*(3), 4–17.
Morin, E. (2001). *Seven complex lessons in education for the future*. Paris: UNESCO.
Nava, R. G. (2001). Holistic education: Pedagogy of universal love (M. N. Rios, & G. S. Miller, Trans., Foundations of holistic education series, Vol. 5). Brandon: Holistic Education Press.
Neill, A. S. (1960). *Summerhill*. New York: Hart.
Neville, B. (1989). *Educating psyche: Emotion, imagination, and the unconscious in learning*. Melbourne: Collins Dove.
Neville, B. (2001). The body of the five-minded animal. In S. Gunn & A. Begg (Eds.), *Mind, body and society: Emerging understandings in knowing and learning*. Melbourne: University of Melbourne.
Neville, B. (2006). Out of our depth and treading water: Reflections on consciousness and culture. *Journal of Conscious Evolution, 2*.
Nielsen, T. W. (2006). Towards a pedagogy of imagination: A phenomenological case study of holistic education. *Ethnography and Education, 1*(2), 247–264.
Nuyen, A. T. (1998). Jean-Francois Lyotard: Education for imaginative knowledge. In M. Peters (Ed.), *Naming the multiple: Poststructuralism and education*. Westport: Bergin and Garvey.
Ornstein, R., & Ehrlich, P. (1991). *New world, new mind: Changing the way we think to save our future*. Glasgow: Paladin.
Orr, D. (1994). *Earth in mind: On education, environment, and the human prospect*. Washington, DC: Island Press.
Palmer, P. (1998). *The courage to teach*. San Francisco: Jossey-Bass.
Peters, M. (Ed.). (1998). *Naming the multiple: Poststructuralism and education* (Critical studies in education and culture series). Westport: Bergin & Garvey.
Piaget, J. (1950/1964). *The psychology of intelligence*. London: Routledge and Kegan Paul.
Pridmore, J. (2004). 'Dancing cannot start too soon': Spiritual education in the thought of Jean Paul Friedrich Richter. *International Journal of Children's Spirituality, 9*(3), 279–291.
Read, H. (1943). *Education through art*. London: Faber and Faber.
Read, H. (1954). Art and the evolution of consciousness. *The Journal of Aesthetics and Art Criticism, 13*(2), 143–155.
Riegel, K. F. (1973). Dialectical operations: The final period of cognitive development. *Human Development, 16*, 346–370.
Rose, K., & Kincheloe, J. (2003). *Art, culture and education: Artful teaching in a fractured landscape*. New York: Peter Lang.
Scott, D. (2000). Spirituality in an integrative age. In V. Kazanjian, H. Kazanjian Jr., & P. Laurence (Eds.), *Education as transformation: Religious pluralism, spirituality, and a new vision for higher education*. New York: Peter Lang Publishing.
Sinnott, J. D. (1998). *The development of logic in adulthood: Postformal thought and its applications*. New York: Springer.
Sinnott, J. D. (2005). The dance of the transforming self: Both feelings of connection and complex thought are needed for learning. *New Directions for Adult and Continuing Education, 108* (Winter), 27–37.
Slaughter, R. (2002). From rhetoric to reality: The emergence of futures into the educational mainstream. In J. Gidley & S. Inayatullah (Eds.), *Youth futures: Comparative research and transformative visions* (pp. 175–186). Westport: Praeger.
Sloan, D. (1983). *Insight-imagination: The emancipation of thought and the modern world*. Westport: Greenwood.

Sloan, D. (1992). Imagination, education and our postmodern possibilities. *ReVision: A Journal of Consciousness and Transformation, 15*(2), 42–53.

Steiner, R. (1904/1959). Cosmic memory: Prehistory of earth and man (GA 11) (1st English ed.) (K. E. Zimmer, Trans.) (Original work published 1904). San Francisco: Harper & Row.

Steiner, R. (1909/1965). *The education of the child in the light of anthroposophy (GA 34)* (2nd ed.) (G. & M. Adams, Trans.) (Original work published 1909). London: Rudolf Steiner Press.

Steiner, R. (1928/1972). *A modern art of education (GA 307)* (3rd ed.) (J. Darrell & G. Adams, Trans.) [14 Lectures, Ilkley, Yorkshire, Aug 5 to 17, 1923] (Original work published 1928). London: Rudolf Steiner Press.

Sternberg, R. J. (1999). *Handbook of creativity*. New York: Cambridge University Press.

Sternberg, R. J. (2001). Why schools should teach for wisdom: The balance theory of wisdom in educational settings. *Educational Psychologist, 36*(4), 227–245.

Subbiondo, J. (2005). An approach to integral education: A case for spirituality in higher education. *ReVision, 28*(2), 18–23.

The Mother. (1955). *On education: Essays on education and self-development, written between 1949 and 1955*. Pondicherry: Sri Aurobindo Ashram Trust.

Thompson, W. I. (2001). *Transforming history: A curriculum for cultural evolution*. Great Barrington: Lindisfarne.

Villaverde, L. E., & Pinar, W. F. (1999). Postformal research: A dialogue on intelligence. In J. Kincheloe, S. Steinberg, & L. E. Villaverde (Eds.), *Rethinking intelligence: Confronting psychological assumptions about teaching and learning* (pp. 247–256). New York: Routledge.

Walkerdine, V. (1988). *The mastery of reason: Cognitive development and the production of rationality*. New York: Routledge.

Wilber, K. (1995/2000). *Sex, ecology, spirituality: The spirit of evolution* (2nd ed., Rev.). Boston: Shambhala.

Woods, G., O'Neill, M., & Woods, P. A. (1997). Spiritual values in education: Lessons from Steiner. *The International Journal of Children's Spirituality, 2*(2), 25–40.

Chapter 7
A Boundary-Crossing Dialogue of Postformal Futures

7.1 Introduction

This chapter offers a series of dialogues to further deepen your understanding of the multiple theoretical facets I have been developing in this book. To set the dialogical scene, interconnections—and distinctions—are indicated between cultural evolutionary approaches that relate to planetary culture as a whole (phylogeny) and developmental psychology approaches related to individual development (ontogeny). The relatively new concepts of integral culture and postformal psychology are shown to be two faces of the one evolution of human consciousness.

The second set of dialogues identifies and maps the convergences and divergences between postformal reasoning and postformal pedagogies, including an analysis of the extent to which Kincheloe and Steinberg's core postformal characteristics align with my theorised postformal reasoning qualities. I then begin a more complex mapping of all of the above relationships to explore how the postformal reasoning qualities and postformal pedagogies intersect with the four evolutionary themes discussed in Chapter 5.

Finally, from the analysis and synthesis, I distil four core pedagogical values: love, life, wisdom and voice. These provide the foundations for my postformal education philosophy, which supports the development of higher stages of reasoning.

7.2 Why a Series of Dialogues?

> Dialogue, as we are choosing to use the word, is a way of exploring the roots of the many crises that face humanity today. It enables inquiry into, and understanding of, the sorts of processes that fragment and interfere with real communication between individuals, nations and even different parts of the same organization. In our modern culture men and women are able to interact with one another in many ways: they can sing dance or play together

J.M. Gidley, *Postformal Education*, Critical Studies of Education 3,
DOI 10.1007/978-3-319-29069-0_7

> with little difficulty but their ability to talk together about subjects that matter deeply to them seems invariably to lead to dispute, division and often to violence. In our view this condition points to a deep and pervasive defect in the process of human thought. (Bohm et al. 1991, Para 1)

I have chosen to use this lengthy quote from David Bohm (1917–1992) and his colleagues to introduce this section because I regard Bohm and his work as a powerful example of the integrative nature of high-level postformal reasoning in action. Although primarily a leading theoretical physicist, Bohm's innovative work spanned quantum theory, neuropsychology, philosophy of mind and activism as he addressed global-societal problems using his dialogue method.

I often wonder at the rich diversity of appearances, values, worldviews and outlooks that we can observe within the "one nature" of our human species. I wonder even more how we can reduce the rich textures of this diversity down to simple binaries like "us" and "them". Perhaps most of us have difficulty comprehending the complexity of pluralism and thus feel compelled to reduce it, for convenience, to simple binaries. Undoubtedly binary logic makes some sense in practical, physical, spatial settings: for example, up and down, left and right, forward and back. However, binaries have less explanatory power the more we move from simple mechanisms that can be explained by classical physics to more complex botanical, zoological and ultimately human life and other noospheric forms. If we bring our full awareness to bear on the complexity of human nature—with its physical, vital, emotional, mental, socio-cultural and moral/ethical/spiritual dimensions—it soon becomes clear that using the simple binary logic of formal reasoning as our highest form of reasoning is far from optimum.

In spite of the vast body of material that has been written about conflict and war, there is a lack of appreciation of the central role of dualistic thinking, based on binary logic, in creating and maintaining conflict. There is even less appreciation of the potential role of postformal reasoning in moving humanity out of the conflict-arousing binary deadlock towards postformal logics such as dialogue, creativity, reflexivity and paradoxical reasoning.

This chapter attempts to open some new doors to understanding higher reasoning through a series of dialogues among the complex theoretical relationships between evolution of consciousness themes, postformal reasoning and postformal manifestations in contemporary education.

7.3 Cultural Evolution and Psychological Development

> Both developmental psychology and evolutionary psychology start with a notion of sequential progress from the simple form of consciousness, which characterises infants and the earliest humans, to the more complex consciousness which characterises mature adults in a postindustrial age. (Neville 2009, p. 69)

This first dialogue explores the interrelationships between cultural evolution (phylogeny) and individual psychological development (ontogeny).

7.3.1 *What do Phylogeny and Ontogeny have in Common?*

[Recapitulation is] . . . the belief that the stage of development of the individual mirror those of the species, and that studying the individual's development will aid our understanding of the species' development: ontogeny recapitulates phylogeny. (Jardine 2006, p. 7)

The theory of recapitulation is a controversial idea that was very popular in the 19th century and came into disrepute by the mid 20th century. It was most commonly used as an evolutionary concept in biology at the turn of the 20th century, and in that domain went out of fashion with more sophisticated theories of genetics. In its most simple form, it is the idea that individual development recapitulates cultural evolution.

Since the main focus of this book is the influence of cultural and psychological developments on educational futures, the biological debates surrounding phylogeny and ontogeny will not concern us here.

This section is a brief general introduction to phylogeny, ontogeny and recapitulation and how they developed in the study of cultural evolution and individual development. The next section looks at current issues with respect to the emergent integral cultural stage discussed in Chapter 2 and the higher-level cognitive abilities of postformal reasoning discussed in Chapter 5. We will consider what light they might throw on recapitulation theory.

7.3.1.1 What is Phylogeny?

[Phylogeny is] . . . the genesis, growth and development of the species. (Jardine 2006).

I have already used the term *phylogeny* several times in relation to cultural evolution. In that context it refers to the cultural development of humans as a whole without regard to any specific cultural, racial or ethnic considerations. As explained in Chapter 2, I chose three theorists of cultural evolution—Steiner, Gebser and Wilber—as my primary sources, with Gebser's model providing the structure of the analysis. To reiterate Gebser's model, he included five structures of consciousness: archaic, magic, mythical, mental-perspectival and integral-aperspectival—the presently emergent culture. To refresh your memory on the parallels between the three approaches, see Chapter 2: Table 2.1. Several other theorists also take an evolutionary—or phylogenetic—view of human culture (Aurobindo 1914/2000; Barfield 1985; Habermas 1979; Jantsch 1981).

7.3.1.2 What is Ontogeny?

[Ontogeny is] . . . the genesis, growth and development of the individual. (Jardine 2006)

The term ontogeny has also been introduced earlier in this book in discussions of individual development. From a psychological—rather than biological—perspective, it encapsulates the idea of individual psychological development through various stages throughout the human lifespan. This concept has been discussed quite fully in Chapter 3 and in Chapter 5 with respect to mature, adult, psychological development. While my focus in Chapter 3 was Piaget's theories of child and adolescent development, we considered a large number of adult development theorists in Chapter 5. Several of these theorists emphasise the ontogenetic—or individual psychological—view of human development (Erikson 1959/1994; Kegan 1994; Kohlberg 1981; Maslow 1971).

7.3.1.3 Hegel, Haeckel and the Controversial Recapitulation Theory

> Inasmuch as he would understand the past and present, [the individual] must pass through all preceding phases of human development and culture, and this should not be done in the way of dead imitation or mere copying, but in the way of living spontaneous self-activity. (Froebel 1887, p. 18)

The notion that ontogeny recapitulates phylogeny is generally attributed to biologist Ernst Haeckel in the late 19th century. However, prior to Haeckel's biological ideas of recapitulation, German Idealism via Hegel and German *Naturphilosophie* offered views about the parallelism between phylogeny and ontogeny. These ideas were taken up by a number of German educational theorists and practitioners, including Johann Heinrich Pestalozzi, Frederich Froebel and Johan Frederich Herbart (Gould 1977/1985). The opening quote of Froebel, cited in Gould, is an expression of how such ideas inspired the educational thought of these 18th- and 19th-century innovators.

Biologist and palaeontologist, Stephen Jay Gould (1941–2002), decided to tackle the controversies in this discussion head-on with his book: *Ontogeny and Phylogeny*. Going beyond biological interpretations of the theory, he pointed to its pervasive influence in child development, education, criminal anthropology, Freudian psychoanalysis and ideologies such as racism (Gould 1977/1985).

As indicated by Gould, the downside is that, like social Darwinism in the 19th century, recapitulation theory came under attack because it was used to support ideologies such as racism. He commented:

> Criminal anthropology and racist ideology used the primitive-as-child argument to reinforce their claims about adults—atavistic deviants or members of lower races, respectively. (Gould 1977/1985, p. 135)

Looking at some of the more positive wider influences of recapitulation theory, Gould noted the uptake of the theory in education. He cited John Dewey's view of recapitulation with regard to educational curricula as follows: "The child is not, educationally speaking, to be led *through* the epochs of the past, but is to be led *by* them to resolve present complex culture into simpler factors, and to understand the *forces* which have produced the present" (Dewey 1911) cited in (Gould 1977/1985).

Gould also discussed Piaget's approach to the phylogeny and ontogeny relationship. He claimed that Piaget's view was more akin to the German *Naturphilosophie*, which claimed a parallel relationship, but not that phylogeny caused ontogeny—which was the Haeckelian view.

In a rather flippant summary of the influence of recapitulation theory on education, Gould made the following comment: "much of the little that is good in modern American education follows an ideal that triumphed with the strong aid of recapitulation" (Gould 1977/1985).

7.3.1.4 Is Recapitulation Theory the only Path to Integration?

> The parallels are real, but phylogeny does not cause ontogeny. Again, two independent sequences follow similar paths under the influence of a common constraint—the structure of the human mind itself. (Gould 1977/1985, p. 147)

Gould is referring to Piaget's position on ontogeny and phylogeny. This parallel relationship appears to be a preferable contemporary path to integrating the two streams. Gebser makes reference to "the parallels between the developmental stages of mankind and those of the individual, in the context of the various structures of consciousness" but does not pursue this in detail (Gebser 1949/1985, p. 58). Gebser's interest appears to focus on grounding the early consciousness in an originary spiritual experience, with limited attention to matters of biological development—he is primarily developing a spiritually oriented, cultural phylogeny.

Steiner was the first to study the symbological—culture and consciousness—relationship between phylogeny and ontogeny (post-Haeckel), prior to Piaget, Freud and Habermas. Steiner applied Haeckel's theories of the relationship between ontogeny and phylogeny in biology to the evolution of culture and consciousness. Steiner, Gebser and Wilber all make significant contributions to this conversation, but none held the simplistic biomechanical view that was understandably discredited.

Steiner claimed that in each new stage of evolution, there is a "recapitulation" of the previous stage in a way that "is something like a repetition of. . .evolution [that] takes place on a higher level" (Steiner 1910/1939, p. 155). He considered this process to be operating at every level of existence, including the previous stages of cosmic existence of the earth (cosmogony), socio-cultural evolution (phylogeny) and individual development (ontogeny).

Wilber wrote significant material on this topic, proposing a complex model of the discredited ontogeny/phylogeny argument (Wilber 1980/1996, 1981/1996). He stated: "The earliest human species was at once a faltering step forward in evolution and an encapsulation of all previous evolution" (Wilber 1981/1996, p. 25). In addition to Steiner and Wilber, several other evolutionary thinkers—including contemporaries—were inspired by the parallels between phylogeny and ontogeny (Combs 2002; Teilhard de Chardin 1959/2002, 1959/2004; Thompson 1998).

Anthropologist Richard Grossinger takes the view that Haeckel was actually dealing in "information theory and deep structure" (Grossinger 2000, p. 330), but because he preceded structuralism, he clothed his theories in natural science. This cybernetic version of recapitulation foreshadowed the scientific notion that a

Table 7.1 Parallels between Gebser's, Piaget's, Postformal and Integrated Models

Phylogeny Ontogeny Integrated	Mythic Concrete Pre-Conventional	Mental Formal Conventional	Integral Postformal Post-Conventional
	Phylogeny – cultural evolution		
Gebser's structures of consciousness	Mythic mode (image)	Mental mode (abstraction)	Integral A-perspectival (integration)
	Ontogeny – psychological development		
Piaget and adult developmental	Piaget: concrete operations	Piaget: formal operations	Postformal reasoning
	Parallels with integrated models		
Kohlberg's moral development	Pre-conventional	Conventional	Post-conventional
Steiner's levels of the mind	Sentient mind (image)	Intellectual mind (abstraction)	Consciousness mind[a] (integration)
Wilber's developmental stages	Pre-rational Mythic	Rational Egoic	Post-rational Integral

Source: Gidley (2007b), Kohlberg (1981), Piaget (1972), Gebser (1949/1985), Steiner (1930/1983) and Wilber (2004)
[a]Steiner also called this stage *consciousness soul.*

complex invisible dimension is infolded within the material world. Bohm's implicate order, Rupert Sheldrake's morphic field and, more recently, Laszlo's Akashic Field require further investigation in this regard (Bohm 1980; László 2006; Sheldrake 2006).

Table 7.1 shows developmental parallels between phylogeny (Gebser), ontogeny (Piaget and adult development) and integrated models (Kohlberg, Steiner and Wilber).

7.3.2 *What do Integral Culture and Postformal Psychology have in Common?*

7.3.2.1 What is Integral Culture?

> Compared to the rest of society, the bearers of Integral Culture have values that are more idealistic and spiritual, have more concern for relationships and psychological

Table 7.2 Reiterating the Key Features of Integral-Aperspectival Consciousness

Integral Consciousness	Extended Interpretation of Integral Culture
Re-integration of the whole person	Originary spiritual presence, magic vitality, mytho-poetic imagination, mental directedness—embodied/enacted through integral transparency.
Integration of dualisms	Such as spirituality and science, imagination and logic, heart and mind, female and male.
Transcending of egotism	Shift from: *small ego* to *pure self* (Wilber); *egoism/egotism* to *higher ego* (Steiner); *egotism/egocentricity* to *ego-freedom* (Gebser).
Transcending linear time	Linear time as a construction of intellectual-mental-rational consciousness (Steiner, Wilber, Gebser).
Planetisation of culture	Teilhard de Chardin coined the term planetisation; importance of global and planetary awareness.
Linguistic self-reflection	Enlivening of language facilitates new consciousness, beyond abstract rationality (Steiner, Gebser).

Source: Gidley (2007b, pp. 111–119)

> development, are more environmentally concerned, and are more open to creating a positive future... The members of this new subculture ... Cultural Creatives... offer hope that we are seeing the emergence of an "Integral Culture" as a successor to Modernism. (Ray 2004, Para 8,14)

The term *integral* is used in a variety of ways in diverse literature, but in this book, primarily according to the usage of Gebser (see Chapter 2). Gebser speaks of it as becoming conscious in oneself and being able to integrate all four previous structures of consciousness: archaic, magic, mythical and mental. He says it is four dimensional—and could be symbolically represented as "a sphere in motion" (Gebser 1949/1985). All the major theorists of the integral culture propose that the first glimmerings were expressed in the Renaissance and that it will continue to grow in critical mass, from now into extended futures.

In Table 7.2 I reiterate the features of integral-aperspectival consciousness as reflected in integral culture, discussed in Chapter 2. The extended interpretations in the right-hand column are from a much larger study (Gidley 2007b, pp. 111–119).

7.3.2.2 What is Postformal Psychology?

> There is general agreement that these postformal (or vision-logic) developments involve at least two or three major stages. Growing beyond abstract universal *formalism* [formal operations], consciousness moves first into a cognition of dynamic relativity and pluralism (early vision-logic), and then further into a cognition of unity, holism, dynamic dialecticism, or universal integralism (middle to late vision-logic). (Wilber 2000, pp. 26–27)

Table 7.3 Reiterating Postformal Reasoning Qualities (Adapted from Table 5.4)

Theorised Postformal Qualities (Gidley)	Extended Interpretation of Postformal Reasoning (Adult Developmental Psychology Research)
Complexity	Incorporating paradox and contradiction
Creativity	Incorporating problem-finding
Dialogical reasoning	Incorporating dialectics, relationality
Ecological reasoning	Incorporating context, process, organicism
Futures reasoning	Incorporating foresight, future mindedness
Higher purpose	Incorporating spirituality, values awareness
Imagination	Incorporating imaginal thinking, mythopoesis
Integration	Incorporating holism, unitary thinking
Intuitive wisdom	Incorporating wisdom, intuition
Language reflexivity	Incorporating construct-aware, voice, language sense
Pluralism	Incorporating non-absolutism, relativism
Reflexivity	Incorporating self-reflection, self-referential thought

Source: Gidley (2007b, 2008b, 2010b, 2010c)

In Chapter 5 I have discussed the qualities associated with postformal reasoning. Ideally when researching, theorising and articulating these qualities, researchers would enact these qualities in their work, instead of expressing them formally. This process would be approaching a postformal psychology.

I now reiterate the twelve postformal reasoning qualities I theorised in Chapter 5: Table 5.1. In Table 7.3, I re-list these qualities (left-hand column) alongside the features others identified (right-hand column) in the original twenty-four features.

7.3.2.3 Synthesising Integral Culture and Postformal Psychology

> As rationality continues its quest for a truly universal or global or planetary outlook… it eventually gives way to a type of cognition I call vision-logic or network-logic… And it is vision-logic that drives and underlies the possibility of a truly planetary culture. (Wilber 1995/2000, pp. 190–191)

Based on the cultural evolution research, it is evident we are entering a new stage of cultural evolution that many refer to as *integral*. Because of this it is now possible for many individuals to not only develop formal operational thinking, but to progress beyond this to incorporate many of the faculties associated with

Table 7.4 Synthesising Integral Culture and Postformal Psychology

Integral Culture and Consciousness	Postformal Reasoning Qualities
Re-integration of the whole person	Integration, imagination, creativity
Integration of dualisms	Complexity, dialogical reasoning
Transcending of egotism	Higher purpose, intuitive wisdom
Transcending linear time	Futures reasoning
Planetisation of culture	Pluralism, ecological reasoning
Linguistic self-reflection	Reflexivity, language reflexivity

Source: Gidley (2007a, 2008a)

postformal reasoning. Only very rare individuals can progress beyond the cognitive level of their own culture. These are the true and great leaders of world culture—and they may exist in any age. Cook-Greuter explained it like this: "At present, mental growth to the postconventional tier and beyond is rare in part because it is not supported by society's prevailing mindset, practices and institutions" (Cook-Greuter 2000, p. 229).

I now explore the relationships between the qualities associated with integral culture and consciousness, reiterated in Table 7.2, and the qualities associated with postformal reasoning, reiterated in Table 7.3. By summarising these relationships as shown in Table 7.4, we can see that there are close parallels between them just as we might expect to find given the parallels we have discovered between phylogeny and ontogeny as a whole. The parallels in Table 7.4 relate specifically to the new culture and consciousness that is arising in our times and that we need to educate for.

A challenge here is that within much integral and postformal research there is bias towards cognicentric content and writing styles, potentially marginalising other types of consciousness research that may reflect and seek to integrate other modes of expression such as affective (Noddings 2005; Sinnott 2005; Zajonc 2005; Nava 2001; Loye 1998), aesthetic (Deleuze and Conley 1992; Derrida 2001; Gidley 2001; Rose and Kincheloe 2003; Roy 2006) or participatory approaches (Ferrer et al. 2005; Hampson 2007; Hart 2000).

7.3.2.4 A Note on Steiner's *Consciousness Soul* and Wilber's *Vision-Logic*

> The true nature of the I [Self] reveals itself only in the consciousness soul. . . . through a certain inner activity. . . if the I wishes to observe itself . . . It must first through an inner

> activity, draw its being out of its own depths in order to have a consciousness of itself. An inner activity of the I begins with a perception of the I, with self-contemplation. (Steiner 1910/1939, p. 31)

> This is the dawning of the age of vision-logic, the rise of the network society, the postmodern, aperspectival, internetted global village. Evolution in all forms has started to become conscious of itself... Kosmic evolution is now producing theories and performances of its own integral embrace. (Wilber 2000, pp. 193–194)

Steiner was one of the first to speak and write about the emergence of a new stage of consciousness beyond abstract, formal, intellectual thinking (Steiner 1904/1993). He spoke of a new "self-reflective consciousness" which cannot only perceive and know the world but become conscious of itself. Adult developmental psychologists refer to this as *reflexivity*—a core quality of postformal reasoning.

What Steiner called *consciousness soul* was a completely new stage of human consciousness by which "the Ego is then able to transform its inner experiences into conscious knowledge of the outer world" (Steiner 1930/1983). Steiner uses the term "I" in relation to the individual observing itself at the consciousness soul stage (Steiner 1910/1939). Wilber uses the abbreviation "I-I" to refer to the "I" who reflects on itself, sometimes also called the "witness" (Wilber 1995/2000). This is clearly Cook-Greuter's "Ego-aware stage"—her first postformal stage.

Wilber coined the term *vision-logic* to describe this stage and it is apt because of its dialectical nature. Wilber has made a significant contribution to the discourse by drawing attention to the emergence of integral consciousness, contemporising and popularising it. His vision-logic foregrounds the dialectical relationship between binary logic and imaginative, visionary or mythic thinking (Hart 1998; Sloan 1983). Wilber describes vision-logic as follows:

> Vision-logic is a higher holon that *operates upon* (and thus transcends) its junior holons, such as simple rationality itself. As such, vision-logic can hold in mind contradictions, it can unify opposites, it is dialectical and non-linear, and it weaves together what otherwise appear to be incompatible notions, as long as they relate together in the new and higher holon. (Wilber 1995/2000)

Wilber's description concurs with Sinnott's view that postformal reasoning enables the ability to operate on different formal logic systems (Sinnott 1998). Interestingly, both Steiner and Wilber used their terms in an integrated manner to characterise both individual and cultural development. Both their meta-perspectives create conceptual bridges between discourses, integrating spiritual models of the layered human being, process-oriented postmodern philosophies, socio-cultural evolution models and developmental psychological models—in Steiner's case an early foreshadowing of contemporary postformal psychology theory.

With respect to our current discussion on phylogeny and ontogeny, Steiner posited that consciousness soul was both (1) a stage that could be attained by all those who seek to develop themselves spiritually and (2) an emergent stage of human consciousness as a whole (Steiner 1971).

7.4 Postformal Psychology and Postformal Education

7.4.1 Postformal Reasoning Qualities and Postformal Pedagogies

In the next stage of analysis and synthesis, I take the twelve clusters of postformal pedagogies that I distilled from the larger group of evolutionary pedagogies in Chapter 6: Table 6.2. I then apply the lens of the twelve postformal reasoning qualities to the list of pedagogies and reorder them to demonstrate their alignment with postformal reasoning (Table 7.5). This strongly suggests that postformal reasoning qualities are already being embedded in the cultural milieu—Foucault's *savoir*—even though this is not a fully conscious and explicit process. Education is becoming postformalised, but is not yet conscious of this, itself.

Table 7.5 Mapping Postformal *Reasoning* and Postformal *Pedagogies*

Theorised Postformal Reasoning Qualities (Gidley)	Postformal *Pedagogies* Re-Ordered to Align with Postformal Reasoning Qualities
Complexity	Complexity in education
Creativity	Creativity in education
Dialogical reasoning	Social and emotional education
Ecological reasoning	Ecological, environmental and sustainability education
Futures reasoning	Futures and foresight education
Higher purpose	Spiritual, transformative and contemplative education
Imagination	Imaginative education
Integration	Integral and holistic education
Intuitive wisdom	Wisdom education
Language reflexivity	Aesthetic, artistic and poetic education
Pluralism	Critical, postcolonial, global & planetary education
Reflexivity	Postmodern and poststructuralist education

Source: Gidley (2007a, 2008a, 2009, 2010a)

7.4.2 Paradoxes of Postformal Research

7.4.2.1 Postformal Reasoning and Kincheloe's Post-formality

> Postformalists draw upon [multiple] analyses, producing in the process a psychology of complexity that accounts for the interaction of self and context, the intricacies of memory and concept building, and the value of cross/multicultural cognitive insights. . . This pursuit of new levels of human possibility is central to the *raison d'être* of postformal education. (Kincheloe 2006, p. 7)

Table 7.6 Postformal Reasoning and Kincheloe and Steinberg's Postformalism

Postformalism **Kincheloe and Steinberg Theorisation**	**Postformal Reasoning Features** **Gidley Theorisation**
• *Etymology*	
The origins of knowledge	Reflexivity (reflection on origins of self)
Thinking about thinking and imagination	Imagination (imagination)
Problem detection (meta-awareness)	Creativity (problem-finding)
• *Pattern*	
Deep patterns and structures	Higher purpose (deeper purpose)
Metaphoric cognition	Intuitive wisdom (higher wisdom)
Connection between mind and ecosystem	Ecological reasoning (ecology)
• *Process*	
Deconstruction—world as text	Language reflexivity (deconstruction)
Logic-emotion links	Integration (head and heart)
Non-linear holism	Complexity (non-linear processes)
• *Contextualisation*	
Attending to the contextual setting	Futures reasoning[a] *historical reasoning*
Particularity and generalisation	Dialogical reasoning (part-whole)
Uncovering the role of power	Pluralism (multiplicity of power)

Source: Gidley (2008b, 2009, 2010c), Kincheloe and Steinberg (1993) Kincheloe et al. (1999a)
[a]I place futures reasoning here, which at first may seem the least likely fit of all the qualities. Although this feature of Kincheloe's model "attending to the contextual setting" is more related to historical context, it does involve a sense of time and therefore is more likely to allow for a futures reasoning element than other qualities.

Important similarities and differences can be found between Kincheloe and Steinberg's "post-formal way of thinking" and the postformal reasoning qualities.

The many similarities are indicated in Table 7.6 where I map Kincheloe and Steinberg's postformalism against the postformal reasoning qualities, theorised in Chapter 5. The analysis also reveals potential gaps in the literature and unidentified features that fall between the "postformal cracks".

Firstly, although Kincheloe and Steinberg do not specify complexity as one of their key terms, when you read both their seminal paper (Kincheloe and Steinberg 1993) and some of Kincheloe's extended writings on the theme (Kincheloe 2006; Kincheloe et al. 1999a), it is clear that complexity is central to their post-formality. In the opening quote, Kincheloe refers to their postformalism as a "psychology of complexity". So complexity is an important similarity.

Secondly, on the surface there appear to be some crucial differences that I want to elucidate. These may be simply terminological differences or may reflect deep conceptual differences. This is what I will attempt to unravel with a hermeneutic analysis of the terms by trying to arrive at their deeper meaning. The main discrepancies in relation to actual qualities are as follows:

- *Origins of Knowledge*: This is part of their core theme of Etymology and does not appear in the psychology research. However, their three-paragraph description of "origins of knowledge" gives it a strong self-reflective quality (Kincheloe and Steinberg 1993, pp. 302–303). Consequently, I relate it to reflexivity. Kincheloe includes "self-knowledge [as] a central feature of postformalism" (Kincheloe 2006, p. 106).
- *Futures Reasoning*: Kincheloe and Steinberg's theory does not include any explicit reference to futures thinking, but then neither does the adult development research. Since this is one of my additions arising from the megatrends of the mind research, it does not indicate a major discrepancy. Futures reasoning only appears in a minor form in the psychology research (Seligman and Csikszentmihalyi 2000). Furthermore, I know from personal communication that Kincheloe was interested in futures thinking and especially in educational futures, although he does not explicitly use futures as one of his core terms.[1]

The third point I want to make is that Kincheloe and Steinberg's post-formality is normative/critical/ethical. These values do not appear widely in the psychology research on postformal reasoning. This is likely to be a feature of the underlying empiricist mindset in psychology, even in the more humanistic and positive sub-fields. If adult developmental psychologists are attempting to establish postformal reasoning qualities by empirical research which is expected to be objective and values-neutral—as empirical psychology research demands—then how can they also take a critical, normative perspective? Can it be that postformal psychology research is actually trapped in the very thing it strives to transcend—the limitations of formal operations? This is a question for further research and I begin to discuss it below in Section 7.4.2.5.

7.4.2.2 Diverging Views of Development and Intelligence

> Starting with the proposition that cognitive development is not a simple, linear process that is biologically determined, postformalism moves directly into a more complex zone than previous approaches to cognition. Because of this complexity, postformalism insists that the idea of universal stage theories designed to describe the process of human development be reworked in a way that accepts a variety of avenues leading us to diverse models of cognitive wisdom. (Kincheloe 2006, p. 9)

[1]Personal email communication from Joe Kincheloe (14th June 2008): "I'm especially interested in your work on futurism. Would you be interested in writing a book on futures and education (broadly defined)"?

Postformal reasoning from the perspective of the psychology research is distinctly developmental—although there are differences within the field regarding the extent to which qualities represent stages.

By contrast Kincheloe and Steinberg's work includes a critique of modernist conceptions of developmentalism. Kincheloe and others refer to what they call "the cultural hegemony of some developmentalist approaches" (Kincheloe et al. 1999b). Kincheloe and Steinberg's primary critique of Piaget's developmentalism—and presumably also of the adult developmental psychology research on postformal reasoning—is that such developmentalism "falls captive to the grand narrative of intelligence" (Kincheloe and Steinberg 1993, p. 298). They explain this in terms of what they see as exclusions from the "community of intelligence" which cluster around "exclusions based on race (the non-White), class (the poor), and gender (the feminine)" (Kincheloe and Steinberg 1993, p. 298).

While these views are normative and healthy in response to the extent of social exclusion in the USA, some postformal education researchers reflect the more extreme cultural relativism found in some schools of postmodern thought, including antipathy to any normative or hierarchical values. Such strong anti-developmentalism that can lead to undervaluing, if not totally ignoring, the adult developmental psychology research on postformal (Malott 2011) must be challenged.

What I find interesting in these statements by Kincheloe is that he has no problem with the idea of cognitive development per se, but only with the dominant "narrative of intelligence" as he puts it. It is clear in several of his writings that he supports the notions of higher-order thinking and evolution of consciousness: "Postformalism asserts that there is no reason why a wide range of people from diverse and sometimes subjugated backgrounds can't learn to engage in a higher order of thinking, a mode of cognition central to the evolution of the human species" (Kincheloe 2006, p. 9). Elsewhere he claims: "The scholarly project of postformalism [is] based on the creation of the highest level of intellectual insight possible" (Kincheloe 2006, p. 20).

Their other critique of the default notion of intelligence is that the highest levels of it are equated with formal operations—or in other words, "mastery of formal logical categories". As I have demonstrated in Chapter 5, in accord with Kincheloe and Steinberg's views, formal operations should no longer be regarded as the highest level of cognitive functioning, as much evidence suggests otherwise, and because of its limitations for complex futures. Although they refer to Piaget's original writings, their adult developmental psychology references were quite limited. Their theory has not had the benefit—giving the timing of publication (1993)—of some of the more recent comprehensive and nuanced approaches to postformal reasoning (Bassett 2005a; Commons and Ross 2008; Sinnott 1998, 2005).

7.4.2.3 Formal or Postformal Presentation of Research

> The theory presented here and in other papers on the Model of Hierarchical Complexity (Commons et al., 1998) makes seven predictions... 1. There are exactly six stages from the beginning of schooling to adulthood in which we find participants performing. 2. Sequentiality of stage is perfect. 3. Absolutely no mixing of stage scores takes place. (Commons and Richards 2002, p. 166)

> Cognitive cubism produces a multidimensional form of knowledge that is always open to new interpretations in its hermeneutical connection to larger social, cultural, political, and cognitive processes. (Kincheloe 2006, p. 155)

Another paradox is that much of the psychology research establishing *postformal* thinking has been framed and presented from a formal, mental-rational mode. Although the content of the psychological research is related to analysing, verifying and elaborating stages of postformal reasoning, much of this research is undertaken from within a *formal* empirical paradigm. The language of the first quote above exemplifies a formal empirical approach as demonstrated by Michael Commons, a leading researcher on postformal stage development. While this formal scientific theorising has clearly contributed a great deal to the discourse by giving it credibility within the academy—which is still largely operating from this mode—it is important that this does not set a biased template for validity of research in this area.

By contrast, the quote from Kincheloe's educational research on *postformality* involves a more complex, postmodern and nuanced approach to language.

Kincheloe and Steinberg attempt to present their research and writing in ways that challenge the formal, modernist, academic paradigm. They warn against the challenges of undertaking postformal research within "formal" settings. In short, the postformal educators research and write more *postformally* than the psychologists.

Referring to the postformal education researcher as a bricoleur, Kincheloe and his co-author Kathleen Berry question rhetorically:

> How does the bricoleur avoid slippage into formalist discourses to describe and interpret the narratives, data, collected knowledge by self and other researchers? How and why can the bricoleur negotiate the borders between formalist and postformalist discourses that recognize the contradictions between and the limitations of both yet produce new insights, social values, structuring devices, and actions? (Kincheloe and Berry 2004, P. 136)

7.4.2.4 Isolationism within the Postformal Terrain

Although Kincheloe and Steinberg's early work made explicit reference to some of the adult developmental psychology work on postformal reasoning, even if only to critique it, later educators drawing on Kincheloe's postformalism seem unaware of this significant psychology research on postformal qualities (Malott 2011). Furthering the rift between the two disciplines, those few adult developmental psychology researchers who are working in an educational arena (Sinnott 1998; Sternberg 2001;

Arlin 1999; Bassett 2005b) demonstrate no awareness of the growing body of literature on post-formal education.

7.4.2.5 A Proposed Complex Postformal Resolution

> Since one of the important features of post-formal thinking involves the production of one's own knowledge it becomes important to note in any discussion of the characteristics of post-formality that few boundaries exist to limit what may be considered post-formal thinking. (Kincheloe and Steinberg 1993, p. 300)

In summary, my dialogue on the similarities and differences between the research on postformal reasoning by adult developmental psychologists and the post-formal cognitive theory of Kincheloe and Steinberg has led me to draw a number of conclusions. Firstly, my research leaves me in no doubt that there are levels of adult reasoning beyond Piaget's formal operations that include multiple postformal reasoning features, which can be clustered into a dozen or so individual qualities. Secondly, while there are many similarities between the qualities identified by psychologists and those identified by Kincheloe and Steinberg, there are also differences as to how they approach post-formality across the two disciplines. Should a *postformal* education philosophy find ways to integrate these contradictions?

As an academic researcher with a professional background in both psychology and education, perhaps I am well placed to create a philosophical and epistemological bridge between the two—or at least begin to articulate the gap. Reflecting on the differences I now distinguish three types of postformal theorising:

- *Empirical postformality*. Under this theme I include the empirical and theoretical cognitive research that uses the formal methods of empirical psychology, mathematics and/or formal logic to establish that it is possible to go beyond its own formality. This approach attempts to be objective and values-neutral. It is not self-reflective, embodied or involved in participating in or enacting its own findings (Arlin 1975; Commons et al. 1982; Kramer 1983; Riegel 1973; Sinnott 1994; Yan and Arlin 1995).
- *Critical postformality*. From this perspective, postformality is both a theoretical and an embodied approach. Researchers working within this view of postformal thought incorporate many of the features of what psychologists call postformal reasoning into the enactment of their work. This approach does not feign objectivity and is explicitly normative in its values (Horn 2001; Kincheloe 2006; Rose and Kincheloe 2003; Steinberg and Kincheloe 2004; Kincheloe and Steinberg 1999; Kincheloe et al. 1999b; Villaverde and Pinar 1999).
- *Philosophical and epistemological postformality*. Neither of these two approaches (empirical or critical postformality) gives adequate recognition to the other. While critical postformalists acknowledge adult developmental theories, they are highly critical of their underlying assumptions. On the other hand even those adult developmental psychologists who have an educational interest

ignore the postformal education literature completely. There is a need for a more embracing approach to postformality, and I propose that more research be undertaken to explore the relationships between them as I have begun to do in this book. My approach, which examines both types of postformality, is epistemological in that it looks at changes in ways of thinking over time, both individually and culturally. It is also philosophical in attempting to grapple with some of the bigger planetary issues that are ignored in the psychology research. Although critical and normative, my approach also sees a place for empirical psychology research given the dominant evidence-based paradigm. This book could be positioned as a humble beginning to such an ambitious project.

7.5 Postformal Psychology and Education and Evolutionary Themes

7.5.1 Postformal Reasoning and Evolutionary Themes

Table 7.7 reiterates the discussions in Chapter 5 that develop the relationships between the evolutionary themes and the postformal reasoning qualities.

Table 7.7 Evolutionary Themes and Postformal Reasoning Qualities

Evolutionary Theme Summary	**Postformal *Reasoning* Qualities**
Theme 1: conscious, compassionate, spiritual development	Higher purpose Dialogical reasoning Integration
Theme 2: mobile, life-enhancing thinking	Imagination Ecological reasoning Futures reasoning
Theme 3: complexification of thinking and culture	Creativity Complexity Intuitive wisdom
Theme 4: linguistic and paradigmatic boundary-crossing	Reflexivity Language reflexivity Pluralism

Source: Gidley (2009)

7.5.2 Postformal Pedagogies and Evolutionary Themes

Table 7.8 reiterates the discussions in Chapter 6 that develop the relationships between the evolutionary themes and the postformal pedagogies.

Table 7.8 Evolutionary Themes and Postformal Pedagogies

Evolutionary Theme Summary	Postformal *Pedagogies*
Theme 1: conscious, compassionate, spiritual development	Spiritual, transformative and contemplative education Social and emotional education Integral and holistic education
Theme 2: mobile, life-enhancing thinking	Imaginative education Ecological, environmental and sustainable education Futures and foresight education
Theme 3: complexification of thinking and culture	Creativity in education Complexity in education Wisdom education
Theme 4: linguistic and paradigmatic boundary-crossing	Postmodern and poststructuralist education Aesthetic, artistic and poetic education Critical, postcolonial, global and planetary education

Source: Gidley (2009)

7.5.3 Postformal Reasoning, Pedagogies and Evolutionary Themes

The next mapping exercise brings together the four evolutionary themes, the postformal reasoning qualities and the postformal pedagogies that best support the development of these qualities (Table 7.9).

Table 7.9 Postformal Reasoning, Evolutionary Themes, Postformal Pedagogies

Postformal *Reasoning*	Evolutionary Themes	Postformal *Pedagogies*
Higher purpose Dialogical reasoning Integration	**Theme 1:** conscious, compassionate spiritual development	Spiritual, transformative, contemplative Social and emotional education Integral and holistic education
Imagination Ecological reasoning Futures reasoning	**Theme 2:** mobile, life-enhancing thinking	Imaginative education Ecological, environmental and sustainable Futures and foresight education
Creativity Complexity Intuitive wisdom	**Theme 3:** complexification of thinking and culture	Creativity in education Complexity in education Wisdom education
Reflexivity Language reflexivity Pluralism	**Theme 4:** linguistic and paradigmatic boundary-crossing	Postmodern and poststructuralist Aesthetic, artistic and poetic Critical, postcolonial, global and planetary

Source: Gidley (2009, 2010a)

7.6 Postformal Psychology, Postformal Education, Themes and Values

> [Goethe's] delicate empiricism has its own version of the phenomenological epoché, and, like Husserl's technique of imaginative variation, it strives to disclose the essential or archetypal structure of the phenomenon through the endowment of human imagination. (Robbins 2006, p. 1)

As I entered more consciously into the interrelationships among the postformal reasoning qualities, the postformal pedagogies and the four evolutionary themes that emerged from the evolution of consciousness discourses, the themes themselves began to reveal their deeper meanings to me. In a manner that resonates with the Goethean notion of "delicate empiricism", the themes, as phenomena, began to speak to me about what they meant in terms of core psychological values and core pedagogical values. I have elsewhere coined the term *delicate theorising* for my theoretical work (Gidley 2010a).

As you will see from the discussion below, summarised in Tables 7.10, 7.11, 7.12 and 7.13, four core values were synthesised from these in-depth analyses: love, life, wisdom and voice. These four qualities when they are taken into the realm of pedagogical values are *central* to my postformal education philosophy.

7.6.1 Evolutionary Themes, Postformal Reasoning and Core Values

In this section, I draw together the findings presented in Chapter 5 including the extensive research by adult developmental psychologists to establish the empirical and theoretical validation of over twenty features of mature adult thinking. I include several additional features that I uncovered through my broader scanning of cultural history and futures studies, and megatrends of the mind research.

My documentation in this chapter of the complex interrelationships, among all these phenomena, builds a convincing case to support the claims in the evolution of consciousness research that something new and qualitatively different is happening in culture and consciousness as this century unfolds.

Table 7.10 offers a glimpse into the process of my theorising that led to the distillation of my core values: love, life, wisdom and voice. While another researcher might interpret the phenomena differently, it is clear to me that these core values and their sub-components are intimately related to both the postformal qualities and the evolutionary themes.

Table 7.10 Evolutionary Themes, Postformal Reasoning and Core Values

Evolutionary Themes and Postformal *Reasoning*	**Core Values**
Theme 1: conscious compassionate spiritual development	***Love***
Higher purpose (putting something else before personal self)	Service
Dialogical reasoning (respecting the views of the "other")	Compassion
Integration (integrating the heart with thinking and action)	Heart
Theme 2: mobile life-enhancing thinking	***Life***
Imagination (bringing our thinking to life)	Vitality
Ecological reasoning (respect for the balance of nature)	Nature
Futures reasoning (responsibility for long-term habitability)	Sustainability
Theme 3: complexification of thinking and culture	***Wisdom***
Creativity (taking novel and multiple perspectives)	Novelty
Complexity (acceptance of contradiction and paradox)	Paradox
Intuitive wisdom (developing one's intuitive knowing)	Intuition
Theme 4: linguistic and paradigmatic boundary-crossing	***Voice***
Reflexivity (reflecting on one's thoughts feelings and values)	Self-knowledge
Language reflexivity (being conscious of our language)	Language
Pluralism (recognising power and worth and their many voices)	Relativism

Source: Adapted from Gidley (2009)

7.6.2 Evolutionary Themes, Postformal Pedagogies and Core Values

Table 7.11 summarises the process of my theorising that led to the distillation of my four core *pedagogical* values: love—an evolutionary force; life—a sustaining force; wisdom—a creative force; and voice—an empowering force. By associating the postformal pedagogies that best align to the evolutionary theme, and partnering them with one of the core pedagogical values and the keywords that arise in the literature related to these values, I begin to build a picture of evolutionary education.

Table 7.11 Postformal Pedagogies, Evolutionary Themes and Core Values

Evolutionary Themes and Postformal *Pedagogies*	**Pedagogical Core Values**
Theme 1: conscious compassionate spiritual development	***Love***
Spiritual, transformative and contemplative education	Reverence
Social and emotional education	Care
Integral and holistic education	Head and heart
Theme 2: mobile life-enhancing thinking	***Life***
Imaginative education	Imagination
Ecological, environmental and sustainability education	Ecology
Futures and foresight education	Foresight
Theme 3: complexification of thinking and culture	***Wisdom***
Creativity in education	Creativity
Complexity in education	Multi-modality
Wisdom education	Layering
Theme 4: linguistic and paradigmatic boundary-crossing	***Voice***
Postmodern and poststructuralist education	Self-reflection
Aesthetic, artistic and poetic education	Silence
Critical, postcolonial, global and planetary education	Multi-cultural

Source: Adapted from Gidley (2009)

7.6.3 Evolutionary Themes, Postformal Reasoning, Pedagogies and Values

Finally, in Table 7.12, I cohere all the meta-components of my philosophy:

- The evolutionary themes that arose from the evolution of consciousness research;
- The postformal reasoning qualities theorised from the adult developmental psychology, cultural evolution and megatrends of the mind research;
- The postformal pedagogies emerging from the three evolutionary waves; and
- The four core pedagogical values I distilled from all of the above.

The application of these core pedagogical values to education is our direction now.

Table 7.12 Themes, Postformal Reasoning, Pedagogies and Core Values

Evolutionary Themes and Postformal *Reasoning*	**Core Pedagogical Values and Postformal *Pedagogies***
Theme 1: *conscious compassionate spiritual development*	***Love:*** *reverence, care, integrating head and heart*
Higher purpose	Spiritual, transformative, contemplative
Dialogical reasoning	Social and emotional education
Integration	Integral and holistic education
Theme 2: *mobile life-enhancing thinking*	***Life:*** *imagination, ecology, foresight*
Imagination	Imaginative education
Ecological reasoning	Ecological, environmental, sustainable
Futures reasoning	Futures and foresight education
Theme 3: *complexification of thinking and culture*	***Wisdom:*** *creative, multi-modal, layered*
Creativity	Creativity in education
Complexity	Complexity in education
Intuitive wisdom	Wisdom education
Theme 4: *linguistic and paradigmatic boundary-crossing*	***Voice:*** *self-reflection, silence, multi-cultural*
Reflexivity	Postmodern and poststructuralist
Language reflexivity	Aesthetic, artistic and poetic education
Pluralism	Critical, postcolonial, global, planetary

Source: Gidley (2007b, 2008b, 2010b, 2010c, 2012, 2013)

7.7 Four Core Pedagogical Values

7.7.1 Pedagogies for Evolving Culture and Consciousness

> And the strength of the thread does not reside in the fact that some fibre runs through its whole length, but in the overlapping of many fibres. (Wittgenstein 1968, p. 32)[2]

[2]I came across this quote from Wittgenstein in *To Dwell with a Boundless Heart: Essays in Curriculum Theory, Hermeneutics, and the Ecological Imagination* (Jardine 1998, p. 25).

Figure 7.1 and Table 7.13 illustrate the complexly interwoven threads of my postformal education philosophy with its multiple fibres of postformal, philosophical, psychological and educational theory. See Figure 6.1 for links to evolutionary themes.

There are many limitations of presenting such complex information in table diagrams and other graphical forms. There are also challenges in presenting the information in text. I am deliberately presenting the information in a variety of forms: (1) to show the light reflecting on the various facets; (2) because individual readers have different learning styles; and (3) to exemplify a multi-modal presentation style that should assist understanding for a diverse audience.

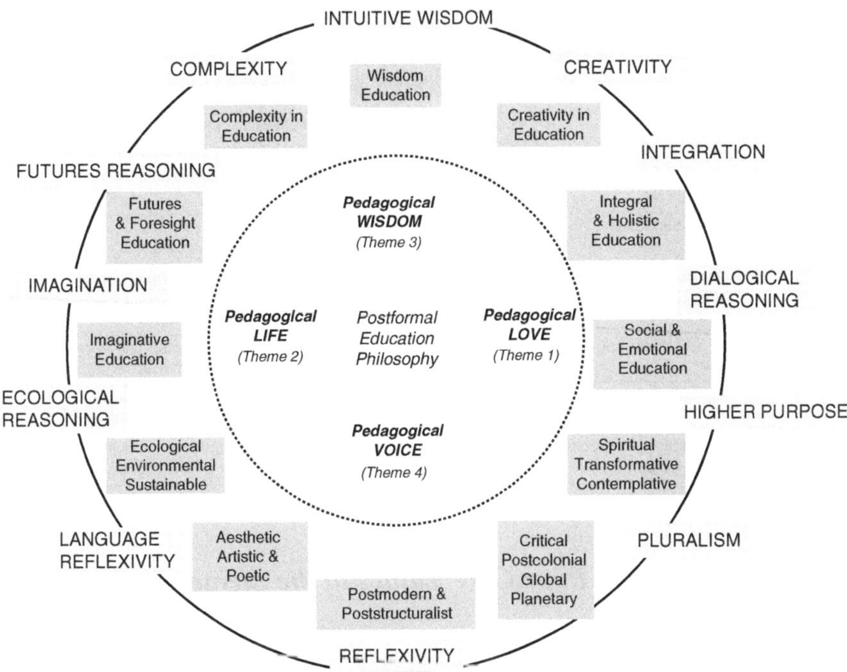

Figure 7.1 Postformal Education Philosophy for Complex Futures (Source: Adapted from: (Gidley 2007b, 2008b, 2010b, 2010c, 2012, 2013)

Table 7.13 Postformal Pedagogies Supporting four Core Pedagogical Values

Postformal Educational Approaches Supporting the *Pedagogy of Love* [Educational styles that emphasise care, contemplation, empathy, love and reverence]	
Integral and holistic education	Includes broad, eclectic holistic education and also specific integral/integrative approaches.
Social and emotional education	There are primarily two types: explicit, conceptual, curricular approaches and implicit, contextual, relational.
Spiritual, transformative and contemplative education	Diversity in spiritual values, non-denominational, and also contemplative and other transformative approaches to learning.
Postformal Educational Approaches Supporting the *Pedagogy of Life* [Educational styles that support shifts from *static* concepts to *living* thinking]	
Imaginative education	Imagination is an important dimension in bringing concepts to life, and thus supporting the development of vitality in thinking.
Ecological, environmental and sustainability education	Approaches grounded in ecological perspectives, environmental awareness, respect for natural surroundings and sustainability.
Futures and foresight education	Encouraging foresight, long-term thinking, and imaginative visioning of preferred futures, not merely perpetuating the past
Postformal Educational Approaches Supporting the *Pedagogy of Wisdom* [Educational styles that stimulate creativity, complexity and multiperspectivality]	
Wisdom education	There are specific educational theories and practices addressed to the cultivation of wisdom.
Complexity in education	Educational approaches that draw from and embrace the science and philosophy of complexity.
Creativity in education	Beyond creativity as an "add-on" in education, and recognising creativity as a fundamental educational underpinning.
Postformal Educational Approaches Supporting the *Pedagogy of Voice/Language* [Encouragement of sensitivity to linguistic, cultural and paradigmatic contexts.]	
Aesthetic, artistic and poetic education	Approaches that cultivate aesthetic sensibility through exposure to and participation in a wide range of artistic activities.
Postmodern and poststructuralist education	Integrating the contributions of continental, especially French, philosophy in identifying the politics of voice and marginality.
Critical, postcolonial, global and planetary education	Further enhancing awareness of dominant political voices and the rights of marginal cultures and sub-cultures to have a voice.

Source: Gidley (2011)

7.7.2 *Applying the Four Core Values to the Steiner National Curriculum*

> Gidley (2009) identifies four core values, which she describes as the "pedagogies of love, life, wisdom and voice." In her view these pedagogies best characterise the discussion of educational futures that are oriented towards the development of further stages of thinking and learning… References taken from Gidley (2009) provide further academic grounding for the Steiner perspectives. (Steiner Education Australia 2011, p. 34)

When the Australian government created its first National Curriculum in 2009, it took the unprecedented step of inviting Steiner Education Australia (and Montessori Australia) to register for approval. My research[3] on the evolution of consciousness

[3]Because of my experience and research, I was engaged as Consultant Research Advisor to this project.

Table 7.14 Postformal Education Philosophy and Australian Steiner Curriculum

Australian National Curriculum	Steiner Curriculum Guidelines	Postformal Education Philosophy (Gidley 2007a, 2008b, 2009, 2011)
	Heart	Pedagogical love
Understanding	Understanding	Love and warmth
Confident and creative individuals	Confident and creative individuals	Warmth, care, relationships, community, belonging, reverence, connectedness.
	Hands	Pedagogical life
Skills	Skills	Life and vitality
Translating theory into practical application	Knowledge transformed into experience.	Process, discovery, movement, ecology. Bringing learning to life imaginatively.
	Head	Pedagogical wisdom
Knowledge	Knowledge	Light of wisdom
Successful Learners	Powerful Learners	Multi-modal learning modes, multiple intelligences, creativity, complexity.
	Moral capacity	Pedagogical voice
Active and informed citizens	Active and informed citizens	Balance through voice/language. Students finding voice, deep knowing.

Source: Adapted from (Gidley 2007a, 2008b, 2009, 2011) and Steiner Education Australia (2011)

and education that led to my theorisation of the four core pedagogical values was included as a philosophical underpinning. The approved Steiner National Curriculum is published online for interested readers (Steiner Education Australia 2011).

The four main categories of the Australian National Curriculum (understanding, skills, knowledge and active and informed citizens) were used in the Steiner Curriculum design as templates for content description and elaboration. Table 7.14 shows how the Steiner Curriculum Project team integrated the four core pedagogical values that underpin my postformal education philosophy and associated research into the overall design of the Steiner National Curriculum. This is an important part of the process of validating a philosophical approach through the lens of theory-in-practice. Further research could establish how successfully it works.

7.8 Concluding Remarks

Part III of this book will expand on these developments as I further articulate my postformal education philosophy—a philosophy created to nurture evolving consciousness. I include numerous rich, creative examples from my—and others'—teaching experience in the evolving *art* of education.

The following four chapters (Chapters 8, 9, 10 and 11) each begin with a conceptual/theoretical discussion of the area of focus, followed by practical examples of how it may be applied in "the classroom"—bearing in mind that "the classroom" is not confined to an actual physical room in a school but rather world as classroom. The conceptual components of each chapter include philosophical and theoretical background to understanding the particular pedagogical value.

The practical examples draw from my own experience and that of other educational theorists, researchers and practitioners.

Since all of these themes are emerging as components of the complex, postformal mindset, they are not mutually exclusive but are complexly interconnected. My decision to treat them in separate chapters relates to my interest in fully honouring each in its particularity and my recognition that most researchers (even postformal ones) do indeed have their favourite emphasis.

While in mainstream education, these four values may seem *peripheral* to the "*real* task" of information acquisition, what I will show you in Chapters 8, 9, 10 and 11 is that they are fundamental values that can potentially rescue education from its current demise as a viable and vital source of cultural renewal.

My educational vision presented in Part III shows how the four pedagogical values—love, life, wisdom and voice—are central to a caring, revitalised, wise education, through explorations of:

- Pedagogical love: an evolutionary force;
- Pedagogical life: a sustaining force;
- Pedagogical wisdom: a creative force; and
- Pedagogical voice: an empowering force.

All four core values and their associated themes, qualities and pedagogies are in dynamic, interrelationship with each other. The postformal education philosophy arising from my research is not static but complexly interwoven and dynamic.

References

Arlin, P. K. (1975). Cognitive development in adulthood: A fifth stage? *Developmental Psychology, 11*(5), 602–606.

Arlin, P. K. (1999). The wise teacher: A developmental model of teaching. *Theory Into Practice, 38*(1), 12–17.

Aurobindo, S. (1914/2000). *The life divine. 2nd American edition* (Originally published in the monthly review *Arya* 1914–1920). Twin Lakes: Lotus Press.

Barfield, O. (1985). *History in English words*. Herndon: Lindisfarne Books.

Bassett, C. (2005a). Emergent wisdom: Living a life in widening circles. *ReVision: A Journal of Consciousness and Transformation, 27*(4), 6–11.

Bassett, C. (2005b, October) Wisdom in three acts: Using transformative learning to teach for wisdom [Electronic version]. In *Sixth International Transformative Learning Conference*, East Lansing, Michigan.

Bohm, D. (1980). *Wholeness and the implicate order*. London: Ark Paperbacks.

Bohm, D., Factor, D., & Garrett, P. (1991). *Dialogue—A proposal*. [Electronic article] http://www.david-bohm.net/dialogue/dialogue_proposal.html. Accessed 31 July 2015.

Combs, A. (2002). *The radiance of being: Understanding the grand integral vision: Living the integral life*. St. Paul: Paragon House.

Commons, M. L., & Richards, F. A. (2002). Organizing components into combination: How stage transition works. *Journal of Adult Development, 9*(3), 159–177.

Commons, M. L., & Ross, S. (2008). What postformal thought is, and why it matters. *World Futures, 64*, 321–329.

Commons, M. L., Richards, F. A., & Kuhn, D. (1982). Systematic and metasystematic reasoning: A case for levels of reasoning beyond Piaget's stage of formal operations. *Child Development, 53*(4), 1058–1069.

Cook-Greuter, S. R. (2000). Mature ego development: A gateway to ego transcendence. *Journal of Adult Development, 7*(4), 227–240.

Deleuze, G., & Conley, T. (1992). *The fold: Leibniz and the Baroque*. Minneapolis: University of Minnesota Press.

Derrida, J. (2001). Structure, sign, and play in the discourse of the human sciences [Electronic version]. In *Writing and difference* (pp. 278–294).

Dewey, J. (1911). Culture epoch theory. In P. Monroe (Ed.), *A cyclopedia of education* (Vol. 2, pp. 240–242). New York: Macmillan.

Erikson, E. H. (1959/1994). *Identity and the life cycle*. New York: Norton.

Ferrer, J., Romero, M., & Albareda, R. (2005). Integral transformative education: A participatory proposal. *Journal of Transformative Education, 3*(4), 306–330.

Froebel. (1887). *The education of man*. New York: D. Appleton.

Gebser, J. (1949/1985). *The ever-present origin*. Athens: Ohio University Press.

Gidley, J. (2001, June). The dancer at the edge of knowledge: Imagination as a transdisciplinary force. In *The 2nd International Philosophy, Science and Theology Festival*, Grafton, NSW, Australia.

Gidley, J. (2007a). Educational imperatives of the evolution of consciousness: The integral visions of Rudolf Steiner and Ken Wilber. *International Journal of Children's Spirituality, 12*(2), 117–135.

Gidley, J. (2007b). The evolution of consciousness as a planetary imperative: An integration of integral views. *Integral Review: A Transdisciplinary and Transcultural Journal for New Thought, Research and Praxis, 5*, 4–226.

Gidley, J. (2008a). Beyond homogenisation of global education: Do alternative pedagogies such as Steiner Education have anything to offer and emergent globalising world? In S. Inayatullah, M. Bussey, & I. Milojevic (Eds.), *Alternative educational futures: Pedagogies for emergent worlds*. Rotterdam: Sense Publishers.

Gidley, J. (2008b). *Evolving education: A postformal-integral-planetary gaze at the evolution of consciousness and the educational imperatives*. PhD dissertation. Southern Cross University, Lismore.

Gidley, J. (2009). Educating for evolving consciousness: Voicing the emergency for love, life and wisdom. In *The International handbook of education for spirituality, care and wellbeing* (Springer International Handbooks of Religion and Education Series). New York: Springer.

Gidley, J. (2010a). Evolving higher education integrally: Delicate mandalic theorising. In S. Esbjörn-Hargens, O. Gunnlaugson, & J. Reams (Eds.), *Integral education: New directions for higher learning* (pp. 345–361). New York: State University of New York Press.

Gidley, J. (2010b). Globally scanning for megatrends of the mind: Potential futures of "futures thinking". *Futures: The Journal of Policy, Planning and Futures Studies, 42*(10), 1040–1048.

Gidley, J. (2010c). Postformal priorities for postnormal times: A rejoinder to Ziauddin Sardar. *Futures: The Journal of Policy, Planning and Futures Studies, 42*(6), 625–632.

Gidley, J. (2011). From crisis to confidence: The development of social and emotional education in Australia. In B. Hey (Ed.), *Social and emotional education: International analysis II* (pp. 69–101). Santander: Fundacione Marcelino Botin.

Gidley, J. (2012). Evolution of education: From weak signals to rich imaginaries of educational futures. *Futures: The Journal of Policy, Planning and Futures Studies, 44*(1), 46–54.

Gidley, J. (2013). Global knowledge futures: Articulating the emergence of a new meta-level field. *Integral Review: A Transdisciplinary and Transcultural Journal for New Thought Research and Praxis, 9*(2), 145–172.

Gould, S. J. (1977/1985). *Ontogeny and phylogeny*. Cambridge, MA: Belknap Press, Imprint of Harvard University Press.

Grossinger, R. (2000). *Embryogenesis: Species, gender and identity*. Berkeley: North Atlantic Books.

Habermas, J. (1979). *Communication and the evolution of society* (T. McCarthy, Trans.). Boston: Beacon Press.

Hampson, G. P. (2007). Integral reviews postmodernism: The way out is through. *Integral Review: A Transdisciplinary and Transcultural Journal for New Thought Research and Praxis, 4*, 108–173.

Hart, T. (1998). A dialectic of knowing: Integrating the intuitive and the analytic. *Encounter: Education for Meaning and Social Justice, 11*, 5–16.

Hart, T. (2000). Deep empathy. In T. Hart, P. Nelson, & K. Puhakka (Eds.), *Transpersonal knowing: Exploring the horizon of consciousness* (pp. 253–270). Albany: State University of New York Press.

Horn, R. (2001). Post-formal design conversation: Designing just and caring educational systems. *Systems Research and Behavioural Sciences, 18*(4), 361–371.

Jantsch, E. (1981). *The evolutionary vision: Toward a unifying paradigm of physical, biological, and sociocultural evolution*. Boulder: Westview Press.

Jardine, D. W. (1998). *To dwell with a boundless heart: Essays in curriculum theory, hermeneutics, and the ecological imagination* (Studies in the Postmodern Theory of Education). New York: Peter Lang Publishing.

Jardine, D. W. (2006). *Piaget and education primer*. New York: Peter Lang.

Kegan, R. (1994). *In over our heads: The mental demands of modern life*. Cambridge, MA: Harvard University Press.

Kincheloe, J. (2006). *Reading, writing and cognition: The postformal basics* (Bold Visions in Educational Research). Rotterdam: Sense Publishers.

Kincheloe, J., & Berry, K. (2004). *Rigour and complexity in educational research: Conceptualising the bricolage* (Conducting Educational Research). Berkshire: Open University Press.

Kincheloe, J., & Steinberg, S. (1993). A tentative description of post-formal thinking: The critical confrontation with cognitive theory. *Harvard Educational Review, 63*(3), 296–320.

Kincheloe, J., & Steinberg, S. (1999). A tentative description of post-formal thinking: The critical confrontation with cognitive theory. In J. Kincheloe, S. Steinberg, & P. H. Hinchey (Eds.), *The post-formal reader: Cognition and education* (Vol. 63, pp. 55–90). New York: Falmer Press.

Kincheloe, J., Steinberg, S., & Hinchey, P. H. (Eds.). (1999a). *The post-formal reader: Cognition and education* (Critical Education Practice). New York: Falmer Press.

Kincheloe, J., Steinberg, S., & Villaverde, L. E. (1999b). *Rethinking intelligence: Confronting psychological assumptions about teaching and learning*. New York: Routledge.

Kohlberg, L. (1981). *Essays on moral development, vol. I: The philosophy of moral development*. San Francisco: Harper & Row.

Kramer, D. A. (1983). Post-formal operations? A need for further conceptualization. *Human Development, 26*, 91–105.

László, E. (2006). *The Chaos point: The world at the crossroads*. Charlottesville: Hampton Roads Publishing Company, Inc.

Loye, D. (1998). *Darwin's lost theory of love: A healing vision for the new century*. Lincoln: iUniverse Inc.

Malott, C. S. (2011). *Critical pedagogy and cognition: An introduction to a postformal educational psychology* (Explorations of Educational Purpose). Dordrecht: Springer.

Maslow, A. H. (1971). *The farther reaches of human nature*. New York: The Viking Press.

Nava, R. G. (2001). *Holistic education: Pedagogy of universal love* (M. N. Rios, & G. S. Miller, Trans., Foundations of holistic education series, Volume 5). Brandon: Holistic Education Press.

Neville, B. (2009). Educating the five-minded animal. In A. C. Scarfe (Ed.), *The adventure of education: Process philosophers on learning, teaching, and research* (pp. 63–80). New York: VIBS Vale Inquiry Book Series.

Noddings, N. (2005). Caring in education. In *The encyclopedia of informal education*. http://infed.org/mobi/caring-in-education/. Accessed 18 Apr 2016.

Piaget, J. (1972). Intellectual evolution from adolescence to adulthood. *Human Development, 15* (1), 1–12.

Ray, P. (2004). The great divide: Prospects for an integral culture. *Yes! Magazine: Powerful Ideas Practical Actions.*

Riegel, K. F. (1973). Dialectical operations: The final period of cognitive development. *Human Development, 16*, 346–370.

Robbins, B. D. (2006). The delicate empiricism of Goethe: Phenomenology as a rigorous science of nature. *Indo-Pacific Journal of Phenomenology, 6*(Special Edition), 1–13.

Rose, K., & Kincheloe, J. (2003). *Art, culture and education: Artful teaching in a fractured landscape*. New York: Peter Lang.

Roy, B. (2006). The map, the gap and the territory. *Integral Review: A Transdisciplinary and Transcultural Journal for New Thought, Research and Praxis, 3*, 25–28.

Seligman, M. E. P., & Csikszentmihalyi, M. (2000). Positive psychology. *American Psychologist, 55*(1), 5–14.

Sheldrake, R. (2006). Morphic fields. *World Futures: The Journal of General Evolution, 62*(1–2), 31–41.

Sinnott, J. D. (1994). Development and yearning: Cognitive aspects of spiritual development. *Journal of Adult Development, 1*(2), 91–99.

Sinnott, J. D. (1998). *The development of logic in adulthood: Postformal thought and its applications*. New York: Springer.

Sinnott, J. D. (2005). The dance of the transforming self: Both feelings of connection and complex thought are needed for learning. *New Directions for Adult and Continuing Education, 108*, 27–37.

Sloan, D. (1983). *Insight-imagination: The emancipation of thought and the modern world.* Westport: Greenwood.

Steinberg, S., & Kincheloe, J. (Eds.). (2004). *Kinderculture: The corporate construction of childhood.* Boulder: Westview Press.

Steiner, R. (1904/1993). *Knowledge of the higher worlds: How is it achieved? (GA 10)* (6th ed.) (D. S. Osmond, & C. Davy, Trans.) (Original German work published 1904). London: Rudolf Steiner Press.

Steiner, R. (1910/1939). *Occult science: An outline (GA 13)* (20th ed.) (M. B. Monges, & H. B. Monges, Trans.) (Original work published 1910). London: Rudolf Steiner Publishing Co.

Steiner, R. (1930/1983). *Metamorphoses of the soul: Paths of experience: Vol. 1 (GA 58)* (2nd ed.) (C. Davy, & C. von Arnim, Trans.) [9 Lectures, Berlin and Munich, March 14 to December 9, 1909] (Original work published 1930). London: Rudolf Steiner Press.

Steiner, R. (1971). *Ancient myths: Their meaning and connection with evolution (GA 180)* (1st English ed.) (M. Cotterell, Trans.) [7 Lectures, Dornach, Switzerland, Jan 4 to 13, 1918]. Toronto: Steiner Book Centre.

Steiner Education Australia. (2011). *Australian Steiner curriculum framework: Vol. 1.* (Educational foundations of Steiner education, pp. 154). Steiner Education Australia.

Sternberg, R. J. (2001). Why schools should teach for wisdom: The balance theory of wisdom in educational settings. *Educational Psychologist, 36*(4), 227–245.

Teilhard de Chardin, P. (1959/2002). *The phenomenon of man.* New York: Perennial.

Teilhard de Chardin, P. (1959/2004). *The future of man.* New York: Image Books, Doubleday.

Thompson, W. I. (1998). *Coming into being: Artifacts and texts in the evolution of consciousness.* London: MacMillan Press Ltd.

Villaverde, L. E., & Pinar, W. F. (1999). Postformal research: A dialogue on intelligence. In J. Kincheloe, S. Steinberg, & L. E. Villaverde (Eds.), *Rethinking intelligence: Confronting psychological assumptions about teaching and learning* (pp. 247–256). New York: Routledge.

Wilber, K. (1980/1996). *The Atman project: A transpersonal view of human development* (2nd ed.). Wheaton: Quest Books.

Wilber, K. (1981/1996). *Up from Eden: A transpersonal view of human evolution* (2nd ed.). Wheaton: Quest Books.

Wilber, K. (1995/2000). *Sex, ecology, spirituality: The spirit of evolution* (2nd ed., Rev.). Boston: Shambhala.

Wilber, K. (2000). *Integral psychology: Consciousness, spirit, psychology, therapy*. Boston: Shambhala.

Wilber, K. (2004). *Introduction to integral theory and practice: IOS basic and the AQAL map*. http://www.integralnaked.org2004

Wittgenstein, L. (1968). *Philosophical investigations*. Oxford: Basil Blackwell's.

Yan, B., & Arlin, P. K. (1995). Nonabsolute/relativistic thinking: A common factor underlying models of postformal reasoning? *Journal of Adult Development, 2*(4), 223–240.

Zajonc, A. (2005, June). Toward an epistemology of love. In *Philosophy science and theology festival*, Grafton, Australia.

Part III
An Evolving Postformal Education Philosophy

Chapter 8
Pedagogical Love: An Evolutionary Force

8.1 Introduction

The journey of this book so far may have been arduous for some of you, as we travelled through a vast territory: historical, cultural, psychological and pedagogical. Much of it has been theoretical and it may have seemed overly complex at times. For this I make no apology. As I said on the first page, the times we are in require radical change. This is not the time to tweak the edges of a failed educational model or ignore the cracks appearing in all of the systems operating on earth: environmental, economic, socio-cultural, political and educational. This is the time to think deeply, feel intensely and have the courage to act.

Having said all that, I imagine that Part III will be easier to read and integrate, if you are an educator, as it is more grounded in educational practice. And yet I expect that many of the concepts will be challenging. In an educational world of high-stakes testing, league tables for primary schools as well as universities, funding cuts, teacher shortages, mass shootings in school campuses and rising rates of depression and suicide among students who miss out on university entrance, how do we decide what should be the core values in education?

As I introduce, discuss and flesh out my four core pedagogical values, I take an unashamedly normative stance. Because I believe it is the most important value that is largely missing from education today, I begin with *pedagogical love*.

After briefly recapitulating the evolutionary themes, postformal reasoning qualities and pedagogies that I associate with this core value, I discuss the philosophical background as to why love should be at centre stage in education. I follow this with an introduction to the contemporary educational approaches that support a caring pedagogy and some experiences and examples from my own and others' practice, ending with some personal reflections on the theme.

J.M. Gidley, *Postformal Education*, Critical Studies of Education 3,
DOI 10.1007/978-3-319-29069-0_8

8.2 Why Love? A Brief Diagnostic

> In the search for truth, the only passion that must not be discarded is love. That is the mission of truth: to become the object of increasing love and care and devotion on our part. (Steiner 1930/1983, pp. 37–38)

Why is love important? Love is central to every form of spiritual path. Even in these very secular times, where essentials and universals have been deconstructed, the late writings of Derrida show that at the end of his life he became aware of, and developed a love of, what he called the "undeconstructible" (Benedikter 2005). The late Derrida, as an older man, is at his philosophical best when speaking about love.[1]

Why do we want to educate with and for love? We live in a cynical global world with a dominant culture that does not value care and empathy. We live under the blanket of a dominant worldview that promotes values that are clearly damaging to human and environmental wellbeing. In many ways our world, with its dominance of economic values over practically all other concerns, is a world of callous values.

What happens when love and care are missing from education? In Chapter 3, I introduced a litany of mental health issues being experienced by young people in Australia, much of the so-called developed world, and increasingly globally. It is not hard to imagine that a lack of love, care and connectedness in education can exacerbate these challenges. In fact "lack of belonging" has been identified in Australian research as a precursor to depression and suicide risk in young people.

What do education and psychology researchers say about love in education? These and other pertinent questions will be explored in this chapter.

8.3 Evolutionary Theme: Conscious, Compassionate, Spiritual Development

In Chapter 5, I introduced four significant themes arising from the evolution of consciousness research. The theme for this chapter promotes conscious, compassionate, spiritual development and includes religious, and particularly post-traditional, post-secular and postmodern spiritual approaches. While the term *spiritual* is still controversial in some philosophical discourse, it is increasingly found in the higher education landscape in the USA through the emergence of contemplative studies programmes and science/spirituality dialogues (Awbrey et al. 2006). Although continental philosophers eschewed notions of spirituality or religion in philosophy, many have referred to a "spiritual turn" (Habermas 2008; Manoussakis 2006).

[1]What Derrida has to say about love: http://www.youtube.com/watch?v=suvpPTMbnAo

Table 8.1 Postformal Reasoning Qualities Aligned to Love

Postformal Reasoning Qualities that relate to Spiritual Development, Contemplation, Compassion	
Higher purpose	There is more to existence than matter and more to life than egocentric desires. Beyond ego-control we become open to inspiration. Through inspiration our higher purpose in life can often be revealed.
Dialogical reasoning	Formal thinking is the ability to debate an argument, ending in win-lose. Dialogical thinking supports real win-win, in which we are free to really listen and finally hear the thoughts and views of others.
Integration	Our world of specialisation and fragmentation requires the ability to integrate, synthesise and take a systems approach. Academia is shifting from disciplinary to transdisciplinary approaches.

8.3.1 Postformal Reasoning Qualities Aligned to Love

To recap earlier discussions, the postformal reasoning qualities aligned to this evolutionary theme are higher purpose, dialogical reasoning and integration (see Table 8.1). In Chapter 7, I theorised that this theme and these qualities are deeply connected with a core value of love.

8.3.2 Postformal Pedagogies that Warm Education

Evolutionary spiritual development and the related postformal qualities are supported by educational styles that emphasise care, contemplation, empathy, love and reverence. In this chapter I show the importance of love in education and discuss some of the educational styles that emphasise care (Noddings 2003), contemplation (Altobello 2007; Brady 2007), empathy (Palmer 1998), love (Nava 2001; Zajonc 2005b) and reverence (Steiner 1909/1965; Whitehead 1916/1967). Related educational approaches include the spirituality in education movement (Glazer 1994; G. Woods et al. 1997; de Souza 2006; Erricker et al. 2001), contemplative and transformative pedagogies (Altobello 2007; Brady 2007; Hart 2001a; Zajonc 2005a); social and emotional education (Goleman 1997); and integral and holistic educational approaches (Esbjörn-Hargens 2006; J. P. Miller 2000; R. Miller 2000). I cohere these interrelated clusters of evolutionary and educational research and practice under the core value of *pedagogical love* (Table 8.2).

Table 8.2 Postformal Pedagogies that Warm Education

Postformal Approaches Emphasising Care, Contemplation, Empathy, Reverence	
Spiritual, transformative and contemplative education…	… reflects diversity in spiritual values and includes contemplative and other transformative approaches to learning.
Social and emotional education…	… is primarily expressed in one of two forms: explicit, conceptual, curricular approaches and implicit, contextual, relational.
Holistic and integral education…	… includes broad, eclectic holistic education and also specific integral/integrative approaches.

8.4 Philosophical Perspectives: Responsible Love, Critical Reverence

> The word 'love' is rarely mentioned in educational circles. The word seems out of place in a world of outcomes, accountability, and standardised tests. (J. P. Miller 2000, p. 31)

Canadian holistic educator, John Miller, quoted here, points to the subjugation of words like love in contemporary educational literature. Paradoxically, the earliest attempts at formal education were almost universally begun by religious organisations. Furthermore, the idea of love is clearly central to spiritual development in most religious and spiritual traditions. In Christianity, Buddhism and Islam, Love and/or Compassion are central indications of Divinity, Allah, Christ- or Buddha-nature. Many educators may dismiss notions of *love* and *reverence* today as being too sentimental or having too much religious significance for secular education. But in spite of the dominance of secularism in the 20th century, spirituality has returned to public discourse in the 21st century. Likewise the notion of love is beginning to reappear in educational conversations. The post-World War II taboos against mentioning spirituality in European philosophical discourse are rapidly dissolving with the spiritual turn in continental philosophy (Manoussakis 2006; Habermas 2008).

I have called this section "responsible love" and "critical reverence" with a view to giving deeper meaning to my broad concept of pedagogical love as a core value for education. My stress on the responsibility that we, as educators, need to attach to love creates distinctions in two directions. Firstly, the way I am using the term *pedagogical love* is not to be confused with the laissez-faire sentimentality that allows children to do as they please.

Secondly, pedagogical love bears a deep responsibility for teachers to be vigilant about personal boundaries so they do not trespass into the intimate spaces of children's emotional, physical and sexual zones. It is not easy today for teachers working with young children to find a safe and appropriate balance between the extremes of inappropriateness that surround us. At one extreme we live in an era where paedophilia has become rampant, particularly in so-called religious schools and communities. At the other extreme the legislative backlash has created situations that are almost as bizarre. In some settings it is illegal for a teacher to even pick up a child who falls and is hurt. This draconian legislation is a failed attempt to try to prevent paedophilia without looking deeply at either the complex societal causes of it or the needs of young children to feel comforted and nurtured when they are injured.

My concept of *critical reverence* may be a way to integrate the critical thinking so valuable for cognitive development with such positive affective states as reverence. Cognitive-affective learning theory provides support for my views (Zajonc 2006). And more recently, discoveries from the emerging field of affective neuroscience about the neuroplasticity of the brain highlight the long-term significance of how children are treated and cared for (or not).[2]

Almost a century ago Whitehead affirmed the significance of reverence in his philosophy of education with the following words.

> The essence of education is. . .religious. . . [it] inculcates duty and reverence. . . And the foundation of reverence is this perception, that the present holds within itself the complete sum of existence, backwards and forward, that whole amplitude, which is eternity. (Whitehead 1916/1967, p. 10)

Whitehead's words are echoed by Gebser, when he describes what he means by integral consciousness: "encompassing all time and embracing both man's distant past and his approaching future as a living present" (Gebser 1949/1985, p. 6). As a forerunner to Whitehead, Steiner gave lectures in 1909 where he explicitly named love and devotion—which he claimed to be the primary components of reverence—as educative forces for humanity in developing the next stage of consciousness.

> The best way of learning to know something is to approach it first of all with love and devotion . . . and when these two emotions are united together they give rise to reverence in the true sense of the word. . . To a child the world is largely unknown: if we are to guide him[/her] towards knowledge and sound judgement of it, the best way is to awaken in him[/her] a feeling of reverence towards it. . . Love and devotion are thus the right guides to the unknown, and the best educators of the soul in its advances from the Intellectual Soul to the Consciousness Soul. . . But this reverence must be led and guided from a standpoint which never shuts out the light of thought. (Steiner 1930/1983, pp. 61–62)

What Steiner meant by *consciousness soul* closely resembles what contemporary adult developmental psychologists call *postformal reasoning*, while Steiner's term intellectual soul resembles formal reasoning. In Chapter 7 I discussed Steiner's use of this terminology to represent postformal reasoning and also noted that Ken Wilber calls this developmental stage *vision-logic*. Jean Gebser refers to it as the *integral-aperspectival* structure of consciousness (Gidley 2007a, 2007b, 2010).

It is notable that in Erikson's three later stages of mature adult development, he refers to the core virtues to be developed as love, care (see Table 8.3) and wisdom (see Table 10.3) (Erikson 1950/1985, 1959/1994).

---

[2]Richard J. Davidson (2010) *The Heart-Brain Connection: The Neuroscience of Social, Emotional, and Academic Learning.* http://www.youtube.com/watch?v=o9fVvsR-CqM&feature=related.

Table 8.3 Erikson's Sixth and Seventh Stages of Mature Adult Development

Stage	Psycho-social Crisis	Basic Virtue	Age
6	Intimacy vs. isolation	Love	Young adult (18–40)
7	Generativity vs. stagnation	Care	Adulthood (40–65)

Barbara Fredrickson's fifteen years of psychology research on the impact of positive emotions has recently involved revisiting some of her earlier research on love. In her new research she refers to love as "positivity resonance between and among people". Here are her concluding comments from this research to date:

> Love, then, may not be just another positive emotion. By virtue of being a single state, distributed across and reverberating between the brains and bodies of two (or more) individuals, love's ability to broaden mindsets and build resources may have substantially greater reach. (Fredrickson 2013, p. 43)

Several holistic educators speak of love and reverence as touchstones for wisdom (Hart 2001b; J. P. Miller 2000; R. Miller 2000), which is a central feature of postformal thinking (Arlin 1999; Sinnott 1994; Sternberg 2001). I further discuss these links in Chapter 10, which is focused on pedagogical wisdom.

Holistic educator Ron Miller notes the significance of love and devotion in the Steiner/Waldorf approach drawing on the research of Mary Richards (1980) who undertook a major exploration of Steiner/Waldorf schooling in the USA. She points to significant structural differences between schooling systems.

> Richards contrasts the Waldorf teacher, as an artist working out of love for children, and their spiritual unfolding, with public school teachers, who are paid employees of large impersonal institutions. Of course, many individual public school teachers are sincerely devoted to their work; the point is that the structure of the system tends to frustrate rather than encourage such devotion. (R. Miller 1990, p. 138)

If love and reverence are so significant to the evolving human consciousness, we might well ask: Why is the word *love* so out of place in educational circles?

British educational researcher Maggie MacLure (2006c) unpacks the heavily quantitative language used to speak about education in the UK, with terms such as objectives, outcomes, standards, high-stakes testing, competition, performance and accountability. What MacLure is characterising is a very powerful neo-conservative backlash in the USA, the UK and Australia in terms of what is considered "good educational research" and consequently "good education". This swing back to neo-fundamentalist positivist and evidence-based research continues to run counter to innovation in education by supporting the status quo (Denzin 2005). MacLure argues that the resistance to the textuality, complexity and diversity of qualitative research that is found in the evidence-based agendas of the audit culture is linked to "deep-seated fears and anxieties about language and desire to control it". In such a context, it is not hard to imagine that words like *love* are likely to create what MacLure calls *ontological panic* among the educational audit-police.

The litany of mental health issues among young people suggests we have pushed many of them to breaking point (Gidley 2005). If young people are to thrive in educational settings, new spaces need to be opened up for softer terms, such as love, nurture, respect, reverence, awe, wonder, wellbeing, vulnerability, care, tenderness, openness and trust. If national governments are serious about wellbeing and spirituality in education—as they claim to be in the UK and Australia—the reductionism and quantification in language needs to be seriously challenged (P. A. Woods and Woods 2002). As Gebser said: "our terminology determines to a certain extent the direction of our thought" (Gebser 1996, p. 84).

In spite of these challenges several educational theorists and practitioners emphasise the importance of *love*—and the role of the heart—in educational settings. Arthur Zajonc has developed an educational and contemplative process that he calls an "epistemology of love" (Zajonc 2006) (see also Section 8.5.1). The term *pedagogical love* has also been used in constructivist educational theory (Hatt 2005), while Mexican holistic education philosopher, Ramon Gallegos Nava, refers to holistic education as a "pedagogy of universal love" (Nava 2001). Notable also are the important contributions of educators such as Nel Noddings with her extensive writings on an "ethics of care", Parker Palmer's "heart of a teacher" and Tobin Hart's "deep empathy" (Hart 2000; Noddings 2005; Palmer 1998). Like Palmer, Noddings links her notion of care to teacher integrity.

> The caring teacher strives first to establish and maintain caring relations, and these relations exhibit an integrity that provides a foundation for everything teacher and student do together… the foundation for successful pedagogical activity… as we listen to our students, we gain their trust and, in an on-going relation of care and trust… they will not see our efforts as "interference" but, rather, as cooperative work proceeding from the integrity of the relation. (Noddings 2005, Para 9)

In a similar vein, the basic premise of Palmer's book *The Courage to Teach* is the significance of teacher identity and integrity, rather than technique. He links both of these qualities with the heart.

> As good teachers weave the fabric that joins them with students and subjects, the heart is the loom on which the threads are tied, the tension is held, the shuttle flies, and the fabric is stretched tight. (Palmer 1998, p. 11)

Focusing on love as the heart of education counter-balances the technologising and commodification of education and resists the censorship of the audit culture.

8.5 Postformal Pedagogies: Promoting Love in Education

> Love allows us gently, respectfully, and intimately to slip into the life of another person or animal or even the Earth itself and to know it from the inside. In this way, love can become a way of moral knowing that is as reliable as scientific insight. Then our highest challenge and aspiration is to learn to love with such selflessness and purity that love becomes a way to true moral insight, one that transcends social construction and biological imperatives. (Zajonc 2014)

Several educational approaches support and promote responsible love in education: spiritual, transformative and contemplative education, social and emotional education, and integral and holistic educational approaches.

8.5.1 Spiritual, Transformative and Contemplative Education

Modern schooling does not serve the spiritual unfoldment of the child. It serves capitalism, nationalism, and a reductionist worldview. (R. Miller 1999, p. 190)

Holistic educator, Ron Miller takes a very definite stand with these opening words. Numerous educational researchers, globally, are now advocating the inclusion of spirituality in education (de Souza 2006; Glazer 1994; J. P. Miller 2000; Milojevic 2005; Palmer 1998; Tacey 2003). In the UK this has been facilitated by changing national education policies, prompting government-sponsored reviews of approaches, such as Steiner education, that include spiritual awareness from a non-denominational perspective (P. A. Woods et al. 2005). The Australian government has taken this even further when they introduced a new National Curriculum in 2009 and decided to approve curriculum streams based on Steiner education and Montessori education (see also Chapter 7).

While individual researchers are beginning to explore existential issues (Webster 2004); "beyond logic" (Hyde 2005) and "beyond rationality" (Stables 2004), there is little evidence of substantial engagement with the evolution of consciousness literature in the spirituality in education discourses.

Arthur Zajonc has developed what he calls an *epistemology of love* based on stages of contemplative inquiry. These stages in Zajonc's epistemology of love include respect, gentleness, intimacy, vulnerability, participation, transformation, *bildung* (education as formation) and insight (Zajonc 2006). In the areas of tertiary, graduate and adult education, an important approach is transformative education, in which transformative personal development is enabled through a climate of mutual trust and caring relationships among teachers and students (Ferrer et al. 2005; Hart 2001a; Montuori 1997).

8.5.2 Social and Emotional Education

The world of feelings can be explored and utilized to enhance how we work and influence our children's future. Whoever is educating the child has to be aware that their feelings and relationships to what they are imparting are intrinsic to the process and have an effect. We cannot really divorce our personalities from the process of teaching. (Clouder 2008, p. 27)

Social and emotional education can be viewed as a curricular intervention or in a more contextual way that involves the whole school and even the parents and wider community (Clouder 2008, p. 37). With respect to the curricular aspect, the main approach to conceptualisation of social and emotional education has arisen from the Collaborative for Academic, Social and Emotional Learning (CASEL) project, co-founded in 1994 by Daniel Goleman and others (Goleman 1997). This approach is strongly skills-based with the primary emphasis on children learning and acquiring several core competencies identified by CASEL including self-awareness, self-management, responsible decision-making, relationship skills and social awareness.

It is important however not to be restricted to the prescriptive, curriculum-based approaches to "social and emotional *learning*" of CASEL and other programmes that focus only on skills. A broader concept of "social and emotional *education*" includes family and community enculturation. The Botín Foundation in Santander, Spain, provides some important guiding parameters (Gidley 2011).

The development of social and emotional education in Australia followed several phases. From the late 1990s, as a response to the youth suicide epidemic, discussion focused on the mental illness and at risk behaviours of young people. This was followed by a gradual shift towards the positive view—of identifying *protective* factors as well as *risk* factors. Positive features of social and emotional wellbeing in children and young people include "resilience, attentiveness, confidence and social skills, and positive affect and self-concept including happiness, self-worth, sense of belonging, and enjoyment of school" (Hamilton and Redmund 2010). This shift away from clinical approaches led to concepts of social and emotional *wellbeing*.

Arising from this positive turn, some significant educational programmes were developed and implemented in Australian schools to deal with mental illness—especially by promoting protective factors. *MindMatters: Leading Mental Health and Wellbeing* was initiated in 2000 to serve Australia's high schools; and *KidsMatter: Australian Primary Schools Mental Health Initiative* was piloted in 2007 and is being expanded. These holistic programmes (e.g. whole child, whole school) grew out of the realisation that the issues are too complex and multi-faceted to be dealt with only by targeted programmes. While the literature on social and emotional learning and education focuses on skills in a transactional manner, rather than love and care as values dimensions, any pedagogy that enriches emotional life is a positive move.

8.5.3 Integral and Holistic Education

> We are convinced that integral approaches to education will contribute to the field of education at large. We see a growing need for frameworks that can unpack and articulate better distinctions around a comprehensive range of pedagogical issues. These frameworks need to be able to hold a variety of tensions in a dynamic balance, as well as be inclusive of diverse ways of engaging in educational endeavours. (Esbjörn-Hargens 2007, p. 3)

Much of what is referred to today as *integral education* has arisen from the application of Sri Aurobindo's integral yoga philosophy to pedagogy. Several contemporary educators have adopted key aspects of this approach in the USA, most notably the California Institute of Integral Studies (CIIS) (Montuori 2006; Subbiondo 2005; McDermott 2005). A double special issue of the journal *ReVision* attempted to broaden integral education beyond a single approach (Esbjörn-Hargens 2006; Montuori 2006; Subbiondo 2005; McDermott 2005; Ferrer et al. 2006). The integral approach emphasised in the special issue arose from Sri Aurobindo's epistemology of knowledge, action and love.

Ken Wilber's integral framework has been applied in some school settings and in the tertiary education sector (Esbjörn-Hargens 2006; Fisher 2007; Gunnlaugson 2004). Drawing on Wilber's integral framework, Sean Esbjörn-Hargens illustrates how Wilber's model has worked for him, teaching a graduate education programme (Esbjörn-Hargens 2006). Esbjörn-Hargens demonstrates the *external* application of AQAL theory and, in addition, implicitly demonstrates a number of qualities of the teacher/author. The case study is tacitly rich with warmth, enthusiasm and creative presence, *internal* qualities vital to developing the *art* of integral education. Yet these considerations are not prioritised in AQAL theory nor have they been made explicit in his paper. Even within integral educational approaches, there is contestation about degrees of cognicentrism versus participatory engagement (Ferrer et al. 2006).

Elsewhere I have attempted to provide a broader approach to integral education, by highlighting the many arts of integral education (Gidley 2010).

A more embracing interpretation of *integral education* would include other integrative and integrally aware approaches such as the *holistic education* movement as well as Steiner, Ralph Waldo Emerson, Owen Barfield and others (Scott 2000; Zajonc 2005a; Montuori 2006; Subbiondo 2005; McDermott 2005). Holistic education has been developing since at least the 1990s, and its leading proponents include John Miller from Toronto and Ron Miller from the USA (J. P. Miller 1988; R. Miller 1999; Forbes 2003; Martin 2004; Nava 2001; J. P. Miller 2000). One of the tensions within the holistic/integral education movement is that some integral educators claim that holistic education is insufficiently integral to address the multiple dimensions that need to be addressed (Esbjörn-Hargens 2006). There have been attempts to integrate holistic and integral approaches (Gidley 2007a; R. Miller 2000, 2005).

8.6 Practical Examples: Letting *Love* into your Classroom

> The heart of Jean Paul [Richter's] understanding of education can be expressed succinctly 'We love to teach and we teach to love'. (Pridmore 2004)

The practical application of these (r)evolutionary ideas seems a far cry from the performance outcomes required by the audit culture. Yet the love of teachers for their children, for the ideas to be conveyed and for learning itself can be nurtured and demonstrated in several ways.

8.6.1 Practice of Responsible Love and Critical Reverence

> Awe, wonder, reverence, and epiphany are drawn forth not by a quest for control, domination, or certainty, but by an appreciative and open-ended engagement with the questions. (Hart 2001b, p. 5)

I now offer some practical ways to enact responsible love and critical reverence by nurturing your relationships with the children in your care in numerous ways. Some of these may seem obvious but are rarely found in pre-service manuals.

- *Acknowledge each individual child*: We all need to feel acknowledged. By taking the time to speak individually to each of your students even if briefly, during each day, you get to know each individual in a practical, friendly way. They will feel acknowledged and have less need to seek attention in inappropriate ways.
- *Connect*: Children often “misbehave” to simply become visible. By making *authentic* eye contact with each child, they feel visible and can relax into that. This is a kind of beholding of the child with “the teacher’s gaze” (Uhrmacher 1993). In my own work I was aware that my gaze held a vision of each child’s potential in dialectical relationship with the reality of where they were, behaviourally or developmentally, in that moment. This draws their souls up like flowers to the sun.
- *Nurture them with beauty*: By creating a beautiful, safe environment, physically, emotionally and psychologically a teacher can provide soul nurture and aesthetic nourishment—as a “gourmet soul chef” perhaps?
- *Guide them*: Teachers who are enacting responsible love and critical reverence will understand that the teacher’s task is to help, guide and nurture the young people in their care (Biesta 2014; Marshak 1997).
- *Commit yourself*: Long-term commitment to children for several years personalises the learning environment. In the USA this is called “looping” during which time the learning environment becomes personalised, more like an extended family than an impersonal factory. Long-term commitment of teachers is central to Steiner education but is now becoming common as looping and personalisation in mainstream education (Eisner 2000; Marshak 1997).
- *Develop community*: The continuity of commitment facilitates the creation of community (Noddings, cited in (Uhrmacher 1997)). It is a conscious attempt to honour the group as well as the individuals. Several educational researchers note the importance of a sense of community in learning (Kessler 2002; Sinnott) and of making everyone feel at home (Chip Wood, cited in (R. Miller 1999) p. 200).
- *Encourage cooperation and collaboration*: Encouraging partnership and cooperation rather than competition is shown to help prevent bullying (Eisler 2001; Goerner 2000). Collaboration will also mitigate against feelings of disconnectedness, which are linked to depression and suicide among young people (Gidley 2001).

8.6.2 Care for Yourselves as Teachers

> Teacher education should be concerned with the formation of the whole person (not, so I wish to emphasise, as a private individual, but as a professional)… Teacher education is not just about the acquisition of knowledge, skills, and dispositions (qualification) or just about doing as other teachers do (socialisation) but starts from the formation and transformation of the person…. (Biesta 2014, p. 135)

Focusing inwardly, we need attend to our own *self-development and self-care*. Foucault pointed out that *self-care* was part of the spiritual path to knowledge for approximately two millennia until the Cartesian split between spirituality and philosophy (Foucault 2005). Some examples of inner work—and self-care—include:

- *Grow your own wisdom*: Read and study inspirational teachings and other wisdom literature to develop your own capacity for inner growth and development.
- *Participate in your own aesthetic development*: Take part in artistic classes in voice, movement, painting, sculpture and drama to promote flexibility of thought, imagination, inspiration and group spirit.
- *Model "practical love" by showing care and respect*: "children learn most profoundly from who their parents, care-givers, and teachers are as people, from the wholeness and rightness of these adults' qualities and actions" (Marshak 1997).
- *Work on the intangibles such as meditation*: In each relationship with each child, include some *inner* work. One of the pedagogical suggestions by Steiner, especially with troubled children, was meditative contemplation, regularly, on each individual child, throughout the school year (Steiner 1982). Mindfulness is another contemporary way to introduce this element into classrooms (Zajonc 2009).
- *Try contemplative lesson preparation for inspiration*: As a personal reflection, my own nightly preparation involved three components: study of the subject material, study of its deeper/broader context and contemplative surrender to being guided by creative inspiration. The latter step in the process invariably provided, as if on cue, new creative inspiration that enriched and enlivened my lessons for the following day.

8.6.3 Inspire a Love of Learning

> As Paulo Freire told me over dinner "there is nothing more important in this world than radical love"… Injecting radical love into this postformal mix provides us with new inroads into the magic of words. (Kincheloe 2006, p. 13)

Finally, we can nurture our own enthusiasm by continually finding new things to learn about. By cultivating our own love of learning, we inspire a love of learning in the children in our care. This creates important links between the cognitive and affective aspects of education—the relationship between love and knowledge (Zajonc 2006). In retrospect, the most interesting lessons I gave were on topics I had to research, afresh, for my lessons. These concepts became warm with the love for learning that I felt while preparing for the children. This is an advantage of not being a slave to textbooks and committing to creating an individualised mode of presentation for each lesson, rather than a mass-produced one. This honours the particularity of each situation and the individual needs of the children.

This responsibly loving approach, as I practised it, in that school with those children, enfolded within it potential for integrating the whole child in a way that could facilitate the evolution of consciousness not just for those individual children but for the culture they will participate in as agents of change throughout their future lives. Such seeds of change can be carried in the colours and textures of a soul-nurturing classroom and in the power of the love in a teacher's gaze.

8.7 Personal Reflections on Pedagogical Love

This section is primarily a personal reflection on how I, as a teacher of children, tried to practise what I call *responsible love* and *critical reverence*. Because this section is personal, it is inwardly focused, teacher-pupil relational, intangible, process-based and somewhat messy. Love itself can be messy. I believe that love is about engagement. That requires being immersed, engrossed and contemplative.

Personal Reflections. *There are several qualities that I strove for that I think contributed to this engrossment of the children in what they were doing. I think the foremost quality is that I felt and enacted a responsible love for them (I am distinguishing here from "sentimental love" which allows children to indulge in whatever they want to do rather than direct them towards what I know; as a responsible adult, it is best for the child's development). I believed that through this, combined with the intellectual and creative effort I made on their behalf, I could "bring out the best in them". I tried always to "see the best in them", to sense their growing points, to go with "what worked" with them and what energised and engaged them, rather than to oppose or force. And yet, much of what I led them to do would not necessarily have been of their own "choice". It was all much subtler than this. I took full responsibility for their education—from my standpoint at the time, I had the knowledge, experience and resources to make the overall decisions in terms of planning the year's work to provide a balance of academic content, suitable for their developmental levels and their skill needs, and to interweave this with the social-emotional dynamics of the class, topical issues of local or global significance, seasonal factors, etc. And to package all this in an imaginative (yet "truthful"), artistic, engaging way, drawing in as many complex threads of possibility as I could at any one time. This usually meant integrating at least two "substantive" knowledge areas (e.g. geometry and natural science, language and* *social science, arithmetic and cultural history, etc.). Simultaneously, in addition to this integrative gesture, whatever the content, it was all packaged (most of the time anyway) in inviting artistic montages that usually included on a daily basis, at least, a new conceptual idea or theme, contained within a story; illustrated by a picture; encapsulated in some poetic prose or poetry; brought to life using music, song, drama or craft; and retold or reenacted by the children in their own language. In the later years material was also discussed either formally as a whole group or informally in quiet conversations.*

Soul-Care as Gourmet Chef for Soul-Hungry Children. *I felt at times as if I were a pedagogical gourmet chef creating and delivering delicious soul food for starving and poisoned children—dishing up colourful, nourishing, tantalising soul food that would both detoxify them from the negative images they were imbibing from the media, TV, socio-political-environmental crisis discourses, and also nourish them and build their soul's resistance to future assault from violent imagery. I could see their souls thriving especially obvious in those who came to me as refugees already wounded from their previous "educational" experiences. Firstly, they would begin to breathe more freely, to lighten up and to recover. Gradually they would begin to see the sense in things, how things fitted together, the meaning in things. One of my underlying tacit-intuitive guidelines was to not give things to children that didn't "make sense." This doesn't mean in any way that I oversimplified things. On the contrary, sometimes I introduced them to very complex things that were way "over their heads" but in a way that they could understand at their level through their mode of understanding (i.e. often in picture or narrative form).*

8.8 Concluding Remarks

In this chapter we found that Steiner claimed a century ago that love, devotion and reverence are profoundly important in educating for new levels of consciousness and that Whitehead, Montessori and Aurobindo agreed. We discussed research by educators, who view love and reverence as touchstones for wisdom, and adult developmental researchers, who view wisdom as central to postformal reasoning. This complexly interwoven relationship between love and wisdom is further illuminated in Chapter 10. Finally, as we go to press, love is appearing as a theme in educational conferences[3] suggesting its rising embeddedness in both theory and practice.

---

[3]An education conference in Aarhus, Denmark, in June 2015 was called "Transforming the Heart of Education". Another Conference on Education for Sustainable Development in Tallinn, Estonia, June 2015 included the theme: "Values in education and ethics of ESD – *What's love got to do with it?*"

References

Altobello, R. (2007). Concentration and contemplation: A lesson in learning to learn. *Journal of Transformative Education, 5*(4), 354–371.

Arlin, P. K. (1999). The wise teacher: A developmental model of teaching. *Theory Into Practice, 38*(1), 12–17.

Awbrey, S., Dana, D., Miller, V., Robinson, P., Ryan, M. M., & Scott, D. K. (Eds.). (2006). *Integrative learning and action: A call to wholeness* (Studies in education and spirituality, Vol. 3). New York: Peter Lang Publishing.

Benedikter, R. (2005). *Postmodern spirituality: A dialogue in five parts*. http://www.integralworld.net/index.html?benedikter1.html. Accessed 28 June 2006.

Biesta, G. J. J. (2014). *The beautiful risk of education*. Boulder: Paradigm Publishers.

Brady, R. (2007). Learning to stop, stopping to learn: Discovering the contemplative dimension in education. *Journal of Transformative Education, 5*(4), 372–394.

Clouder, C. (2008). Introducing social and emotional education. In C. Clouder (Ed.), *Social and emotional education. An international analysis*. Santander: Fundacion Marcelino Botin.

de Souza, M. (2006). Educating for hope, compassion and meaning in a divisive and intolerant world. *International Journal of Children's Spirituality, 11*(1), 165–175.

Denzin, N. (2005). The first international congress of qualitative inquiry. *Qualitative Social Work, 4*(1), 1105–1111.

Eisler, R. (2001). Partnership education in the 21st century. *Journal of Futures Studies, 5*(3), 143–156.

Eisner, E. (2000). Those who ignore the past...: 12 easy lessons for the next millennium. *Journal of Curriculum Studies, 32*(2), 343–357.

Erikson, E. H. (1950/1985). *Childhood and society*. New York: Norton.

Erikson, E. H. (1959/1994). *Identity and the life cycle*. New York: Norton.

Erricker, J., Ota, C., & Erricker, C. (Eds.). (2001). *Cultural, religious and social differences: New perspectives for the 21st century*. Brighton: Sussex Academic Press.

Esbjörn-Hargens, S. (2006). Integral education by design: How integral theory informs teaching, learning and curriculum in a graduate program. *ReVision, 28*(3), 21–29.

Esbjörn-Hargens, S. (2007). Integral teacher, integral students, integral classroom: Applying integral theory to graduate education. *AQAL Journal of Integral Theory and Practice, 2*(2), 72–103.

Ferrer, J., Romero, M., & Albareda, R. (2005). Integral transformative education: A participatory proposal. *Journal of Transformative Education, 3*(4), 306–330.

Ferrer, J., Romero, M., & Albareda, R. (2006). The four seasons of integral education: A participatory proposal. *ReVision, 29*(2), 11.

Fisher, R. M. (2007). Ken Wilber and the education literature: Abridged annotated bibliography. *Paths of Learning*. http://www.feareducation.com/pdfs/techpap27.pdf. Accessed 20 Apr 2016.

Forbes, S. H. (2003). *Holistic education. An analysis of its ideas and nature*. Brandon: Solomon Press/Foundation for Educational Renewal.

Foucault, M. (2005). *The hermeneutics of the subject: Lectures at the Collège de France 1981–1982*. New York: Palgrave MacMillan.

Fredrickson, B. L. (2013). Positive emotions broaden and build. In P. Devine & A. Plant (Eds.), *Advances in experimental social psychology*. Elsevier: Burlington Academic Press.

Gebser, J. (1949/1985). *The ever-present origin*. Athens: Ohio University Press.

Gebser, J. (1996). The conscious and the unconscious: A misleading choice. *Integrative Explorations Journal, 3*, 84–85.

Gidley, J. (2001). An intervention targeting hopelessness in adolescents by promoting positive future images. *Australian Journal of Guidance and Counselling, 11*(1), 51–64.

Gidley, J. (2005). Giving hope back to our young people: Creating a new spiritual mythology for western culture. *Journal of Futures Studies, 9*(3), 17–30.

Gidley, J. (2007a). Educational imperatives of the evolution of consciousness: The integral visions of Rudolf Steiner and Ken Wilber. *International Journal of Children's Spirituality, 12*(2), 117–135.

Gidley, J. (2007b). The evolution of consciousness as a planetary imperative: An integration of integral views. *Integral Review: A Transdisciplinary and Transcultural Journal for New Thought, Research and Praxis, 5*, 4–226.

Gidley, J. (2010). Evolving higher education integrally: Delicate mandalic theorising. In S. Esbjörn-Hargens, O. Gunnlaugson, & J. Reams (Eds.), *Integral education: New directions for higher learning* (pp. 345–361). New York: State University of New York Press.

Gidley, J. (2011). From crisis to confidence: The development of social and emotional education in Australia. In B. Hey (Ed.), *Social and emotional education: International analysis II* (pp. 69–101). Santander: Fundacione Marcelino Botin.

Glazer, S. (Ed.). (1994). *The heart of learning: Spirituality in education.* New York: Jeremy P. Tarcher/Putnam.

Goerner, S. (2000, July). Rethinking education in the light of great change. *New Horizons for Learning.*

Goleman, D. (1997). *Emotional intelligence: Why it can matter more than IQ.* New York: Bantam.

Gunnlaugson, O. (2004). Towards an integral education for the ecozoic era. *Journal of Transformative Education, 2*(4), 313–335.

Habermas, J. (2008). *Between naturalism and religion: Philosophical essays.* London: Polity Press.

Hamilton, M., & Redmund, G. (2010). *Conceptualisation of social and emotional wellbeing for children and young people, and policy implications: A research report for the Australian Research Alliance for Children and Youth and the Australian Institute of Health and Welfare.* Sydney: Social Policy Research Centre University of New South Wales.

Hart, T. (2000). Deep empathy. In T. Hart, P. Nelson, & K. Puhakka (Eds.), *Transpersonal knowing: Exploring the horizon of consciousness* (pp. 253–270). Albany: State University of New York Press.

Hart, T. (2001a). *From information to transformation: Education for the evolution of consciousness.* New York: Peter Lang.

Hart, T. (2001b). Teaching for wisdom. *Encounter: Education for Meaning and Social Justice, 14* (2), 3–16.

Hatt, B. E. (2005). Pedagogical love in the transactional curriculum. *Journal of Curriculum Studies, 37*(6), 671–688.

Hyde, B. (2005). Beyond logic – Entering the realm of mystery: Hermeneutic phenomenology as a tool for reflecting on children's spirituality. *International Journal of Children's Spirituality, 10* (1), 31–44.

Kessler, R. (2002). Nurturing deep connections. *School Administrator, 59*(8), 22–26.

Kincheloe, J. (2006). *Reading, writing and cognition: The postformal basics* (Bold visions in educational research). Rotterdam: Sense Publishers.

MacLure, M. (2006). The bone in the throat: Some uncertain thoughts on baroque method. *International Journal of Qualitative Studies in Education, 19*(6 November–December), 729–745.

Manoussakis, J. P. (2006). *After God: Richard Kearney and the religious turn in continental philosophy* (Perspectives in continental philosophy). New York: Fordham University Press.

Marshak, D. (1997). *The common vision: Parenting and educating for wholeness.* New York: Peter Lang.

Martin, R. A. (2004, April). Holistic education: Research that is beginning to delineate the field. In *American Education Research Association,* San Diego, CA.

McDermott, R. (2005). An Emersonian approach to higher education. *ReVision: A Journal of Consciousness and Transformation, 28*(2), 6–17.

Miller, J. P. (1988). *The holistic curriculum.* Toronto: OISE Press.

Miller, J. P. (2000). *Education and the soul: Towards a spiritual curriculum.* Albany: State University of New York Press.

Miller, R. (1990). *What are schools for? Holistic education in American culture.* Brandon: Holistic Education Press.

Miller, R. (1999). Holistic education for an emerging culture. In S. Glazer (Ed.), *The heart of learning: Spirituality in education.* New York: Putnam.

Miller, R. (2000). Education and the evolution of the cosmos [Electronic version]. *Caring for new life: Essays on holistic education.*

Miller, R. (2005). Philosophical sources of holistic education [Electronic version]. *Deðerler Eðitimi Dergisi (Journal of Values Education), 3*(10), 9.

Milojevic, I. (2005). Critical spirituality as a resource for fostering critical pedagogy. *Journal of Futures Studies, 9*(3), 1–16.

Montuori, A. (1997). Reflections on transformative learning: Social creativity, academic discourse and the improvisation of inquiry. *ReVision, 20*(1), 34–37.

Montuori, A. (2006). The quest for a new education: From oppositional identities to creative inquiry. *ReVision, 28*(3), 4–17.

Nava, R. G. (2001). *Holistic education: Pedagogy of universal love* (M. N. Rios, & G. S. Miller, Trans., Foundations of holistic education series, Vol. 5). Brandon: Holistic Education Press.

Noddings, N. (2003). *Happiness and education.* Cambridge: Cambridge University Press.

Noddings, N. (2005). Caring in education. *The encyclopedia of informal education.* http://infed.org/mobi/caring-in-education/. Accessed 18 Apr 2016.

Palmer, P. (1998). *The courage to teach.* San Francisco: Jossey-Bass.

Pridmore, J. (2004). 'Dancing cannot start too soon': Spiritual education in the thought of Jean Paul Friedrich Richter. *International Journal of Children's Spirituality, 9*(3), 279–291.

Richards, M. C. (1980). *Toward wholeness: Rudolf Steiner education in America.* Middletown: Wesleyan University Press.

Scott, D. (2000). Spirituality in an integrative age. In V. Kazanjian, H. Jr., & P. Laurence (Eds.), *Education as transformation: Religious pluralism, spirituality, and a new vision for higher education.* New York: Peter Lang Publishing.

Sinnott, J. D. (1994). Development and yearning: Cognitive aspects of spiritual development. *Journal of Adult Development, 1*(2), 91–99.

Sinnott, J. D. (n.d.). *Teaching as nourishment for complex thought: Approaches for classroom and practice built on postformal theory and the creation of community.* Towson University, Psychology Department.

Stables, A. (2004). Responsibility beyond rationality: The case for rhizomatic consequentialism. *International Journal of Children's Spirituality, 9*(2), 219–225.

Steiner, R. (1909/1965). *The education of the child in the light of anthroposophy (GA 34)* (2nd ed.) (G. & M. Adams, Trans.) (Original work published 1909). London: Rudolf Steiner Press.

Steiner, R. (1930/1983). *Metamorphoses of the soul: Paths of experience: Vol. 1 (GA 58)* (2nd ed.) (C. Davy, & C. von Arnim, Trans.) [9 Lectures, Berlin and Munich, March 14 to December 9, 1909] (Original work published 1930). London: Rudolf Steiner Press.

Steiner, R. (1982). *Meditatively acquired knowledge of man (GA 302a)* (T. van Vliet, & P. Wehrle, Trans.) [4 Lectures, Stuttgart, Germany, Sept 15 to 22, 1920] Forest Row: Steiner School Fellowship Publications.

Sternberg, R. J. (2001). Why schools should teach for wisdom: The balance theory of wisdom in educational settings. *Educational Psychologist, 36*(4), 227–245.

Subbiondo, J. (2005). An approach to integral education: A case for spirituality in higher education. *ReVision, 28*(2), 18–23.

Tacey, D. (2003). *The spirituality revolution: The emergence of contemporary spirituality.* Sydney: Harper Collins.

Uhrmacher, B. P. (1993). Making contact: An exploration of focused attention between teacher and students. *Curriculum Inquiry, 23*(4), 433–444.

Uhrmacher, B. P. (1997). Evaluating change: Strategies for borrowing from alternative education. *Theory Into Practice, 36*(2), 71–78.

Webster, S. (2004). An existential framework of spirituality. *International Journal of Children's Spirituality, 9*(1), 7–19.

Whitehead, A. N. (1916/1967). *The aims of education*. New York: Free Press.

Woods, G., O'Neill, M., & Woods, P. A. (1997). Spiritual values in education: Lessons from Steiner. *The International Journal of Children's Spirituality, 2*(2), 25–40.

Woods, P. A., & Woods, G. (2002). Policy on school diversity: Taking an existential turn in the pursuit of valued learning? *British Journal of Educational Studies, 50*(2), 254–278.

Woods, P. A., Ashley, M., & Woods, G. (2005). *Steiner schools in England*. Bristol: Department for Education and Skills.

Zajonc, A. (2005a, February 13). Love and knowledge: Recovering the heart of learning through contemplation. In *Contemplative practices in education: Making peace in ourselves and peace in the world*, Columbia University.

Zajonc, A. (2005b, June). Toward an epistemology of love. In *Philosophy science and theology festival*, Grafton, Australia.

Zajonc, A. (2006). Cognitive-affective connections in teaching and learning: The relationship between love and knowledge. *Journal of Cognitive Affective Learning, 3*(1), 1–9.

Zajonc, A. (2009). *Meditation as contemplative enquiry: When knowledge becomes love*. Great Barrington: Lindesfarne Books.

Zajonc, A. (2014). Love as Ethical Insight. *Mind and Morality: Where do they Meet?*

Chapter 9
Pedagogical Life: A Sustaining Force

9.1 Introduction

If love is the most important value in my educational philosophy, life comes a close second. In just a few years, public warnings about the increasing likelihood of severe effects of climate crisis have become much more insistent. While it is hard to imagine the environmental impact of the current sea level rise predictions, the social, cultural and especially psychological impacts will be far greater. And yet governments, corporations and the general public continue to ignore the warnings like a child who covers their eyes thinking they cannot be seen.

If a more caring, life-enhancing consciousness could assist the restoration of our fragile planetary ecosystem, how might educators achieve this?

This chapter begins by reiterating the important evolutionary theme that would shift our thinking from static mechanistic metaphors to life-enhancing ones. I refresh the reader on the postformal qualities and pedagogies that support this shift before discussing the philosophical underpinnings of a life-promoting education. An introduction to the most life-supporting educational approaches today is followed by examples from my teaching experience and that of other alive and vital educators.

I finish with some personal reflections on the importance of pedagogical life.

9.2 Why Life? A Brief Diagnostic

> All education is the development of genius... The three factors of genius are the habit of action, the vivid imagination, and the discipline of judgment. (Whitehead 1919, p. 41)

Why is life important? This may seem like a rhetorical question. Why do we send satellites into space looking for life in other parts of the solar system? Life as a core value is so fundamental to human existence that it is overlooked. We should not

J.M. Gidley, *Postformal Education*, Critical Studies of Education 3,
DOI 10.1007/978-3-319-29069-0_9

underestimate the beneficial effects of enlivening education, or as Whitehead notes in the opening quote, its potential in developing genius in our young people.

Why do we want to educate with and for life? We live in a world with a globalising culture that does not value life in its many dimensions: the environment, the health and vitality of its children and young people, or the wellbeing of socio-cultural life in general. We must ask ourselves how has this come to be. Since the publication of Julien Offray de La Mettrie's (1748) *L'Homme Machine*, mechanistic metaphors of human and nature have dominated science and philosophy.

What happens when life and vitality are missing from education? When we offer children a lifeless and stale education, we not only destroy their vitality but also dumb them down. The excesses of the industrial era have depleted resources, polluted our air and water to the extent that climate crisis is recognised as a global geo-political issue. We have altered the biosphere to the extent that our planetary homeland may in the foreseeable future become inhospitable for human habitation. How can children and young people be expected to contend with catastrophic futures?

So how can we re-enliven education? This chapter explores the creative use of the imagination in education as a way of enlivening thinking and breaking with outdated models from the past. By moving beyond narrow, abstract intellectualism as the main mode of instruction, we can revitalise teachers and young people.

9.3 Evolutionary Theme: Mobile, Life-Enhancing Thinking

This evolutionary theme transcends static mechanistic thinking and promotes fluid, life-enhancing thinking. At the heart of this new thinking is the active imagination. Imagination is evident in all the organic, process-oriented, postmodern and poststructuralist philosophies (Bergson 1911/1944; Deleuze and Guattari 1994; Derrida 2001; Whitehead 1929/1985). The movement beyond the Newtonian building-block universe is evident in the new science theories, such as Einstein's relativity, quantum physics and systems sciences. The shift from simple mechanistic metaphors to complex organic metaphors is found in the new biology theories of chaos, complexity, self-organisation and emergence (Goodenough and Deacon 2006; Jantsch 1980; László 2006; Varela et al. 1993).

9.3.1 Postformal Reasoning Qualities Aligned to Life

The features of postformal reasoning that I align with this evolutionary stream are imagination, ecological reasoning and futures reasoning (especially long-term thinking) (see Table 9.1). For a more detailed version of these qualities, see Table 5.4. The connection between this theme, these qualities and pedagogies and the core value of life is discussed in Chapter 7.

9.3.2 Postformal Pedagogies that Revitalise Education

In this chapter, I stress the central importance of educating with imagination to promote life and vitality in the children and young people we work with. While several educational approaches support the movement from *static* concepts to *living* thinking, the nurturing of an active imagination is a fundamental catalyst. Numerous educators have stressed the significance of imagination in bringing concepts to life (Egan 1990; Eisner 1985; Gidley 2001; Neville 1989; Nielsen 2006; Sloan 1983; Whitehead 1916/1967). Life and its metaphors are also emphasised in pedagogies grounded in ecology and sustainability (Jardine 1998; Orr 1994) and futures thinking and foresight (Gidley et al. 2004; Hicks 2002). Arguably, the resuscitation of education will require a revival of living thinking in educational philosophy. I cohere these related clusters of evolutionary and educational research under the core value of *pedagogical life* (Table 9.2).

Table 9.1 Postformal Reasoning Qualities Aligned to Life

Postformal Reasoning Qualities that promote Organic, Ecological, Life-enhancing Thinking	
Imagination	Einstein said: "Imagination is more important than knowledge... Knowledge is limited but imagination encircles the world". Imagination is a portal to higher-order thinking and vital to envisioning alternative futures.
Ecological reasoning	Whitehead's process philosophy makes clear that "existence" cannot be abstracted from "process". In a similar way, living things cannot be extracted from the broader context of life—that is ecological reasoning.
Futures reasoning	While it is commonly thought that futures studies is an attempt to predict the future based on extrapolation from present day trends, this is only one of several epistemological approaches to futures reasoning.

Table 9.2 Postformal Pedagogies that Revitalise Education

Postformal Approaches that Shift from *Static* Concepts to *Living* Thinking	
Imaginative education...	... regards imagination as an important dimension in bringing concepts to life and supporting the development of vitality in thinking.
Ecological, environmental and sustainability education...	... includes approaches grounded in ecological perspectives, environmental awareness, respect for nature and sustainability.
Futures and foresight education...	... encourages foresight, long-term thinking and imaginative visioning of preferred futures, not merely perpetuating the past.

9.4 Philosophical Perspectives: Imagination as Living Thinking

> Present-day thinking is directed essentially to the dead world... The intellectualistic thinking current since the middle of the fifteenth century [is] a corpse... There is a real tendency today to embalm thinking so that it becomes pedantically logical, without a single spark of fiery life. (Steiner 1956, Lecture V, ¶ 9, 25)

9.4.1 German Lebensphilosophie and French Poststructuralism

The turn of the 20th century was a time when several philosophers, particularly in Europe, were moving beyond mechanistic metaphors to organic metaphors of thinking—known in German as *Lebensphilosophie*—or *life-philosophy*. This period was punctuated by Eduard Suess' notion of the *biosphere* (Suess 1875), Bergson's *élan vital* (Fraser et al. 2005), Whitehead's *process thinking* (Gare 1999), William Dilthey's *life-nexus*, Edmund Husserl's *life-world*, Steiner's notion of *living thinking* and, more recently, Deleuze's *lines of flight* (St. Pierre 2004).

The genealogical roots of ideas about the relationship between creative, productive, human thinking and the organic, life processes of nature go back to Goethe's *delicate empiricism*, Schiller's aesthetics and Schelling's *nature philosophy*. Schelling was inspired by the feeling that the ideas that appear in his imagination are also the creative forces of nature's process (Steiner 1901/1973). Steiner honoured the influence of Goethe's *metamorphosis* and Schelling's *naturphilosophie* and *intellectual imagination* in his notions of organic/living thinking (Steiner 1901/1973). Schelling himself was influenced by the philosophical imagination of German mystic Jacob Boehme (Steiner 1901/1973, p. 158), whose cosmology has also influenced Basarab Nicolescu's transdisciplinarity (Nicolescu 1991). Schelling's philosophical integration of *spirit*, *nature* and *intellectual imagination* had a significant philosophical influence on both Steiner and Wilber and also on both deconstructive and reconstructive streams of postmodern philosophy (Gare 2002). In summary, these continental philosophers proposed that to make thought living required imagination and a process view of thinking—they were trying to approach the source of creative life. However, the dominant mechanistic models of science led to the sidelining of this small philosophical flourishing of organic/process/living thinking.

Contemporary philosopher of imagination, Richard Kearney, has undertaken substantial research into the major theorists of imagination in modern European thought. Referring to these thinkers as "pathfinders of a new hermeneutic", he discusses at length the perspectives on imagination arising since Husserl declared in 1900 "the act of imagining to be the very life-source of essential truth". Beyond Husserl's phenomenological imagination, Kearney also identifies ontological imagination (Heidegger), existential imagination (Sartre), the poetical imagination (Bachelard), dialectical imagination (Merleau-Ponty), hermeneutical imagination (Ricoeur) and the postmodern imagination (Lacan, Althusser, Foucault, Vattimo, Kristeva, Lyotard). He then advances his own theories on the narrative imagination and its relationship to ethics, providing a philosophical foundation for both imagination and story/narrative in education (Kearney 1998).

Kearney's research on the complex genealogy of the imagination goes back much further than the modern European era. He refers to Plato's view that "imagination (eikasia) is nothing more than an imitation of the visible world, which is itself a mere shadow of the forms" (Kearney 1998, p. ix). He also summarises Aristotle's view that "imagination, in short... [is] the passage between sense experience and reason" (Kearney 1998, p. ix).

Continuing my own research on the philosophical background to imagination, I found that the synthesising nature of imagination was identified as early as the 3rd century CE in Plotinus' *conceptual imagination* (Warren 1996). Philosophers have used the term imagination to denote complex, potentially higher-order forms of thinking. The German idealists and romantics, particularly Goethe, Schiller and Schelling, extended the conceptual efforts of Plotinus.

In the early 20th century, Steiner's work with imaginal thinking—building on Goethe's *creative imagination* and Schelling's *intellectual imagination*—explicitly linked *imagination* with the evolution of consciousness (Steiner 1905/1981). Steiner claimed that: "For the world conception of Goethe and Schiller, truth is not only contained in science, but also in art" (Steiner 1901/1973, p. 142). According to Steiner, Goethe believed that "only men with imagination can attain the highest stages of knowledge". He claimed that Goethe calls these men the "comprehensive [and] contemplative in contrast to the merely intellectual-inquisitive, who have remained on a lower stage of cognitive life" (Steiner 1901/1973, p. 144).

Jürgen Habermas expanded on the synthesising nature of Kant's concept as follows:

> It is well known that Kant connected the concept of knowledge with the synthetic accomplishments of the productive imagination and of the understanding, through which the manifold of sensations and representations are organised into a unity of experiences and judgements. Apprehension within intuition, reproduction within imagination, and recognition within the concept are spontaneous actions that run through the manifold, take up its elements, and combine them into a unity. (Habermas 1992, p. 12)

Deleuze and Guattari advanced the project of bringing philosophy to life through conceptual creativity. They proposed that "philosophy is the art of forming, inventing, and fabricating concepts ... [and although] sciences, arts, and philosophies are all equally creative ... only philosophy creates concepts in the strict sense... philosophy is the single point where concept and creation are related to each other" (Deleuze and Guattari 1994, pp. 2–11). And yet, as they reveal elsewhere, concepts themselves are not closed, finished, "ready-made", but rather, "concepts are centers of vibration, each in itself and every one in relation to all the others" (p. 23). Morin's work is also a vital contribution to the evolution of a more living philosophy (Morin 2001, 2005; Morin and Kern 1999).

9.4.2 Imagination: A Well-Spring of Vitality

> The challenge that the notion of the vital—in whatever form it takes—poses then, is a challenge to all kinds of reductionism: sociological and cultural no less than biological. (Fraser et al. 2005, p. 6)

Imagination as I use the term is an activity that enables conceptual vitality—it can bring concepts to life. The term imagination can be used to depict complex, higher-order forms of thinking as discussed above or, disparagingly, to mean inferior to reason/formal thinking. Douglas Sloan (1983) draws on David Bohm's distinction between "the deep act of imagination in insight from what he calls *imaginative fancy*" (p. 144). Like Goethe and others, Sloan views imagination as a "higher order of consciousness" and the organ of cognition that "will break through these obstacles and unlock for our thinking the way to its deepest sources" (Sloan 1983, p. 180). Sloan continues:

> The cultivation of imagination does not mean the rejection of hard, lucid thought. It is, rather, the bringing of thought to life, permeating concepts and abstractions with life-giving images and inner energies through which thinking can penetrate and participate in the fullness of reality. (p. 192)

From the numerous interpretations I have encountered, Sloan's (1983) characterisation of *insight-imagination* best approaches my understanding of the kind of imagination that is needed to bring life into our thinking as a way of renewing our relationships with our world and thus our education. Sloan's "Insight-Imagination [can be best] understood as the involvement of the whole person—thinking, feeling, willing, valuing—in knowing..." (Sloan 1983, p. xiii).

Continuing the idea that there is a relationship between insight and imagination, Zajonc quotes Ralph Waldo Emerson from his essay "The Poet":

> This insight, which expresses itself by what is called Imagination, is a very high sort of seeing, which does not come by study, but by the intellect being where and what it sees, by sharing the path, or circuit of things through forms, and so making them translucid to others. (Zajonc 2005, p. 6)

This translucing quality of Emerson's "imaginative insight" has a very similar flavour to one of Gebser's characterisations of integral thinking, where he says: "Integral reality is the world's transparency, a perceiving of the world as truth: a mutual perceiving and imparting of truth of the world and of man and all that transluces both" (Gebser 1949/1985, p. 7).

Sloan's depiction of the dialectical nature of imagination links it to Wilber's vision-logic and the paradoxical nature of postformal reasoning:

> The wholeness presented in imagination is more the living unity of a tension of opposites... it is essential that the incompatibles, or polarities, not be overcome one by the other, nor

> that they be swallowed up and dissolved in sameness, but that they be maintained together in all their strength. And in that tension between them the imagination grasps a larger meaning and deeper connection than appears in either separately... The wholeness of imagination revealed in the tension of polarities is akin to the unity of the human being. (Sloan 1983, pp. 156, 159)

Sloan is encapsulating the paradoxical nature of higher-order imagination. This is remarkably similar to what Wilber says about "vision-logic":

> [V]ision-logic can hold in mind contradictions, it can unify opposites, it is dialectical and nonlinear, and it weaves together what otherwise appear to be incompatible notions, as long as they relate together in the new and higher holon, *negated* in their partiality but *preserved* in their positive contributions. (Wilber 1995/2000, p. 191)

Wilber's term—*vision-logic*—is a dialectical term for postformal reasoning that re-integrates the *vision* of imaginative thinking with the *logic* of formal thinking. It archetypally represents what the new consciousness stands for. For Gebser, the re-integration of the imagination is the conscious awareness and concretion of the mythical structure. Steiner had a complex view of imagination. He regarded the conscious cultivation of the *imagination* as crucial in psycho-spiritual development and a key feature of the emergent consciousness (Steiner 1905/1981).

Imagination is linked with postformal development by some adult developmental psychology researchers (Bassett 2005; Cook-Greuter 2000; Sinnott 2005). Through activating the *imagination* in our thinking, we not only enliven concepts, but we bring the significance of *life* back into centre focus in our *lifeworld*, enhancing vitality and wellbeing.

9.5 Postformal Pedagogies: Promoting Life in Education

> A thinking that is fragmenting, detached, and rigid will continue to give us a world that is increasingly broken, alien, and dead. The possibility of a living, harmonious, and meaningful world can only be grasped and realised by a thinking and knowing that are themselves living, whole and engaged. (Sloan 1983, p. xiii)

Several educational approaches support the movement from *static* concepts to *living* thinking and, in the process, help to re-enliven education and increase the vitality of young people. In addition to approaches that emphasise the importance of imagination in its own right, life and its metaphors are also cultivated in pedagogies grounded in ecology and sustainability and futures thinking and foresight.

9.5.1 Imaginative Education

> The living human being... demands a living kind of thinking... You must get your head so strong again that it can stand not only logical, abstract thinking, but even living thinking. You must not immediately get a buzzing head when it is a matter of thinking in a living

> way... pure intellectualism had dead thinking. The purpose of this dead thinking was the materialistic education of the West. (Steiner 1967b, Chapter III, ¶ 16)

The use of imagination and metaphor in education draws from a philosophical stream of thought that flows from Plato to Schiller, Rudolf Steiner and, in the 20th century, Elliot Eisner (Eisner 1985; Schiller 1954/1977; Steiner 1981, 1990). Steiner/Waldorf education is a highly imaginative pedagogical approach. Research has shown that Australian Steiner-educated students, while holding similar fears and concerns about the future to other students, had a greater capacity to envisage positive preferred futures. In spite of identifying many of the same global problems of environmental destruction, social injustice and threats of war that concern mainstream youth, most of the Steiner-educated students felt empowered to do something to create their preferred futures (Gidley 1998a, 1998b). They were able to develop richer and more detailed images of their preferred futures than mainstream-educated students, who had general ideas about positive things they would like to see happen, but were unable to translate them into detail (Eckersley 1996; Francis Hutchinson 1996). In spite of the power of negative media images of dystopian futures, the balance provided by cultivating positive imagination in a young person can transcend the negative and fearful imagery.

Arguably, the foremost proponent of imaginative education is Canadian educational theorist Kieran Egan. Egan's developmental model for imaginative education includes five stages: somatic, mythic, romantic, philosophic and ironic. Burnie Neville has compared Kegan's stages with both Gebser's structures of consciousness and Robert Kegan's orders of consciousness (Neville 2001). Table 9.3 shows a parallel view of those relationships and builds on Tables 3.1 and 7.1.

A number of other contemporary educators take the view that imagination must play a crucial role if education is to become the transformative experience it could be. These educators include Jack Miller from Toronto, Ron Miller from the USA, Bernie Neville and Thomas Nielsen from Australia (Nielsen 2006; J. P. Miller 1988; R. Miller 1999; Egan 1989; Neville 1989).

Table 9.3 Parallels among Jean Gebser, Robert Kegan and Kieran Egan

Gebser's Cultural Evolution	**Robert Kegan's Orders of Thinking**	**Kieran Egan's Imaginative Education**
Archaic (Pre-history)	First order Impulsive mind	Somatic
Magical consciousness (Ice Age)	Second order Instrumental mind	Mythic
Mythic consciousness (Agrarian era) (Ice Age–500 BCE)	Third order Socialised mind	Romantic
Mental/rational mode (500 BCE–1,500 CE)	Fourth order Self-authoring mind	Philosophic
Integral consciousness (1,500 CE > the future)	Fifth order Self-transforming mind	Ironic

Source: Egan (1997), Gebser (1949/1985), Gidley (2008) and Kegan (1994)

9.5.2 Ecological, Environmental and Sustainability Education

> Ecopedagogy, or "Earth's Pedagogy", as Moacir Gadotti calls it, emerges now as a project for a New Ecologically-Sustainable Civilization that *children* and *young people* can undertake….with the help of educators and people everywhere. There are many sciences—mathematics, history, economics…but ecopedagogy is a new kind of scientific inquiry into how we can best produce a more just, more ecological and peaceful sustainable civilization. (Grigorov 2012, p. 14)

Ecopedagogy grew out of the First Earth Summit in Brazil in 1992 and has been growing as a movement since then. Since 1950, while the global rural population less than doubled, the global urban population grew five times. By 2010 the global urban population had overtaken the global rural population for the first time in human history. Such rapid urbanisation has placed enormous stresses on urban resources, and the very viability of the urban lifestyle. What are the psycho-socio-cultural and environmental costs of this development? Is this sustainable and how can we educate young people to prepare them for the complexity and unpredictability of what will ensue? Morin's ecological philosophy provides an important grounding for the new complex thinking that will be needed to transform education sufficiently (Morin 2001; Morin and Kern 1999) and is worthy of further attention for those interested.

Making an explicit link between imaginative education and ecological education, David Jardine introduces the concept of the "ecological imagination" in education (Jardine 1998). Ecological education requires ecological reasoning, which I theorise as a postformal reasoning quality. It is thinking that has a context, a sense of connectedness and a sense of meaning. Guevara and Ord (1996) suggest that the search for meaning has three aspects:

- A sense of belonging found through context;
- A sense of relationship and connectedness;
- An ability to make a contribution (p. 711).

Youth researchers claim that a lack of meaning can be linked to disempowerment (Eckersley 1995; Gidley 2005). If education contextualises information into a meaningful form through stories, and other imaginative modes, this may contribute to students' meaning-making capacities, in turn empowering them. This seems to be borne out by the research with Steiner-educated students discussed in the previous section. The processes of Steiner education provide both the sense of belonging through context and the sense of relatedness. Perhaps these provide the confidence to make a contribution, which in turn enhances the sense of meaning in one's life that further motivates empowerment and positive action.

In the UK, David Hicks and Cathie Holden's work has led to futures thinking being taken into the new national curriculum area of citizenship education (Hicks 2001; Holden 2002). Citizenship education is part of the education for sustainability movement and has helped join together environmental education innovators

(Sterling 2001; Fien 1998; Orr 2001; Morin and Kern 1999; Orr 1994) with educational futurists (Francis Hutchinson 1992; Hicks 1995). This creates links between education for sustainability, citizenship education and futures education. Other integrative manoeuvres have been attempted between postformal complex reasoning, ecology and creativity (Montuori 1997, 2003; Morin 2001).

9.5.3 *Futures Studies and Foresight Education*

> Philosophy of education must always make place for that which cannot be foreseen as a possibility, that which transcends the realm of the possible. (Biesta 2014, p. 52)

The scope of the futures studies in education discourse includes three areas: (1) research with young people (mostly in school settings) which explores their views and visions of their futures; (2) the teaching of futures concepts, tools and processes in school settings; and (3) the speculative research into transformative educational models and approaches which have futures reasoning and foresight as part of their worldview. Much of the educational futures work with young people has sustainability as a central theme. A special issue of the journal *Futures* on educational futures is a good place to start for further reading on futures studies in education (Gidley 2012; Gidley et al. 2004).

Imagination is an important focus of futures education and features prominently in futures studies literature (Hicks 1995, 1998; Gidley 1998a; Stewart 2002; Milojevic 2005; Gidley et al. 2004; Slaughter 1991). Elise Boulding pointed to the work of Fred Polak and his diagnosis of a decline in the West's imaging capacity as being fundamental to the inability of policy-makers, scholars and the general public to picture a humanly desirable postnuclear world (Boulding 1988). Examining Polak's linking of images of the future with history, Boulding gives a possible explanation for the disempowerment our young people feel today:

> Utopian optimism has characterised the Western worldviews of recent centuries—but not of the last few decades. In eras when pessimism combines with a sense of cosmic helplessness the quality of human intentionality declines, and with it, the quality of imagery of the 'not yet'. Societies in that condition live bounded by the present, with no social dynamic for change available to them. (Boulding 1988, p. 20)

Boulding claimed that the strengthened and enriched imagination is a key aspect of action-oriented futures thinking. She notes a "possible relation among vividness or concreteness of imagery, intensity of affect and action readiness" (Boulding 1988, p. 34). Boulding and her colleague Warren Ziegler used imaging workshops to transform negative images of feared futures into positive images of preferable ones thereby using envisioning as an empowerment process (Boulding 1988; Ziegler 1991). Australian researchers have undertaken similar work with young people using positive imaging of the future to empower marginalised youth (Wildman et al. 1997; Gidley 2001, 2002).

9.6 Practical Examples: Bringing Education back to Life

> The problem of keeping knowledge alive, of preventing it from becoming inert… is the central problem of education… the solution which I am urging, is to eradicate the fatal disconnection of subjects which kills the vitality of our modern curriculum. There is only one subject-matter for education, and that is Life in all its manifestations. (Whitehead 1916/1967, pp. 4–5)

In spite of the rich possibilities of imagination discussed above, mainstream education seems caught within what Whitehead called the "inert ideas" in education. He noted: "we must beware of what I will call 'inert ideas'… ideas that are merely received into the mind without being utilized … or thrown into fresh combination… Education with inert ideas is not only useless: it is … harmful" (Whitehead 1916/1967, p. 1). Jean-Francois Lyotard referred to this as "the already said" when he discussed the dominance of the performativity principle in education, with its overemphasis on skill development in the postmodern world (Lyotard 2004). Ironically, Lyotard, who first drew attention to the demise of the grand narratives of modernity, also points to the importance of developing the imagination as a way to bring movement and change into a performance-oriented world system—a system designed to perpetuate conceptual inertia.

A resurgence of interest in imagination is evident in both postmodern philosophical circles (Abbs 1994; Deleuze and Conley 1992; Derrida 2001; Kearney 1998; Lyotard 2004; St. Pierre 2004; Whitehead 1919) and educational circles (Frank Hutchinson 1993; Eisner 1985; Broudy 1987; Egan 1990; Gidley 2009; Nielsen 2006; Neville 1989; Sloan 1992; Nuyen 1998; Giroux 1998; Abbs 1994).

Using imagination to bring concepts to life has been central to Steiner pedagogy for almost one hundred years, as a catalyst for the evolution of consciousness through both individual development and cultural regeneration (Gidley 1998a; Nielsen 2006; Sloan 1992; Stehlik 2008). While the cultivation of logic and rationality was significant in overcoming the deficiencies of earlier mythic consciousness, e.g. dogma and superstition (Gidley 2007), the dominance of narrow instrumental rationality, at the expense of other faculties, is a psychic prison for children and young people. In formal education the notion of *training* children is often used. The term *training* in educational settings is a behaviourist metaphor, and I prefer not to use it in relation to the education of children. If we only educate in an intellectual abstract way, presenting dry finished concepts, we are potentially stunting their conceptual development and ability to think flexibly by fundamentalising concepts as dogmatic, unchanging *facts*.

By contrast, educational approaches that foreground *conceptual imagination* can be forces for *conceptual vitality*. If the child's imagination is stimulated through bringing concepts to life, the concepts themselves can begin to breathe and grow with children, so they evolve to meet children's developmental potential. Because imagination is more fluid than formal categorisation, it allows thinking to flow around boundaries rather than be stopped by category barriers. This supports flexible, complex, process-oriented thinking and a smooth transition to higher levels of reasoning at the appropriate developmental moment.

Perhaps Steiner's and Whitehead's ideas sowed seeds for Lyotard's movement beyond the already-said (Lyotard 2004) and Deleuze and Guattari's living philosophical concepts (Deleuze and Guattari 1994). Deleuze, in his affirmative philosophy, challenges us "to bring something to life, to free life from where it is trapped, to trace lines of flight" (Deleuze (1990/1995, pp. 140–141), cited in (St. Pierre 2004, p. 287)).

Could more imagination assist us in freeing education from where it is trapped?

Pointing to these educational imperatives, Sloan quotes philosopher Mary Warnock: "I have come very strongly to believe ... that it is the cultivation of the imagination which should be the chief aim of education, and in which our present system of education more conspicuously fails" (Sloan 1983, p. 191).

9.6.1 Imagination as a Portal to Pedagogical Life

> Education today is filled with broken paradoxes, and with their lifeless results. The great challenge of integrative education is to "think the world together," not apart, so that education can become the life-giving enterprise it was meant to be. (Palmer 2007, Abstract)

I want to speak about two aspects to the art of cultivating *pedagogical life*:

1. Firstly, I want to promote the idea that imagination brings concepts to life—that we can create living thinking by cultivating imagination—as a way of "thinking the world together" as Palmer suggests;
2. Secondly, I refer to practical activities that explicitly honour life (see Section 9.6.2).

Clearly, the cultivation of imagination is vital to being able to "think the world together". There are several ways to facilitate this development in children:

- *Teacher imagination*: In order to bring a concept to life with imagination, the teacher needs to *be imaginative*. In practical terms the healthy development of a teacher's imagination can be cultivated through such artistic activities as painting, creative writing, poetry and storytelling to increase the likelihood of inspired teaching practice (Gidley 2003, 2004; Leonard and Willis 2008). There is a substantial body of educational literature that supports teachers using imagination in education (and of fostering it in children), yet somehow it is not reaching mainstream education. In terms of learning theory, Harry Broudy examined the indirect yet crucial role of imagery and imagination in forming part of what he calls the *allusionary base* of learning. (Broudy 1987) Here he refers to the conglomerate of concepts, images and memories available to us to provide meaning in what we hear or read.

  Could it be that the lack of meaning experienced by many of our youth today is related to an education that does not provide the images and context needed to develop a rich allusionary base? Broudy explains that this context of meaning may be enriched through poetry, literature, mythology and the arts and comprises the stock of meaning with which we think and feel.

- *Storytelling*: The cultivation of imagination is primarily nurtured in children through creative storytelling and "pedagogy permeated with the arts and an aesthetic sensitivity" (Sloan 1992, p. 47). In Steiner schools, particularly throughout the primary schooling stage, the teachers use the narrative form to present much of the material they introduce (Steiner 1967a, 1982). Such stories may run for a day, a week, a month or even a year, the extent and diversity of content to be included being limited only by the versatility and imagination of the teacher. Stories, once established in children's imaginations, may be revisited, and familiar characters can be developed to a new level of sophistication. Doctoral research focused on this aspect of Steiner pedagogy provides a worthwhile illumination of the cultivation of imagination in education, through "drama, exploration, storytelling, routine, arts, discussion and empathy" (Nielsen 2006). A unique pedagogical process that differentiates Steiner education is that writing is introduced first through pictures and pictograms prior to the abstract Roman alphabet. In my experience this *soft version of recapitulation theory* supports evolution of consciousness in a meaningful way so that when children do learn to read the more abstract text, they are able to read for meaning and thus are less likely to be functionally illiterate.

  A distinction needs to be made between stories (in contemporary children's literature, movies and television) that use fantasy images unrelated to real life and images that are grounded in a real-life context. Suitable stories may draw on mythological characters and archetypes from the literature from all historical periods and the entire pool of cultural material at the teachers' disposal. American educational research as early as the 1980s and 1890s indicates that the use of metaphors and images, especially through storytelling, is a valuable educational tool (Anderson 1985; Arnheim 1989; Egan 1988; Eisner 1985; Uhrmacher 1992).
- *Imagination as the shadow of the Academy*: There is a sense in which standard academic thinking is dead thinking. The formality required of standard academic writing is underpinned by formal operations, based on formal logic with its bounded categories and conceptualisations. Formal academic writing is the epitome of formal thinking in our culture. Because imagination is not cultivated and honoured in a healthy way, it comes out in an unhealthy way in our society through media, advertising images, images of violence and fear and horror. It could be said that imagination has become the shadow—the disowned self—of the academy and indeed the dominant global culture. Yet imaginative educators and carefully designed school environments can help to balance the impact of negative mass media on children's wellbeing through providing critically reconstructed images of the good, beautiful and true and by strengthening each child's own "image-making powers" (Sloan 1992).

  The imagination like the intellect and the physical body needs appropriate content to develop in a healthy manner. The healthy effects of this positive use of imagination on young people's views and visions of the future and sense of empowerment have been found in research with Steiner-educated students in Australia (Gidley 1998a, 2002). See also Imaginative Education section earlier.

- *Image and the media*: Imagination is not of itself positive or negative. Its impact on the child depends on the content and context. The power of "the image" is well known to the advertising industry, and futures researchers point to its transformative power (Boulding 1988; Gidley 1998a; Jenson 1996; Polak 1973). We live in a global cultural milieu, bombarded by pre-packaged images created by corporations to sell their products (Giroux 2001; Steinberg and Kincheloe 2004) and where imagination is cultivated in an unhealthy way through dystopian media images of violence and fear. Yet much of mainstream education seems unaware of the impact of these dystopian images. Since the advent of TV, video and computer games (originally designed to train and desensitise soldiers before sending them off to the killing fields), children and youth are consistently and exponentially exposed to violent images (Grossman et al. 1999). More recently with the ubiquity of mobile phones and the proliferation of Apps, children and young people are barely able to escape the technological mediation of their experiences. The American Medical Association and American Academy of Paediatrics made a joint statement: "The prolonged viewing of media violence can lead to emotional desensitization towards violence in real life" (Callahan and Cubbin 2000). Several researchers critique the damaging effects of overexposure to negative media images (Clouder et al. 2000; Grossman et al. 1999; Healy 1998; Marshak 1997; Pearce 1992), while from critical pedagogy the call is for more critical awareness (Healy 1999; Milojevic 2005; Spina 2004; Steinberg and Kincheloe 2004). Recent research includes positive, altruistic games (Klisanin 2003).

9.6.2 Practical Approaches that Enliven Curricula

> It is 'intuitive and imaginative powers (which) are the midwives to new forms of thought and conduct, new vistas and even new social institutions and systems'... Science relies heavily on both intuition and imagination, and scientists testify to their own indebtedness to the aesthetic. (Rose and Kincheloe 2003, p. 124)

In addition to cultivating the child's imagination, we can encourage life-enhancing values in education and affirm and enhance vitality and wellbeing through promoting *pedagogical life* in the following practical ways:

- *Creative handwork* is central to traditional and indigenous enculturation practices and used pedagogically for over a century (Dewey 1972; Montessori 1916/1964; Steiner 1928/1972);
- *Postmodern, postindustrial architecture* (Jencks 1997) creates imaginative, postformal and aesthetic spaces along with creative interior design;

- *Rhythm*: Attention to rhythmical, cyclical, organic time vs. fast, mechanical time helps to pace education more in line with our humanness. An example is the slow school movement (McGill 2005);
- *Practice nature care*: Ecological awareness will not automatically be instilled in children by talking about it. It is enhanced by caring for plants, small animals and other sentient beings (Orr 1994). Create a school herb or vegetable garden and introduce some suitable domestic pets into the campus. This develops respect for nature through the *ecological imagination* and reverence for life (Jardine 1998).

9.7 Personal Reflections on Pedagogical Life

Reflecting on my personal experience of bringing education to life for children, I offer two practical examples from the Steiner school I founded where we engaged children in activities that brought science to life for them.

Personal Reflections. *In the new design of the Daystar Steiner School playground, in rural Australia we decided to introduce the idea of "playing for science". This was back in the mid-1980s when alternative energy was still a relatively new idea. The school was centred in a community of new rural settlers, mostly urban refugees from an urban lifestyle they did not support. The idea of encouraging the children to learn about alternative energy was appealing to both teachers and parents alike. The school was creatively designed and built out of stone and timber to create a natural, organic environment for the children.*

The playground was vast and set within kilometres of farmland and natural bushland. The children had free spirits like their parents and were full of energy. It occurred to us that we could harness some of that bursting childish energy, which can sometimes create chaos for teachers in classrooms, to create alternative energy. This way even the young, primary school children could learn some very important lessons in physics through their bodily kinetic activity, which they would only later on, in high school, learn about in a more conceptual way when they studied physics theories.

Project 1: Swinging for Light. *With the help of a low-impact alternative energy expert from the local region, a swing set was designed and built which was like no other. When the children swung on the swings, once their kinetic energy built up to a certain degree, a light bulb fitted into the frame of the swing set would light up. To the children, this was pure magic. And yet it was a magic that they had created with their own energy, while they were playing!*

Project 2: Playing for Science. *In a second project, we built a large stone structure with a water wheel at the top and a series of sculpted clay-fired flow form basins through which water flowed down the structure like a waterfall, into a pond at the bottom, nestled into a sandpit beside a see-saw. When children rode the* *see-saw, the kinetic energy of their weight moving the see-saw up and down pumped water up, turning the water wheel and pouring water down through the flow forms. The children were again empowered to experience the force of their own energy transforming into another kind of energy—physics through imaginative play.*

9.8 Concluding Remarks

> The one fundamental principle of education—that the pupils are alive, and not mere portmanteaus to be neatly packed. (Whitehead 1919, p. 43)

Without a habitable planet for our children's children in another century, what point is there to all the science and technology, all the new computer software, all the mobile value-added services, all the profits in all the financial dealings swirling through the stock markets and all the high-stakes testing of our young people?

Believe it or not, it is that serious. While I am not by nature a doomsayer, I have come to realise in the last decade that unless we educate our children to appreciate, respect and value life on earth—the only planet we know of so far that can support human life—then we have failed them.

We have seen in this chapter that the leading edge of science and philosophy are life-affirming and life-promoting. Why then give our children the dry stale concepts of the already-known. Why not give them concepts that live and breathe as they do, through their lively imaginations, through ecological awareness and through a sense of the importance of the long-term view.

In the next chapter, we will build on our base of pedagogical love and life, to create the philosophical foundations for a wise education.

References

Abbs, P. (1994). *The educational imperative: Defense of Socratic and aesthetic learning*. London: RoutledgeFalmer.

Anderson, J. (1985). *Cognitive psychology and its implications*. New York: W.H.Freeman and Co.

Arnheim, R. (1989). *Thoughts on art education*. Los Angeles: Getty Centre for Education in the Arts.

Bassett, C. (2005, October). Wisdom in three acts: Using transformative learning to teach for wisdom [Electronic version]. In *Sixth international transformative learning conference*, East Lansing. Michigan.

Bergson, H. (1911/1944). *Creative evolution* (A. Mitchell, Trans.). New York: Macmillan & Co.

Biesta, G. J. J. (2014). *The beautiful risk of education*. Boulder: Paradigm Publishers.

Boulding, E. (1988). Image and action in peace building. *Journal of Social Issues, 44*(2), 17–37.

Broudy, H. S. (1987). *The role of imagery in learning*. Los Angeles: The Getty Centre for Education in the Arts.

Callahan, G., & Cubbin, N. (2000, November 11–12). Scream tests. *The Australian Magazine*, pp. 20–27.

Clouder, C., Jenkinson, S., & Large, M. (2000). *The future of childhood*. Gloucestershire: Hawthorn Press.

Cook-Greuter, S. R. (2000). Mature ego development: A gateway to ego transcendence. *Journal of Adult Development, 7*(4), 227–240.

de La Mettrie, J. O. (1748). *L'Homme machine*. Leyden: Elie Luzac.

Deleuze, G. (1990/1995). *Negotiation: 1972–1990* (M. Joughin, Trans.). New York: Columbia University Press.

Deleuze, G., & Conley, T. (1992). *The fold: Leibniz and the Baroque*. Minneapolis: University of Minnesota Press.

Deleuze, G., & Guattari, F. (1994). *What is philosophy?* (First published in French 1991) (H. Tomlinson, & G. Burchell, Trans.) (A series in social thought and cultural criticism). New York: Columbia University Press.

Derrida, J. (2001). Structure, sign, and play in the discourse of the human sciences. *Writing and Difference* (A. Bass, Trans.) (pp. 278–294). London: Routledge.

Dewey, J. (1972). *The early works, 1882–1898* (Vol. 5). Carbondale/Edwardsville: Southern Illinois University Press.

Eckersley, R. (1995). Values and visions: Youth and the failure of modern Western culture. *Youth Studies Australia, 14*(1), 13–21.

Eckersley, R. (1996). *Having our say about the future: Young people's dreams and expectations for Australia in 2010 and the role of science and technology*. Australian Science and Technology Council.

Egan, K. (1988). Metaphors in collision: Objectives, assembly lines and stories. *Curriculum Inquiry, 18*(1), 63–86.

Egan, K. (1989). *Teaching as story-telling*. Chicago: Chicago Press.

Egan, K. (1990). *Romantic understanding: The development of rationality and imagination, ages 8–15*. London: Routledge.

Egan, K. (1997). *The educated mind: How cognitive tools shape our understanding*. Chicago: The University of Chicago Press.

Eisner, E. (1985). *The educational imagination: On the design and evaluation of school programs* (2nd ed.). New York: Macmillan.

Fien, J. (1998). Environmental education for a new century. In D. Hicks & R. Slaughter (Eds.), *World yearbook 1998: Futures education*. London: Kogan Page.

Fraser, M., Kember, S., & Lury, C. (2005). Inventive life: Approaches to the new vitalism. *Theory, Culture and Society, 22*(1), 1–14.

Gare, A. (1999). Speculative metaphysics and the future of philosophy: The contemporary relevance of Whitehead's defence of speculative metaphysics. *Australasian Journal of Philosophy, 77*(2), 127–145.

Gare, A. (2002). The roots of postmodernism: Schelling, process philosophy, and poststructuralism. In C. Keller & A. Daniell (Eds.), *Process and difference: Between cosmological and poststructuralist postmodernisms*. New York: SUNY Press.

Gebser, J. (1949/1985). *The ever-present origin*. Athens: Ohio University Press.

Gidley, J. (1998a). Prospective youth visions through imaginative education. *Futures: The Journal of Policy, Planning and Futures Studies, 30*(5), 395–408.

Gidley, J. (1998b). Youth futures: Transcending violence through the artistic imagination. In S. Inayatullah & P. Wildman (Eds.), *Futures studies: Methods, emerging issues and civilizational visions. A multi-media CD ROM*. Brisbane: Prosperity Press.

Gidley, J. (2001, June). The dancer at the edge of knowledge: Imagination as a transdisciplinary force. In *The 2nd International Philosophy, Science and Theology Festival*, Grafton.

Gidley, J. (2002). Holistic education and visions of rehumanized futures. In J. Gidley & S. Inayatullah (Eds.), *Youth futures: Comparative research and transformative visions* (pp. 155–168). Westport: Praeger.

Gidley, J. (2003, September). Empowering teachers to work with imagination. In *3rd international soul in education conference*, Byron Bay.

Gidley, J. (2004, May). Imagination and integration: Empowering teachers and children. In *Council of Government Schools Organisations (COGSO), 4th annual conference*, Darwin, NT, Australia.

Gidley, J. (2005). Giving hope back to our young people: Creating a new spiritual mythology for western culture. *Journal of Futures Studies, 9*(3), 17–30.

Gidley, J. (2007). Educational imperatives of the evolution of consciousness: The integral visions of Rudolf Steiner and Ken Wilber. *International Journal of Children's Spirituality, 12*(2), 117–135.

Gidley, J. (2008). *Evolving education: A postformal-integral-planetary gaze at the evolution of consciousness and the educational imperatives*. PhD dissertation Southern Cross University, Lismore.

Gidley, J. (2009). Educating for evolving consciousness: Voicing the emergency for love, life and wisdom. In *The international handbook of education for spirituality, care and wellbeing* (Springer international handbooks of religion and education series). New York: Springer.

Gidley, J. (2012). Evolution of education: From weak signals to rich imaginaries of educational futures. *Futures: The Journal of Policy, Planning and Futures Studies, 44*(1), 46–54.

Gidley, J., Bateman, D., & Smith, C. (2004). *Futures in education: Principles, practice and potential* (AFI monograph series 2004, Vol. 5). Melbourne: Australian Foresight Institute.

Giroux, H. A. (1998). Series foreword. In H. A. Giroux (Ed.), *Naming the multiple: Poststructuralism and education*. Westport: Bergin & Garvey.

Giroux, H. A. (2001). *Stealing innocence: Corporate culture's war on children*. New York: Palgrave Macmillan.

Goodenough, U., & Deacon, T. W. (2006). The sacred emergence of nature. In P. Clayton (Ed.), *Oxford handbook of science and religion* (pp. 853–871). Oxford: Oxford University Press.

Grigorov, S. K. (2012). *International handbook of ecopedagogy for students, educators and parents: A project for a new eco-sustainable civilization*. Sophia: Bulgarian Centre for Sustainable Local Development and Ecopedagogy.

Grossman, D., Degaetano, G., & Grossman, D. (1999). *Stop teaching our kids to kill: A call to action against TV, movie and video violence*. New York: Random House.

Guevara, K., & Ord, J. (1996). The search for meaning in a changing work context. *Futures: The Journal of Policy, Planning and Futures Studies, 28*(8), 709–722.

Habermas, J. (1992). *Postmetaphysical thinking: Philosophical essays*. Cambridge: Polity Press.

Healy, J. M. (1998). *Failure to connect: How computers affect our children's minds—and what we can do about it*. New York: Touchstone.

Healy, J. M. (1999). *Endangered minds: Why children don't think and what we can do about it*. New York: Simon and Schuster.

Hicks, D. (1995). Envisioning the future: The challenge for environmental educators. *Environmental Education Research, 1*(3), 1–9.

Hicks, D. (1998). Identifying sources of hope in post-modern times. In D. Hicks & R. Slaughter (Eds.), *World yearbook of education 1998: Futures education*. London: Kogan Page.

Hicks, D. (2001). *Citizenship for the future: A practical classroom guide*. Surrey: World Wildlife Fund-UK.

Hicks, D. (2002). *Lessons for the future* (Futures and Education Series). London: Routledge.

Holden, C. (2002). Citizens of the new century: Perspectives from the United Kingdom. In J. Gidley & S. Inayatullah (Eds.), *Youth futures: Comparative research and transformative visions* (pp. 131–142). Westport: Praeger.

Hutchinson, F. (1992). Making peace with people and planet: Some important lessons from the Gandhian tradition in educating for the 21st century. *Peace, Environment and Education, 3*(3), 3–14.

Hutchinson, F. (1993). Educating beyond fatalism and impoverished social imagination: Are we actively listening to young people's voices on the future? *Peace Environment and Education, 4* (4), 36–57.

Hutchinson, F. (1996). *Educating beyond violent futures*. London: Routledge.

Jantsch, E. (1980). *The self-organising universe: Scientific and human implications of the emerging paradigm of evolution*. New York: Pergamon Press.
Jardine, D. W. (1998). *To dwell with a boundless heart: Essays in curriculum theory, hermeneutics, and the ecological imagination* (Studies in the postmodern theory of education). New York: Peter Lang Publishing.
Jencks, C. (1997). *The architecture of the jumping universe: A polemic: How complexity science is changing architecture and culture*. West Sussex: Wiley.
Jenson, R. (1996). The dream society. *The Futurist, 30*(3), 9–13.
Kearney, R. (1998). *Poetics of imagining: Modern to post-modern*. Edinburgh: University Press.
Kegan, R. (1994). *In over our heads: The mental demands of modern life*. Cambridge, MA: Harvard University Press.
Klisanin, D. (2003). *Designing media with intent: Evolutionary guidance media for the creation of planetary consciousness*. Ph.D., Saybrook Graduate School and Research Center, California.
László, E. (2006). *The chaos point: The world at the crossroads*. Charlottsville: Hampton Roads Publishing Company.
Leonard, T., & Willis, P. (Eds.). (2008). *Pedagogies of the imagination: Mythopoetic curriculum in educational practice*. Berlin: Springer.
Lyotard, J.-F. (2004). *The postmodern condition: A report on knowledge*. Manchester: Manchester University Press.
Marshak, D. (1997). *The common vision: Parenting and educating for wholeness*. New York: Peter Lang.
McGill, J. (2005). *Reflecting on the pace of schooling*. http://www.torontowaldorfschool.com/pdf/refpace.pdf. Accessed 7 Dec 2006.
Miller, J. P. (1988). *The holistic curriculum*. Toronto: OISE Press.
Miller, R. (1999). Holistic education for an emerging culture. In S. Glazer (Ed.), *The heart of learning: Spirituality in education*. New York: Putnam.
Milojevic, I. (2005). *Educational futures: Dominant and contesting visions*. London: Routledge.
Montessori, M. (1916/1964). *The Montessori method*. New York: Schoken Books.
Montuori, A. (1997). Reflections on transformative learning: Social creativity, academic discourse and the improvisation of inquiry. *ReVision, 20*(1), 34–37.
Montuori, A. (2003). The complexity of improvisation and the improvisation of complexity: Social science, art and creativity. *Human Relations, 56*(2), 237–255.
Morin, E. (2001). *Seven complex lessons in education for the future*. Paris: UNESCO.
Morin, E. (2005). RE: From prefix to paradigm. *World Futures: The Journal of General Evolution, 61*, 254–267.
Morin, E., & Kern, A. B. (1999). *Homeland earth: A manifesto for the new millennium* (S. Kelly, & R. Lapoint, Trans.). (Advances in systems theory, complexity and the human sciences). Cresskill: Hampton Press.
Neville, B. (1989). *Educating psyche: Emotion, imagination, and the unconscious in learning*. Melbourne: Collins Dove.
Neville, B. (2001). The body of the five-minded animal. In S. Gunn & A. Begg (Eds.), *Mind, body and society: Emerging understandings in knowing and learning*. Melbourne: University of Melbourne.
Nicolescu, B. (1991). *Science, meaning and evolution: The cosmology of Jacob Boehme*. New York: Parabola Books.
Nielsen, T. W. (2006). Towards a pedagogy of imagination: A phenomenological case study of holistic education. *Ethnography and Education, 1*(2), 247–264.
Nuyen, A. T. (1998). Jean-Francois Lyotard: Education for imaginative knowledge. In M. Peters (Ed.), *Naming the multiple: Poststructuralism and education*. Westport: Bergin & Garvey.
Orr, D. (1994). *Earth in mind: On education, environment, and the human prospect*. Washington, DC: Island Press.
Orr, D. (2001). *The nature of design*. Oxford: Oxford University Press.

Palmer, P. (2007). The precision of poetry & the passion of science: An education in paradox uncovering the heart of higher education. In *Integrative learning for compassionate action in an interconnected world*, San Francisco.

Pearce, J. C. (1992). *Evolution's end: Claiming the potential of our intelligence*. San Francisco: Harper.

Polak, F. (1973). *The image of the future* (E. Boulding, Trans.). San Francisco: Jossey-Bass.

Rose, K., & Kincheloe, J. (2003). *Art, culture and education: Artful teaching in a fractured landscape*. New York: Peter Lang.

Schiller, F. (1954/1977). *On the aesthetic education of man—in a series of letters* (First published in 1795). New York: Frederick Ungar Publishing.

Sinnott, J. D. (2005). The dance of the transforming self: Both feelings of connection and complex thought are needed for learning. *New Directions for Adult and Continuing Education, 108*, 27–37.

Slaughter, R. (1991, June). Changing images of futures in the 20th century. *Futures,* 499–515.

Sloan, D. (1983). *Insight-imagination: The emancipation of thought and the modern world.* Westport: Greenwood.

Sloan, D. (1992). Imagination, education and our postmodern possibilities. *ReVision: A Journal of Consciousness and Transformation, 15*(2), 42–53.

Spina, S. U. (2004). Power plays: Video games' bad rap. In S. Steinberg & J. Kincheloe (Eds.), *Kinderculture: The corporate construction of childhood*. Boulder: Westview Press.

St. Pierre, E. A. (2004). Deleuzian concepts for education: The subject undone. *Educational Philosophy and Theory, 36*(3), 283–296.

Stehlik, T. (2008). Thinking, feeling and willing: How Waldorf Schools provide a creative pedagogy which nurtures and develops imagination. In T. Leonard & P. Willis (Eds.), *Pedagogies of the imagination: Mythopoetic curriculum in educational practice*. Berlin: Springer.

Steinberg, S., & Kincheloe, J. (Eds.). (2004). *Kinderculture: The corporate construction of childhood*. Boulder: Westview Press.

Steiner, R. (1901/1973). *The riddles of philosophy (GA 18)* (4th ed.) (Original work published 1901, and republished with addition in 1914). Spring Valley: The Anthroposophic Press.

Steiner, R. (1905/1981). *The stages of higher knowledge (GA 12)* (L. Monges & F. McKnight, Trans. 1967) (Original work published 1905). Spring Valley: Anthroposophic Press.

Steiner, R. (1928/1972). *A modern art of education (GA 307)* (3rd ed.) (J. Darrell & G. Adams, Trans.) [14 Lectures, Ilkley, Yorkshire, Aug 5 to 17, 1923] (Original work published 1928). London: Rudolf Steiner Press.

Steiner, R. (1956). *Supersensible influences in the history of mankind (GA 216)* (D. S Osmond, & O. Barfield, Trans.) [6 Lectures, Dornach, September 22 to October 1, 1922]. London: The Rudolf Steiner Publishing Co.

Steiner, R. (1967a). *Discussions with teachers, lectures, 1919*. London: Rudolf Steiner Press.

Steiner, R. (1967b). *The younger generation: Education and spiritual impulses in the 20th century (GA 217)* (R. M. Querido, Trans.) [13 Lectures Stuttgart, October 3 to 15, 1922]. New York: Anthroposophic Press.

Steiner, R. (1981). *The renewal of education through the science of the spirit: Lectures, 1920*. Sussex: Kolisko Archive.

Steiner, R. (1982). *The kingdom of childhood: Lectures, 1924*. New York: Anthroposophic Press.

Steiner, R. (1990). *Toward imagination: Culture and the individual (GA 169)* (S. H. Seiler, Trans.) [7 Lectures, Berlin, June 6 to July 18, 1916] New York: Anthroposophic Press.

Sterling, S. (2001). *Sustainable education*. Bristol: Schumacher Briefings.

Stewart, C. (2002). Re-imagining your neighbourhood: A model of futures education. In J. Gidley & S. Inayatullah (Eds.), *Youth futures: Comparative research and transformative visions* (pp. 187–196). Westport: Praeger.

Suess, E. (1875). *Die Entstehung Der Alpen* [The origin of the Alps] Vienna: W. Braunmuller.

Uhrmacher, B. (1992). Coming to know the world through Waldorf education. In *American Educational Research Association conference* (p. 24), San Francisco, unpublished.
Varela, F., Thompson, E., & Rosch, E. (1993). *The embodied mind: Cognitive science and human experience*. Cambridge, MA: The MIT Press.
Warren, E. W. (1996). Imagination in Plotinus. *The Classical Quarterly, 16*(2), 277–285.
Whitehead, A. N. (1916/1967). *The aims of education*. New York: Free Press.
Whitehead, A. N. (1919). Discussion upon fundamental principles of education. *Process Studies, 14*(1), 41–43.
Whitehead, A. N. (1929/1985). *Process and reality*. New York: Free Press.
Wilber, K. (1995/2000). *Sex, ecology, spirituality: The spirit of evolution* (2nd ed., Rev.). Boston: Shambhala.
Wildman, P., Gidley, J., & Irwin, R. (1997). Visions as power: Promises and perils of envisioning desired futures with marginalised youth. *Journal of Applied Social Behaviour, 3*(2), 15–24.
Zajonc, A. (2005, February 13). Love and knowledge: Recovering the heart of learning through contemplation. In *Contemplative practices in education: Making peace in ourselves and peace in the world*, Columbia University.
Ziegler, W. (1991). Envisioning the future. *Futures, 23*(5), 516–527.

Chapter 10
Pedagogical Wisdom: A Creative Force

10.1 Introduction

I consciously invite you to engage with the core value of pedagogical wisdom third, after love and life, because I believe that wisdom flourishes in educational contexts already imbued with reverence-care-love and life-filled conceptual imagination. While pedagogical love essentially involves bringing the heart back into education, and pedagogical life engages both the imagination and the hands—in handwork, gardening, nature care—pedagogical wisdom is the most cognitive of the core values. Wisdom requires the head as well as the heart. Yet paradoxically, even a brilliant intellect—if it lacks heart and ethics—is not always wise. So wisdom is integrative, it is complex and it is creative. Wisdom does not follow the straight and narrow but meanders, pauses and looks around corners seeing what surprises. So how do we educate for wisdom? That is what I hope you will discover in this chapter.

After a brief diagnostic, I reiterate the evolution of consciousness theme, the postformal qualities and the postformal pedagogies that I conceptually weave into my tapestry of wisdom. The main sections of this chapter explore the philosophical importance of wisdom, educational approaches that encourage and support it, many practical examples from educators of how to cultivate wisdom and some personal reflections on how I have worked creatively, complexly and multi-modally in my educational endeavours with children and young people.

10.2 Why Wisdom? A Brief Diagnostic

> Teachers therefore need not simply to be competent, but also to be educationally wise. Such wisdom is to be understood as a "quality" of the person. (Biesta 2014, p. 8)

J.M. Gidley, *Postformal Education*, Critical Studies of Education 3,
DOI 10.1007/978-3-319-29069-0_10

Why is wisdom important? The notion of *wisdom*—for millennia a central concept in the perennial philosophies (or wisdom traditions)—seems to have lost its way as an aspirational virtue. The modern era of hyper-rationality and hyper-specialisation has been a reductive process in which the pre-modern unitive worldview of inherited, or revealed, "wisdom" has been superseded by bits—and, more recently, bytes—of information. Yet wisdom has been attracting a resurgence of interest, particularly at the philosophical intersections between postformal developmental psychology, education and spirituality discourses. Perhaps, after the long-term privileging of cognitive over emotional or vital ways of knowing in the academic arena, the reductionist trend is beginning to be reversed.

Why do we want to educate with and for wisdom? We live in a global world with a dominant culture that no longer values wisdom. It could be said that the dominant 21st-century worldview is replete with stupid rather than wise values, signified by corporate greed, climate crises, environmental degradation and huge economic disparity. Is this what we want for our children and their grandchildren? What do we aspire towards? An education for wisdom includes creativity, multi-modal learning and complexity, all of which are discussed below.

What happens when wisdom is missing from education? Fragmentation of knowledge is one of the more prevalent by-products of the loss of wisdom. Borrowing heavily from industrial era metaphors, education is now marketed as the product in a globally competitive *knowledge industry*. This globalisation of knowledge frequently reflects commodification and homogenisation, whereby outmoded models and approaches are transplanted as if they were fast-food franchises with little regard to the quality of the learning experience for students or the cultural context in which the model is implanted. Referred to as the global knowledge economy, such approaches are locked into short-termism, stasis and homogenisation.

What do education and psychology researchers say about wisdom in education? Wisdom is a complex, elusive dimension but is attracting growing interest among adult developmental and transpersonal psychologists and educators working with postformal thinking. These developments are explored here.

10.3 Evolutionary Theme: Complexification of Thinking and Culture

The idea that wisdom is a stage of human development can be approached from at least two perspectives—cultural evolutionary theories and adult developmental psychology theories. Both approaches point to complexification of human thinking and consciousness, and both explicitly identify new stage/s, structures or movements of consciousness. The most acknowledged path to wisdom is through the cultivation of creative, multi-perspectival standpoints and the integration of complex thinking including embracing paradox and contradiction.

10.3.1 Postformal Reasoning Qualities Aligned to Wisdom

The particular features of postformal reasoning that I align with wisdom are creativity, complexity and intuition (the very heart of wisdom) (see Table 10.1). For a more comprehensive understanding of these qualities, see Table 5.4. In Chapter 7 you will have seen that I cohere these qualities as aspects of wisdom.

10.3.2 Postformal Pedagogies that Create Wise Education

There are specific educational theories addressing the cultivation of wisdom (Falcone 2000; Hart 2001a, 2001b; Sternberg 2001). Pedagogies that emphasise creativity (Neville 1989; Sloan 1992) and complexity (Davis 2004; Morin 2001) also facilitate the cultivation of wisdom. Numerous learning modes can be explored as steps towards wisdom through engaging with multiple intelligences (Gardner 1996).

I also wish to disrupt a little with some surprising pedagogical concepts. In the serious business of education and learning, squeezed on either side by the audit culture and high-stakes testing, such concepts as laughter (Johnson 2005), play (Schwartz 1999; Derrida 2001; Ota et al. 1997), dancing (Pridmore 2004), jouissance (Kincheloe 2006) and happiness (Noddings 2003) seem remote. Such creative human literacies can contribute to a flexibility and lightness of cognition as facets of the core value of *pedagogical wisdom* (Table 10.2).

Table 10.1 Postformal Reasoning Qualities Aligned to Wisdom

Postformal Reasoning Qualities that Promote Wisdom through Complexity of Thinking and Culture	
Creativity	Creativity is the ability to see things from novel perspectives. Psychology research found that creativity is declining during childhood in the USA.
Complexity	Complexity involves the ability to hold multiple perspectives in mind. In a complex interconnected world, changing one thing affects everything else.
Intuitive wisdom	It takes a highly developed individual to know the difference between accurate intuition and other types of instinctive reaction. Intuition is higher wisdom.

Table 10.2 Postformal Pedagogies that Create Wise Education

Postformal Approaches through Creativity, Complexity and Multiple Perspectives	
Creativity in education...	... goes beyond creativity as an "add-on" in education and recognises creativity as a fundamental educational underpinning.
Complexity in education ...	... includes educational approaches that draw from and embrace the science and philosophy of complexity.
Wisdom education ...	... also involves some specific educational theories and approaches that directly address the cultivation of wisdom.

10.4 Philosophical Perspectives: Wisdom as Waking up to Multiplicity

> Wisdom is defined as the application of tacit as well as explicit knowledge as mediated by values toward the achievement of a common good through a balance among (a) intrapersonal, (b) interpersonal, and (c) extrapersonal interests, over the (a) short and (b) long terms, to achieve a balance among (a) adaptation to existing environments, (b) shaping of existing environments, and (c) selection of new environments. (Sternberg 2001, p. 231)

The notion of *wisdom*—for millennia a central concept in the perennial philosophies (or wisdom traditions)—is a complex, elusive dimension. The Greek Stoic philosophers defined philosophy itself as the striving after wisdom. And they defined wisdom in turn as the knowledge of things divine and human. There are numerous definitions of wisdom, even within psychology.

Developmental psychologist and wisdom researcher Robert Sternberg has developed a "balance theory of wisdom" as described in the opening quote. According to Vana Prewitt, Sternberg's theory built on his earlier definition: "wisdom is evidenced during conflict that requires a balanced perspective of multiple points of view and fair judgment" (Prewitt n.d.). As one might expect from a quality as multi-faceted as wisdom, even Sternberg himself describes it in many different ways. In quite simple terms, he says it is enhanced by the cultivation of "openness to experience, reflectivity upon experience, and willingness to profit from experience" (Sternberg 2005, p. 21). He also characterises wisdom as the application of intelligence, creativity and knowledge (Sternberg 2005).

Deirdre Kramer claims that wisdom has been conceptualised as:

> (1) a rare, highly exercised and developed form of cognitive expertise about the domain of human affairs that allows for multiple conduits or (2) a constellation of personal attributes reflecting a high degree of cognitive, affective, and behavioral maturity that allows for an unusual degree of sensitivity, broad-mindedness, and concern for humanity. (Kramer 2000, p. 83)

Elsewhere Sternberg confirms the importance of balancing and integrating the cognitive, conative/behavioural and affective aspects of human abilities (Sternberg 2005). This echoes Steiner's thinking/head (knowledge), the feelings/heart (love) and the hands/will (action) (Steiner 1927/1986, 1909/1965), which must have been influenced by the "head, heart and hands" approach of Swiss educator Johann Heinrich Pestalozzi (1746–1827). Sri Aurobindo's integral yoga with its threefold path of *knowledge*, *love* and *action* and the integral education model inspired by it is also aligned. Wilber's *Big Three*—based on Plato's Truth, Beauty and Goodness—represent similar archetypes (Wilber 1995/2000). How a postformal educational philosophy might integrate the ideals of Truth, Beauty and Goodness is discussed in Chapter 11: Pedagogical Voice. Wisdom researcher Carol Bassett has extended the archetypal three to four wisdom dimensions: discerning (cognitive), respecting (affective), engaging (active) and transforming (reflective) (Bassett 2005a, p. 7).

Adult developmental psychologists claim that complexity, multi-perspectivality, creativity, dialectical thinking, relativism, self-reflexivity, ability to deal with uncertainty, complexity, contextualism and problem-finding have all been linked to wisdom (Arlin 1999; Labouvie-Vief 1990; Sinnott 1994; Sternberg 2001; Yan and Arlin 1995). Psychologist Jan Sinnott views wisdom as a complex and integrative characteristic of postformal thought, explicitly connecting it with spirituality and creativity (Sinnott 1998). Kaufman and Baer (2005) characterise creativity as the ability to see things from novel perspectives reinforcing Sternberg's and Sinnott's links between wisdom, creativity, complexity and ability to take multiple perspectives.

The importance of creativity in human psychology was emphasised by Arthur Koestler in his seminal work, *The Act of Creation* (1964/1989). Koestler argued that there is an inverse relationship between creativity and rational thinking and that creativity is suppressed by the "automatic routines of thought and behaviour that dominate" our lives, foreshadowing the notion of creativity as a postformal feature. While creativity was generally ignored by psychologists in Koestler's time, a resurgence of interest among psychologists and educators (Kaufman and Baer 2005; Sinnott 1998, 2005; Sternberg 1999) has linked creativity to postformal thinking and transformative learning (Montuori 1997, 2006). Koestler's observations on the tension between reason and creativity are supported by recent psychological research indicating that creativity and imagination are declining during childhood—in contrast to most aspects of cognitive development (Kaufman and Baer 2006). This raises the question as to whether it may be the process of schooling itself with its focus on the acquisition of knowledge and the production of correct (rather than imaginative) answers, which promotes this decline (Kaufman and Baer 2006).

Further to Kaufman and Baer's research, more recent psychological research has found that creativity as measured by the Torrance Tests of Creative Thinking (TTCT) has significantly declined in the USA over the last two decades (Kim 2011). The researcher proposes that the reason for this decline is the pressure on young people to compete in standardised high-stakes tests and subsequent loss of freedom. It is likely that similar results would be found in the UK, where poet and professor of creative writing Peter Abbs notes:

> Most of the educational changes made during the last two decades under the nationalised curriculum have engineered a vast prescriptive system of convergent learning ... at the expense of the potential creativity of the overloaded learner. Pupils and students are now driven through a series of preconceived programs to emerge as convergent members of the consumer society; I would rather have them go through a series of transformative experiences to enter a cultural democracy as reflective citizens and radical contributors to the workplace. (Abbs 2003, p. 1–2)

The situation in China is much worse, where it is reported that "suicide in the wake of disappointing results in the state university placement exams is the fifth leading cause of death in China" (Sherman 2012).

In Erik Erikson's later stages of mature adult development, as discussed in Chapter 8 (see Table 8.3), he refers to the basic virtues to be developed as love,

Table 10.3 Erikson's Eighth Stage of Mature Adult Development

Stage	Psycho-social Crisis	Basic Virtue	Age
8	Ego integrity vs. despair	Wisdom	Maturity (65+)

care and finally wisdom (Erikson 1950/1985). Table 10.3 demonstrates Erikson's placement of wisdom as the most mature virtue—to be developed in later life, post sixty-five years of age (Stage 8). Erikson regarded wisdom as the successful resolution of the growing tension during older age between despair and ego integrity.

Finally, wisdom is about *waking up*—to our own presence and the presence of others. The complex wisdom embedded in the art of education demands being awake in every moment. According to Steiner in 1922:

> Waldorf School Education is not a pedagogical system but an Art—the Art of awakening what is actually there within the human being... First of all, the teachers must be awakened, and then the teachers must awaken the children and young people... what matters is a question of awakening, for evolution has made human beings fall into a sleep that is filled with intellectualistic dream... The awakening must be sought within the human being himself. (Steiner 1967, p. 23–28)

Echoing Steiner's sentiments, Tobin Hart refers to Henri David Thoreau's notion of the value of being able to live even one day "deliberately".

> The deliberateness he [Thoreau] refers to implies moving beyond habits of thought, perception, and deed to be fully centred and awake throughout the day. Education for wisdom is not about simply being taught but about *waking up*. Waking up requires a certain kind of energy, certain capacities for taking the world into our consciousness. (Hart 2001b, p. 10)

The evolutionary significance of this waking up is poignantly brought home in the last lines of poet Christopher Fry's poem: "Sleep of Prisoners".

> ... It takes
> So many thousand years to wake,
> But will you wake for pity's sake!

10.5 Postformal Pedagogies: Promoting Wisdom in Education

In addition to educational approaches that explicitly educate for wisdom in its own right, wisdom is also cultivated by pedagogies that emphasise creativity and complexity in education. Such multi-modality can include many surprising features.

10.5.1 Creativity in Education

> I am interested in education as itself a creative "act" or, to be more precise, in education as an act of creation, that is, as an act of bringing something new into the world, something that did not exist before. (Biesta 2014, p. 11)

With these words, Biesta aligns himself with Whitehead in that he sees education itself as a creative act and creativity as not just something to be added on or cultivated. This makes practical sense in the context of educational psychology research on creativity by Kaufman and Baer, who operationalise creativity as the ability to see things from novel perspectives. Their disturbing psychological research showing the decline of creativity and imagination in childhood does not augur well for the development of wisdom in later life (Kaufman and Baer 2006). Kaufman and Baer are continuing their research into whether this decline in creativity can be attributed to modern education or to other factors. Building on Sternberg's and Sinnott's links between wisdom, creativity, complexity and ability to take multiple perspectives, the question we need to ask is: "How might education be more creative and thus nurture wisdom more effectively?"

Integral educator Alfonso Montuori is a strong voice in the area of creativity in higher education. He makes a case for the metaphor of jazz improvisation as a way to think about creativity in education (Montuori 2003). He also points to the close relationship between creativity and complexity, both of which he sees as important directions for the development of higher consciousness (Montuori 2003; Montuori et al. 2004). Montuori has developed an educational research methodology called creative enquiry, which he argues leads students beyond instrumental formal learning to a love of learning (Montuori 1998).

Arguably, wisdom can be nurtured by pedagogical approaches that acknowledge *multiple intelligences* (Gardner 2001) and/or multiple *lines* of ability (Wilber 2004). Further reading on the importance of multiple perspectives and their integration can be found in special issues of the journal *Futures* on transdisciplinarity (Klein 2004) and global mindset change (Gidley 2010). Creativity is an important feature of Steiner education, as we will see in later sections. Kaufman and Sternberg's (2006) international creativity research also found aesthetic orientation to be a personality trait associated with creativity. This suggests a role for aesthetic education in cultivating wisdom, as indicated by post-formal educators (Rose and Kincheloe 2003). Aesthetic education is discussed in Chapter 11 as we circle through the interweaving landscape of postformal pedagogies.

10.5.2 Complexity in Education

> Pertinent knowledge must confront complexity. *Complexus* means that which is woven together... Complexity is... the bond between unity and multiplicity. Developments proper to our planetary era confront us more frequently, ineluctably with the challenge of complexity. (Morin 2001, p. 15)

My approach to complexity in education is inspired by French philosopher and sociologist Edgar Morin's *third-generation complexity theory* which goes beyond the mathematical and cybernetic approaches of first- and second-generation complexity science (Alhadeff-Jones 2008; Morin 2005; Nicolescu 2002). Morin is a leading thinker on complexity in educational futures (Morin 2001), his writings being particularly favoured in Latin America, where he has founded a university based on his complex education philosophy.[1] Morin distinguishes his approach from complexity sciences which he calls "restricted complexity, to differentiate it from that wider and humanist holding, which defines it as a method of new thinking, valid to understand the nature, society, reorganize human life, and to find solutions to the crisis of contemporary humanity" (Morin 2015, Para 5). Morin's multiversity in Mexico applies advanced complexity thinking in higher education.

In 2008 a special issue of the journal *Educational Philosophy and Theory* was published on "Complexity Theory and the Philosophy of Education" and edited by Michael Peters. Mark Mason suggested that educational research informed by complexity theory might be concerned with "connectionist holistic, non-linear" perspectives, rather than "input–output, 'black-box' causal modelling" (Mason 2008, p. 4). Mike Radford echoed Mason's claim stating that: "Complexity theory, with its emphasis on non-linear and dynamic interactions between multiple variables, within indeterminate and transient systems, supports the case for a connectionist and holistic analysis" (Radford 2008, p. 144). These papers support my theorisation that complexity is one of several interconnected postformal reasoning qualities which need to inform educational theory. In other papers, Inna Semetsky undertakes a rereading of Dewey in the light of complexity theory, while Mark Olssen views Foucault as a complexity theorist (Semetsky 2008; Olssen 2008). William Doll focuses on the potential impact of complexity theory on curriculum development and instruction so that it becomes "open, dynamic, relational, creative, and systems oriented…with an integration of the rational/scientific with the aesthetic/spiritual" aspects (Doll 2008, p. 190).

Wilber's integral framework could offer theoretical coherence to wisdom in education, but there is an art to how this works in practice (Rose and Kincheloe 2003; Steiner 1928/1972). Kincheloe refers to what he calls a *complex aesthetics* that creatively integrates the multiple perspectives to facilitating higher-order thinking.

> As teachers think about the relationship between the aesthetic and the intellectual, they develop pedagogical strategies that encourage engagement… It is a collaborative endeavor to aestheticize the familiar and to intellectualize the aesthetic. This involves the recognition of multiple ways of knowing which assists more students to discover that they are imaginative, creative and smart. (Rose and Kincheloe 2003, p. 46)

[1]The Real World Multiversity of Edgar Morin is also called The World Centre of Higher Learning for Social Transformation. http://www.multiversidadreal.edu.mx

10.5.3 Wisdom Education

> Wisdom is distinguished from bare intellect especially by its integration of the heart... We might even think of wisdom as the power of the mind to honor the insights of the heart... Such qualities as the ability to listen, empathise, and [be] comfort[able] with ambiguity are associated with wisdom. (Hart 2001b, p. 2–5)

Sternberg builds on his balance theory discussed earlier to develop sixteen principles for teaching wisdom in schools. It is beyond the scope of this small introduction to describe them all, but they include role-modelling wisdom, encouraging students to think about, critique and integrate their own values, to think dialogically and dialectically and to avoid self-interest (Sternberg 2001, p. 238). Secondly, Sternberg proposes several procedures for teachers to follow in teaching wisdom. These include: "read classic works of literature and philosophy"; engage students in class discussions to help them to develop dialogical thinking so that they can understand "significant problems from multiple points of view and understanding how others could conceive of things [differently]" (Sternberg 2001, p. 238). Teachers would also emphasise "critical, creative and practical thinking in the service of good ends" (Sternberg 2001, p. 238). Sternberg distinguishes his approach to teaching wisdom from a standard "constructivist approach to learning" in that students of wisdom "must be able to construct knowledge not only from their own point of view, but to construct and sometimes reconstruct it from the point of view of others" (Sternberg 2001, p. 238). Finally, he presents the outline of a wisdom-related curriculum. For those interested in pursuing Sternberg's approach, I would recommend reading his article "Why Schools Should Teach for Wisdom" (Sternberg 2001).

Patricia Arlin takes a different approach and focuses on what a wise teacher might be like. She arrives at five characteristics related to the five wisdom characteristics indicated by Baltes and Smith (1990) and adapts them to education.

What Arlin concludes from her research is that the characteristics that distinguish otherwise good or even *expert* teachers from *wise teachers* are anchored in "current developmental psychology theories of wisdom" (Arlin 1999, p. 16). Expanding on this point she claims:

> Wise teachers are described as having a sense of context, an understanding of relativism, and an appreciation for uncertainty. Since contextualism, relativism, and uncertainty are characteristics of mature adult thought, it appears that teacher personal and professional development may be a special case of general cognitive and social development. (Arlin 1999, p. 16)

It is notable that Arlin uses several of the key postformal qualities to identify her wise teachers. Wisdom educator Caroline Bassett (2005b) proposes three approaches: "wisdom as cognitive functioning, wisdom associated with various personal attributes, and wisdom understood as exceptional self-development" (Bassett 2005b). She contextualises Sternberg's approach within the first but omits Sinnott's research. Bassett situates her own work in the third approach, which she associates with postformal thinking, transformative learning and aesthetics/creativity. She claims that through affect, aesthetic education also contributes to wisdom (see Chapter 11: Section 11.5.2). Jan Sinnott's approach to education is more generally focused on developing complex postformal thought than specifically targeted at wisdom. However, it is worth noting that in her work with college students, she emphasises postformal qualities such as dialogical reasoning, complexity, synthesis and the honouring of the student as a *whole person* (Sinnott 2002).

Tobin Hart has developed an elegant theoretical model designed to align education to the evolution of consciousness. His model of learning goes through six successive *microgenetic* stages from: "information gathering to learning as knowledge building… [then] to learning that involves, successively, intelligence, understanding, wisdom and finally transformation" (Hart 2006, p. 104).

10.6 Practical Examples: Weaving a Wisdom Culture

> Good teachers…are able to weave a complex web of connections among themselves, their subjects, and their students so that students can learn to weave the world for themselves. The methods used by these weavers vary widely: lectures, Socratic dialogues, laboratory experiments, collaborative problem solving, creative chaos. The connections made by good teachers are held not in their methods but in their hearts—meaning heart in its ancient sense, as the place where intellect and emotion and spirit and will converge in the human self. (Palmer 1998, p. 11)

This next section focuses on the creative voices of educators who have cultivated pedagogical wisdom as an *art* through their creativity, adaptability and professional judgement. The ability to teach with, and for, wisdom cannot be measured by the evidence-based auditing of teachers' "skills and competencies" as some nations are proposing. It can however be developed in teachers through a variety of ways and means that will be offered below. Biesta refers to "the crucial role of judgement in always new, open, and unpredictable situations" (Biesta 2014, p. 120). An education suitable for complex futures, as I propose in this book, requires the development of just such judgement, which I call *pedagogical wisdom*. Biesta calls it educational "virtuosity" which he argues should be "at the very heart of education" (Biesta 2014, p. 120). My notion of pedagogical wisdom is, I believe what Biesta refers to as:

> A virtue-based conception of teaching and teacher education one that focuses on educational wisdom and the ways in which, through teacher education, we can help teachers become educationally wise. (Biesta 2014, p. 120)

Creative and complex thinking are inevitably enhanced when we take multiple perspectives and honour multiple ways of knowing (Gardner 1984/2011, 1996). Whitehead, cited by Hart, places creativity at the forefront of everything:

> Whitehead referred to creativity as the ultimate category—the category necessary to understand all other processes. That is, creation as a movement into novelty is the basic process of existence. (Hart 2006, p. 121)

And yet almost one hundred years after Whitehead, and in spite of the evolutionary waves of educational change we discussed in Chapter 6, MacLure bemoans the situation in the UK and beyond where "... state-sponsored intolerance of difference and complexity is now part of the story of education policy and research funding in many countries" (MacLure 2006a, p. 731).

Kincheloe makes the interesting point that it was because of what I called the second evolutionary wave—the alternative movements of the 1970s—that conservative interests began to fear a loss of control. He refers to this as the "recovery movement" in the USA and explains it as follows:

> By the mid-1970s a conservative counter-reaction—especially in the US—to these liberation movements was taking shape with the goals of "recovering" what was perceived to be lost in these movements... Thus, the politics, cultural wars, and educational and psychological debates, policies, and practices of the last three decades cannot be understood outside these efforts to "recover" white supremacy, patriarchy, class privilege.... (Kincheloe 2006)

To counter-balance this rise of neo-conservatism, we need to hear the creative voices of educators who have cultivated pedagogical wisdom as an *art*. MacLure's (2006b) art is her critical passion. She claims "Interruptive methods are needed to try to crack... the inertia coded in the pedagogic encounter" (MacLure 2006a, p. 731). She proposes a *baroque* educational philosophy, drawing on the educational philosophy of Deleuze, as a creative way to interrupt and resist closure (Deleuze and Conley 1992). In her keynote address to the Australian Educational Research Association Conference in Adelaide Australia, she summarised some key features of this creative model as: "entangled, disruptive, defamiliarises traditional education, artistic aesthetic and literary". MacLure further noted that by utilising "dislocation of time and space...[and] periodic interruptions of the 'other'" baroque educational philosophy offers "resistance to audit culture...[and] disrupts closure seeking" (MacLure 2006b).

It is intriguing to see how many of MacLure's *baroque* features resemble Steiner education—often regarded as quaintly anachronistic. Yet from MacLure's (2006c) perspective, this "defamiliarisation" with the "mythic immediacy of the educational present" is of immense value in moving beyond the "closure-seeking tendencies" of the audit culture. So how might such "left-field" aesthetic approaches as Steiner education or Deleuze's *baroque* philosophy lead to wisdom, postformal thinking or even qualify as "good education"? Some practical examples follow.

10.6.1 Multi-modal and Interconnected

> Being able to see and perceive in multiple ways is necessary for a great artist, an artful teacher and higher order thinkers in general. To see the self, objects, students ad infinitum from multiple perspectives and in the process discern the significance of each perspective and, importantly, their relationship to one another rests at the heart of expanded forms of cognition. (Rose and Kincheloe 2003, p. 144)

It may seem challenging and even paradoxical to recommend that teachers utilise multi-modal ways of presenting ideas, concepts and values and at the same time integrate them in such a way that their underlying interconnectedness becomes visible. And yet what may be most effective in cultivating wisdom in education is embracing complex thinking and creativity to represent knowledge from multiple perspectives while showing their integral interconnectedness through our creative artfulness. This can be assisted by approaches that acknowledge *multiple intelligences* (Gardner 2001), or *lines* of ability (Wilber 2004).

> In my view, if we are to encompass adequately the realm of human cognition, it is necessary to include a far wider and more universal set of competences than has ordinarily been considered. And it is necessary to remain open to the possibility that many—if not most—of these competences do not lend themselves to measurement by standard verbal methods, which rely very heavily on a blend of logic and linguistic abilities. (Gardner 1984/2011, p. xxviii)

The integration of multiple perspectives is enabled especially through the arts (see Chapter 11) and through imagination (see Chapter 9). The crucial point is that in "post-formal" thinking, these qualities and processes are not separate but already integrally interwoven.

Notions of creativity-based integration and aesthetic interconnectedness in education have been appearing in the literature for at least a decade. The scenarios described by Noddings below and Palmer earlier are representative of processes that have been implemented in Steiner schools for a century:

> Mathematics teachers, for example, must be able to draw on philosophy, biography, history, fiction, poetry, science, art, music, and current events. In doing this competently, teachers help students to make connections between school studies and great existential questions. (Noddings 2005, Para 13)

And if we go back further in time, we are reminded that the idealist approach was inspired by Herbart's integrative curriculum. Are we coming full circle?

10.6.2 Cultivating Broad Creativities

> Postformal thought ... is linked to creative production by virtue of its ... multiple views of reality and its multiple solutions, definitions, parameters, and methods during problem solving... [also combining] subjective and objective understanding... the same sorts of processes [can be observed] under the rubrics of wisdom. (Sinnott 1998, p. 271)

Effectively, wisdom is enhanced if we ensure that children learn critically under-appreciated human values and a diversity of modes of thinking, doing and being through cultivating a broad range of "creativities". Other ways to ensure that children develop a creative, wise, multi-perspectival experience of learning include the honouring of the often-subjugated humanistic values, play and laughter.

- *Value of play*: Awareness of the value of play in education goes back two centuries to German romantic philosophers, particularly Schiller (1954/1977) and Jean Paul Richter (Pridmore 2004; Schiller 1954/1977). Schiller regards what he called the play-drive as being a crucial force in balancing the excesses of reason and the excesses of the senses. In the fourteenth letter of his 1794 book *On the Aesthetic Education of Man*, Schiller famously stated: "...man only plays when in the full meaning of the word he is a man, and he is only completely a man when he plays..." (Schiller 1954/1977). Born just a few years after Schiller, Jean Paul claimed that: "spiritual education is essentially counter-cultural, that it is promoted by play and that it is grounded in love" (Pridmore 2004, p. 279). Dutch historian and cultural theorist Johan Huizinga wrote about the cultural significance of play in his book *Homo Ludens* (1938). German philosopher of hermeneutics, Georg Gadamer, building on the German romantic lineage, also wrote about the significance of play in the appreciation of art (Gadamer 1960/2005). Contemporary North American educator Eugene Schwartz (1999) sees play as a foundation for conceptual knowledge. Kincheloe and Steinberg (1993) link it to postformality. Play can be philosophically grounded by the *jouissance* of poststructuralist word play (Derrida 2001; Kristeva 1982) and integral developmental theory (Gordon and Esbjörn-Hargens 2007). Kincheloe, citing Kristeva, makes a significant link between Hermes and play in education.

> Hermes, the playful trickster, mysteriously pops up everywhere with his fantasies, surprise inspirations, and other gifts of the imagination; they are ours for the taking if we can hold onto the silence long enough to listen to him, if we have not let social expectations crush our propensity for play. (Kincheloe and Steinberg 1993, p. 304)

- *What about games?* While the topic of games could be a subsection of "play", the influence of video gaming in youth culture is such that I will briefly address it separately. While substantial literature suggests that violent video games have a destructive influence on children (Benoit 2000; Clouder et al. 2000; Grossman et al. 1999; Healy 1998; Pearce 1992), Stephanie Urso Spina contests this, arguing that this is only part of the picture:

> Video games serve young people as social, cognitive, and psychological tools, as signs of individual and social identity, as meaning-full experience... [and with reference to some of the 'unspeakable horrors' contained in some of them] ... I would encourage game designers and corporations to imagine and develop new games that marshal all the creative and technological sophistication currently mesmerising kids while engaging the self-expressive and even altruistic impulses. (Spina 2004, p. 278)

A new genre of altruistic games is emerging which will balance the dominant violent game genre (Klisanin 2003). From a futures perspective, Buckminster Fuller's World Game could provide just this possibility. In addition, German strategy games are another way to introduce into schools a balance to the extracurricular influence of violent video games, which would also contribute to the development of complex systems thinking. A whole genre of postformal game playing is just waiting to be discovered by the educational world. For example, non-violent strategy board games could playfully contribute to the development of postformal, complex systems thinking in adolescence.

- *Happiness, humour and laughter*: Perhaps even more subjugated in most mainstream education settings are notions such as *wellbeing* and *happiness* (Abbs 2003; Eckersley et al. 2006; Noddings 2003), *laughter*, *humour* and even *frivolity* (Johnson 2005; Koestler 1964/1989; MacLure 2006c; Kincheloe 2006). Koestler notes the relationship between humour, laughter and creativity (Koestler 1964/1989), while Helen Johnston and Maggie MacLure point to laughter and frivolity as indicators of healthy resistance to the performativity of the audit culture, the latter drawing on Derrida's archaeology of the frivolous (Johnson 2005; MacLure 2006c).

  Nel Noddings draws on the Dalai Lama, William James and John Dewey to challenge the Aristotelian foundations of our education system based on the hierarchical valuing of rational intellectual pursuits at the expense of many other human qualities and experiences, in particular happiness (Noddings 2003). It is encouraging to see these broader human literacies opening up through the creativity of postformal educational offerings.

10.7 Personal Reflections on Pedagogical Wisdom

As I reflected during the writing of this book on how I personally tried to cultivate the ground so that wisdom could grow, I realised that my approach had been particularly multi-modal. In reflecting on this chapter, I also asked myself: "What would a wise education feel like to children and teachers?"

Personal Reflections. *In my own pedagogical practice, I continually danced between disciplinary emphasis and transdisciplinary contextualisation: conceptually, through imaginative vitality; visually, through a picture or diagram; imaginatively, through the narration of a story, poem, song, dance or role-play; and/or experientially, through handwork, gardening or off-campus excursions. My planning was not held rigidly but always open to change in the moment to accommodate current issues or needs. As well as the overall class "programme" I was always aware of the individual differences in capability and motivation. So how did this translate into the children being engrossed? I think it also relates to the pedagogical art of how one presents and works with the material and processes. Here are some reflections.*

Wise Education from a Child's Perspective

Children would enjoy learning—love of learning.

Children would find meaning in what they learn—things would "make sense" because they would see how things "fitted together" (finding meaning in a fractured, postmodern world).

Children would develop self-confidence by learning that they were good at many things.

Children would feel that their whole being was valued and engaged not just their intellect or physical prowess.

Children would often not want to go outside when it was recess or lunchtime because they were so engrossed in what they were doing.

They were proud of the work they produced.

They engaged in "whole processes" for many things rather than just segments of processes.

Much of the time there was energy in the room—a buzz of engagement. The room was not silent and it was not generally noisy, but conversation between children took place during lessons as they might discuss what they were doing.

Wise Education from a Teacher's Perspective
Teachers would feel creative and inspired as they would feel that they were taking part in a co-transformation process.

Teachers would feel empowered as their sovereignty increased—they would find that they were more creative than they thought.

10.8 Concluding Remarks

They say you can't put an old head on young shoulders, and it is important to be clear that in this chapter I am not trying to turn children into "wise elders" before their time. Conversely, by letting children play and move and be active and mobile when they are young, and by stimulating their imaginations, their creativity and their senses of care, justice and fun while they are still children, we will help them to become wise as elders. Only if we learn to see content and concepts from multiple perspectives in childhood will we be able to see multiple perspectives in adulthood. Wisdom is essentially about being able to see things from multiple points of view.

By grounding this chapter in the educational domain, we can also bring greater insight to the core value of pedagogical wisdom. Much of the educational work we have reviewed involves recognising the importance of integrating the ways of knowing of the heart with our analytical, intellectual way of knowing if we are to work towards wisdom. This reflects the idea that wisdom cannot be separated from love, life and language. In the next chapter, we bring all four together, but with the special focus of Chapter 11 being on voice and language.

References

Abbs, P. (2003). *Against the flow: The arts, postmodern culture and education.* London: RoutledgeFalmer.

Alhadeff-Jones, M. (2008). Three generations of complexity theories: Nuances and ambiguities. *Educational Philosophy and Theory, 40*(1), 66–82.

Arlin, P. K. (1999). The wise teacher: A developmental model of teaching. *Theory into Practice, 38*(1), 12–17.

Baltes, P. B., & Smith, J. (1990). Toward a psychology of wisdom and its ontogenesis. In R. J. Sternberg (Ed.), *Wisdom, its nature, origins and development* (pp. 87–120). Cambridge: Cambridge University Press.

Bassett, C. (2005a). Emergent wisdom: Living a life in widening circles. *ReVision: A Journal of Consciousness and Transformation, 27*(4), 6–11.

Bassett, C. (2005b, October). Wisdom in three acts: Using transformative learning to teach for wisdom [Electronic version]. In *Sixth international transformative learning conference*, East Lansing, Michigan.

Benoit, M. (2000). The Dot. Com kids and the demise of frustration tolerance. In C. Clouder, S. Jenkinson, & M. Large (Eds.), *The future of childhood*. Gloucestershire: Hawthorn Press.

Biesta, G. J. J. (2014). *The beautiful risk of education*. Boulder: Paradigm Publishers.

Clouder, C., Jenkinson, S., & Large, M. (2000). *The future of childhood*. Gloucestershire: Hawthorn Press.

Davis, B. (2004). *Inventions of teaching: A genealogy*. Mahwah: Lawrence Erlbaum Associates.

Deleuze, G., & Conley, T. (1992). *The fold: Leibniz and the Baroque*. Minneapolis: University of Minnesota Press.

Derrida, J. (2001). Structure, sign, and play in the discourse of the human sciences. *Writing and Difference* (A. Bass, Trans.) (pp. 278–294). London: Routledge.

Doll, W. (2008). Complexity and the culture of curriculum. *Educational Philosophy and Theory, 40*(1), 190–212.

Eckersley, R., Wierenga, A., & Wyn, J. (2006). *Flashpoints and signposts: Pathways to success and wellbeing for Australia's young people*. Canberra: Australia 21.

Erikson, E.H. (1950/1985). *Childhood and society*. New York: Norton.

Falcone, G. J. (2000). *The relationship of postformal thought to conceptions of wisdom as mediated by age and education*. Ed.D., Rutgers The State University of New Jersey – New Brunswick and University of Medicine and Dentistry of New Jersey, New Jersey.

Gadamer, H.-G. (1960/2005). *Truth and method* (J. Weinsheimer, & D. Marshal, Trans., New York) (2nd Rev. ed.). London: Continuum International Publishing Group.

Gardner, H. (1984/2011). *Frames of mind: The theory of multiple intelligences*. New York: Basic Books.

Gardner, H. (1996). Probing more deeply into the theory of multiple intelligences. *NASSP Bulletin, 80*(583), 1–7.

Gardner, H. (2001, March 13). *An education for the future: The foundation of science and values*. Paper presented at The Royal Symposium Convened by Her Majesty, Queen Beatrix, Amsterdam.

Gidley, J. (2010). Globally scanning for megatrends of the mind: Potential futures of "Futures Thinking". *Futures: The Journal of Policy, Planning and Futures Studies, 42*(10), 1040–1048.

Gordon, G., & Esbjörn-Hargens, S. (2007). Are we having fun yet? An exploration of the transformative power of play. *Journal of Humanistic Psychology, 47*(2), 198–222.

Grossman, D., Degaetano, G., & Grossman, D. (1999). *Stop teaching our kids to kill: A call to action against TV, movie and video violence*. New York: Random House.

Hart, T. (2001a). *From information to transformation: Education for the evolution of consciousness*. New York: Peter Lang.

Hart, T. (2001b). Teaching for wisdom. *Encounter: Education for Meaning and Social Justice, 14* (2), 3–16.

Hart, T. (2006). From information to transformation: What the Mystics and Sages tell us education can be. In S. Inayatullah, I. Milojevic, & M. Bussey (Eds.), *Neohumanist educational futures: Liberating the pedagogical intellect*. Tamsui: Tamkang University Press.

Healy, J. M. (1998). *Failure to connect: How computers affect our children's minds—and what we can do about it*. New York: Touchstone.

Johnson, H. (2005). Counteracting performativity in schools: The case for laughter as a qualitative redemptive indicator. *International Journal of Children's Spirituality, 10*(1), 81–96.

Kaufman, J. C., & Baer, J. (2005). *Creativity across domains: Faces of the muse*. Mahwah: Lawrence Erlbaum Associates.
Kaufman, J. C., & Baer, J. (2006). *Creativity and reason in cognitive development*. New York: Cambridge University Press.
Kaufman, J. C., & Sternberg, R. J. (2006). *The international handbook of creativity*. New York: Cambridge University Press.
Kim, K. H. (2011). The creativity crisis: The decrease in creative thinking scores on the Torrance Tests of Creative Thinking. *Creativity Research Journal, 23*(4), 285–295.
Kincheloe, J. (2006). *Reading, writing and cognition: The postformal basics* (Bold Visions in Educational Research). Rotterdam: Sense Publishers.
Kincheloe, J., & Steinberg, S. (1993). A tentative description of post-formal thinking: The critical confrontation with cognitive theory. *Harvard Educational Review, 63*(3), 296–320.
Klein, J. T. (2004). Prospects for transdisciplinarity. *Futures, 36*(4), 515–526.
Klisanin, D. (2003). *Designing media with intent: Evolutionary guidance media for the creation of planetary consciousness*. Ph.D., Saybrook Graduate School and Research Center, California.
Koestler, A. (1964/1989). *The act of creation*. London: Arkana.
Kramer, D. A. (2000). Wisdom as a classical source of human strength: Conceptualization and empirical inquiry. *Journal of Social and Clinical Psychology, 19*(1), 83–101.
Kristeva, J. (1982). *Desire in language: A semiotic approach to literature and art*. New York: Columbia University Press.
Labouvie-Vief, G. (1990). Modes of knowledge and the organization of development. In M. Commons, C. Armon, L. Kohlberg, F. A. Richards, T. A. Grotzer, & J. D. Sinnott (Eds.), *Adult development, volume 2: Models and methods in the study of adolescent and adult thought* (pp. 43–62). Westport: Praeger.
MacLure, M. (2006a, November–December). The bone in the throat: Some uncertain thoughts on baroque method. *International Journal of Qualitative Studies in Education, 19*(6), 729–745.
MacLure, M. (2006b). 'The bone in the throat': Some uncertain thoughts on baroque method. In *Engaging Pedagogies, AARE 2006 International Education Research Conference*, Adelaide.
MacLure, M. (2006c). Entertaining doubts: On frivolity as resistance. In J. Satterthwaite, W. M. Martin, & L. Robert (Eds.), *Discourse, resistance and identity formation*. London: Trentham.
Mason, M. (2008). Complexity theory and the philosophy of education. *Educational Philosophy and Theory, 40*(1), 4–18.
Montuori, A. (1997). Reflections on transformative learning: Social creativity, academic discourse and the improvisation of inquiry. *ReVision, 20*(1), 34–37.
Montuori, A. (1998). Creative inquiry: From instrumental knowing to love of knowledge. In J. Petrankar (Ed.), *Light of knowledge*. Oakland: Dharma Publishing.
Montuori, A. (2003). The complexity of improvisation and the improvisation of complexity: Social science, art and creativity. *Human Relations, 56*(2), 237–255.
Montuori, A. (2006). The quest for a new education: From oppositional identities to creative inquiry. *ReVision, 28*(3), 4–17.
Montuori, A., Combs, A., & Richards, R. (2004). Creativity, consciousness, and the direction for human development. In D. Loye (Ed.), *The great adventure: Toward a fully human theory of evolution* (pp. 197–236). Albany: SUNY Press.
Morin, E. (2001). *Seven complex lessons in education for the future*. Paris: UNESCO.
Morin, E. (2005, June 26). Restricted complexity, general complexity. In "*Intelligence de la complexite: Epistemologie et pragmatique*", Cerisy-La-Salle, France. Centre d'Etudes Transdisciplinaires. Sociologie, Anthropologie, Histoire.
Morin, E. (2015). *What is the complex thought?* Accessed 17 Aug 2015.
Neville, B. (1989). *Educating psyche: Emotion, imagination, and the unconscious in learning*. Melbourne: Collins Dove.
Nicolescu, B. (2002). *Manifesto of transdisciplinarity* (K.-C. Voss, Trans.) (Suny series in western esoteric traditions). New York: SUNY Press.
Noddings, N. (2003). *Happiness and education*. Cambridge: Cambridge University Press.

Noddings, N. (2005). Caring in education. *The Encyclopedia of Informal Education*. http://infed.org/mobi/caring-in-education/. Accessed 18 Apr 2016.

Olssen, M. (2008). Foucault as complexity theorist: Overcoming the problems of classical philosophical analysis. *Educational Philosophy and Theory, 40*(1), 96–117.

Ota, C., Erricker, C., & Erricker, J. (1997). The secrets of the play ground. *Pastoral Care in Education, 15*(4), 19–24.

Palmer, P. (1998). *The courage to teach*. San Francisco: Jossey-Bass.

Pearce, J. C. (1992). *Evolution's end: Claiming the potential of our intelligence*. San Francisco: Harper.

Prewitt, V. (n.d.). *The constructs of wisdom in human development and consciousness*. http://www.psy.pdx.edu/PsiCafe/Areas/Developmental/CogDev-Adult/OD-Wisdom.pdf. Accessed 7 Oct 2006.

Pridmore, J. (2004). 'Dancing cannot start too soon': Spiritual education in the thought of Jean Paul Friedrich Richter. *International Journal of Children's Spirituality, 9*(3), 279–291.

Radford, M. (2008). Complexity and truth in educational research. *Educational Philosophy and Theory, 40*(1), 144–157.

Rose, K., & Kincheloe, J. (2003). *Art, culture and education: Artful teaching in a fractured landscape*. New York: Peter Lang.

Schiller, F. (1954/1977). *On the aesthetic education of man—in a series of letters* (First published in 1795). New York: Frederick Ungar Publishing.

Schwartz, E. (1999). *Millennial child: Transforming education in the twenty-first century*. New York: Anthroposophic Press.

Semetsky, I. (2008). On the creative logic of education, or: Re-reading Dewey through the lens of complexity science. *Educational Philosophy and Theory, 40*(1), 83–95.

Sherman, Z. (2012). *The curiosity of school: Education and the dark side of enlightenment*. Toronto: Penguin Canada.

Sinnott, J. D. (1994). Development and yearning: Cognitive aspects of spiritual development. *Journal of Adult Development, 1*(2), 91–99.

Sinnott, J. D. (1998). *The development of logic in adulthood: Postformal thought and its applications*. New York: Springer.

Sinnott, J. D. (2002). Teaching as nourishment for complex thought: Approaches for classroom and practice built on postformal theory and the creation of community. In N. L. Diekelmann (Ed.), *First, do no harm: Power, oppression, and violence in healthcare* (pp. 232–272). Madison: University of Wisconsin Press.

Sinnott, J. D. (2005). The dance of the transforming self: Both feelings of connection and complex thought are needed for learning. *New Directions for Adult and Continuing Education, 108* (Winter), 27–37.

Sloan, D. (1992). Imagination, education and our postmodern possibilities. *ReVision: A Journal of Consciousness and Transformation, 15*(2), 42–53.

Spina, S. U. (2004). Power plays: Video Games' bad rap. In S. Steinberg & J. Kincheloe (Eds.), *Kinderculture: The corporate construction of childhood*. Boulder: Westview Press.

Steiner, R. (1909/1965). *The education of the child in the light of anthroposophy (GA 34)* (2nd ed.) (G. M. Adams, Trans,) (Original work published 1909). London: Rudolf Steiner Press.

Steiner, R. (1927/1986). *Truth, beauty, goodness (GA 220)* [Lecture, Dornach, Switzerland, Jan 19, 1923] [Electronic version] (Original work published 1927).

Steiner, R. (1928/1972). *A modern art of education (GA 307)* (3rd ed.) (J. Darrell, & G. Adams, Trans.) [14 Lectures, Ilkley, Yorkshire, August 5–17, 1923] (Original work published 1928). London: Rudolf Steiner Press.

Steiner, R. (1967). *The younger generation: Education and spiritual impulses in the 20th century (GA 217)* (R. M. Querido, Trans.). [13 Lectures Stuttgart, October 3–15, 1922]. New York: Anthroposophic Press.

Sternberg, R. J. (1999). *Handbook of creativity*. New York: Cambridge University Press.

Sternberg, R. J. (2001). Why schools should teach for wisdom: The balance theory of wisdom in educational settings. *Educational Psychologist, 36*(4), 227–245.

Sternberg, R. J. (2005, Winter). Older but not Wiser? The relationship between age and wisdom. *Ageing International, 30*(1), 5–26.

Wilber, K. (1995/2000). *Sex, ecology, spirituality: The spirit of evolution* (2nd ed., Rev.). Boston: Shambhala.

Wilber, K. (2004). *Introduction to integral theory and practice: IOS basic and the AQAL map.* http://www.integralnaked.org

Yan, B., & Arlin, P. K. (1995). Nonabsolute/relativistic thinking: A common factor underlying models of postformal reasoning? *Journal of Adult Development, 2*(4), 223–240.

Chapter 11
Pedagogical Voice: An Empowering Force

11.1 Introduction

Perhaps the most surprising of my core values is pedagogical voice. Why voice you might ask? And we will discuss this below. I have to admit that this one was a surprise to me as well. As I worked through my grounded theory process of clustering the postformal reasoning qualities and sorting out which of the evolutionary themes they related to, I began with only the other three. The first three qualities of love, life and wisdom emerged from the literature in quite a clear and bold way. At first I thought my theorising was complete. But this partial closure was unsatisfying. There were loose ends that did not seem to fit the other core values: qualities like pluralism and relativism, reflexivity and especially Suzanne Cook-Greuter's "construct-aware". Of course these renegades could have all been gathered under wisdom, but this left me feeling uncomfortable.

The situation with the postformal pedagogies was even more disturbing. Where would I place critical pedagogy, postcolonial and global education, postmodern and poststructuralist approaches, artistic and poetic education? I think it was poststructuralism that gave me the key insight into the importance of voice and language in the mix. Secondly, the emphasis on the discourse of power and marginal voices in critical pedagogy gave a further clue. Finally, the refinement of language sensibility in Peter Abbs' poetic education brought the *AHA moment*. It must have come to me as an inspiration, but once the idea arrived it was then obvious. I realised that pedagogical voice was the missing link, meaning voice in its broadest sense, as I indicate below. Even an education that is caring, lively and wise will not be effective in the long run if young people are not empowered to find their voice.

In this chapter, as with the previous three, I reiterate the evolutionary theme, and the related postformal reasoning qualities and pedagogies before entering the philosophical discussion. On the practical side, I discuss the educational approaches

J.M. Gidley, *Postformal Education*, Critical Studies of Education 3,
DOI 10.1007/978-3-319-29069-0_11

that awaken voice and language awareness and share some examples from my own and others' teaching experience, finishing with personal reflections.

11.2 Why Voice? A Brief Diagnostic

> Communication between human beings [is] not a process of transportation of information from one mind to another, but is rather to be understood as a process of meaning and interpretation. It is a process that is radically open and undetermined—and hence weak and risky. (Biesta 2014, p. 26)

Why is the human voice important? No matter where we live in the world today, the human voice is predominantly mediated by technology. Children born in the last fifteen to twenty years in affluent countries have never known a world without communication technologies of all kinds. But even in Africa, television has replaced the grandmother in the role of family storyteller, and the mobile phone is replacing face-to-face conversation everywhere.

Why do we want to educate with an awareness of voice and language? Marshall McLuhan claimed decades ago that every advance in technology dulls a former human capacity. The increasing reliance of young people on the sound bytes of the media and the truncated "spelling" of mobile phone text messages as their primary modes of communication dramatically limits the richness of their language development. By contrast, a live human educator telling children stories or facilitating Socratic dialogues with adolescents offers the rich nuances of voice, intonation, eye contact, gestures, facial expression, body language, emotional response and soul warmth. The mode and content of language that we expose children to not only create the foundations of their language but also their thinking patterns and worldviews. Put simply, for young people, having a voice is empowering.

What happens when we are unconscious of our voice and language in education? There is growing evidence that children who are overexposed to screen-mediated forms of communication from an early age become increasingly disconnected from the world around them and become disempowered. A growing number of kindergarten children have delayed language, arguably linked to reduction in real human-voice contact. This is an educational time bomb that will explode in coming decades unless we rehumanise our relationship to voice and language.

What does research say about voice and language in education? Educational, psychological, sociological and philosophical research will be explored in this chapter to gain insights into the under-appreciated importance of being conscious of what we say to young people and how we say it: our pedagogical voice.

11.3 Evolutionary Theme: Linguistic and Paradigmatic Boundary-Crossing

In this chapter we further explore the evolutionary academic and educational movement beyond fragmentation and disciplinary isolationism and towards more integration—particularly through transdisciplinarity. One of the challenges that has emerged from this literature is the difficulty in communicating across different disciplines, epistemologies and paradigms (Eckersley et al. 2006; Grigg et al. 2003). An evolutionary philosophy of education that can overcome this challenge requires tremendous sensitivity to linguistic, cultural and paradigmatic contexts. An important insight of French postmodern and poststructuralist philosophies is the awareness of context in terms of how we language the world. *Language reflexivity*—or construct-awareness—is a significant feature of postformal reasoning (Cook-Greuter 2000; Gidley 2009).

11.3.1 Postformal Reasoning Qualities Aligned to Voice Awareness

The features of postformal reasoning that are aligned to boundary-crossing are reflexivity, language reflexivity and pluralism (or in other words multi-vocal awareness) (see Table 11.1). The extended characteristics of these features are discussed in Chapter 5, Table 5.4, where I cohere these qualities under voice.

11.3.2 Postformal Pedagogies that Empower Multiple Voices

In this electronic age of "voice" mail, "chat" rooms and "talking" computers, perhaps the least valued of evolutionary forces is the human voice itself. Yet

Table 11.1 Postformal Reasoning Qualities Aligned to Voice Awareness

Postformal Reasoning Qualities that cross Disciplinary, Linguistic and Paradigmatic Boundaries	
Reflexivity	The ability to reflect on, and become conscious of, one's own thoughts, feelings, actions and values. Only mature adults can master the postformal trait of reflexivity in times of pressure, stress and uncertainty.
Language reflexivity	Awareness of our language is a subtle but important postformal feature. "The language habit... [is] a barrier to further development if it remains unconscious, automatic and unexamined".
Pluralism	The notions of *pluralism* and *relativism* are postmodern moves beyond empirical science as THE epistemology. The concept of multiple voices paves the way for social and cultural diversity in personal and civic spheres.

Table 11.2 Postformal Pedagogies that Empower Multiple Voices

Postformal Approaches Sensitive to Aesthetics, Language, Culture and Paradigm	
Postmodern and poststructuralist education [*approaching truth*]	. . . includes contributions of continental, especially French, philosophy in identifying the politics of voice and marginality.
Aesthetic, artistic and poetic education [*appreciating beauty*]	. . . cultivates aesthetic sensibility through exposure to and participation in diverse artistic activities and reflection on the aesthetics of the world.
Critical, postcolonial, global and planetary education [*applying goodness*]	. . . enhances awareness of dominant political voices and the rights of marginal cultures and sub-cultures to find their voices.

without its presence, little children cannot even learn to speak. Several significant 20th-century thinkers have drawn attention to the developmental and evolutionary significance of self-reflection and creativity in how we language the world (Abbs 2003; Barfield 1985; Derrida 2001; Gadamer 1960/2005; Gangadean 1998; Thompson 1998).

Arguably, the *linguistic turn* in philosophy has not yet significantly influenced formal education. Yet we can encourage this empowering capacity of *language reflexivity* to develop through postmodern and poststructuralist (Elkind 1998; Peters 1998); aesthetic, artistic and poetic (Abbs 2003; Read 1943; Rose and Kincheloe 2003); and critical, postcolonial, global and planetary pedagogies (Freire 1970; Giroux 1992). I cohere these threads under the core value of *pedagogical voice*.

In an additional philosophical manoeuvre, I note that these three contemporary educational styles can also be regarded as having relationships with the Platonic philosophical virtues of Truth, Beauty and Goodness (see Table 11.2).

11.4 Philosophical Perspectives: The Linguistic Turn

> The poetics of education . . . calls for the endless acts of cultural reincarnation—acts which enable students to see with new eyes and to speak with new tongues. (Abbs 2003, p. 17)

In this chapter I use the term *pedagogical voice* as a broad palette to include *family resemblances*[1] among postformal developments in language and linguistics, speech education, the range of voices of teachers and children, the empowerment and human agency notion of "finding one's voice", education in awareness of sound and silence and, most importantly, consciousness of how we "language the world" (Gadamer 1960/2005).

---

[1]*Family resemblances* was used by Wittgenstein (1968) to refer to the "complicated network of similarities, overlapping and criss-crossing" found in different word uses and meanings (Wittgenstein 1968, p. 32).

Consciousness of how we language the world was popularised in philosophical discourses with the *linguistic turn* (Rorty 1967). The *linguistic turn* was influenced by Ferdinand De Saussure's *linguistic structuralism* (Lyotard 2004; Matthews 1996; Wittgenstein 1968), the *language-games* of Ludwig Wittgenstein's (1968) later *anti-dogmatic* philosophy and the notion of *metanarratives* by Lyotard (2004). Several French philosophers in the poststructuralism mode deepened consciousness of language (Deleuze 1968/1994; Derrida 2001; Foucault 1986; Kristeva 1982). Likewise, transpersonal researcher Rosemary Anderson's *intuitive inquiry* elucidates the uniqueness and particularity of the individual "human voice" in research (R. Anderson 1998, p. 81).

Consciousness of language is a key indicator of postformal reasoning. Both Steiner and Gebser emphasised the significance of language awareness, poetic expression and creativity as part of the new consciousness.

Plato's *Republic,* especially the dialogues with Socrates, marked the end of poetry and image as primary ways of languaging the world and the beginning of the formalisation of philosophy as the new epistemology for the mental-rational consciousness. In a recursive, parabola-shaped re-integration, Gebser claims that the new consciousness is to be birthed through poetry, yet a new kind of *conscious* poetry. In the context of Gebser's and Steiner's views on consciousness evolution, poetry as an artistic condensation of language opens the awareness to a simultaneous experience—*concretion*—of all the consciousness structures. Wilber also identifies the role of language in the new consciousness. However, unlike Steiner and Gebser, he does not emphasise the central importance of poetry and artistry in language.

The re-integration of philosophy and poetry in Western European culture was begun in the late 18th century by English and German romantic philosopher-poets such as Blake, Schelling, Novalis and the Schlegel brothers (Richards 2002; Royce 1892/2001; Steiner 1901/1973). Gebser affirms this in the following quote:

> Our new situation requires new means of description and statement. The new components which have irrupted into our reality demand new 'concepts'... This urgent necessity was perceived and described shortly after the French Revolution by two great figures, Novalis and Hufeland. (Gebser 1949/1985, p. 306)

The enlivening of language was unquestionably a major focus for Steiner in facilitating the birth of the new consciousness, beyond abstract rationality. He stressed the need to awaken the artist in us when it comes to language if we hope in the future to be able to express our experiences of spiritual awareness.

> We have to create ... an immediate connection between *what* we want to say and *how* we want to express it. We have to re-awaken the linguistic artist in us in all areas. ... Each sentence will be seen as a birth, because it must be experienced inwardly in the soul as immediate form, not simply as a thought. (Steiner 1934/1983, pp. 15–16)

Steiner wrote and lectured extensively about the conscious development of language and speech and their significance for human evolution (Steiner 1904/1959, 1961, 1984). He saw speech education as a central part of a healthy evolutionary pedagogy, and the emphasis on oral as well as written language has remained a core component of Steiner/Waldorf education. Steiner also developed a complex, enlivening movement art called *eurythmy* based on his advanced understanding of how consciousness co-evolves with speech and language (Steiner 1931/1984). Eurythmy is a largely undiscovered postformal art form with the potential to enhance higher-order consciousness through complex creativity and body-mind integration. It can be enacted artistically—with speech or music—or therapeutically. Research into the potential of eurythmy in systems theory has begun (Deijmann n.d.). Such vitalising artistic practices need to be recognised at a time when low vitality is a chronic human condition. Eurythmy could be philosophically located within the emergent *aesthetic literacies* arising from the critique of *narrow literacies* (Gale 2005).

Gebser continued this emphasis on creative language development as central to the evolutionary shift in consciousness claiming it is reflected in new more conscious types of poetry.

> Here again we find, not a loss of ego and the poet as an instrument of the Muses, but a growing above and beyond the mental ego to freedom from the ego: to that freedom which is the guarantor of the spiritual...Whereas poetry from antiquity until the Renaissance proceeded from the 'musing' capabilities of the poet ... we find a renunciation of this type of creativity after the French Revolution beginning with Novalis that becomes increasingly and pervasively conscious in its expression. (Gebser 1949/1985, p. 327)

Cook-Greuter supports this stance using the term *construct-aware* to characterise the reflexive feature of postformal language development. She refers to the ego becoming "transparent to itself" at this ego-aware stage (Cook-Greuter 2000, p. 235). In this way she echoes Geber's concept of transparency as one of the features of higher-order, integral thinking, whereby Gebser claims that: "Integral reality is the world's transparency" (Gebser 1949/1985, p. 19).[2]

I use the term *language reflexivity*, with a similar meaning to Cook-Greuter's construct-aware. In addition to Cook-Greuter's work, several other significant 20th-century thinkers, including the French poststructuralists, have drawn attention to the construction of language and its significance in evolution of consciousness (Barfield 1985; Subbiondo 2003; Thompson 1998). Academic and poet, Peter Abbs, argues that there is a spiritual crisis in education and culture and proposes that the language awareness of postmodernity can be increasingly infused with creativity, through the arts in a poetics of education (Abbs 2003). One of the forms of creative language emerging from the poststructuralist philosophers is the use of *neologisms* (Derrida 2001; Gangadean 1998; St. Pierre 2004). Another is the concept of *polysemy*, which is about the "multiple meanings, connotations, connections to other concepts... that particular words possess" (Kincheloe 2006, p. 11).

One of the ways that the *subjective-objective* approach to knowledge can play itself out in language is through *intertextuality*. Although the term *intertextuality* is often associated with the work of de Saussure, it was coined by Bulgarian-French

[2]The full quote from Gebser on this idea can be found in Chapter 9.

philosopher, Julia Kristeva, in France in the late 1960s (Orr 2003). Kristeva's linguistic theorising reflects both the artistry of the mosaic and the rigour of postformal logics, not the least demonstrating postformal language reflexivity. Kristeva's intertextuality also includes other distinct features, such as focusing on "interconnection of ideas where previously none existed" (Orr 2003, p. 24).

11.5 Postformal Pedagogies: Voicing Truth, Beauty and Goodness

Being that can be understood is language. Gadamer Aphorism

The move beyond mental-rationality to integral-postformal culture and consciousness requires an integration of the search for *truth*—via scientific and philosophical epistemologies; with *beauty*—via artistic/aesthetic sensibilities; and with *goodness*—via participatory embodiment and critical enactment of the truth claims that we profess (see Table 11.2). This is a foundational point—often overlooked—that could ground postformal-integral-planetary consciousness in a *concretion*[3] of all consciousness modes, rather than a primarily conceptual abstraction of what integrality might be.

Several educational approaches support and cultivate an awareness of language and voice in education. These include postmodern and poststructuralist educational approaches—which deconstruct and reconstruct in the search for truth; aesthetic, artistic and poetic education—which refine the senses in ways that lead to an appreciation of beauty; and critical, postcolonial, global and planetary education approaches—which include normative values that aim to create a more just world by applying goodness. The first aims to build explicit awareness of how power is constructed through language, including self-reflection; the second assists with enriching, refining and developing more conscious and nuanced language; and the critical cluster of pedagogies particularly emphasises diversity, pluralism and empowering of marginal voices.

Kincheloe, through both his postformal education and his bricolage, applies a strong integrative lens to this significant cluster of pedagogies, building bridges between aesthetic, critical, postmodern and postformal (Kincheloe and Steinberg 1993; Rose and Kincheloe 2003).

[3]Gebser uses the term *concretion* to mean an experiencing in fully awake consciousness of all the previous structures in the same moment.

11.5.1 Postmodern and Poststructural Pedagogies: Approaching Truth

> Whereas modern childhood was defined in terms of differences between age groups, postmodern childhood is identified with differences within age groups. This metamorphism of our conception of childhood has radically transformed educational practice quite independently of any reform movement or agenda. (Elkind 1998, p. 1)

Educational psychologist David Elkind is referring to some general shifts in educational policy and practice that have occurred within US schooling as a result of changing conceptions of childhood in the postmodern era. Most notably, the changes he highlights first include changes to language. He notes that "the introduction of bilingual classes" arises from increased awareness of multi-cultural differences. More educational space needs to be allocated today to the learning of multiple languages and learning about diverse cultures given the inevitability of cultural pluralism in our multicultural global world. Several educational researchers have attended to this issue particularly in relation to emerging issues surrounding spirituality in education (de Souza 2006; Inayatullah 2002; Milojevic 2005). Elkind also points to the need to individualise curriculum so that at one end of the cognitive spectrum it meets the needs of "gifted and talented" students, and at the other end it serves the needs of children with special learning needs and different learning styles. Elkind sees the postmodern spirit as being best exemplified "in our main streaming and inclusion of children with special needs-a group excluded in the modern era" (Elkind 1998, p. 9). He also notes that postmodernism has led to the "modification of our textbooks and of our language to eliminate gender bias" (Elkind 1998, p. 9).

Education researcher, Zhihe Wang, contributes to the conversation as he draws from a Whiteheadian constructive postmodern educational approach to reconfigure Chinese education. Wang claims that Whitehead's "constructive postmodern education may offer an effective antidote to modern test-oriented education" in China. The problems he cites with the current education model include its fragmentation and narrowness; the overemphasis on second-hand knowledge through book learning; the dominance of scientism over imagination and creativity; and the rigidity of abstract concepts compared to process philosophy. One of the most important issues for Wang is that "from a point of view of organic philosophy, constructive postmodern thinkers view the students as living human being instead of machine[s]" (Wang 2004, p. 6). Other forms of reconstructive postmodernism may also contribute to the discourse (Griffin 2002; Kegan 1994).

> Poststructuralism as a contemporary philosophical movement offers a range of theories (of the text), critiques (of institutions), new concepts, and forms of analysis (of power) which are relevant and significant for the study of education... In part the significance of poststructuralism for education lies in the fact that it can be construed as a philosophical reaction against a *scientistic* social science. (Peters 1999, pp. 1, 4)

In his introduction to the book, *Naming the Multiple: Poststructuralism and Education*, as in the preceding quote, educational philosopher, Michael Peters, stresses that poststructuralism cannot be pinned down to a "single methodology, philosophy or body of theory". It is this very aspect of poststructuralism that makes it both so challenging to the modernist education paradigm and so exciting to critical, postmodern, postformal educators who resist modernist education and want to create something completely new. I regard the discourse of poststructuralism in education to be closely aligned to the deconstructive postmodern stream. It aims to challenge, to disrupt, even to unravel all of the old certainties that modernism clings to. But does it build a new educational approach—or perhaps multiple new educational approaches?

Some critical pedagogical theorists consider postmodern, and particularly poststructuralist, pedagogies to be too affected by what they call *ludic postmodernism*, with too little engagement with praxis and *historical materialism* (Eryaman 2006; McLaren and Farahmandpur 2003). Clearly, postmodern and poststructuralist approaches to education add rich dimensions to the diverse gathering of postformal pedagogies and will likely continue to develop over this century.

11.5.2 Aesthetic, Artistic and Poetic Education: Appreciating Beauty

> Art—or, to use a more exact phrase, aesthetic experience—is an essential factor on which Homo Sapiens has depended for the development of his highest cognitive faculties. (Read 1954, p. 143)

Sir Herbert Read (1893–1968) was a powerful advocate for art in education as this quote indicates. The moral, cultural and integrative value of aesthetic education has been known since the time of Plato and has been promoted by philosophers such as Kant, Schiller, Goethe and Schelling through to Steiner and Read in the 20th century and Rose and Kincheloe in recent times. Research and practice of 20th-century art educationists and psychologists support the value of artistic education for cognitive development and the development of meaning in life (J. Anderson 1985; Broudy 1987; Arnheim 1989; Eisner 1985). As discussed in Chapter 2, both Schiller and Read claimed that art/aesthetics should be the very *basis* of education (Read 1943; Schiller 1954/1977). Read also points to reverence as "a religious spirit or attitude that it is inculcated by music, dance and the arts" (Read 1943, p. 222). Art educators emphasise in particular the importance of aesthetics in balancing cognicentrism in education (Abbs 2003; Eisner 1985; Read 1943). Through art, drama and movement, students can see the complex paradoxes of "both/and" relationships, not just the binaries of "either/or".

Steiner regarded the creative arts as a foundation to teaching that gives meaning to every subject and promotes intrinsic motivation and positive self-esteem, rather than just something that could be taught as isolated subjects in themselves. He linked the artistic education of the child with the development of initiative (Steiner 1964, 1976, 1981).

In my own teaching experience, I was continually interweaving between the conceptual content and the multiple ways it could be presented artistically. I found the creative use of a range of artistic media to be the most practical and productive way to foster a multi-faceted and yet integrated worldview. Through art, drama and movement, students learn to see the world from multiple points of view and understand complex interrelationships, which helps them to make sense of the world and ultimately empowers them to find their own personal voice. Critical educators stress the pedagogical value of art, noting it should be more than a mere "add-on" in education.

> Artful teachers and their students begin an intellectual journey that explores the ways meaning is made, consciousness is constructed and social, cultural and political change occurs. This is a profoundly different process of education from the transference of predigested data that now occurs in technical standards-driven education. (Rose and Kincheloe 2003, p. 32)

11.5.3 Critical, Postcolonial, Global and Planetary: Applying Goodness

> Central to such a project is the issue of how pedagogy might provide cultural studies theorists and educators with an opportunity to engage pedagogical practices that are not only transdisciplinary, transgressive, and oppositional, but also connected to a wider project designed to further racial, economic, and political democracy. (Giroux 1998, p. x–xi)

In his foreword to the book series on "Critical Studies in Educational Culture", critical education theorist Henri Giroux makes clear why I have linked critical pedagogy with the Platonic concept of the good through my notion of *applying goodness*. Giroux's *cultural pedagogical practice* includes broader forms of enculturation across such sites as the mass media, in addition to school and university education. He notes how within these diverse contexts "education makes us both subjects of and subject to relations of power" (Giroux 1998, p. xi). Gert Biesta, in his writing on emancipation, explains how the "emancipatory interest of critical pedagogies focuses on the analysis of oppressive structures, practices, and theories", whereby critical education theorists such as Giroux, Michael Apple and Peter McLaren claim that "emancipation can be brought about if people gain an adequate insight into the power relations that constitute their situation" (Biesta 2014, p. 81).

One of the leading inspirations for *critical pedagogy*, particularly in North America, was Brazilian educational philosopher, Paulo Freire (1921–1997), most notably in his book *Pedagogy of the Oppressed* as a way of educating oppressed adults in Latin America (Freire 1970, 1995). His approach was picked up by educators, particularly in the USA, who were looking for alternatives to mainstream education that were more socially just and equitable for the marginalised members of society. Critical educators Kincheloe and McLaren discuss how creativity, criticality, futures orientation and postformality are applying goodness through taking "part in a process of critical world making, guided by the shadowed outline of a dream of a world less conditioned by misery, suffering and the politics of deceit" (Kincheloe and McLaren 1994, p. 154). Kincheloe and Steinberg went on to develop Freire's critical pedagogy into their postformal education.

Postcolonial educational literature points to the broader global issue of the export of this model to the rest of the world (Gidley 2001a, 2001b; Jain 2000; M. Jain and S. Jain 2003; Jain et al. 2001; S. Jain and M. Jain 2003) and the *hidden curriculum* that growing numbers of children and young people, globally, imbibe from the mass media (Gatto 1992; Gidley 2002; Giroux 2001; Healy 1998; Pearce 1992; Steinberg and Kincheloe 2004).

Global or planetary education is an emerging approach, but its sensibility infuses the work of several contemporary educators (Gidley 2007; Laszlo 2000; Montuori 1999; Morin 2001; Sloan 1992). It also includes educators whose focus is the environmental ecology of the planet (Fien 1998, 2002; Hicks 1995; Jardine 1998; Ornstein and Ehrlich 1991) or the social ecology of the planet, including the globalism, postcolonialism, multiculturalism and multilingualism discourses (Boulding 1990; Dighe 2000; Gangadean 2006; Gidley 2004; Miller 1993; Milojevic 2002; Mische 1986; Yihong 2005). Cosmopolitanism is a significant feature of planetary consciousness and it would be beneficial to cultivate this perspective in school contexts.

11.6 Practical Examples: Finding one's Pedagogical Voice

> On better days we struggle to tear off the tacky film, which covers our educational and poetic aspirations, resist the counterfeit version of consciousness and struggle to locate the smothered springs of renewal. (Abbs 2003, p. 28)

11.6.1 Silent Spaces and Sensitive Sounds

> So much of a schooling system that is negative is silenced by virtue of schools offering silence as a positive non-coercive choice... Schools need silence to overcome their structures such that people in schools can find new meanings of their own and communal togetherness born of choices and democracy. Silence can teach children about living in the world in ways conducive to peaceful co-existence. A silent curriculum with loud effects. (Lees 2013, p. 3)

What kinds of environments are we providing for our children? The world of sound and tone—which incidentally is carried on the air—is heavily polluted today, just like the particle pollution in the air. How often do urban children hear birds or insects sing, wind whistle, creeks babble or waves break? Attention to sound education has been severely neglected, other than through the obvious formal process of music education. We can begin with very young children by allowing them to "hear a pin drop" or taking them to environments where they can actively listen to natural sounds. Arguably, a joyful teacher starting a class with a song is far less likely to attract resistance than one who shouts to be heard.

In our noise-polluted urban worlds, it is a huge challenge to draw conscious attention to sound, let alone begin to refine and educate the delicate senses in relation to it. By contrast, an educational environment where spoken human language is valued over written and electronic voices for young children may provide an antidote. Poems, singing, drama and natural conversation are all vocal methods that can greatly benefit the development of written language. Additional oral methods include chanting, oration, re-telling stories, tongue twisters and word play. Learning a second or third language is invaluable for enhancing sound awareness and ability to see things from multiple perspectives, not to mention expanding awareness of the cultural *other*. This awareness is also fundamental to dialogical reasoning.

Consciousness of how we voice ourselves with children also makes space for silence, which can be a very powerful arena for holding the space for children to be themselves. British education researcher Helen Lees claims that what she calls "strong silence" offers "a way for children to appreciate their own natural inner resources in a world of mainly media-driven externalising tendencies of the self" (Lees 2012, p. 10). By strong silence Lees means non-coercive, participatory silence, not the kind imposed coercively on children by teachers, which she refers to as "weak silence". Lees clarifies what she means as follows: "A coercive educational silence is used to control or manipulate circumstances… the stare, the sharp pregnant pause, the look, the subtle movement of a hand. This is not silence—it is control" (Lees 2012, p. 63). Other terms for Lees' strong silence include "deep/contemplative/slow silence" (p. 69). Canadian education theorist David Jardine also stresses the importance of cultivating silent spaces in our classrooms.

> We must begin to believe again that silence may be our most articulate response. Silence must become possible again. In the midst of silence, a word, a gesture, a cry, can finally *mean* something, because we can finally hear, finally listen. (Jardine 1998, pp. 30–31)

Kincheloe and Steinberg (1993) make a similar point, referring to the respect the ancient Greeks had for moments of silence, perceiving them as representing the presence of Hermes.

> Ancient Greeks … were fascinated by the lulls of profound silence that periodically spread across a room filled with conversation. The Greeks postulated that at such moments Hermes had entered the room. By silencing the everyday babble, Hermes allowed the Greeks to tap their imagination, fears, hopes and passions. (Kincheloe and Steinberg 1993, p. 304)

When so much education has become reduced to *vocational training*, it might be useful to consider that the word *voc*ation—from *voce*—originally meant *spiritual calling*. For teachers, it might also be useful to consider how we are facilitating the kind of deep listening that might enable children to hear such a calling (Hillman 1996). A fundamental component of most, if not all, spiritual discipline is contemplation, meditation or prayer. While not recommending meditation for children, listening practices, observation of nature and the inner stillness of absorption in a creative activity—e.g., painting, wood carving, weaving—are foundations for stillness, open mindedness and open heartedness. Recently silence itself has become a territory of interest and research in education, but it is well beyond the scope of this chapter to discuss this research in detail. For a very good study of strong silence in education, see *Silence in Schools* (Lees 2012).

11.6.2 Languaging the World into Being

> What I see as essential for education [is] the presence of a teacher, not just as a fellow learner or a facilitator of learning, but as someone who, in the most general terms has to bring something to the educational situation that was not really there already. (Biesta 2014, p. 6)

Educational philosopher, Gert Biesta, takes a controversial stand for the important role of a teacher—in the midst of contemporary constructivist and child-centred approaches in education, which overly value notions of "communities of practice" and "learning communities" (Biesta 2014). I agree with Biesta's stand and would go further to say that the authentic human presence of the teacher can only be experienced through the language and voice of the teacher and at times the silences an artful teacher can create between their words. The significance of "teacher presence" is emphasised by Parker Palmer and Rachel Kessler, particularly in her work with teachers and young people (Kessler 2000a, 2000b; Palmer 1998). Others refer to the importance for children's wellbeing of teachers being fully present rather than absent-minded (Uhrmacher 1993).

In a pedagogical environment where teachers are reflexively conscious of their own language and voice and respectful of children's voices, the space can be opened for children to voice their hopes and fears, interests and dreams. The honouring of children's voices in education is in line with the UNESCO project *Education for All through Voices of Children*. In the context of high-stakes testing and performance outcomes, *pedagogical voice* and *language reflexivity* are not high on educational agendas. Speaking to children in ways that demonstrate love and devotion and that evoke reverence, awe and wonder can be stepping stones to wisdom—and to higher awareness generally.

How much more conscious might we be of how we "word" ideas and concepts with children, whose mobile consciousness we are shaping and moulding? To my knowledge little research has been undertaken on the pedagogical affects of different types of language on children. However, the work of Marshall Rosenberg on non-violent communication points to the need for this to occur. Anecdotal evidence from my work as a school psychologist suggests that there is a significant increase in speech impairment in young children in recent years. Research suggests that sustained exposure to electronic "voices"—television, computers and electronic games—may impair early speech development (Clouder et al. 2000; Healy 1998; Pearce 1992). While not advocating the elimination of the latter, more creative attention to the nuances of the *living word* could facilitate postformal language sensibility at appropriate developmental moments.

11.7 Personal Reflections on Pedagogical Voice

The following is an example from my experience of how the use of simple words ("sun juice") if filled with meaning through an imaginative context can be transformative of a child's consciousness (perhaps for life). Discovering the extraordinary in the ordinary through nurturing "radical amazement".

Personal Reflections. *One of the richest memories from my teaching career was the Winter Solstice festival in the mid-eighties where I worked the "miracle" of "turning oranges into sunballs full of Sun juice". Along with other teachers, I had created an inspired "environment" for our festival that included turning our small classroom into a simulacra of a mystical cave made of a draped parachute and other cloths which could only be entered by crawling into a tunnel made of increasingly darkly coloured silk (violet, indigo). Our school was young, small and intimate and the children were aged between around five and eight years old. Once the children, led by a teacher, ventured inside the room-sized "cave", their eyes grew large as they witnessed pockets of crystals lit by live, flickering, candle light (carefully guarded of course). After they had explored the cave and the crystals with their eyes and hands, tangibly, sensually, experiencing what the mystics of all traditions know, that the "Light can be found in and through the darkness", they were led out of the cave back into the "Sunlight" through another tunnel, this one made of red-, orange- and golden-coloured silks. As each child was re-entering the "outside world" of their classroom, after this communion with mystery, arriving at this new place of "sun renewal" on the other side of darkness (reminiscent of the "dark night of the soul"), they were reverently handed something magical—a bright, half-spherical, golden-orange cup—with the simple words "would you like some sun juice?" Each child carefully took this mysterious object in their hands, held it to their lips and squeezed the sweet "sun juice" into their mouths. They were experiencing wonder and awe. I will never forget the face and eyes of one child, who in another setting would be classified as autistic spectrum disordered. I am quite sure he was transformed by this experience and would never again eat an ordinary orange in quite the same way.*

A critical, pragmatic voice might ask: "What is the point of deluding children into thinking they are drinking sun juice? Don't they need to learn scientific facts so that we can measure what they know in order to grade them?" My response would be that this creative, imaginative gesture, one that fills the child's soul with wonder, can make a great contribution to developing their respect for nature and indeed for developing their evolving, ecological consciousness.

11.8 Concluding Remarks

In this chapter I have gone against the grain of much of what happens in schools today. Over several decades, global societal pressures by way of the mass media have led us further away from the human voice than ever before in history and more into a technology-mediated world, which bypasses human presence. Since the advent of television, followed by computers, the now ubiquitous mobile phone and soon-to-be wearable technology, young people born this century have little option but to be attached to technological limbs. We do not yet know the long-term effects of this mediated lifestyle, but we do know that "digital detox" vacations are an emerging form of tourism.

While there is a counter-thread to my concerns in that mobile media and new technological platforms such as Facebook, YouTube and Twitter have been instrumental tools in empowering young people in some cases, for example, the Arab Spring, it is also the case that these movements have not been sustainable. The technologies themselves are just tools, and the young people who use them need to be educated and empowered to use them for higher purpose.

As educators we carry a developmental—even evolutionary—responsibility to educate with care, with vitality and with wisdom. Ultimately we succeed in this (or fail) through our choice of words, our tone of voice, the timing of our silences, our authentic presence and how well we enable children to express theirs.

References

Abbs, P. (2003). *Against the flow: The arts, postmodern culture and education*. London: RoutledgeFalmer.

Anderson, J. (1985). *Cognitive psychology and its implications*. New York: W.H. Freeman and Co.

Anderson, R. (1998). Intuitive inquiry: A transpersonal approach. In W. Braud & R. Anderson (Eds.), *Transpersonal research methods for the social sciences: Honoring human experience*. Thousand Oaks: Sage Publications.

Arnheim, R. (1989). *Thoughts on art education*. Los Angeles: Getty Centre for Education in the Arts.

Barfield, O. (1985). *History in English words*. Herndon: Lindisfarne Books.

Biesta, G. J. J. (2014). *The beautiful risk of education*. Boulder: Paradigm Publishers.

Boulding, E. (1990). *Building a global civic culture: Education for an interdependent world*. Syracuse: Syracuse University Press.

Broudy, H. S. (1987). *The role of imagery in learning*. Los Angeles: The Getty Centre for Education in the Arts.

Clouder, C., Jenkinson, S., & Large, M. (2000). *The future of childhood*. Gloucestershire: Hawthorn Press.

Cook-Greuter, S. R. (2000). Mature ego development: A gateway to ego transcendence. *Journal of Adult Development, 7*(4), 227–240.

de Souza, M. (2006). Educating for hope, compassion and meaning in a divisive and intolerant world. *International Journal of Children's Spirituality, 11*(1), 165–175.

Deijmann, W. (n.d.). *More on systems thinking, personal mastery and eurythmy*.

Deleuze, G. (1968/1994). *Difference and repetition* (First published in French 1968). New York: Columbia University Press.

Derrida, J. (2001). Structure, sign, and play in the discourse of the human sciences. *Writing and Difference* (A. Bass, Trans.) (pp. 278–294). London: Routledge.

Dighe, A. (2000). Diversity in education in an era of globalization. In M. Jain (Ed.), *Learning societies: A reflective and generative framework*. Udaipur: Shikshantar: The People's Institute for Rethinking Education and Development.

Eckersley, R., Wierenga, A., & Wyn, J. (2006). *Flashpoints and signposts: Pathways to success and wellbeing for Australia's young people*. Melbourne: Australia 21.

Eisner, E. (1985). *The educational imagination: On the design and evaluation of school programs* (2nd ed.). New York: Macmillan.

Elkind, D. (1998). Schooling the postmodern child. *Research Bulletin, 3*(1), 1–9.

Eryaman, M. Y. (2006). Editorial statement: Understanding critical pedagogy and Peter McLaren in the age of global capitalism. *International Journal of Progressive Education, 2*(3), 6–7.

Fien, J. (1998). Environmental education for a new century. In D. Hicks & R. Slaughter (Eds.), *World yearbook 1998: Futures education*. London: Kogan Page.

Fien, J. (2002). *Teaching and learning for a sustainable future*. Paris: UNESCO.

Foucault, M. (1986). Text/context of other space. *Diacritics, 16*(1), 22–27.

Freire, P. (1970). *Pedagogy of the oppressed*. New York: Herder and Herder.

Freire, P. (1995). *Pedagogy of hope: Reliving pedagogy of the oppressed*. New York: Continuum International Publishing Group.

Gadamer, H.-G. (1960/2005). *Truth and method* (J. Weinsheimer, & D. Marshal, Trans., New York) (2nd Rev. ed.). London: Continuum International Publishing Group.

Gale, R. (2005). Aesthetic literacies and the "Living of Lyrical Moments". *Journal of Cognitive Affective Learning, 2*(1), 1–9.

Gangadean, A. (1998). *Between worlds: The emergence of global reason* (Revisioning Philosophy, Vol. 17). New York: Peter Lang.

Gangadean, A. (2006). A planetary crisis of consciousness: From ego-based cultures to a sustainable global world. *Kosmos: An Integral Approach to Global Awakening, V*(2), 37–39.

Gatto, J. T. (1992). *Dumbing us down: The hidden curriculum of compulsory schooling*. Philadelphia: New Society.

Gebser, J. (1949/1985). *The ever-present origin*. Athens: Ohio University Press.

Gidley, J. (2001a). 'Education for All' or education for wisdom? In M. Jain (Ed.), *Unfolding learning societies: Deepening the dialogues*. Udaipur: Shikshantar.

Gidley, J. (2001b). Globalization and its impact on youth. *Journal of Futures Studies, 6*(1), 89–106.

Gidley, J. (2002). Global youth culture: A transdisciplinary perspective. In J. Gidley & S. Inayatullah (Eds.), *Youth futures: Comparative research and transformative visions* (pp. 3–18). Westport: Praeger.

Gidley, J. (2004). The metaphors of globalisation: A multi-layered analysis of global youth culture. In S. Inayatullah (Ed.), *The causal layered analysis (CLA) reader: Theory and case studies of an integrative and transformative methodology*. Taipei: Tamkang University.

Gidley, J. (2007). Educational imperatives of the evolution of consciousness: The integral visions of Rudolf Steiner and Ken Wilber. *International Journal of Children's Spirituality, 12*(2), 117–135.

Gidley, J. (2009). Educating for evolving consciousness: Voicing the emergency for love, life and wisdom. In *The international handbook of education for spirituality, care and wellbeing* (Springer International handbooks of religion and education series). New York: Springer.

Giroux, H. A. (1992). *Border crossing: Cultural workers and the politics of education*. New York: Routledge.

Giroux, H. A. (1998). Series foreword. In H. A. Giroux (Ed.), *Naming the multiple: Poststructuralism and education*. Westport: Bergin & Garvey.

Giroux, H. A. (2001). *Stealing innocence: Corporate culture's war on children*. New York: Palgrave Macmillan.
Griffin, D. R. (2002). Introduction to SUNY series in constructive postmodern thought. In *Process and difference: Between cosmological and poststructuralist postmodernisms* (pp. vii–xi). New York: SUNY Press.
Grigg, L., Johnston, R., & Milson, N. (2003). *Emerging issues for cross-disciplinary research: Conceptual and empirical dimensions*. Canberra: DEST, Commonwealth of Australia.
Healy, J. M. (1998). *Failure to connect: How computers affect our children's minds—and what we can do about it*. New York: Touchstone.
Hicks, D. (1995). Envisioning the future: The challenge for environmental educators. *Environmental Education Research, 1*(3), 1–9.
Hillman, J. (1996). *The soul's code: In search of character and calling*. New York: Random House.
Inayatullah, S. (2002). Youth dissent: Multiple perspectives on youth futures. In J. Gidley & S. Inayatullah (Eds.), *Youth futures: Comparative research and transformative visions* (pp. 19–30). Westport: Praeger.
Jain, M. (Ed.). (2000). *Unfolding learning societies: Challenges and opportunities*. Udaipur: Shikshantar: The People's Institute for Rethinking Education and Development.
Jain, M., & Jain, S. (Eds.). (2003). *McEducation for all?* Udaipur: Shikshantar.
Jain, M., Miller, V., & Jain, S. (Eds.). (2001). *Unfolding learning societies: Deepening the dialogues* (Vimukt Shiksha, Vol. April 2001). Udaipur: The People's Institute for Rethinking education and Development.
Jain, S., & Jain, M. (Eds.). (2003). *The dark side of literacy* (Resisting the Culture of Schooling, Vol. IV). Udaipur: The People's Institute for Rethinking education and Development.
Jardine, D. W. (1998). *To dwell with a boundless heart: Essays in curriculum theory, hermeneutics, and the ecological imagination* (Studies in the Postmodern Theory of Education). New York: Peter Lang Publishing.
Kegan, R. (1994). *In over our heads: The mental demands of modern life*. Cambridge, MA: Harvard University Press.
Kessler, R. (2000a). *The soul of education: Helping students find connection, compassion and character at school*. Alexandria: Association for Supervision and Curriculum Development.
Kessler, R. (2000b). The teaching presence. *Virginia Journal of Education, 944*(2), 7–10.
Kincheloe, J. (2006). *Reading, writing and cognition: The postformal basics* (Bold Visions in Educational Research). Rotterdam: Sense Publishers.
Kincheloe, J., & McLaren, P. (1994). Rethinking critical theory and qualitative research. In N. Denzin & Y. Lincoln (Eds.), *Handbook of qualitative research* (pp. 138–154). Thousand Oaks: Sage Publications.
Kincheloe, J., & Steinberg, S. (1993). A tentative description of post-formal thinking: The critical confrontation with cognitive theory. *Harvard Educational Review, 63*(3), 296–320.
Kristeva, J. (1982). *Desire in language: A semiotic approach to literature and art*. New York: Columbia University Press.
Laszlo, K. C. (2000). *Creating the conditions for the design of evolutionary learning community: A participatory and co-creative exploration of educational images for a sustainable and evolutionary future*. Ph.D., Saybrook Graduate School and Research Center, California.
Lees, H. (2012). *Silence in schools*. London: Trentham Books, Institute of Education Press.
Lees, H. (2013). *The art of being together in schools through silent stillness?* [Electronic article]. https://www.academia.edu/2556935/The_art_of_being_together_in_schools_through_silent_stillness. Accessed 20 July 2015.
Lyotard, J.-F. (2004). *The postmodern condition: A report on knowledge*. Manchester: Manchester University Press.
Matthews, E. (1996). *Twentieth century French philosophy*. Oxford: Oxford University Press.

McLaren, P., & Farahmandpur, R. (2003). Breaking signifying chains: A Marxist position on postmodernism. In D. Hill, P. McLaren, M. Cole, & G. Rikowski (Eds.), *Marxism against postmodernism in educational theory*. Lanham: Lexington Books.

Miller, R. (Ed.). (1993). *The renewal of meaning in education: Responses to the cultural and ecological crisis of our times* (CD-ROM ed.). Brandon: Great Ideas in Education.

Milojevic, I. (2002). *Futures of education: Feminist and post-western critiques and visions*. PhD thesis. University of Queensland, Brisbane.

Milojevic, I. (2005). *Educational futures: Dominant and contesting visions*. London: Routledge.

Mische, P. (1986). Age of global transformation: A challenge to educators. *Renaissance Universal Journal, 5*(2–3), 36/38–39/11.

Montuori, A. (1999). Planetary culture and the crisis of the future. *World Futures: the Journal of General Evolution, 54*(4), 232–254.

Morin, E. (2001). *Seven complex lessons in education for the future*. Paris: UNESCO.

Ornstein, R., & Ehrlich, P. (1991). *New world, new mind: Changing the way we think to save our future*. Glasgow: Paladin.

Orr, M. (2003). *Intertextuality: Debates and contexts*. Cambridge: Polity Press.

Palmer, P. (1998). *The courage to teach*. San Francisco: Jossey-Bass.

Pearce, J. C. (1992). *Evolution's end: Claiming the potential of our intelligence*. San Francisco: Harper.

Peters, M. (Ed.). (1998). *Naming the multiple: Poststructuralism and education* (Critical Studies in Education and Culture Series). Westport: Bergin & Garvey.

Peters, M. (1999). Poststructuralism and education. In M. Peters, T. Besley, A. Gibbons, B. Žarnić, & P. Ghiraldelli (Eds.), *Encyclopaedia of educational philosophy and theory* [Electronic article]. http://eepat.net/doku.php?id=poststructuralism_and_philosophy_of_education. Accessed 16 Apr 2015.

Read, H. (1943). *Education through art*. London: Faber and Faber.

Read, H. (1954). Art and the evolution of consciousness. *The Journal of Aesthetics and Art Criticism, 13*(2), 143–155.

Richards, R. J. (2002). *The romantic conception of life: Science and philosophy in the age of Goethe*. Chicago: University of Chicago Press.

Rorty, R. (1967). *The linguistic turn: Essays in philosophical method*. Chicago: University of Chicago Press.

Rose, K., & Kincheloe, J. (2003). *Art, culture and education: Artful teaching in a fractured landscape*. New York: Peter Lang.

Royce, J. (1892/2001). Josiah Royce's the spirit of modern philosophy, lecture 6: The romantic school in philosophy. Accessed 7 Feb 2004.

Schiller, F. (1954/1977). *On the aesthetic education of man—in a series of letters* (First published in 1795). New York: Frederick Ungar Publishing.

Sloan, D. (1992). Imagination, education and our postmodern possibilities. *ReVision: A Journal of Consciousness and Transformation, 15*(2), 42–53.

St. Pierre, E. A. (2004). Deleuzian concepts for education: The subject undone. *Educational Philosophy and Theory, 36*(3), 283–296.

Steinberg, S., & Kincheloe, J. (Eds.). (2004). *Kinderculture: The corporate construction of childhood*. Boulder: Westview Press.

Steiner, R. (1901/1973). *The riddles of philosophy (GA 18)* (4th ed.) (Original work published 1901, and republished with addition in 1914). Spring Valley: The Anthroposophic Press.

Steiner, R. (1904/1959). *Cosmic memory: Prehistory of earth and man (GA 11)* (1st English ed.) (K. E. Zimmer, Trans.) (Original work published 1904). San Francisco: Harper & Row.

Steiner, R. (1931/1984). *Eurythmy as visible speech (GA 279)* (Rev. ed.) (V. & J. Compton-Burnett, Trans.) [15 Lectures, Dornach, Switzerland, June 24 to July 12, 1924] (Original work published 1931). London: Rudolf Steiner Press.

Steiner, R. (1934/1983). *Metamorphoses of the soul: Paths of experience: Vol. 2 (GA 59)* (2nd ed.) (C. Davy, & C. von Arnim, Trans.) [9 Lectures, Berlin, Jan. 20 to May 12, 1910] (Original work published 1934). London: Rudolf Steiner Press.

Steiner, R. (1961). *Verses and meditations*. London: Rudolf Steiner Press.

Steiner, R. (1964). *The arts and their mission (GA 276)* (L. D. Monges, & V. Moore, Trans.) [8 Lectures, Dornach, Switzerland and Oslo, Norway, May 18 to June 9, 1923]. Spring Valley: The Anthroposophic Press.

Steiner, R. (1976). *Practical advice to teachers: Lectures, 1919*. London: Rudolf Steiner Press.

Steiner, R. (1981). *The renewal of education through the science of the spirit: Lectures, 1920*. Sussex: Kolisko Archive.

Steiner, R. (1984). *The realm of language and the lost unison between speaking and thinking (GA 162)* (Rev. ed.) (G. Karnow, & A. Wulsin, Trans.) [2 Lectures, Dornach, Switzerland, July 17 & 18, 1915]. Spring Valley: Mercury Press.

Subbiondo, J. (2003). Lexicography and the evolution of consciousness: A study of Owen Barfield's history in English words. *Historiographia Linguistica, 30*, 407–427.

Thompson, W. I. (1998). *Coming into being: Artifacts and texts in the evolution of consciousness*. London: MacMillan Press Ltd.

Uhrmacher, B. P. (1993). Making contact: An exploration of focused attention between teacher and students. *Curriculum Inquiry, 23*(4), 433–444.

Wang, Z. (2004). *An antidote to modern test-oriented education: Toward a constructive postmodern education*. Paper presented at the Forum for Integrated Education and Educational Reform, Santa Cruz.

Wittgenstein, L. (1968). *Philosophical investigations*. Oxford: Basil Blackwell's.

Yihong, F. (2005). From globalization 3.0 to integral university 3.0: Higher education in a changing learning landscape. In *UNIQUAL 2005*, Norway.

Chapter 12
Meta-Reflections

12.1 Introduction

With this book I have begun to create a postformal education philosophy focusing on love, life and wisdom, for educators who speak from their full humanity. If you as a reader are genuinely interested in creating educational settings that support evolution of consciousness, I have left you with much to think about.

I offer some concluding reflections here but not a lockstep shortcut to what I have already said. Let me be clear. There are no shortcuts to evolving education.

What masquerades as education today must be seen for what it is—an anachronistic relic of the industrial past. Unless we resolve to rehumanise education so its core purpose becomes once again to develop whole human beings who care, who have and respect life, who exercise wisdom and who have the courage to voice their truths to those who would corrupt our futures, then we should forget about the whole idea of education altogether. Nothing less will suffice, if our young people are to become whole enough to navigate the complex futures they will ineluctably inherit.

12.2 This is not a Shortcut to Reading the Book

Part I (Chapters 1, 2, 3 and 4) was intended to stretch the minds of educators, researchers, students and parents who are serious about their children's education. Chapter 2 took you out of the classroom to imagine life at the beginning of human time and speculate on how children learned to take part in their families, tribes and societies in those ancient times. Upon return from that journey in time, I hope you were able to see the schools of today very differently and to realise that everything we do with children in the name of education is up for negotiation. None of it is fixed and all of it needs to be recreated at every moment if children are to learn to

J.M. Gidley, *Postformal Education*, Critical Studies of Education 3,
DOI 10.1007/978-3-319-29069-0_12

live in unpredictable tomorrows. In Chapter 3 I took you on a journey through the cognitive life of individuals using developmental psychology as a lens. This should have left you with the view that nothing is finished with adolescence, and perhaps also with questions about cognitive development after adolescence. Chapter 4 was designed as a big picture overview of education, to go beyond your already-known educational mindset, to create a wide-open space in which to consider some of the deeper questions, such as: "Who are we educating?" and "What are we educating for?"

I hope you found Part II to be dense, complex and intriguingly interwoven. In Chapter 5, you met adult developmental psychologists who demonstrate higher-order modes of cognition in mature adults. You were led through my theorisation of postformal reasoning qualities and my mapping of these qualities onto evolutionary themes. I introduced you in Chapter 6 to postformal education researchers and a large number of evolutionary pedagogies, demonstrating how they related to both the evolutionary themes and the postformal reasoning qualities. Finally, in Chapter 7, I invited you into a series of inter-related dialogues among the various facets and layers of leading-edge cultural, psychological and educational research. It is for you to judge whether I fulfilled my aim in this chapter: to integrate and cohere these multi-stranded, evolutionary expressions from culture, psychology and education by revealing them as interwoven facets of the evolution of consciousness.

In Part III, I developed my theory of four core pedagogical values that arose at the intersections between the evolutionary themes, postformal reasoning qualities and postformal pedagogies. You will have seen that these four core values—love, life, wisdom and voice—are central to my postformal education philosophy. In case I did not make it clear enough, I do not want you to see the core values as formal concepts or "containers" but as dynamic centres of psychological, educational, and ultimately cultural, activity. Their role is to enable a delicate theoretic coherence between the plurality of innovations on the periphery of the educational discourse and a unity at the centre: a postformal education philosophy for complex futures.

12.3 Personal Reflections

I am probably more attached to this book than I should be. There are a number of reasons for this:

Firstly, it has taken nearly ten years to write, if I include the years of doctoral research that merged seamlessly with the writing and rewriting of the actual book.

Secondly, it contains insights from four decades of professional and academic work in education, psychology and futures studies, in all educational levels and sectors and in many parts of the world. It is the voice of my life experience.

Thirdly, I was personally invited to write this book by the late Joe Kincheloe whose own writing I had studied and admired for years before his invitation in 2008.

Fourthly, after Joe's untimely death in late 2008, the responsibility of writing a book that would appropriately reflect the significance of his life's work for educational futures, and how much he had inspired my own, weighed heavily.

12.4 A Qualifier: What this Book is not about

The book is not about teacher education, though I would love to design a course around the four core pedagogies of my postformal education philosophy.

The book is not about educational policy, though policy-makers could draw policy from the philosophy that lies at the heart of the book.

The book is not about small changes in an obsolete system but about co-evolving a radically new education that is complexly human and simply divine.

12.5 In Short...

Through this book I offer to the education discourse insights from the evolution of consciousness research about the significance of the global mindset shift. From cultural evolution I reveal an emergent integral culture, and from adult developmental psychology I theorise a dozen postformal reasoning qualities. I engage in a series of dialogues between the evolutionary thematic threads, the postformal reasoning qualities and postformal pedagogies. I distil what arises at the intersection into four core pedagogical values: love, life, wisdom and voice, placing these values at the heart of my postformal education philosophy. Finally, I articulate across four chapters how we can strengthen the evolving consciousness of young people so they develop the passion, the vitality, the wisdom and the courage to face what is coming.

Name Index

J.M. Gidley, *Postformal Education*, Critical Studies of Education 3,
DOI 10.1007/978-3-319-29069-0

Subject Index

J.M. Gidley, *Postformal Education*, Critical Studies of Education 3,
DOI 10.1007/978-3-319-29069-0

Lightning Source UK Ltd.
Milton Keynes UK
UKOW06n0714140916

282955UK00013B/292/P